JUDAISM IN LATE ANTIQUITY

PART FIVE

THE JUDAISM OF QUMRAN:
A SYSTEMIC READING OF THE DEAD SEA SCROLLS

VOLUME TWO

HANDBOOK OF ORIENTAL STUDIES
HANDBUCH DER ORIENTALISTIK

SECTION ONE
THE NEAR AND MIDDLE EAST

EDITED BY

H. ALTENMÜLLER · B. HROUDA · B.A. LEVINE · R.S. O'FAHEY
K.R. VEENHOF · C.H.M. VERSTEEGH

VOLUME FIFTY-SEVEN

JUDAISM IN LATE ANTIQUITY

PART FIVE

THE JUDAISM OF QUMRAN:
A SYSTEMIC READING OF THE DEAD SEA SCROLLS

VOLUME TWO

JUDAISM IN LATE ANTIQUITY

EDITED BY

ALAN J. AVERY-PECK, JACOB NEUSNER

AND

BRUCE D. CHILTON

PART FIVE

THE JUDAISM OF QUMRAN:
A SYSTEMIC READING OF
THE DEAD SEA SCROLLS

VOLUME TWO

World View, Comparing Judaisms

BRILL
LEIDEN · BOSTON · KÖLN
2001

Die Deutsche Bibliothek – CIP-Einheitsaufnahme

Handbuch der Orientalistik. – Leiden ; Boston ; Köln : Brill.
Teilw. hrsg. von H. Altenmüller. – Teilw. hrsg. von B. Spuler. –
Literaturangaben
Teilw. mit Parallelt.; Handbook of oriental studies
Abt. 1. Der Nahe und Mittlere Osten = The Near and Middle East /
hrsg. von H. Altenmüller ...
Teilw. hrsg. von B. Spuler
Bd. 57. Judaism in late antiquity
Pt. 5. The Judaism of Qumran. A Systemic Reading of the Dead Sea
Scrolls. Vol. 2. World view, comparing judaisms. 2001

Judaism in late antiquity / ed. by Alan J. Avery-Peck, Jacob
Neusner and Bruce Chilton – Leiden ; Boston; Köln : Brill 2001
(Handbook of oriental studies : Abt. 1, The Near and Middle East ;
Literaturangaben
Pt. 5. The Judaism of Qumran. A Systemic Reading of the Dead Sea Scrolls.
Vol. 2. World view, comparing judaisms– 2001
(Handbook of oriental studies : Abt. 1, The Near and Middle East ;
Bd. 57)
ISBN 90–04–12003 3

Library of Congress Cataloging-in-Publication Data

Library of Congress Cataloging-in-Publication Data is also available.

ISSN 0169-9423
ISBN 90 04 12003 3

© *Copyright 2001 by Koninklijke Brill NV, Leiden, The Netherlands*

*All rights reserved. No part of this publication may be reproduced, translated, stored
in a retrieval system, or transmitted in any form or by any means, electronic,
mechanical, photocopying, recording or otherwise, without prior written
permission from the publisher.*

*Authorization to photocopy items for internal or personal use is granted
by Brill provided that the appropriate fees are paid directly to
The Copyright Clearance Center, 222 Rosewood Drive, Suite 910
Danvers MA 01923, USA.
Fees are subject to change.*

PRINTED ON ACID-FREE PAPER IN THE NETHERLANDS

TABLE OF CONTENTS

Preface vii

PART 3. WORLD VIEW

9. What Did the Jews of Qumran Know about God and How Did They Know It? Revelation and God in the Dead Sea Scrolls 3
   Edward M. Cook, Cincinnati, Ohio
10. The Torah at Qumran 23
    Philip R. Davies, University of Sheffield
11. The Shape of the "Bible" at Qumran 45
    Peter W. Flint, Trinity Western University
12. Biblical Interpretation at Qumran 105
    Craig A. Evans, Trinity Western University
13. History and Eschatology at Qumran: Messiah 125
    Todd S. Beall, Capital Bible Seminary
14. Wisdom at Qumran 147
    Torleif Elgvin, Lutheran Theological Seminary

PART 4. COMPARING JUDAISMS

15. Paul's and Qumran's Judaism 173
    Heikki Räisänen, University of Helsinki
16. The Gospel of John and the Community Rule of Qumran: A Comparison of Systems 201
    Adriana Destro & Mauro Pesce, University of Bologna

PART 5. CONCLUSION

17. Reading the Scrolls Systemically 233
    Bruce D. Chilton, Bard College

General Index to Volumes 1-2 247
Index of Ancient Sources to Volumes 1-2 255

PREFACE

These volumes ask of the documents of the Dead Sea Library found at Qumran a simple question: how does each participate in a shared Judaic religious system? We propose a systemic reading of the Scrolls within the working hypothesis that all of them in one way or another rest upon a cogent Judaism: a world view, way of life, theory of the social entity, "Israel," that coheres in responding to a single urgent question with a self-evidently valid answer. The opening chapter defines precisely what is meant by "a systemic reading," or an account of "a Judaism." The analysis of the data of the Dead Sea Scrolls within the now-defined categories of systemic analysis of a religious system of the social order then asks how diverse writings hold together to make a single coherent statement, to stand for a religious system possessed of integrity and cogency.

Our account of the world view of the Judaism adumbrated by the Qumran library covers principal questions addressed to any Judaic religious system: doctrine of God, Torah (including the issue of Scripture and the interpretation of Scripture), matters of history, wisdom, and mysticism. When it comes to the way of life, we include first of all the evidence of the material culture of the community—and here, whatever the status of the library writings, we do deal with a well-attested community—and then turn to practical matters of religious conduct. How the community's world view comes to realization is suggested by its treatment of the calendar, by its provision of laws that concern women, by questions of cultic and secular purity, by its piety and forms of worship and views of Temple and sacrifice, and the like. Finally, with the community's definition of "Israel" and of itself in relationship to "Israel" (or of itself as constituting "Israel" tout court!), inclusive of Israelites excluded from this "Israel," we gain an account of the theory of who and what is Israel that animates the particular Judaism represented in these writings.

All systemic description, analysis, and interpretation requires an exercise of comparison, e.g., between and among Judaic religious systems or Judaisms. For that purpose, we include the comparison of the systems of Paul and Qumran, on the one side, and John and Qumran, on the other. The comparison of the Rabbinic system represented by the Mishnah and related writings with the Qumran system—even at the level of comparing structures of category-formations—is at a primitive level, though the comparison of details of the Halakhah of Qumran with the Halakhah of the Mishnah and related writings has made commendable progress. The conclusion then points to some of the principal results of systemic study of a well-attested Judaism in antiquity and suggests where we now stand.

We therefore undertake a systemic description of the Judaic religious system that (as a matter of hypothesis here) animates the library found by the Dead Sea. What we have done is to synthesize knowledge within a structure meant to hold together diverse doctrines and patterns of action within a single construct, as a cogent, working system: the social culture of a particular community. We have selected evidence of a single venue for that purpose and attempted to read the evidence whole and within the hypothesis that this reading is legitimated by the social setting in which the evidence is preserved. We then realize one approach to the study of Judaism, namely, the systemic one, which insists that we define Judaism as a set of religious systems not as a single, unitary, harmonious body of doctrine and practice, continuous with Scripture and encompassing nearly everybody within a large and capacious frame.

But what about the opposite view, the analytical one? Do we not also insist upon differentiating evidence into its distinct components, each representing a Judaic system in its own terms? Indeed, we do, and in the previous volume within this series, Part Four, *Death, Afterlife, Resurrection, and the World to Come in the Judaisms of Late Antiquity*, we did just that. So that other, analytical approach also has served in this account of Judaism in late antiquity. How did the analysis go forward among the diverse writings, all of them classified as Judaic? What we did was to ask one and the same question to the greater part of the bodies of data produced by Judaisms in antiquity.

We inquired as follows for the case that we chose: since opinion on life-after-death occurs in most writings attributed to Judaic origin in ancient times, do all the sources concur on some few points, which we may call "Judaism" and its doctrine on the matter at hand? Or do the diverse sources represent only the communities that produced and preserved them, not "Judaism" all together and all at once? Accordingly, the method of this volume forms a mirror-image of its predecessor. In *Death, Life-after-Death, Resurrection, and the World-to-Come in the Judaisms of Late Antiquity*, we contrasted accounts of a single topic put forth by diverse bodies of Judaic writing in ancient times. With an account of Scripture's diverse pictures in hand, we reviewed how Judaic writings of various classes present their ideas on the same topic. We divided by language or venue or type of writing: Jewish writings in Greek—apocalyptic literature, apocrypha and non-apocalyptic pseudepigrapha, Philo and Josephus; the picture set forth in the Dead Sea Scrolls viewed as a coherent statement; the account of the matter in the Gospels, providing the perspective of Jewish followers of Jesus; the evidence of inscriptions and of the Targums to the Pentateuch, and the perspectives of the two principal phases of Rabbinic Judaism, Mishnah, then Talmudic and Midrashic.

Each précis limited itself to one body of evidence. That allowed us to see the diversity of opinion on a single topic set forth by various writings, each representing the religious system of its writers and of the community that valued those writings and preserved them. The volume then formed an experiment to test the proposition that a single Judaism is to be discerned within, behind, and among the conflicting writings of various persons, representative of diverse groups. No harmony of opinion can be identified, and if there is a single common Judaism, what it can have held on so central a question as life-after-death, beyond an exceedingly low common denominator of conviction, is not readily defined.

In this volume we have done the opposite. We concentrate on a single corpus of evidence, the writings found in the library of Qumran, and ask specialists in the study of that library to contribute to generalizations about the system as a whole. Each was invited to describe the part of the matter on which he or she specializes. The essays then coalesce thematically, all dealing with the same community. They come together to form a systematic account of the religious system that animates those diverse writings. We defined the assignments so as to produce a coherent picture of the way of life, the world view, and the theory of the social entity, "Israel," that all together emerge from the library of Qumran. Our working hypothesis is that these writings can be asked to speak of a common Judaic religious system, to attest to parts of a single whole, a Judaism. That is why we read the documents all together and all at once and combine the evidence yielded by distinct scrolls. That is only to test the working hypothesis at hand. Others may wish to differentiate and analyze where we have synthesized, to challenge the notion that governs here, a reading in quest of a single coherent world view, a cogent picture of a way of life, and a theory of who and what is Israel that pervades all the documents. With the editors and authors of this volume they will get no argument. Each reading has its merits, and both are absolutely necessary for the religious study of the Dead Sea Library, which here becomes systematic and encompassing.

What we think we have proved in the five parts of this work is that the study of Judaism in late antiquity forms a principal part of the academic study of the history of religion. Because of the methodological problems that inhere in the pertinent evidence—problems of the religious study of religion, not only the philological, linguistic, archaeological, anthropology, political, cultural, theological, or sociological study of religious data for the purposes of philology, linguistics, archaeology, anthropological, political science, culture, theology, or sociology—Judaism claims a position in the very forefront of subjects that reward systematic academic inquiry. But philology, linguistics, archaeology, and the rest are not religion and do not represent the study of religion. Each field of learning has its distinctive contribution to make; each selects its data and interprets it in response to methods and issues particular to its own epistemic logic. And so is the case for the religious study of Judaism, that is, the study of Judaism in the comparison of religions and for the history of religion.

Not only so, but the position that it demands for itself is defined autonomously, not only or mainly in comparison and contrast (whether religious or theological) with earliest Christianity. And it is to be defined in terms of the study of religion, the complex of religious systems we call "Judaism"—that, and not the history of the Jews or their ethnic culture, whether then, whether now. Indeed, whether the study of the Jews' ethnic culture and history in ancient times yields important results for the study of culture and history in antiquity is not for us to say, since we do not work in that field. Recent results strike us as limited in their academic value and interest, but great historical work on the Jews as a historical entity has been done and, in some subdivisions of ancient history, continues to go forward. Nonetheless, much is lost to the comparative study of religion and the history of religion, when the comparative study of religion leaves in the hands of ethnic inquiry the matter of Judaism, the religion. Then by "Judaism" people mean "the history of the Jews" or aspects of their ethnic affairs (some of them indeed bearing on matters of interest to the study of the religion, Judaism, many of them not). They do not mean what people mean when they study Christianity or Graeco-Roman paganism, Zoroastrianism or Islam,

Manichaeism or Mandaeism, or any other religion of late antique venue.

With this part we conclude the series, Judaism in Late Antiquity, which has accomplished its goals. We promised an account of the sources for the study of late antique Judaism, a picture of the historical syntheses that they yield, and then three parts devoted to special problems: issues and debates (in four volumes); a review of death and life-after-death as portrayed by late antique Judaisms, and a picture of a particular Judaic religious system of special interest, the one expressed in the writings of the Dead Sea Library, in the present part (in two volumes). The editors have no further plans at this time to augment their handbook of ancient Judaism but welcome suggestions on further problems worthy of systematic consideration under their auspices. Professor Avery-Peck calls attention, further, to the *Annual of Rabbinic Judaism*, of which he is editor-in-chief, for studies of problems particular to Rabbinic Judaism from antiquity to our own day. That journal, devoted to a particular Judaism over the whole of its history, forms yet another medium for discussion and debate on the history of Judaism.

The editors express their thanks to E.J. Brill for sustaining this project through so many parts and volumes and to the editors of the Handbuch der Orientalistik for including the project in their series. We appreciate both the comments that they made on specific essays and the free hand they accorded us to plan and execute the project, under their auspices, in the way we thought proper and appropriate. Brill's editors, past and present, stood by the work and patiently brought it to realization, in volume after volume, doing their job with that high level of professionalism and efficiency for which Brill has made itself famous. No agency of culture or higher education or scholarship—whatever the sponsorship, wherever located—makes a greater contribution to the study of Judaism than does E.J. Brill, and Judaism is not the only religious tradition that can make such a statement.

Professors Neusner and Chilton express their gratitude to Bard College, and Professor Avery-Peck to the College of the Holy Cross, for research grants and general support that make the scholarly work possible. The editors are grateful, most of all, to the contributors to this and the four prior parts of the work. They gave us their best work, they gave it to us on time, and they trusted us to produce a worthy medium for their scholarship. In response, we have aimed at establishing an academic medium for our subject in which important questions come under civil, significant debate, issues get aired, diverse, conflicting viewpoints get a fair hearing, and colleagues gain perspective on a critical component of a principal part of Western civilization: that comprised by the religion, Judaism, from Scripture to our own times.

Jacob Neusner
Bard College

Alan J. Avery-Peck
College of the Holy Cross

Bruce D. Chilton
Bard College

PART 3

WORLD VIEW

9. WHAT DID THE JEWS OF QUMRAN KNOW ABOUT GOD AND HOW DID THEY KNOW IT?
Revelation and God in the Dead Sea Scrolls

Edward M. Cook
Cincinnati, Ohio

If, according to a standard philosophical formula, knowledge is "justified true belief," then one can talk about knowledge, or propositions offered as knowledge, in three different ways: their content (what is believed), their veridicality, and their justification. When the topic is religious knowledge, people have tended lately to talk about justification to the exclusion of all else. The methods of justifying religious belief are generally said to be two: faith and reason. Reason includes everything that a person can think of for himself, without relying on outside information or help, while faith, in this cognitive sense, denotes the acceptance of information or help gained from some source outside the self. Reason is often compared to the sense of sight, in that people often feel that they can "see for themselves" and so need no other informant, while faith is more easily likened to hearing, and the act of faith consists of "taking someone's word" for something. Both of them are kinds of knowledge, with their own kinds of justification. A "rational" approach will emphasize foundational axioms common to all, while a "fideistic" approach will give reasons for trust in the external source of knowledge, reasons usually grounded in the relational (trustworthiness of the revealer), the traditional (inspiration of a sacred text), or experiential (personal encounter with the divine).

Judaism and Christianity, as revealed religions, ultimately must justify their claims to knowledge by faith, although historically reason has played no inconsiderable role. The group that collected the Dead Sea Scrolls, as a form of Judaism, was no exception. Indeed, one of the interesting things about the Qumran group was their insistence that their faith, their assent to their own understanding of divine revelation, was a participation in the knowledge of God. "Knowledge," as an organizing concept, was as crucial for them as "faith" was for Christianity, and for much the same reasons: possession of "knowledge" was the thing that saved you. Paraphrasing Paul, they would have said, "By grace you are saved through knowledge, and that not of yourselves. It is the gift of God." And they were more inclined to stress the *causes* of their belief by the grace of God, rather than their *reasons* for them. In this they anticipate in some ways the philosophical austerity of Calvin, who said:

> Let it therefore be held as fixed, that those who are inwardly taught by the Holy Spirit acquiesce implicitly in Scripture; that Scripture...deigns not to submit to proofs and arguments, but owes the full conviction with which we ought to receive it to the testimony of the Spirit.[1]

It is likewise typical for the scroll writers to thank God for letting them, or causing them, to have knowledge of him: you have favored me with a spirit of knowledge (1QH 6:25).[2] Such favor, God's gift of knowledge, never ceases to astonish the psalmist of the *Hodayot*. How can a mere mortal have knowledge of the divine? Humanness entails the kind of limitations that separate one from God. We mortals are but dust (1QH 19:3, 1QS 11:21, etc.); we are made out of it (1QH 11:21), we dwell in it (1QH 11:13), some of us crawl in it (1QH 13:27), and ultimately all of us will return to it (1QH 18:4, 12, 12:26, 31, 22 iv.11, etc.). We are also clay vessels[3] (1QH 9:21, 11:24, 12:29, 19:3, 20:26, 21:12, etc.), with an element of water added to the mixture (1QH 9:21, 11:24). Not only that, but humanity is corrupt and sinful, not only a vessel of clay and kneaded with water (1QH 9:21), but also (1QH 9:22-23):

> An intimate of shame and a spring of filth, a melting pot of iniquity and a structure of sin, a spirit of error, perverted without understanding and terrified by righteous judgments.

These concepts—shame, filth, iniquity, and sin—recur often in the Scrolls' conception of human nature.[4] The Manual of Discipline can

---

[1] *Institutes of the Christian Religion*, I, 7.5 (trans. Henry Beveridge, Grand Rapids, 1989), p. 72.

[2] References to the Hodayot use the new system of numbering the columns; see Johann Maier, *Die Qumran-Essener: Die Texte vom Toten Meer*, I (Munich, 1995), pp. 45-47, and the literature cited there.

[3] Eduard Lohse, *Die Texte aus Qumran* (Munich, 1971), points the Hebrew word as asphalt, bitumen (*ḥemar*), but it is clearly clay (*ḥomer*), as comparison with Is. 29:16, 64:7, and Job 33:6 demonstrates.

[4] For "shame" (*'erwah*), see also 1QH 20.25, 5.15; "filth" (*niddah*), 1QS 4:5, 10, 22, 5:19, etc.; 1QH 4:19, 19:11, 20:25, etc.; "iniquity" (*'awon*), see especially *'awon basar*, "iniquity of flesh" (1QS 11:12) and also 1QH 9:25, 27, 32, 12:29 (man is in sin from the womb, *hw' b'wwn mrḥm*), etc.; "sin," *haṭa'ah*, 1QH 9:22, 25; also "impiety" (*peša'*), 1QS 4:11, 10:11, 11:9, 1QH 11:21, 12:35, 17:13, 21:16, 22:4, etc.

even speak of "filth of the human" and "sin of humanity" (1QS 11:14-15) in a way that makes it clear that these are innate characteristics. The Damascus Document also mentions the "sin of humanity" and the "impure ways" of mortals (CD 3:17).

With the twin barriers of finitude and sinfulness, it would seem that man could come to know God and his ways only by a miracle. That, of course, is what the sectarians claimed. In a miraculous act of condescension, God communicated true knowledge of himself and his ways to some (but not all) sinful humans.

An example of the pattern is readily available in tracing the uses of the phrase *sod 'emet* in the texts. Hebrew *sod* means a group of friends characterized by mutual intimacy or by common interests, often translated "council" but equally well expressed by English "circle" or "company." It can also mean private knowledge shared by such a group, hence, by an understandable homophony, their "counsel" but also translatable as "secret." The phrase *sod 'emet*, then, could be translated "secret of truth" or perhaps simply "knowledge of truth," reliable knowledge, with the nuance that such knowledge is inside information. Given the psalmist's view of human nature, it is not surprising that he believes that *sod 'emet* belongs alone to the God of knowledge (1QH 9:27), and it dwells with him (4Q286 fg. 1, 2:7); indeed, according to 4Q417 fg. 2, 1:8 (= 4Q418 fg. 43, 6), the God of knowledge is himself *sod 'emet*.[5] Because of their sin he has hidden the source of insight and *sod 'emet* from men (1QH 13:26). But although mankind is dirt and dust, still God makes some know *sod 'emet* (1QH 10:4), in particular, those with whom he is pleased (1QH 19:9), including the psalmist himself (19:4). In fact, God makes *sod 'emet* strong or firm in his heart (13:9). The psalmist can even become the very personification of *sod 'emet*: you made me the knowledge of truth and insight (*sod 'emet ubinah*) to the upright of way (1QH 10:10). Thus something that is initially claimed to be a characteristic of God can, by God's grace, become an attribute of one of his servants.

The word *binah* ("insight, understanding") may provide another example. If God is the custodian of *sod 'emet*, he is also the source of understanding (*mqwr bynh*) (4Q286 fg. 1, 2:6) and he cherishes it (*'l*

---

[5] The text reads: *'l hd'wt swd 'mt*. F. García Martínez translates "God will spread knowledge of the foundation of truth" (*The Dead Sea Scrolls Translated* [Leiden, 1992], p. 390), but this is incorrect in almost every word.

dwrš bynh) (4Q418 fg. 88, 6).⁶ Because of their sin he has hidden the fountain of understanding (*mʿyn bynh*) from men (1QH 13:26), and the psalmist himself is by nature "without understanding" (*blwʾ bynh*) (1QH 9:22), as are all men. Even the benighted soothsayers have not grown wise in understanding (*bbny lʾ hskltm*, 4Q300 fg. 1, 2:2), nor those who are foolish in heart (*[ks]yly lb lʾ ybynw ʾlh*, 1QH 9:37). How could the spirit of flesh gain understanding, except through God? (1QH 5:13, 20:33). But through God's favor, some come to share in the understanding of God himself, so the psalmist can say to God, "I know these things through your understanding" (*ʾlh ydʿty mbyntkh*, 1QH 9:21; see also 1QH 6:12, 13, 7:12), echoing the prayer of the whole community ("we know these things through your understanding," *ʾlh ydʿnw mbyntkh*, 1QM 10:10). The heart of the psalmist is the new location of *binah*, for God has opened up the heart (1QH fg. 4:12) and put it there (1QH 10:17, 6:8). Now those who have been gifted in this way are truly *mebinim*, those who have understanding. In the long wisdom composition from Cave 4, the novice is addressed over and over again as *mebin* (4Q416 fg. 4:3, 4Q417 fg. 2, 1:1, 14, 18, 4Q418 fg. 69, 2:15, fg. 81:15, fg. 123, 2:5, fg. 168:4, etc.). It is for those made wise to give understanding (*lhbyn*) and to teach all the sons of light (1QS 3:13).

Another Hebrew root is a key element in the Qumran understanding of religious knowledge: *sekel*, "intelligence, learning, awareness." In the Scrolls, *sekel* is generally referred to as a human endowment; although it is only attained by the gift of God (1QH 18:6), and we are told that he is, or has, a storehouse of *sekel* (4Q286 fg. 1, 2:7), we never hear that only God has *sekel* or the like. God is praised for giving the psalmist awareness of knowledge (*skl dʿh*, 1QH 19:28), and one can pray that God will enlighten your heart with the *sekel* of life (1QS 2:3). But it admits of degrees; one can have more, or less, of *sekel*. According to the psalmist, people will "know you [God] according to their *sekel*" (1QH 9:31). For this reason, members of the sect can be ranked according to their intelligence (1QS 5:23). Each new member is examined with respect to his *sekel* (1QS 5:21) and then

---

⁶ The context is damaged, and this text may mean "God seeks among [...]," as I translated in M. Abegg, E. Cook, M. Wise, *The Dead Sea Scrolls: A New Translation* (San Francisco, 1996), p. 388. It certainly does not mean "God seeks knowledge"! (García Martinez, op. cit., p. 392). The sense "seek with care, care for" is well attested for the root *drš*.

ranked in order according to his *sekel* (1QS 5:21-23). If so, someone with a high level of insight would be at the top of the list, among the leaders of the group. These are the *maskilim*, the wise, for whom, and no doubt by whom, several of the Scrolls were written. The *maskil*, according to the Manual of Discipline, shall have an important teaching role in the community; because of his insight and advanced standing, he has authority to "advance someone according to his *sekel*" (1QS 9:15-16), he must guide the members of the group "into knowledge" (9:18) "and thus educate them (*lhskylm*) in the mysteries of wonder and truth" (9:18) and "educate them (*lhskylm*) in all that is found to do in this time" (9:20). We will return to the *maskilim* later, but for now it should be noted that the revelation of God's will described in the *Hodayot* as coming directly, as it were, can also be mediated indirectly to the group members through the *maskil*.

Enough examples have been given to demonstrate a pattern of revelation as conceived in the Qumran literature: Although human nature as commonly found is too weak or sinful to understand God or his ways, God through his grace can transfer his own knowledge to certain chosen individuals, and these in turn can serve as sources of the knowledge of God.

But still the exact mode of revelation may seem vague, and indeed the Scroll writers have a love for inexplicit generalities in their theological expression that makes a clear construal of their thought difficult. What exactly were they *doing* when they received revelation? Did they hear an audible voice, or did they see or hear figures in a vision, or in a dream? Did they experience trances, or see miracles, or what? The question is important, because they claimed to have a revelation that the rest of Israel did not have, and we must try to understand what made them think it was a revelation and why only they had it.

We may continue by underlining the primarily *intellectual* terms they use to describe their knowledge and the way they acquired it. They have "knowledge," "understanding," and "insight" in abundance, but the use of terms denoting sense perception is less common. Even when the Scrolls talk about "seeing," it is usually intellectual perception that is meant. The speaker in the Damascus Document announces that he will "open the eyes" of his hearers "to see and understand the deeds of God" (CD 2:14) and then goes on to an overview of Israel's past. Similarly the psalmist of the *Hodayot* speaks of people seeing God's righteousness (1QH 6:16), glory (1QH 18:20), and jealousy (4Q427 fg. 7, 2:15), and, in the Manual, of his wonders (1QS 11:3), deep secrets (11:19), and eternal being (1QS 11:19). As for hearing, they have "heard the secrets of God" (1QM 16:15), but this is not stated in such a way as to suggest a literal audition; instead it was "long ago" (*m'z*). The Damascus Document speaks of the members of the group, whose eyes God has uncovered "to hidden things" and whose ears they themselves have opened "for deep things" (4Q268 fg. 1, 7-8), but the upshot once again is cognitive, not experiential: "so they understood (*wybynw*) all the things to come before they will happen to them." The idiom "to uncover the ear" is common in the texts but is used figuratively. When the psalmist says, "You have uncovered my ears to wonderful mysteries" (1QH 9:21), he means no more than the preceding sentence, "I know these things through your understanding."

On the rare occasions when they describe a literal vision or audition, it is either in the remote past or the future. At Sinai, God spoke with Israel "face to face" and appeared "in burning flame from above and stood on the mountain" (4Q377 fg. 1, 2:6-8). During the last battle with darkness, the high priest will pray and describe Israel as "a people learned in law...hearers of the glorious voice, beholders of holy angels" (1QM 10:10-11). But this time is not yet fulfilled.

Therefore the scroll writers are reluctant to claim they have literally heard the voice of God or have seen a supernatural vision. God speaks only to figures of the biblical past. "God spoke to Habakkuk" (1QpH 7:1); "you spoke through Moses" (1QH 4:12); "he spoke to Moses" (4Q252 fg. 1 4:2), "he spoke through Ezekiel" (CD 19:11), "you spoke to us long ago...through your anointed ones you spoke to us" (1QM 11:6, 8), "the word of YHWH came to Ezekiel" (4Q285 fg. 1 1), and so on. They do not say in the *Hodayot* or elsewhere, "God spoke to me," "God (or an angel) appeared to me," "the word of the Lord came to me." It is worth insisting on this point, because it has sometimes been the custom among scholars to ascribe to the faith of Qumran a belief in a special revelation of their own. We must use terms carefully here; "revelation," in the sense that I use it, refers to God's disclosure of himself to certain human vessels, informing them of his character and purposes; these disclosures may be preserved in writing or through oral tradition. Distinct from this is what we may call "inspiration," "illumination," or "enlightenment," in which the human subject is divinely led to believe, understand, and accept the revelation hitherto ignored, disbelieved, or misunderstood. Accordingly, I do not believe that the Qumran writers claimed to have received a new revelation, but they did claim, in all their comments about "knowledge," to have reached, through God's grace, a level of enlightenment not attained by other groups.

A question that is difficult to answer is raised by the existence of "revelatory" literature that is non-canonical, that is, outside *our* canon. It is impossible to determine which pseudepigraphical texts, if any, were considered canonical by the Qumran group. It is likely that Jubilees was, and perhaps some of the Enoch literature; but it is rare for the explicitly sectarian texts to ground any of their beliefs in references to clearly extra-canonical revelations, even when one would most expect them to. The difficulty I am speaking of comes into view most clearly in a contrast between two texts that present the same doctrine in decidedly different ways. I refer to the Vision of Amram and the Manual of Discipline.

One of the most purely theological sections of the Dead Sea Scrolls is the so-called "Treatise of the Two Spirits" in the Manual of Discipline (1QS 3:13-4:26), in which the "nature of all the sons of men" (3:13) is described as a contest between the two great powers of Light and Darkness, Good and Evil, personified in two mighty angelic beings called the "Spirit of Truth" (also the "Prince of Lights") and the "Spirit of Evil," or the "Angel of Darkness" (3:18-19). In other texts, the good and evil angels are called, respectively, Melchizedek (11Q13) and Melchiresha (4Q280 fg. 1). The same theological account of human destiny is given in narrative fashion in the Vision of Amram. At Qumran, the genealogical line connecting Levi with Moses—that is, Levi, Kohath, Amram—is supplied with a series of narratives of the "testamentary" genre, and the Vision tells of a "vision of a dream" that Amram had:

> There were two figures arguing over me...and holding a great dispute over me. So I asked them, "How is it that you have authority over me?" And they said, "We rule and have authority over all the human race...." I lifted my eyes and saw one of them, whose appearance was dreadfully frightening; his clothing was multicolored and very dark... and I saw another and he was pleasant in his appearance, and his face was laughing and he was covered in white... [7]

Amram discovers that these two figures are Melchizedek (presumably, for the fragmentary text does not preserve his name) and Melchiresha. Here we have what appears to be a central doctrine of

---

[7] The translation is mine, taken from *The Dead Sea Scrolls: A New Translation*, p. 435.

the Qumran group on the occasion of its first revelation, which is made to the father of Moses and Aaron. The interesting features of this text in the present discussion are two. First, the actual revealing of this doctrine does not seem to have been very important to the authors of the other texts. The Manual of Discipline in the Treatise of the Two Spirits does not appeal to the authority of Amram for teaching, and the dream vision of Amram is not mentioned anywhere else in the Dead Sea Scrolls as a ground for belief in the doctrine of the two spirits. The texts, taken together, give the impression that the theological exposition of the two-spirit doctrine in the Manual and the narrative portrayal of it in the Vision are alternate ways of presenting the same idea, not as a theological development of a historically given revelation. But, on the other hand, the revelatory vision is not located in the present or in the recent past, but in the biblical period, within a line of figures whose custody of revelation was undisputed within Judaism, i.e., the family of Moses and Aaron. The texts present a doctrine whose authority, if one cared to look for it, was grounded in the context of biblical revelation, not in contemporary personal reception of new divine disclosures.

In fact, all throughout the testamentary literature in the Dead Sea Scrolls, one finds an emphasis on the *ancient* transmission of revelation that matches the Scrolls' writers' reluctance to claim new revelation. For instance, in the Testament of Kohath (4Q542), Kohath, the son of Levi and father of Amram, charges Amram to take care of the writings that Levi had received and passed on to Kohath, "for in them is great merit for you when they are transmitted with you" (fg. 1 ii 13). Likewise, in the Words of Levi, Levi's son, probably Kohath, is admonished to protect "many revelations.... Examine them and seek and know what will befall you. But do not damage them by erasure or wear.... Do not bring shame on the priestly headplate" (4Q541 fg. 24, 2:3-5).[8] In a fragmentary text that also seems to be from a "testament," the author exclaims, "Who will write these words of mine in a book that does not wear out?" (4Q536 fg. 1, 2:12). Thus even the pseudepigraphical texts point the reader back to canonical Scripture and particularly to the two Levites *par excellence*, Moses and Aaron, and the revelation given to Moses, the Torah.

---

[8] Cf., the translation in *The Dead Sea Scrolls*, p. 260. The translations of this fragment vary widely; I believe the one I have given is more justifiable than the others.

After the Torah came the prophets, who are cited as the "seers of truth" in the Damascus Document (CD 2:12). Those who enter the community swear to do God's will as commanded "by Moses and by his servants the prophets" (1QS 1:3; cf. 8:16). No member of the community is called a prophet. Probably none was even called a "seer," although this is not so clear.[9] One very important member of the group was called the "Teacher of Righteousness," and much has been claimed for this figure, including that the community viewed him as a prophet. But the texts are very careful not to say he is a prophet; rather, he was an inspired exegete. According to the Habakkuk Commentary, God granted the Teacher the power "to interpret all the words of his prophets, by whom God has told everything that is to come on his people Israel" (1QpHab 2:8-10). It is the prophets who have done the foretelling, not the Teacher. He has performed the key task of unlocking the secrets of the prophets (1QpHab 7:5), because God has "made him know" those secrets. But it is not said that he "spoke" (*dbr*) to the teacher, but to the prophet (1QpHab 7:1).

This might seem to be a minor difference, and some will understandably want to claim the title "revelation" for the Teacher's work as well as for the prophets'. The Habakkuk Commentary comes close to saying exactly that when it associates the Teacher's message with "the mouth of God" (1QpHab 2:2);[10] but it does not quite say the Teacher's message is *directly* from the mouth of God, and nowhere else is there a clear implication that the Teacher was the recipient of new disclosures from God, although he may have been the first properly to understand the old disclosures. This is no more (and no less!) than many modern scholars would claim for themselves or their mentors, although divine aid is not usually mentioned in such a context.

There are indeed passages in which the prophets alone are credited with the revelation and the interpreter, honored elsewhere, is wholly absent. In the War Scroll, God's "anointed ones, the seers of foreordained times" (1QM 11:8) are the conduit through which the information about the wars of the end-time reached Israel: "From of old you proclaimed to us the time of your mighty blow against the

---

[9] Some of the contexts in which the word for "seer" is used are damaged or otherwise incomplete.

[10] The passage has some gaps; the usual restoration is "they have not [obeyed the words of] the Teacher of Righteousness from the mouth of God" (cf., *The Dead Sea Scrolls*, p. 116).

Kittim, saying...," followed by the citation of Is. 31:8. Someone must have told them that the Assyrians of the biblical passage were the Kittim, and someone must have suggested that the time of fulfillment was near; but that someone, whether the Teacher himself or one of his followers, recedes completely behind the prophetic text, which is God speaking.

The Teacher, therefore, is a key figure for the Qumran group, but only key in a way that a leading rabbi is key for his followers. He is an inspired interpreter, and this was no small distinction for a group that so prized written revelation, but he differed only in the degree, not the kind, of his inspiration. For it seems clear that the *maskil* was a type of teacher of which the Teacher of Righteousness was a particularly distinguished example; or, conversely, that the Teacher had achieved a degree of insight that any *maskil* might legitimately aspire to. As noted above, the Teacher had been granted special insight into the "mysteries" of the prophets; but the *maskilim* are also custodians of God's mysteries, as stated in 1QS 9:18: "The *maskil* must guide them with knowledge and instruct them in the mysteries of wonder and truth." In fact, as a type, the *maskil* is far more prominent in the Qumran documents than the Teacher of Righteousness. Two sections of the Manual of Discipline are given over to describing the *maskil's* duties (1QS 9:12-21, and 1QS 9:21-10:5) and the final hymn of the Manual (10:6-11:22) is his ideal confession. The manifest links between this hymn and the psalms of the *Hodayot* suggest that the latter, too, are the ideal speakers of its compositions (and not, as is often asserted, the Teacher of Righteousness). Indeed, the heading "for the *maskil*" appears as at least one heading in the *Hodayot* (4Q427 fg. 2+3 2:5 = 1QH 20:4). The same heading also appears throughout the Songs for the Sabbath Sacrifice (4Q400-407, 11Q17), the Songs of a Sage (4Q510-511), and arguably in the first line of the War Scroll.

The use of the term *maskil* in some of the so-called "sapiential" scrolls hints at the true relationship of the *maskil* and the *mebin*, mentioned above. The address "you, O *mebin*," occurs repeatedly throughout them; the sapiential works are clearly books for them to learn from. Within them the *mebin* is encouraged to "accept instruction from all your *maskilim*" (4Q418 fg. 81, 17), or admonished that a good student "will accept the rebuke of a *maskil*" (4Q421 fg. 1a 2:11-12). The *mebinim*, then, are the students, the disciples, the novices. Another term for students may be suggested. One of the texts is titled

"Words of the *Maskil* to the Students." The last words are usually translated "sons of dawn (*šḥr*)," but the root *šḥr* in the sapiential texts means "study" or "inquiry." Thus: "study (*šḥr*) these things always" (4Q417 fg. 2, 2:12), the wicked "have not sought insight" (*l' šḥrw bynh*, 4Q418 fg. 55, 5), the one who desires wisdom "should not seek it (*yšḥrnh*) with a deceitful mind" (4Q525 fg. 2, 3). If the "sons of *šḥr*" are those characterized by seeking, or inquiry, i.e., students—then the *maskil*, quite simply, is "the teacher." The teacher is "a mediator of knowledge of wonderful mysteries...a spring of knowledge for all *mebinim*" (1QH 10:13, 18).

It would appear, therefore, that the teacher-student relationship is more important in the Qumran group than has hitherto been suspected. It gives us the beginnings of an answer to the question, "What were they doing when they received revelation?" The answer, at least in most cases, simply is, "Listening to the voice of a human teacher or studying the holy books." And it gives us another angle to go back and appreciate the rather exalted language of the Qumran psalmists when they talk about God's gift of knowledge: "God has placed in my heart a spirit of knowledge and understanding, truth and righteousness" (4Q444 fg. 1, 3); "you have favored me with a spirit of knowledge" (1QH 6:25); "I know these things through your understanding...and thus you bring me near to your understanding" (1QH 6:12-13); "I know these things through your understanding, for you have opened my ear to wonderful mysteries" (1QH 9:21); "I, your servant, have gained knowledge through the spirit you placed in me" (1QH 5:24-25); and others of the same import could be quoted for pages. These statements are a theological understanding of what happens when someone becomes a member of the group and begins to learn its doctrine. Although knowledge is mediated by a teacher, it is understood to be given directly by God.

The teachers themselves were once students and received their doctrine through the spoken voice; but they may also study the Scripture for themselves and propound interpretations of their own. Such was the case with the Teacher of Righteousness, and in such a way, no doubt, the Qumran group came to have its identity. The same theology obtains in these instances, as seen above: God makes known his "secrets" through the written word to those who, through his own providential guidance, are able to understand it. But there is no claim to a special new revelation. All "direct" disclosures are ascribed to the biblical period and to biblical figures.

God

With such a belief system, it is not surprising that the group's doctrine of God, while containing special emphases and innovations, does not stray greatly from biblical foundations. As in the Bible, the divine attributes that come in for the most attention are the relative attributes—those that are exercised towards the creation—and not the absolute attributes, that describe God in his essential being. In the Damascus Document, it is true, a certain liturgy begins with the address to God, "You are the All" (*'t hw' hkwl*)—which sounds quite metaphysical (cf., 4Q266 fg. 18 5:9).[11] But it continues in this vein (4Q266 fg. 18, 5:9-12):

> In your hands is all, and you are the maker of all things, who established the peoples by their families, and languages, and nations, and made them wander in the trackless waste; but you chose our ancestors and gave to their seed the laws of your truth, and the judgments of your holiness, which a man shall do and live.

The liturgy moves rapidly from an absolute attribute to concrete facts of creation and redemption. And the language it uses for those concrete facts is biblical language. "Made them wander in the trackless waste" is from Ps. 107:40; "chose our ancestors...seed" recalls Deut. 4:37, 10:15; "which a man shall do and live" is from Lev. 18:5 (or Ezek. 20:11ff., Neh. 9:29).

Hence the God of Qumran is unmistakably the God of the Bible. This is not to say that the Scrolls do not have their characteristic emphases or even novelties. They do; but they never wholly detach themselves from the scriptural umbilical cord. For them, God is most emphatically the "God of Israel" (1QS 3:24, and often).

As the God of Israel, he is known by his covenant name YHWH. Scholars once thought that the tetragrammaton was used at Qumran only in the biblical texts; the release and publication of all the material shows that it was more widespread. But it is still mainly used, if not solely in canonical texts, then in texts imitating or commenting on those texts, such as Jubilees or other pseudepigraphical works. (A notable exception is the liturgy in 4Q493 fg. 3 6: "You are the Lord, you chose our fathers long ago.") The word *Elohim* is used in a similar way, in biblical or pseudo-biblical contexts, or less commonly in a

---

[11] A similar statement is found in Sirach 43:27: "The sum of our words is: He is the all (*hw' hkwl*)." The context deals with the creation of the world.

sermon or prayer. The preferred term for "God" in the central texts of the group is *El*, a word with ample biblical precedent but less common in the canon than in the Scrolls. As in the Bible, the concept of God's name itself has a special significance: "the honored name" (1QS 6:27), "your great name" (1QM 11:2), "I will praise your name" (1QH 20:3), "the glorious name of your godhead" (4Q287 fg. 2 8), and many times.

The epithets of God usually follow a biblical pattern as well. The word "lord" (*'adon*) is well attested, both in a personal address (*'adonay*, "my Lord") in psalms or prayers, and in general attributions (e.g., "lord of all," 4Q409 fg. 1 1:8). In the Aramaic texts, *mare* ("lord") is used in a number of combinations, most notably in the prayer of Abraham: "Blessed are you, God Most High, lord (*mry*) of all ages, for you are lord (*mrh*) and ruler over all…" (1QGenAp 20:13). "Most high" appears both in combination ("God Most High," e.g., 1QH 12:31) and alone (e.g., "knowledge of the Most High," 1QS 4:22 [cp. Num. 24.16], "Torah of the Most High," 4Q525 fg. 3, 2:4). The biblical expression "Lord of Hosts" (*yhwh ṣbʿwt*) is rare and occurs only in pseudepigraphical works (e.g., 4Q385 fg. 2, 8; note that "pseudo-Ezekiel" uses the expression, while canonical Ezekiel does not!).

More important than such terminology, however, is the underlying conception of God. The foundation of Qumranian thought about God is his rule of the universe, which is understood both spatially and temporally—spatially, in that all parts of the universe are under his control; and temporally, in that all of history has been subjected to his will. I say *has been subjected*, not *is subject*; for the course of history, no less than the movements of the heavenly bodies, in the thought of the scroll writers, has been foreordained by God.

The exemplification of such a theology lies ready to hand on almost every page of the Scrolls. The introduction to the programmatic "Two-Spirit Treatise" (1QS 3:13-4.26) is typical (1QS 3:15-17):

> All that is now or ever shall be originates with the God of knowledge. Before things come to be, he has ordered all their designs, so that when they do come to exist—at their appointed times as ordained by his glorious plan—they fulfill their destiny, a destiny impossible to change. He controls the laws governing all things, and he provides for all their pursuits.[12]

---

[12] Translation of Michael Wise in Abegg, Cook, Wise, *The Dead Sea Scrolls: A New Translation*, p. 129.

Such a doctrine is not an innovation within Judaism. Ben Sira says, "All things were known unto him or ever they were created; and in like manner also after they were perfected" (23:20). Judith prays, "You have designed the things that are now, and those that are to come. What you had in mind has happened; the things you decided on presented themselves and said, 'Here we are!' For all your ways are prepared in advance, and your judgment is with foreknowledge" (Judith 9:5-6, NRSV). All these Jewish writers could point to biblical texts that form a basis for the idea that God's plan is behind all things. Does not Jeremiah confess that "a man's way is not his own, nor may a man walk and direct his own steps" (Jer. 10.23)? Likewise, in the book of Proverbs, they could read that "a man's mind may plan his way, but the Lord determines his steps" (Prov. 16:9). "As I have intended, so it has been; and as I have planned, it will come to pass" (Is. 14:24).

God exercises his rule equally in the world of nature as in the world of men. The same language is used for each. In the hymn that concludes the Manual of Discipline, the psalmist declares that he will bless God "according to law engraved forever" (1QS 10:6)—and that law, as the next few lines show, is the law of the unfolding of time in the rhythm of day and night, the four seasons, the years by groups of seven, and the Jubilees (1QS 10:7-9). This engraved law is not "the law of nature," as if "nature" (a concept not explicitly articulated at this point in history) had a different law—no, the engraved law is also the law by which the psalmist himself is judged: "my sin is before my eyes according to the engraved law" (1QS 10:11). There is no difference between the natural law and the moral law at Qumran, no distinction between creation and history, for all are equally the expressions of the will of God.

Therefore biblical passages that describe God's creative power in nature are pressed into service in the Scrolls to apply to human destiny. In Job 28:25, God makes a weight for the wind (*ruaḥ*) and distributes the waters by measure; in 4Q434 fg. 1, 1:10, he creates the human spirit (*ruḥam*) by measure and distributes their words by weight. Similarly, "you determine their spirit by weight" (4Q415 fg. 11, 8). All of history is likewise determined, for the very dispensations of time have a measure and weight (4Q418 fg. 77, 3).

It can be observed that passages praising the God of creation pass easily and unconsciously to passages praising the God of redemption. For instance, in the War Scroll, a psalmist exclaims, "Who is like you, God of Israel?" and goes on to praise his work in creating the people Israel (1QM 10:8-11), the heavenly bodies (11-12), the earth, seas, beasts, and man (12-14), dividing the nations into groups (14), and establishing the seasons of the year (15). Then he recalls God's work in subduing Goliath and the Philistines (11:1-3) and thanks God in advance for his promise of victory over the forces of evil (8-15). After all, all these things have been foretold by the prophets (7, 11). Finally his thought returns to the hosts of heaven, the angels, in God's glorious abode (12:1) and the multitudes of the redeemed who are among them (12:2). All this, he avers, comes from God's mercies as shown in his covenant, which is "engraved for them with a living pen" (12:3).

In the *Hodayot*, the teacher who is the psalmist affirms that the order of the universe shares in the oneness and immutability of God. He speaks of "the order made firm by the mouth of God and the destiny of all that is; and it shall come to pass, and nothing else; besides it there was nothing, and never shall be, for the God of knowledge determined it, and there is no other with him" (1QH 20:9-11). This is unmistakably reminiscent of Is. 45:5: "I am the Lord, and there is none else; besides me, there is no god." At Qumran, monotheism implied determinism. If there was one all-powerful God, what could stand in the way of his will? If there were no other god, then there could be no other plan; besides his plan, there is no plan. "Without him nothing is done" (1QS 11:11).

The rule of God is enabled by his power. The terms most often used are "might" (*gbwrh*) and "power" (*kwḥ*). "In your power," says the psalmist, "is all might" (1QH 19:8). "Who is like you in power?" (1QM 13:13). "There is none equal to you in power" (1QH 18:10). Humankind, regrettably, does not understand the great power of God (1Q34 fg. 3, 2:4), but the redeemed are victorious through God's might, not through their own power (1QM 11:4). Through God's mercy to his elect, "all his creatures will know the power of his might" (1QH 12:32), a might utterly without equal (1QH 18:10). God's "strength" (*'wz*) is also praised: "you support me with your strength" (1QH 15:6). Biblical metaphors are fully exploited; the Scrolls have no aversion to speaking of God's "mighty hand" (1QM 3:8), "the power of your hand" (1QM 11:1), "the great hand of God" (1QM 1:14), which is lifted up (1QM 18:3) and placed on the enemies' neck (1QM 19:3).

God's rule is that of a king. He is the "king of glory" (1QM 12:8;

4Q403 fg. 1, 1:31) and kingship is his (1QM 6:6). He is the king of kings (4Q403 fg. 1, 1:34), the king of truth (4Q404 fg. 5, 6), king of gods (4Q 405 fg. 23, 1:13), the king of holiness (4Q405 fg. 23, 2:11), and the glory of his kingly rule is the subject of angelic praise (4Q400 fg. 2, 1). Those on earth whom he has chosen may join in this praise: "Ascribe greatness to our God, and glory to our king!" (4Q427 fg. 7, 1:15). He is majestic and awe-inspiring (4Q372 fg. 1, 29).

The admiration of God's royal power is not, or not only, the homage of weakness to power; God's power is not disconnected from his righteousness. The link between power and righteousness comes to expression in the concept of judge. As ruler, God has the power to pass judgment; perfectly righteous and holy, his sentences are always just. Therefore the psalmist can say, echoing the words of Job, "Who can be in the right against you when he is judged?" (1QH 15:28; cp. Job 9:2, 25:4). In his "hand" is the power to judge all that lives (1QS 10:16-17). His judgment against wickedness is inevitable (4Q416 fg. 1, 10); he calls the wicked to account for their iniquity (1QH 6:24); indeed, he calls the whole earth to account and gives the wicked what they deserve (CD 7:9).

At the beginning of the Damascus Document, God's just ways with erring mankind are spelled out. God has a "case" against all flesh and will pass judgment on all who reject him (CD A 1:2), an expression again echoing the words of Scripture (Jer. 25:31). This adverse sentence against the wicked is closely connected with the wrath of God. The wicked will be judged "by the furious wrath of the God of vengeance" (1QS 4:12). It will be inscribed on the trumpets of God's army: "His wrath will not abate until the wicked are destroyed" (1QM 3:9). Disease can be a sign of God's wrath: "in your wrath are all the judgments of disease" (1QH 19:8). In the time of the end, God will use fire as an instrument of his wrath. He will judge the wicked with "fire of brimstone" (1QpHab 10:5) and condemn them to the gloom of everlasting flame (1QS 2:8).

Although "wrath" is a term from the realm of emotion, once again in the Scrolls God's wrath is not disconnected from his righteousness. The "fire of brimstone" does not break out in a storm of rage; first God brings the wicked to justice, then passes sentence, and only then is the guilty doomed to the fiery punishment (1QpHab 10:3-5). It is because of "the darkness of his deeds" (1QS 2:6) that the wicked may expect the darkness of eternal flame. Therefore God is the "God of vengeance" (1QS 4:12) on the wicked, and the group members pray that God will "show [the wicked] an angry face for vengeance" (1QS 2:9). God's "hatred" is also an expression of his righteousness. He "hates" iniquity forever (1QH 6:25), he "abominates" the council of darkness (1QS 4:1), he "hates and abominates" the false teachers and his anger is hot against them and their followers (CD 19:31-32).

In general, though, the Scrolls dwell far more on the kindness of God and his willingness to forgive. The great "attribute formulary" of the Bible—"a God merciful and compassionate, slow to anger and abounding in kindness and loyalty" (Exod. 34:6)—echoes like the peal of a bell throughout the writings of the Qumran group. It is quoted explicitly in 1QH 8:24-25, and its view of God underlies all the praise of the scroll writers. "Blessed are you, God of compassion and mercy!" (1QH 19:29). When God judges his people, he will do it "with grace...with copious compassion and an abundance of forgiveness" (1QH 14:9). He brings near his followers "by forgiveness...by the abundance of your goodness and your copious compassion" (1QH 15:30). Because of God's goodness, he shows forgiveness and mercy to all whom he approves (1QH 19:9). God's tender care for the faithful is like a father for his children—or even like a mother: "you rejoice over them, like she who pities her baby, and like a nurse, you support in your bosom all your creatures" (1QH 17:36).

As in the attribute formulary, he is "slow to anger" or patient. "Patience is with him, and an abundance of forgiveness" (CD 2:4). He is indeed glorious in his patience (4Q301 fg. 3, 4). Accordingly, he is able to turn from his wrath. If a man is truly penitent, "then God will see and his anger will subside and he will pass over your sins" (4Q417 fg. 1, 1:15). God has shown mercy to the poor (4Q434 fg. 1, 1:5-6):

> He has not given them into the power of cruel tyrants,
> Nor judged them with the wicked,
> Nor aroused his anger against them,
> Nor destroyed them all in his wrath.
> His fierce wrath has not blazed out against all,
> And he has not judged them in the fire of his zeal.[13]

The mercies of God are his *ḥasadim*, variously translatable as "love," "kindness," "favor," or "grace."[14] He is the "God of grace" (1QM

---

[13] Translation mine, in ibid., p. 395.

[14] The scroll writers favored the plural form for this word when speaking of an attribute of God, in this respect differing from biblical usage, although the singular form is also used.

14:8), for he has shown to Israel the mercies of his grace (1QS 2:1). There is an abundance of grace on all the children of truth (1QS 4:5), and they must rely on God's grace forever (1QS 4:4, 10:16, 1QH 12:37). "By your grace," says the psalmist, "you save my soul" (1QH 10:23), "by your grace you have not abandoned me" (1QH 17:7), "God's grace is my eternal salvation" (1QS 11:12), "in your grace there is hope" (1QS 17:14). Closely allied in concept is the *raḥamim* of God, his compassion. The two terms are virtually interchangeable; one may speak of "the grace of compassion (*ḥsd rḥmym*) on Israel" (1QS 1:22) and then of the "compassion of his grace" (*rḥmy ḥsdw*) (1QS 2:1; see also the citations from 1QH 14:9 and 15:30 above).

Together these comprise God's "goodness" (*ṭub*). "In the greatness of his goodness" he will atone for sins (1QS 11:14), he cleanses the pious from their transgression (1QH 15:30), shows great forgiveness (1QH 19:9). A man may be righteous only through God's goodness (1QH 5:22-23); therefore, says the psalmist, "my soul delights in your great goodness!" (1QH 19:6). Again, all these expressions are redolent of Scripture, e.g., Is. 63:7: "I will mention the grace of the Lord, the praise of the Lord...and his great goodness to the house of Israel, who repaid them with compassion, and according to the abundance of his grace."

Finally, the "righteousness" of God is shown in his forgiveness of the repentant. Although we might expect a word usually glossed as "righteousness" to be primarily linked with judgment, it is not so. As in the Bible, God's *ṣedaqah* has primary reference to his vindication of those who belong to him; only so can a sentence like "may the wicked not enter your righteousness" (Ps. 69:29 [Heb.: 28]) make sense. Hence the Qumran psalmist can say, "by his righteousness he effaces my sins...from the fountain of his righteousness is my judgment" (1QS 11:3, 5), "he has judged me by his true righteousness and by his great goodness he atones for all my sins" (1QS 11:14). "By your righteousness you made me stand in your covenant" (1QH 15:19-20). It is a synonym for salvation, so that in the last days "salvation and righteousness will be revealed to those who fear God" (CD 20:20).

In the thought of the Scrolls, then, God's wrath falls justly on the wicked, but his grace and goodness are shown to the pious, who indeed cannot be the pious without God's prior choice of them "before ever they were" (1QS 3:15). But if "nothing is done without you" (1QS 11:11, 1QH 9:20, 18:9), then the wicked were destined to be the way they are, too. In some way, then, is God is the author of darkness? This conclusion, which is both logical and apparently mandated by Scripture ("I form light and create darkness, make peace and create evil," Is. 45:7), is not quite drawn by the scroll writers. In the "Two-Spirit Treatise," it is the angel of darkness—indeed created by God (1QS 3:25)—who causes humanity to walk in wickedness; but from another point of view, human wickedness causes itself: "To you, God of knowledge, belong all the works of righteousness and true counsel; but to man belongs the service of iniquity and deeds of deceit" (1QH 9:26-27).

And yet the dualism that is part of the Qumran monism goes very deep. In the recently published fragment 4Q392, it is stated (4Q392 fg. 1, 4-7) that

> God created darkness, but light is his, and in his dwelling place shines perfect light, and all gloom is inactive in his presence, so he has no need to divide light and darkness. But for the sons of men he divided them, giving light by day in the sun, and at night, by the moon and stars. With him is light unsearchable...for all the works of God are double.[15]

Although the dualism between light and darkness reaches back to the initial decree of God, the preference of God for light reaches back to the same moment. Therefore God's plan encompasses both light and darkness, and the ethical paths corresponding to each of them, but his plan also entails an eventual end to the power of darkness, which is given dominion for a time.

Why God should make this kind of plan in the way he does is a question not asked, for the theological is swallowed up by the doxological. It is enough that God is in control, that he favors the forces of light, and that by his goodness he has included obedient Israel—that is, the members of the Qumran group—in his plan for eventual triumph.

The purpose of God's plan, its goal, is the glory of God. He spread

---

[15] The translation is mine, based on the text in B. Wacholder and M. Abegg, *A Preliminary Edition of the Unpublished Dead Sea Scrolls, Fascicle Two* (Washington, 1992), p. 38. The text published by F. Garcia Martinez and E. Tigchelaar (*The Dead Sea Scrolls Study Edition* [Leiden, 1998]) differs in some material readings, particularly in the word "double," which they read as "wonderful." The Wacholder-Abegg text seems more correct. Ben Sira likewise says, "Look upon all the works of the Most High; two and two, one against another" (36:15), and in the *Testament of Asher* it reads, "God has granted two ways to the sons of men... Accordingly, everything is in pairs, the one over against the other" (T. Asher 1:3-4).

out the heavens for his glory (1QH 9:10), teaches the pious for his glory (1QH 14:10), and, most particularly, chooses the elect from dust for his glory: "What is one who returns to dust, that he should have strength? Only for your glory have you done all these things" (1QH 18:12). "You have done these wonders for your glory" (1QH 23:16). It is only right that the ultimate purpose of God should also be the purpose of the elect: "all my song is for the glory of God" (1QS 10:9). "I will tell of your glory among the sons of men" (1QH 18:6). And indeed it is God's purpose that the elect not only show their glory, but tell of it: you made them "so that they would tell of your glory" (1QH 5:17). The *sola gratia* of the gift of knowledge is magnified only for the ultimate intent of the creation, the glory of God.

What did the Jews of the Dead Sea Scrolls know about God, and how did they know it? They did not believe knowledge of God was possible apart from revelation, and they did not believe that revelation was accessible or comprehensible without the active intervention of God within them. They knew about God what the Bible told them, through the agency of their teachers, whom they saw as servants of the Torah. In very natural and even prosaic processes of study and learning, they saw the power of God marking them out for salvation, overcoming their creaturely limitations and forgiving them their sin. From that time onward, they saw themselves as growing in knowledge of God and the Torah, sharing in the praise of God offered by all the forces of Light, and looking forward to the consummation of his plan, when "wickedness will vanish forever and righteousness will be manifest like the sun" (1Q27 1:6). The ultimate justification of their belief—and therefore its claim to be knowledge—rested on the hope and expectation of that consummation.

10. THE TORAH AT QUMRAN

Philip R. Davies
University of Sheffield

The following account addresses three questions: What does the word "Torah" refer to in the Qumran literature? What are the contents or substance of this "Torah" as understood in these writings? And how does Torah function in them?

To allow us to deal with the last two of these questions and by way of a review of the scriptural Mosaic Torah, I begin considering separately two dominating themes of that Torah: covenant and holiness. To a large extent, though Deuteronomy and Leviticus (where the bulk of the legal, as opposed to narrative, material is found) express both themes, Deuteronomy is primarily a book of covenant, and Leviticus one of holiness. Although crude word counts are not an infallible index, it is indicative that the word "holy" (*qadosh*) appears nine times in Deuteronomy but ninety-four times in Leviticus; while "covenant" (*berit*) is used twenty-seven times in Deuteronomy, and ten times in Leviticus. More tellingly, the two books offer distinct definitions of Israel and its relationship to its God, predicated respectively on the notion of Israel as God's legally constituted partner and as an extension on earth of the holiness of God.

Underlying and informing the individual rulings in Leviticus and Deuteronomy is a system. Deuteronomy offers an essentially forensic definition of Israel's religion (though the word "religion" is probably too narrow) as a legal contract between a patron deity and a client nation, and it focuses on the social obligations of Israelites to each other and on the administrative and executive functions of a properly regulated society (warfare, justice, slavery, debt). These are formulated as exemplary rules, though there are also general principles: one God, one sanctuary and one nation. Obeying the regulations and the principles will guarantee Israel divine approval and protection. Accordingly, the so-called "Deuteronomistic History" in the books of Joshua–Kings narrates the fortunes of Israel and Judah in terms of the obedience of its leaders (and sometimes its population) to the requirements of the Deuteronomic covenant, which it takes to be exclusive allegiance to Israel's God, a single sanctuary, and severance from any cultural influences from its "Canaanite" neighbors. Put simply: Deuteronomic ideology holds that Israel and God are tied together by a legal relationship of which the obligations are protection on God's side and obedience on Israel's. The exclusive covenant also severs Israel from the other nations.

For Leviticus, the relationship between Israel and its God is predicated on the fact that God is holy so that his people must also be holy. Breach of holiness on Israel's part effects a rupture of the relationship. Accordingly, Leviticus specifies the manner in which holiness is to be preserved in Israel, focussing on the activities of the priesthood, but, especially in the second part of the book (chs. 17-26), extending this to the people as a whole, and—an issue of equal importance—to the land. Thus, observance of sabbatical years and of proper tithing, for example, maintain the holiness of the land. The interpretation in Leviticus of Israel's absence in exile is correspondingly appropriate: as a sabbath for the deserted land: "Then the land shall enjoy its sabbatical years while it lies desolate, while you are in the land of your enemies; then the land shall rest, and enjoy its sabbatical years. While it remains desolate, it shall have the rest it did not have on your Sabbaths, when you were residing in it" (Lev. 26:34-35).

Of course, any understanding of Torah in the period of the Qumran Scrolls (predominantly first century B.C.E.-first century C.E.) will have viewed the two themes as interlinked. We shall see that "covenant" remains a crucial category, and "covenant" remains the formal structure by which membership of the communities described in the Qumran literature is defined. But these communities are sustained most importantly by the maintenance of holiness. In the Qumran literature, not only Sabbaths but all holy times must be rigorously observed: exile was understood as the result of old Israel's failure to do this, and the same neglect will lead to future punishment. Still, as we shall see, it is fruitful to deal with covenant and holiness as separate topics within a discussion of Torah at Qumran.

What Does "Torah" Mean in the Qumran Scrolls?

> They shall recruit him with the oath of the covenant which Moses made with Israel, the covenant to return to the Torah of Moses with all heart and soul, to that which is discovered to be [required to be] done during the whole period of wickedness (CD 15:8-10).

And when he has taken it upon himself to return to the Torah of Moses with all heart and soul [....] if he transgresses. All that has been revealed of the Torah to the population of the camp—if he errs in this, then the overseer shall inform him and make an order concerning him... (CD 15:12-14).

Therefore a man shall take it upon himself by an oath by his life to return to the Torah of Moses, for in it everything is specified. And the detail of the periods of Israel's blindness to all these things is specified in the book of the divisions of times into their Jubilees and weeks. But on the day when a man takes it upon himself to return to the Torah of Moses, the angels Mastema will depart from him, so long as he fulfils his words (CD 16:1-5).

Whoever joins the council of the community shall enter the covenant of God in the sight of all those who have pledged themselves. He shall take it upon himself by an oath to return to the Torah of Moses, according to all that commanded, with all heart and soul, by all that has been revealed of it to the Zadokite priests, the keepers of the covenant and seekers of His will (1QS 5:7-9).

The quoted passages show that in both the Damascus community/communities (represented primarily in the Damascus Document, CD) and in the Yahad (represented in one layer of the Damascus Document but most fully in the Community Rule, 1QS), the Torah of Moses is the fundamental obligation; indeed, both documents explain the reason for the use of the word "return:" the Israel beyond their boundaries does *not*, in their view, obey the Mosaic Torah. And since obedience to that Torah is what constitutes the true Israel, these communities represent, in their own view, the only true Israel.

In seeking to demonstrate that the historical society of Israel is in error, the Damascus Document constantly quotes from Scripture, especially the books of Moses. These books, recognized as containing the will and commandments of God to Israel, are shared between those inside the "Damascus" community and the larger society that claims to be "Israel." Whatever the origins and evolution of the written corpus of Mosaic Torah, by the time the Qumran documents are composed these constitute a fairly fixed text, nearly always written on five scrolls. In the Qumran caves, there are remnants of fifteen scrolls of Genesis, seventeen of Exodus, thirteen of Leviticus, eight of Numbers, and twenty-nine of Deuteronomy. (Of the other books of the Masoretic scriptural canon, only Isaiah and Psalms are represented by more than a total of eight.)

Recruits to the Damascus and Yahad communities are thus required to *return* to the Torah that is already written in the books of Moses that all Israel possesses. Is it, then, the case that these communities possessed further texts they believed also belonged to the Torah of Moses, of which those outside were deprived? The book of Jubilees has been suggested by some scholars as a possible candidate. For Jubilees does claim to originate from Moses, and it is cited authoritatively in CD 16:2-3 (cited above), precisely in the middle of a passage about returning to the Torah of Moses. Moreover, in speaking of both the Torah and Jubilees, the word *meduqdaq* (translated here as "specify") is used. Indeed, the word *perush*, which is used throughout CD to indicate its specific understanding and application of Torah, is also used of Jubilees here.

Ben Zion Wacholder[1] has also claimed that the Temple Scroll (11QT) functioned as Torah for the communities of the Qumran texts, noting that in it God speaks in the first person. He suggests that according to the Qumran authors God gave to Moses two Torahs, one contained in the old scriptural books, the other to be revealed at the end of time, contained in the Temple Scroll. The five books of Moses, he suggests, were valid only until and unless contradicted by the new Torah.

I do not agree that either of these texts was represented or understood as part of the written text of the Mosaic Torah. I prefer a different account of the relationship between these and the five scriptural books of Moses. As far as Jubilees is concerned, I would certainly accept that its contents probably expressed what the Qumran writers believed to be the substance of Mosaic Torah; and the same is true of the Temple Scroll, even though it contains items not referred to in the scriptural text. But the alternatives of "being Torah" and "not being Torah" are actually invalid. In the Genesis Apocryphon from Qumran Cave 1 we have a retelling, with much embellishment, of part of the narrative of Genesis. This document is generally understood to be midrashic and certainly not a replacement of the scriptural narrative itself. It seems reasonable to read the Temple Scroll and the book of Jubilees likewise as midrashic. Both documents are substantially rewritings of the scriptural text, Jubilees following the narrative sequence, the Temple Scroll following its own topical sequence of laws. Jubilees is largely a haggadic midrash (to use

---

[1] B.Z. Wacholder, *The Dawn of Qumran. The Sectarian Torah and the Teacher of Righteousness* (Cincinnati, 1983).

the terminology familiar in Rabbinic scholarship), like the Genesis Apocryphon, although its import is halakhic; while the Temple Scroll is halakhic. Jubilees is not, however, presented in CD as part of Mosaic Torah, since it is mentioned separately.

The issue, then, is not about obedience to additional books of Torah. Rather it is about the correct understanding of Torah. The crux of the problem lies in the manner in which that understanding is reached, for the Torah cannot be obeyed without being properly understood. Let us begin with some explicit examples. The Damascus Document, in its accusation that Israel has been led astray by Belial and does not observe the Torah, offers the following cases (4:20-5:11):

1. marrying two women in their lifetime, "although the basis in creation is 'male and female he created them.'" The argument, which is about remarriage,[2] is supported by another text from Genesis, "two by two they came into the ark."

2. marriage between an uncle and a niece: "although Moses said 'You shall not approach your mother's sister; she is your mother's kin,' the commandment about incest is written concerning males, but means females as well (Heb.: *wekahem hanashim*, 5:10)."

Here one observes the application of exegetical rules, of the kind made explicit in the *middot* of the Rabbinic literature, though the second instance, in which what the Torah says about males applies to females as well, is not found there. Nor are rules of exegesis anywhere spelled out systematically.

These instances show that, rather than citing a different Torah of Moses that its community holds, the Damascus Document condemns Israel, or its leaders, for failing to observe the Mosaic Torah it possesses. Moreover, a survey of the collections of laws in the same document does not reveal any that are not either explicitly or implicitly derived from the scriptural Torah.[3] In many cases, the scriptural text that forms the basis for the ruling is actually cited. What we find in the laws of CD seems to me to be the earliest recorded instance of

---

[2] There has been a long scholarly argument about whether the text implies divorce (and thus the possibility of remarriage) or polygamy. I take the view that it means precisely what it says: no second wife, either simultaneously or sequentially. See "Marriage and the Essenes," in my *Behind the Essenes. History and Ideology in the Dead Sea Scrolls* (Atlanta, 1987), pp. 73-85.

[3] See "Halakhah at Qumran," in my *Sects and Scrolls: Essays on Qumran and Related Topics* (Atlanta, 1996).

a Jewish community drawing up a code of behavior for its members that is based explicitly on the Mosaic Torah. (As Jacob Neusner has comprehensively shown, even the later Mishnah itself largely did not originate through exegetical procedures.[4])

Here a brief comment on the development of Torah in Second Temple Judaism is required. For it may seem to many students of early Judaism to be a truism that Jews always defined themselves by adherence to the Mosaic Torah and attempted to live by it. But this is not demonstrable. Rather, in the wake of the Hasmoneans' success in achieving national independence, differences that must already have existed over the definition of what it meant to be a servant of the God of Israel surfaced. While this debate took place in the context of disagreements about the extent of accommodation with Hellenistic cultural values, in which the Hasmoneans themselves displayed a high degree of latitude, both Hellenism and political independence forced a deeper and ultimately far more significant issue: how to (re-)constitute the nation *as the scriptural Israel*. Among the groups engaged in this quest are those already known (or soon to be known) as Pharisees and Sadducees as well as those responsible for the Qumran literature. The debate was not entirely new, for Greek and Greek-Jewish writers were already describing the Jews as an ancient race with an ancient political constitution drawn up by their founder Moses. Now, however, those living in Judea were becoming acutely conscious that this "constitution" could not be formulated in general terms, nor could any consensus be achieved in the face of the cultural and political challenges now offered.

It is in the context of this reassertion of the Mosaic Torah as definitive of Judaism, and a reassertion of Israel as covenanted to its God and unique among the nations, that we observe attempts to turn Torah into what the rabbis will call *halakhah*: a system of regulations for the conduct of everyday life. While we can see that the books of Moses were already in the second century the subject of learned study (see ben Sira 39:1-5) and the basis of a personal piety (see Ps. 1, of uncertain but probably Hellenistic date), in the Qumran Scrolls we see the Torah of Moses as something to which individual Israelites should *return*, and *not in any individual capacity* but as members of the true Israel constituted as an ordered society. Before Torah becomes the defining category of Israel's life under the rabbis, a Judaism, in

---

[4] See, e.g., Jacob Neusner, *History of the Mishnaic Law of Purities* (Leiden, 1977).

Neusner's famous words, of the Dual Torah, it emerges as a *sectarian* phenomenon.

Comparison and contrast with the rabbis is useful at this point, since they return us to the question of how precisely the scriptural Torah could be extended into halakhah. The Rabbinic system was explicated in a literary corpus of halakhot and in a discrete second stage, again as Neusner has shown, by presenting them as an "oral Torah" passed from Moses through an unbroken line of tradition to the rabbis themselves.[5] Since the Mishnah contains statements of rabbis, the notion of the "oral Torah" from Moses is a theological and not a historical one. But the claim that the contents of the Mishnah are Mosaic Torah is entirely sober.

I do not wish to impose a Rabbinic system or a Rabbinic hermeneutic onto an earlier Judaic one. The differences are as instructive as the similarities. But there are two hermeneutical principles that the rabbis share with the Qumran writers: that the scriptural Torah contains everything, both explicitly *and implicitly*; and that whatever is derived from it has the same authority as the scriptural Torah. This perception leads us to realize that the word *Torah* refers not only to the written text but also to what that text implicitly means. In that sense, one may suppose that the contents of the Temple Scroll or the book of Jubilees could be called "Torah," because these express what the scriptural Torah of Moses means to the authors. But this understanding does not entail that these writings were regarded as part of, or an addition to, the five books of Moses. Rather, in the term used by the Damascus Document itself, they contain *perush ha-Torah*, the precise understanding and application of that Torah, an account of its proper meaning for the true Israel.

I conclude the first part of this section, then, by stating that for the Qumran writers, there was a scriptural canon of Mosaic Torah in five books, shared and acknowledged by all Jews. However, as CD has it, "in it everything is specified:" there remained both the opportunity and the necessity of drawing, understanding, and following its implications, which are equally part of Torah.

But the picture is not complete, for the language of Torah in the Qumran literature also includes talk of revelation. Here again our discussion can be illuminated by comparing and contrasting the case

---

[5] For a concise resume of Neusner's work on the evolution of Rabbinic halakhah, see his *Judaic Law from Jesus to the Mishnah* (Atlanta, 1993).

of the Mishnah. I earlier offered an example of a dispute over remarriage and uncle-niece marriage in CD 4-5. There the argument was made through a hermeneutical deduction, based on an explicit principle: masculine language does not necessarily exclude application to females. But in another passage rather different language seems to be applied. The origins of the community in the aftermath of the destruction and exile under Nebuchadnezzar are described as follows (CD 3:12-16):

> But with those who adhered to the commandments of God, who were left over of them [sc., those of the old Israel killed or exiled], God established his covenant with Israel for ever, by revealing (*legalot*) to them the hidden things (*nistarot*) in respect of which Israel had gone astray: his holy Sabbaths and his glorious set festivals, his righteous decrees and his true ways, and the requirements of his will "which a man shall do and live by" (citing Lev. 18:5); he laid them open (*pataḥ*) before them....

In a detailed study of Qumran law, Schiffman[6] has argued that the Dead Sea literature shows that the group (he does not discern more than one group) assimilated non-scriptural material into their halakhah by using the concepts *nigleh* and *nistar*, respectively "revealed" and "hidden," the former being the simple meaning of Scripture revealed at Sinai and available to all Israel, the latter hidden knowledge of the Torah, available to the sect only by inspired biblical exegesis. (Schiffman goes further in suggesting that these exegetically derived laws were eventually composed into *serakhim*, lists of sectarian laws and were then redacted into such collections as CD and 4Q159 —the so-called "Ordinances.")

Although I would disagree with Schiffman that the disciplinary rules in 1QS were ever regarded as Mosaic Torah, his analysis seems to be cogent at least for the "Damascus" writings (CD, the 4QD mss). The language of "revelation" is there clear enough. Schiffman is also correct, in using the term "inspired biblical exegesis," to underline that the "revelation" referred to in CD 3:12-16 is not a new Torah but a clarification of the old (in which "Israel had gone astray"). The exegetical character of this revelation is most fully explicated in CD 6:2-8:

> But God remembered the covenant of the first ones and raised from Aaron men of understanding and from Israel men of wisdom, and he

---

[6] L.H. Schiffman, *The Halakhah at Qumran* (Leiden, 1975).

made them hear (him) and they dug a well: the "well which the princes sank, which the nobles of the people dug, with the scepter and the staff" (citing Num. 21:18). The well is the law (*Torah*) and those who dug it are the returners/captivity of Israel (*shebi/shabe yisrael*) who left the land of Judah and dwelt in the land of Damascus...and the staff is the Interpreter of the Law (*doresh ha-Torah*).

The divine revelation to the surviving Israel thus took the form of a new Torah, but the Torah was derived ("dug") by exegesis (*derash, midrash*). Nevertheless, it is inescapable that the passage cited wishes to parallel the original giving of Torah to Moses and to the old Israel with the new revelation of the proper meaning of Torah to the new Israel. The scheme is remarkably similar to that exploited by Ezra (Neh. 8:8), with the difference that the interpretation comes via inspiration.

In other words, while the full meaning of the Mosaic Torah was implicit in the written text of Scripture and could be spelled out, as explained earlier, that meaning was not always acquired by means of exegetical rules but sometimes by means of direct divine inspiration. Thus, all exegesis of Torah could be regarded, for the purposes of sectarian ideology, as "revealed" to it, whether or not explicit principles were applied in its derivation. And, as explained earlier, the "inspired exegeses" produced Torah.

But here we need to discriminate between the practice of the "Damascus" community and that of the Yahad. The need for authority over the application of the community's law is met, according to the Damascus Document, by three institutions: the priest, who is consulted over objects lost and found, "because the finder does not know the rule (*mishpat*) regarding it" (CD 9:15); the *mebaqqer*, more widely responsible for implementing discipline and also for "everything in which a man sins against the Torah" (CD 9:16-17); and ten "judges of the congregation," four from the tribe of "Levi and Aaron" (*sic*) and six from Israel, who are "instructed in the book of *hhgw*, and in the teachings of the covenant (*yesudey ha-berit*)." The identity of the mysterious "book of *hhgw*" remains disputed; it is probably a collection of community rulings. Attempts to identify it with a known Qumran manuscripts have not so far achieved any great support. Of more importance to note here is that the administering of Torah is divided among different institutions, thereby negating the possibility of an overriding of the text of Torah by any individual or any single "revelation." The Torah is applied "by the book" and not by proclamation, and the halakhot of the Damascus community are written. As CD 6:2-8 makes clear, the "revelation" applies to the work of the "Interpreter of the Law" and is not an ongoing feature of the life of the community.

But revelation does lie again in the future. For one highly important feature of the Torah of the Damascus Community remains to be noted, and it will be explained in the final section. The phrase "Torah for the period of wickedness" is frequently used in CD, and the "period of wickedness" is the epoch that lasts from the punishment under Nebuchadnezzar up to the "end of days." The divine wrath is manifested in the unleashing of Belial upon Israel and will be fulfilled in the final punishment of the wicked. Meanwhile, the members of the "Damascus covenant" will walk (*halakh*) according to their understanding of Torah "in all the period of wickedness...until the rise of one who will teach righteousness at the end of days." The punishment on the wicked will thus be balanced by the bringing of true righteousness, something that the interim "Torah for the period of wickedness" cannot fully achieve. And past revelation of the true will of God to the community's founder will be fulfilled by the complete revelation of righteousness at the "end of days."

But there are texts from Qumran that reflect a situation in which this expected fulfillment has taken place and a "teacher of righteousness" has appeared. This figure is not mentioned at all in the manuscripts of the Community Rule, but he does appear in a few passages from the Damascus Document that, I have argued,[7] stem from the Yahad and reflect its ideology, not that of the framers of the bulk of CD. Indeed, the difference between the "Damascus" community and the Yahad, which I shall consider in the final section below, stems precisely from the fact that the former anticipated an eschatological teacher, while the Yahad began life as a group following a leader who claimed to be that figure. Thus, material from the Yahad refers to the "teacher" in the past.

Because of the authority of this figure with respect to the Torah, the balance maintained in CD between the authority of the scriptural Torah, that of the body of originally inspired interpretation, and that of an individual figure is upset. Let me then illustrate the peculiar place of this now present "teacher" with respect to the Mosaic Torah (CD 20:27-28; 31-32):

---

[7] *The Damascus Covenant: An Interpretation of the Damascus Document* (Sheffield, 1983).

> All those who hold fast to these rules by going in and out according to the Torah (*'al pi ha-Torah*), and listen to the voice of the teacher...and are instructed in the former commandments (*mishpatim*) by which the men of the *yahad* (?) were judged and pay heed to the voice of the teacher....

The "voice of the teacher" has here been set alongside both the Torah and also what I would understand to be the community's scripturally-derived regulations (*mishpatim*), which are contained in the second part of CD (pp. 9-16), and which, I suggest, represented its *perush ha-Torah*, its own exegetically-derived application of Torah. On what basis this individual has, or is given, the right to speak with equal authority to the Torah we shall investigate later. However, his arrival marks a crucial step in the evolution of Qumran sectarianism and introduces into his new Yahad a notable qualification in the status of the Torah. For the Habakkuk *pesher* attributes inspired interpretation of the words of the prophets to this figure, suggesting that his authority was what we would call "charismatic;" and presumably this authority, derived directly from a claim to divine inspiration, would apply also to his interpretation of Torah: for it is his *voice* (*qol*) that must be obeyed in matters of law, not his interpretation: the vocabulary is, I think, significant. I shall argue presently that the diminution of the role of Torah in the Yahad is a remarkable and hitherto unremarked phenomenon, to be vividly contrasted to the crucial importance of Torah in the Damascus community

Accordingly, in 1QS, while the Torah of Moses receives lip service, the emphasis lies rather on the esoteric knowledge imparted to members by their instructor, the *maskil*. Thus, the behavior of the members of the Yahad is regulated by those who, after his death, stand in the place of the "teacher of righteousness," alongside the Torah:

> And thus he shall enter into the covenant so as to act according to all those statutes (*huqqim*) for the Yahad, the holy congregation (*'edah*). They shall examine their spirits (*ruahot*) within the Yahad, comparing each other by insight and works in the Torah according to the sons of Aaron who pledge themselves within the Yahad to uphold the covenant (1QS 5:20-22).

The various other redactions of the Community Rule that we now possess from Cave 4 show us differences in this authority over the meaning of the Torah (for this is what I take the text to mean), and the "multitude of Israel" still appears after the passage just cited in

1QS. But the historical development in the structures of the Yahad, and/or in the redaction of this document that follows the death of the teacher cannot be pursued here. The essential point to be grasped is that even after this teacher died, the place taken by his voice was filled by others. The high authority of the Mosaic Torah was not restored. Torah remained subject to sectarian authority.

What Is the Substance of the "Torah" in the Qumran Scrolls?

In this section, as previously explained, I shall consider the major themes of the Mosaic Torah as presented in the Qumran literature under the general headings of "covenant" and "holiness."

Covenant

According to Deuteronomy (and also Exodus) the establishment of the Sinai (Horeb) covenant is constituted by the giving of the Torah that represents the legal basis for Israel's relationship with its God. This contract confirms God's choice of Israel as his own people; disobedience to it will lead to annulment of that choice.

The rhetoric of the Damascus Document draws heavily upon the theme of covenant. In its opening account of the history of Israel, it contrasts the dismal failure of the "covenant of the first [people]" (*berit ha-rishonim*, CD 1:4; 4:9) with a "new covenant" that was made with the survivors from the destruction that ended the first covenant. This new covenant is called the "covenant in the land of Damascus" (CD 19:33-4), and those who entered it "went out of the land of Judah and dwelt in the land of Damascus" (CD 6:5). The meaning of "Damascus" is highly controversial and will not be considered here.[8] But the Torah the members of that community believed they exclusively understood and obeyed had been, they believed, given to their founder by revelation. As (re-)chosen by God and as the true adherents to God's will, this community was the true Israel. Therefore, their identity needed to be established in the same way that of the first Israel had been: by a covenant. However, this new covenant is expressed in terms of continuity as well as contrast with the previous one (CD 3:10-13):

---

[8] For discussion, see *Sects and Scrolls*, pp. 95-11.

> Through it [their stubbornness of heart] the first members of the covenant (*ba'ey brit ha-rishonim*) sinned and were handed over to the sword, because they forsook the covenant of God, chose their own desire and behaved in the stubbornness of their heart, each one doing his own desire. But with those who adhered to the commandments of God, who were left over from them, God established his covenant with Israel for eternity.

The "new covenant" is also a revival of the former one, made with the remnant of that former Israel. It retains the same written texts of the Torah of Moses and has the right to call itself Israel. So far, the ideology may seem straightforward. But there is a crucial difference: the "new covenant" is not made with a people assembled on a mountain. It is a covenant with a group, and every new adherent of that group must individually "enter the covenant." It is an elective covenant, entered after conversion (hence the use of the verb *shub*, which connotes repentance as well as return); and it is a sectarian covenant, since it excludes those outside the group who do not "return" or "repent" and yet would also call themselves "Israel" and claim allegiance to the covenant.

We would expect to find, as we do, an account in the Qumran texts of the ceremony in which this covenant is offered to new members and reaffirmed with existing members. Among Jews generally the giving of the Torah is associated with the feast of Booths (see Deut. 31:9), but the covenant in the Qumran texts is associated with the feast of Weeks (Pentecost). Although there is no account of such a ceremony in the Cairo manuscripts of the Damascus Document, two of the fragments from Qumran mention an event at this time, the third month of the Qumran calendar (4Q266 fragment 11 and 4Q270 fragment 7):

> And all [the inhabitants] of the camps shall assemble in the third month and shall curse whoever turns aside, to the right [or left] from the Torah.

A much fuller account appears in 1QS 1, which opens with a lengthy statement of the requirements of members of the "council of God:" they must observe what was commanded by Moses and the prophets, "devote themselves to do the statutes (*huqqim*) of God in the "covenant of mercy" (*berit hesed*), and hate all the "children of darkness." There follows (1QS 1:16-2:26) an account of a covenant ceremony. When new members "cross over into the covenant" (*'oberim beberit*) the priests praise God and recall his deeds, with the entrants answering, "Amen." The Levites then recount the sins of Israel, and the entrants confess. The priests then bless the members of the covenant, and the Levites curse those under Belial's domination. Finally, curses are uttered against those who would backslide. This ceremony is to take place every year.

This account of a ceremony in the Yahad does not convey the ambiguity of continuity/discontinuity present in the Damascus Document: the link with the "old" covenant is minimal. The language of "old Israel" and "new Israel," detectable in the Damascus Document, is submerged here under a new dualism, explicated in the following section (1QS 3:13-4:26) on light and dark, truth and falsehood, righteousness and wickedness. The God of Israel now becomes the "God of knowledge," who has chosen the children of light from the beginning of time; and while the covenant ceremony draws quite obviously on the model of Deut. 27, the nature of the covenant of the Yahad and its teaching owe less to the categories of obedience to the written Mosaic Torah and more to the esoteric "knowledge" imparted by the community's leaders. The scriptural distinction between "Israel" and "gentiles" is, from the perspective of the *yahad*, theologically almost irrelevant compared to that between those inside and those outside the realm of God's saving "mystery." This dramatic shift in the understanding of covenant in the *yahad* texts parallels the shift in the nature of its teaching away from the Mosaic Torah alone towards an esoteric body of knowledge that anticipates in many ways the gnostic religious doctrines of later centuries. The *yahad* is not the remnant of Israel, not the true Israel, hardly an "Israel" at all. "Israel" and its God have virtually become metaphors in a new dualistic religion: God standing for both the principle of good and the high god; Israel for those preordained to the "party of light."

Holiness

The requirements of the "Damascus Covenant" are conveniently summarized in CD 6:12-7:6. They are as follows:
1. not to "light the Temple altar in vain" by failure to observe the "Torah for the period of wickedness"
2. to keep apart from the "children of perdition"
3. to abstain from money gained illicitly through wrong vows, donations to the Temple, or by extortion of the poor

4. to "distinguish between the clean and the unclean," between the profane and the holy
5. to keep Sabbaths and fast days as prescribed in the "Damascus covenant"
6. to set aside holy offerings as prescribed
7. to love fellow-members of the community ("brothers") as oneself
8. to refrain from illicit sexual activity
9. to keep away from all forms of uncleanness (*teme'ot*) and not defile one's holy spirit (*ruaḥ qedoshaw*)

The list concludes that all who follows these principles, "in holy perfection" (*betamiym qodesh*) will be sustained forever by God. The laws contained in CD 9-16 and now more fully represented in the Cave 4 manuscripts confirm that the concept of holiness was rooted in the community's understanding of its covenant.

Indeed, the requirements of holiness are intensified. The Mosaic Torah distinguishes clearly between the requirements laid upon ordinary Israelites and those pertaining to the priesthood who were in regular immediate contact with the sphere of the divine. But it is already well-known that in the late Second Temple period there emerged groups that, although not of the priesthood, took upon themselves some of the obligations of "Levitical purity," as if they were serving at the Temple. A similar phenomenon is observable in the Qumran writings. The reasons for this development in either case are unclear, but it seems probable that voluntary or imposed restrictions on Temple access by the groups represented in the Qumran texts are an important factor. The language of "lighting the altar in vain" (CD 6:12) probably represents exactly that position. But the Yahad appears to have taken a further step by making "Temple" a metaphor for itself and its cult for its daily life (see further below).

The publication of the Cave 4 text 4QMMT[9] throws a quite dramatic light on the issue. The original claim of the editors, Qimron and Strugnell, that this is the text of a letter from the "teacher of righteousness" to his enemy the "wicked priest" is now disputed. But in the view of most scholars, the contents of this (reconstructed) text offer a key insight into the process by which the Qumran communities came into existence. The main substance of the reconstructed text comprises a set of statements on issues in which the writers

---

[9] E. Qimron and J. Strugnell, *Qumran Cave 4 V: Miqsat Ma'aseh Ha-Torah* (Oxford, 1994). The text is also sometimes referred to as the "Halakhic Letter."

("we") and addressees of the document ("you") differ. These issues include ritual purity: the status of gentile offerings, slaughter of animals, the "red heifer" ritual, membership of those physically defective from the congregation, the treatment of lepers, the capacity of running liquids to convey uncleanness (*nitsoq*), tithing, the presence of dogs in Jerusalem, and contact with corpses. Also dealt with are intermarriage and entry into the congregation.

The text not only introduces the kind of debate on individual issues (and some of the language) that will become familiar in the Rabbinic literature but also implies quite clearly a tradition of dispute over the interpretation of scriptural rules pertaining to holiness. These issues range widely but largely concern matters pertaining to priestly activity. They are called in the text itself, "some matters regarding application of the Torah" (*miqtsat maʿasey ha-Torah*). The text invites the addressee, who is apparently a ruler of Israel (most likely one of the Hasmonean kings), to abandon the practices currently in force and adhere to the rulings of the writers.

It is unimportant for our purposes whether or not the rulings presented by the writers point to a "Sadducean" tradition, as a number of commentators maintain.[10] More important is that this disagreement over the maintenance of Israel's holiness seems to underlie, at least in part, the emergence of sectarian societies governed by this tradition. It is logical (and logic is at the moment all we have to follow) that 4QMMT represents an attempt to (re)instate an ousted priestly tradition, the failure of which was, we can suggest, likely to lead to secession on the part of its adherents. The contents of the Damascus Document are indeed consistent with a sectarian community emerging from these conditions: its criticism of the leaders of Israel, and of the Temple regime in particular, but also its veneration of the Temple itself and, most significantly, the creation of a segregated Israel in which the "correct" traditions can be followed.

Deuteronomy suggests, and the history remembered in CD is meant to prove, that disobedience to God's Torah brings disaster. But according to Leviticus, a lack of holiness in Israel and in the land given to Israel will also result in disaster. That ideology that divides the world into the realms of purity and impurity, holiness and un-

---

[10] E.g., J. Sussmann, in Qimron and Strugnell, DJD X, pp. 179-200; L. Schiffman, "The New Halakhic Letter [4QMMT] and the Origins of the Dead Sea Sect," in *Biblical Archaeologist* 53, 1990, pp. 64-73.

holiness, is paramount in the Damascus Document, and those laws relating to the maintenance of holiness arguably represent the bulk of the laws contained in it. They also form the subject matter of many other Qumran texts, including not only the lengthy Temple Scroll but smaller lists of purity regulations such as several fragments known as 4QTohorot A-G. In the Yahad, the implicit dualism of the Leviticus system into holy and unholy, clean and unclean is transformed into a cosmic dualism of good and evil: again, we see a process of metaphorizing taking place.

In connection with the theme of holiness, we must also mention both the calendar and the city and Temple of Jerusalem. As is well-known, the calendar promoted in the Qumran writings is one whose year comprises three hundred and sixty-four days. This total, being divisible by seven, allows feast days and Sabbaths to occur on precisely the same days each year, thus avoiding the difficulties encountered when Sabbaths and feast-days coincide of establishing the priority of the rules of one over the other. It is the sabbatical aspects of this "solar" calendar that preserve its deepest significance. The Sabbath itself is certainly the subject of a good deal of legislation, and its proper observance is paramount. But Sabbaths do not apply only to days. This can be perceived from the book of Jubilees, in which the calendar is applied to the events of Genesis. For Jubilees also divides the calendar of world history into "weeks" of seven years and Jubilees of forty-nine. These units of measurement are already available in Deuteronomy and Leviticus, but they do not have, as they do in Jubilees, or in the Enoch literature, where the same calendar appears, the calendrical significance, according to which the history of the world has a predetermined end. That end is calculated, according to most of the extant (Qumranic and non-Qumranic) literature, as a period of four hundred and ninety years or ten Jubilees from the time of the Babylonian deportation: thus Daniel (which makes no mention of a solar or any other calendar) and the Melchizedek text from Cave 11 (11QMelch), while the Enochic "Apocalypse of Weeks" (1 Enoch 93+91) commences (like Jubilees) with Creation. The eschatological calculations implicit in this calendar are mostly outside our topic, except in respect of the "law for the period of wickedness," which is discussed below in the next section. The main importance of the calendar is that it defines and protects the holiness of times; but a calendar also constitutes an issue on which it is difficult for any reconciliation: observing the wrong calendar means lack of holiness for Israel and the land, breaking of the covenant, and thus divine punishment. How different calendars were accommodated prior to the sectarian division is an interesting question. How, indeed, was the Jerusalem Temple run in these circumstances?

Deuteronomy insists on a single place of worship as a key covenant condition, but the role of the Temple in Torah is associated most closely with the theme of holiness: its core, the Holy of Holies, is the most holy place on earth, site of the presence of God. Leviticus presents the cult (representing the Temple as the wilderness tent and tabernacle) as the locus of covenant mediation. These two emphases merge in the high status enjoyed by the city, the Temple, and its cult in the late Second Temple period. For CD the defiling of the sanctuary by its priesthood is named again and again as a key issue. 4QMMT names it as the "chief of the camps," suggesting perhaps that it was also the site of the main settlement of the "Damascus" community. In both CD and 4QMMT, Jerusalem is named the "city of the sanctuary;" in the Temple Scroll the holiness of the Temple extends to the city, and thus in CD 12:43 we also find a ban on sexual intercourse inside Jerusalem.

But however much the Qumran Scrolls embrace the notion of a reformed Temple cult and maintain a keen interest in the proper rules for this cult, effectively it became necessary to sublimate this vital symbol of Judaism's relationship to its God. In the Damascus Document, this is done by arguing that the Temple can be used only by those obedient to the true law: they will "light the altar in vain" unless they are careful to behave according to the "specifications of the Torah for the period of wickedness" (CD 6:13-14). But the Yahad seems to have abandoned the Temple cult entirely. The language of the cult was reapplied to the community itself, as a "holy house for Aaron" or "house of perfection and truth," where atonement and "sweet fragrance" shall be offered up in obedience and suffering (1QS 8:5-12). In the light of this ideology we may understand the "Songs of the Sabbath Sacrifice" or "Angelic Liturgy" texts (4Q400-407) that describe the performance of the heavenly liturgy and probably betray an increasing interest by the Yahad in this transcendental worship as a substitute for the earthly cult authorized only for the chosen city of Jerusalem.

To conclude this section, it needs to be underlined that I have been careful to distinguish between the "Damascus" community and the Yahad, i.e., between CD and 1QS (and their respective recensions, mostly from Cave 4) and other manuscripts that appear to belong to the sphere of one or the other. The most important distinction between the two sets of texts thus created, as far as Torah is concerned, seems to be as follows: in the "Damascus" community the Torah, albeit according to a particular tradition of interpretation, remains the guiding principle of a sectarian organization that regards itself as the true Israel; but the documents of the Yahad, while using the phrase "Torah of Moses," lay increasing emphasis on the authority of community leaders, beginning with the "teacher of righteousness," and develop a sectarian ideology of esoteric knowledge, of preordained election to light or darkness, in which the role of Torah is increasingly irrelevant to the system. I shall attempt to explain in the final section how this stems partly from the "messianic" origin of this sect.

How Does Torah Function in the Qumran Scrolls?

In this final section I want to consider the place of Torah within the Judaic systems on Qumran. As usual, I begin with the Damascus Document and the crucial passage, 6:2-11:

> But God remembered the covenant of the first ones and raised from Aaron men of understanding and from Israel men of wisdom, and he made them hear (him) and they dug a well: the "well which the princes sank, which the nobles of the people dug, with the scepter and the staff" (citing Num. 21:18). The well is the law (*Torah*) and those who dug it are the returners/captivity of Israel (*shebi/shabe yisrael*) who left the land of Judah and dwelt in the land of Damascus...and the staff is the Interpreter of the Law (*doresh ha-Torah*), as Isaiah said: "Who brings forth a tool for his work." And the nobles of the people are those who have come to dig the well with the staves that the Staff made, to walk in them during the whole period of wickedness, and other than these they shall not obtain until there shall arise one teaching righteousness at the end of days

This is a crucial passage, because it expressed forcefully the belief that the community of "Damascus" lives by a Torah *with a beginning and an end*. By "Torah" here I do not mean the text of the Mosaic Torah, but the application and expression of that Torah that has become necessary because of the anger of God against Israel. But necessary only for that period, the beginning of which is the revelation to the "interpreter of the law" and the end the arrival of "one teaching righteousness" at the "end of days." This Torah endures for the "period of wickedness."

The idea that the Torah of Moses, however interpreted, should be provisional in any sense seems strange to a student of ancient Judaism, and yet it is dictated by the requirements of a situation in which the full Torah cannot be observed. The anger of God, initiated at the end of the old covenant, still lies on Israel, and for this reason Belial is loose until the final judgment falls on them. The remnant, the new Israel, who possess the true Torah, however, lives between this punishment and their salvation. According to CD 12:23, the members of the Damascus community will "walk in these (sc., their laws) during the period of wickedness *until there shall arise a messiah of Aaron and Israel.*" The messiah is thus the one "teaching righteousness" according to CD 6:11. Hence, the messiah is the "teacher of righteousness" or, conversely, the "teacher of righteousness" is a messiah.

The arrival of this "teacher" in a historical personage (whom we cannot identify), and his acceptance by some and rejection by others among the "Damascus" community, necessarily creates a new movement. Within the circle of his followers, his own messianic authority is added to that of the "Torah for the period of wickedness." This is why CD 20:27 (one of the sections of CD bearing the marks of revision within the Yahad) lays the "voice of the teacher" alongside the Torah. For the Yahad the "period of wickedness" is over, the end is near—until this person dies. According to CD 20:13-14, this event has now taken place (the necessity of a diachronic reading of this document is here dramatically evident!). This leads first to disorientation, as the expected "end of days" has not materialized:

> And from the day of the gathering in of the teacher of the Yahad (reading *yoreh hayahad*) to the end of all the men of war who returned with the "man of the lie" is forty years or so. And in this period the anger of God will be kindled against Israel, as it says, "no king and no prince and no judge and no-one to instruct in righteousness" (citing Hos. 3:4).

Instead, the text continues, the members of the community will *instruct each other, "until salvation and righteousness shall be revealed for those who fear God"* (CD 20:20). Thus, cognitive dissonance takes the form of postponement of the end of forty years. But what thereafter?

A number of other eschatological scenarios can be detected in the Qumran Scrolls: both the Rule of the Congregation (1QSa) and the

War Scroll (1QM) anticipate a restored congregation (*'edah*) of Israel, including women and children. Both these documents rehearse biblical patterns, the War Scroll specially of the structure of Israel as a war-camp (Num. 1-10:10). Messianic beliefs also vary: instead of the single teacher-messiah of the "Damascus" community, a doctrine of two messiahs emerges as the main expectation, though messianic ideas do not seem to function any longer as of great importance.

We are, of course, confronting in these scrolls not only texts from the Yahad but from the "Damascus" community, which presumably continued after the formation of these followers of the "teacher." What relationship remained between the two sects is not clear. But while the one seems to have modeled itself on the biblical Israel, adopted the Torah of Moses (as understood and interpreted by itself), and continued to await a messiah who would bring the restoration of Israel, the other, with its messiah dead, continued to drift away from an understanding of itself as an Israel bound by Torah, adopting a dualistic system in which a "God of knowledge" pre-ordained those of light and darkness, revealing to them his secrets. Whether this latter system at some point ceases to be Judaic is an interesting, though unanswerable, question.

But this essay should be concluded with a return to the topic of Torah. It was earlier observed that the "Damascus" community anticipated a (single) messiah who would teach righteousness, and the context of that statement implies that the "Torah for the period of wickedness" would no longer obtain. It is thus possible to infer a belief that the Mosaic Torah itself was an interim dispensation, an idea that Saul/Paul of Tarsus would take to an extreme. Or it might be inferred that the Torah would be fully restored, along with the Temple cult. My own preference is for something more ambitious: that there would be some form of transformation, not merely of Torah, Temple, land, or Israel, but of the condition of humanity itself. The "end of days" would also see the abolition of wickedness and, presumably, the end of evil. The distinction between the holy and unholy, one of the pillars of the Torah as understood in this community, would no longer apply.

Such a belief is in fact expressed in the so-called Berakhot text, 11Q14:9-11: "And for you the land will produce excellent fruits; and you shall eat them and be filled. In your land there shall be no miscarriage, no sickness, drought and disease will not occur to your crops...evil will vanish from the land (earth?). For God is with you...."

Indeed, the dualistic sermon of 1QS 3-4 takes a similar vision for the children of light, though less poetically expressed.

Thus, within both of the systems discerned here in the Qumran Scrolls, the place of Torah may, despite different paths taken, be expected to change if not vanish in a new state of affairs. Was the doctrine that the Torah was eternal not embraced at Qumran? Here would commence another interesting line of contrast with the understanding of Torah among the rabbis. But on one statement, Rabbinic Judaism and Christianity will also agree: until the messiah comes, Torah is the will of God and the life of Israel.

11. THE SHAPE OF THE "BIBLE" AT QUMRAN

Peter W. Flint
Trinity Western University

This essay deals with the overall shape and contents of the Scriptures at Qumran. The first section deals with appropriate terminology in view of ambiguous or inaccurate language often employed in relation to the Bible and the canonical process. This is followed with a profile of the various books that were regarded as Scripture by the Qumran community. (Some attention will also be paid to the textual form of specific books, but a systematic treatment of this topic is beyond the scope of the present essay.) The final section considers the criteria according to which the specified writings were viewed as Scripture at Qumran. The essay closes with a select bibliography listing editions of the biblical scrolls and the relevant secondary literature. An Appendix then offers a complete index of passages in the biblical and Apocryphal Scrolls.

1. *The Quest for Appropriate Terminology*

The Dead Sea Scrolls are divided into two main groups: the "biblical" scrolls and the "non-biblical" scrolls. This division, however, is from a modern perspective and is made simply to facilitate different types of research by scholars (e.g., studies on the biblical text, Judaism at the start of the Common Era). However, some scholars writing on the "biblical" scrolls persist in using language that presupposes the closure of the Hebrew canon prior to 200 B.C.E.—although the diversity of Scriptures found among the Scrolls shows that the Writings (and possibly the Prophets)[1] had not been finalized by the end of the Qumran era (68 C.E.).[2] It will thus be most helpful to

---

[1] See section 2.1 below.
[2] The *terminus ad quem* is fixed by the apparent destruction of the Qumran settlement by the Romans in the late Spring (April?) or early Summer (June?) of 68 C.E.

examine in their historical perspective commonly-used terms and to suggest more apposite ones.

1.1 *Canon* and *Bible*

Together with their corresponding adjectives, these terms have various senses in English[3] and in biblical scholarship,[4] giving rise to confusion in the discussion of both *canon* and the authoritative status of the biblical scrolls from the Judaean Desert. As several scholars have pointed out,[5] clear and precise terminology is necessary for constructive discourse in this area. For the discussion that follows, it will be useful to detail the three main canons of the Hebrew Bible/Old Testament.

Table 1: The Jewish, Protestant, and Roman Catholic Canons of the Hebrew Bible/Old Testament

Jewish TANAK (24)	Protestant O.T. (39)	Roman Catholic O.T. (46)
Torah (5)	*Pentateuch* (5)	*Pentateuch* (5)
Genesis	Genesis	Genesis
Exodus	Exodus	Exodus
Leviticus	Leviticus	Leviticus
Numbers	Numbers	Numbers
Deuteronomy	Deuteronomy	Deuteronomy

---

[3] This wide range of meaning is most evident with respect to "canon." Definitions given by *Webster's New International Dictionary* (p. 328a) include: "a decree...made by ecclesiastical authority;" "a collection or authoritative list of books accepted as holy scripture;" "the authentic works of a writer;" "a basic general principle or rule generally accepted as true, valid and fundamental;" "a general mathematical rule, formula or table;" "a norm, criterion, model, or standard for evaluating...." In addition, further philosophical, musical, and liturgical meanings are listed.

[4] According to Bruce Metzger, *The Canon of the New Testament. Its Origin, Development, and Significance* (Oxford, 1987), p. 36, Brevard Childs uses "canon" with three different meanings: a fixed collection of books, the final form of a book or a group of books, and a principle of finality and authority. See also Eugene Ulrich, "The Canonical Process, Textual Criticism, and Latter Stages in the Composition of the Bible," in M. Fishbane and E. Tov, eds., *"Sha'arei Talmon." Studies in the Bible, Qumran, and the Ancient Near East Presented to Shemaryahu Talmon* (Winona Lake, 1992), pp. 267–291, esp. p. 269, n. 6.

[5] For example, T.A. Hoffman, "Inspiration, Normativeness, Canonicity, and the Unique Sacred Character of the Bible," in *CBQ* 44, 1982, pp. 447–469; and Ulrich, "Canonical Process," pp. 2–3.

Prophets (8)
Joshua
Judges
Samuel
Kings
Isaiah
Jeremiah
Ezekiel
Book of the Twelve
  Hosea
  Joel
  Amos
  Obadiah
  Jonah
  Micah
  Nahum
  Habakkuk
  Zephaniah
  Haggai
  Zechariah
  Malachi

Writings (11)
Psalms
Job
Proverbs
Ruth

Song of Songs
Ecclesiastes

Lamentations
Esther
Daniel
Ezra-Nehemiah
Chronicles

Historical Books (12)
Joshua
Judges
Ruth
1 & 2 Samuel
1 & 2 Kings
1 & 2 Chronicles
Ezra
Nehemiah
Esther

Poetry/Wisdom (5)
Job
Psalms
Proverbs
Ecclesiastes
Song of Songs

Prophets (17)
Isaiah
Jeremiah
Lamentations

Ezekiel
Daniel

Hosea
Joel
Amos
Obadiah
Jonah
Micah
Nahum
Habakkuk
Zephaniah
Haggai
Zechariah
Malachi

Historical Books (16)
Joshua
Judges
Ruth
1 & 2 Samuel
1 & 2 Kings
1 & 2 Chronicles
Ezra
Nehemiah
Tobit
Judith
Esther + Additions
1 & 2 Maccabees

Poetry/Wisdom (7)
Job
Psalms
Proverbs
Ecclesiastes
Song of Songs
Wisdom of Solomon
Ecclesiasticus

Prophets (18)
Isaiah
Jeremiah
Lamentations
Baruch + Letter of Jeremiah
Ezekiel
Daniel + Prayer of Azariah, Song of the 3 Young Men, Susanna, Bel and the Dragon
Hosea
Joel
Amos
Obadiah
Jonah
Micah
Nahum
Habakkuk
Zephaniah
Haggai
Zechariah
Malachi

The basic meaning of canon is a "reed," but its two extended meanings in classical Greek, "norm" and "list," are pertinent for biblical studies.[6] Although the term occurs thrice in the Septuagint[7] and four times in the New Testament,[8] its only significant usage in the present context is Gal. 6:16, which says that Christians live by one *kanon* (*kanōn*) or normative rule of life. In the early Church, the notion of *kanon* as a norm soon became prominent due to early disputes[9] and was also used for binding decisions.[10] In addition to a norm, the term was sometimes used for widely accepted lists of Scriptures. Such closed lists of *kanonizomena* became invested with ecclesiastical status, giving rise to the twofold meaning of *kanon* that prevailed in later theology: "norm" for the Church, and "list" of sacred writings of the Old and New Testaments.[11] Implicit is the notion of reflexive judgment on the part of the church authorities and compilers, who declared certain lists to be normative and sacred. "Canon" is thus to be regarded as a technical term with several distinct components.[12]

---

[6] "Canon" transliterates the Greek *kanōn*, which derives from a Semitic word for "reed" (cf., Greek *kánna*, Hebrew *qana*, and Arabic *qanāh*. Note also the English term "cane"). In classical usage, the basic sense of "reed" yields to that of "straight rod" or "bar," with the literal meaning of a measuring tool (e.g., a measuring stick used in building). Metaphorically, the term becomes a "norm" or "ideal" or "standard" of excellence (e.g., to denote the perfect human figure in sculpture or the basis for knowing what is true or false in philosophy). Finally, the term can signify a "table" or "list" (e.g., a chronological timetable or a mathematical series). See R.E. Brown and R.F. Collins, "Canonicity," in *NJBC*, pp. 1034–54 (§66.1–101), esp. p. 1035 (§66.5); and H.W. Beyer, "*kanōn*," in *TDNT*, vol. 3, pp. 596–602.

[7] Mic. 7:4; Jud. 13:6; 4 Macc. 7:21 (The last is a figurative reference to philosophical rule.)

[8] 2 Cor. 10:13, 15, 16; and Gal. 6:16.

[9] For instance, Clement (96 C.E.) employs the term in an ethical and homiletical context (1 Clem. 7:2), and Irenaeus (ca. 180) uses the "canon of truth" to describe the binding truth of the Gospel, attested by the Scriptures and tradition (*Against Heresies* 1.9.4–5; 3.2.1; 3.11.1.).

[10] For example, the decisions reached at Nicaea (325 C.E.) were termed "canons," which functioned as normative rules of life for Christians.

[11] In the early fourth century (in his letter to Carpian) Eusebius uses *kanones* for chronological timetables and for lists of Gospel references, although he refers to his own listing of New Testament books as a *katalogos* (*Ecclesiastical History* 3.25; 6.25). Our earliest extant list is in the Muratorian Fragment (late second century), but it is only with lists from the later fourth century—those of Athanasius, Augustine, and the councils of Hippo and Carthage III—that general agreement with respect to their contents is reached in much of the Church. Athanasius, for instance, distinguishes between the *kanonizomena* (canonical books) and the apocrypha.

[12] See Ulrich, "Canonical Process," pp. 269–270; and James Barr, *Holy Scripture: Canon, Authority, Criticism* (Philadelphia, 1983), p. 50.

Since a definition of "canon" should thus include the elements of norm, list, and reflexive judgment, I propose the following (with due acknowledgement to Sid Leiman):[13] "A canon is the closed list of books accepted retrospectively by a group (especially Jews or Christians) as authoritative and binding for religious practice and doctrine."

Two points need to be made. First, this definition recognizes that different groups have different canons, whether in the ordering of materials (Jews vs. Christians) or in the inclusion or exclusion of specific books (Roman Catholics vs. Jews and Protestants). Second, "books" here refers to literary works rather than their specific form.[14] To term a book such as the Psalter, Jeremiah, or Exodus "canonical" need not mean that only one form of that book may qualify. Different forms can be canonical at the same time: for example, the (shorter) Septuagint version of Jeremiah is viewed as Scripture by the Greek Orthodox Church, while most other Churches and Judaism accept the (longer) version preserved in the Masoretic Text.

The word Bible[15] usually denotes a book consisting of writings that are generally accepted by Jews or Christians as inspired by God and thus of divine authority; however, more general,[16] narrow,[17] or technical[18] meanings are also possible. The problem with using this term

---

[13] Cf., Sid Leiman, *The Canonization of Hebrew Scripture* (Hamden, 1976), p. 14: "A canonical book is a book accepted by Jews as authoritative for religious practice and/or doctrine, and whose authority is binding upon the Jewish people for all generations."

[14] Ulrich, "Canonical Process," p. 273, points out that "canon" is concerned with "the literary opus, and not the particular wording of that opus."

[15] From *biblia*, plural of *biblion*, the diminutive of *biblos*, "papyrus" or "book." Biblos is a loanword from the Egyptian, first denoting the papyrus reed, later the inscribed paper or scroll, and finally the writing as a book, letter, record, or statute. It is also used for individual books (e.g., Psalms in Acts 1:20) or groups of books (e.g., the whole Law in Mark 12:26). The diminutive form *biblion* is used especially for a scroll or writing, for nonbiblical writings, libraries, archives, chronicles, epistles, and for documents. With reference to the Old Testament, to; *biblion* can denote the Law (e.g., Gal. 3:10) or a single book (cf., Luke 4:17), but the plural *ta biblia* seems to indicate several OT books in 2 Tim. 4:13. Later, *ta biblia* is used for the entire canon, which for Christians includes the New Testament. Special senses of biblivon are also evident in the Book of Revelation. See G. Schrenk, "βιβλός, βιβλίον," in *TDNT*, vol. 1, pp. 615–620.

[16] "A book containing the sacred writings of [any] religion" (*Webster's Dictionary*, 211c).

[17] For example, the Torah.

[18] "A library or collection of books" (*Webster's Dictionary*, 211c).

for writings prior to the second century C.E. is that it implies the completion of the Jewish Scriptures, and their existence in one book or collection at that time. These presuppositions, however, are inaccurate with respect to the Second Temple period in general and to the Qumran era in particular and pertain only to a later date. No completed Bible existed at Qumran, and it is incorrect to say that the collection preserved in the Masoretic Bible had been finalized and intentionally closed prior to the community's demise in 68 C.E.

1.2 *Apocrypha and Pseudepigrapha*

The terms Apocrypha and Pseudepigrapha each have several layers of meaning, which gives rise to ambiguity and confusion for both scholar and general reader alike. The most common use of Apocrypha denotes those books or parts of books that appear in Roman Catholic Bibles but not in Jewish or Protestant ones (see Table 1 above). The term is thus used differently by different groups, since the books so categorized by Protestants and Jews are accepted as biblical by Catholics, who term them the Deutero-Canonicals. Furthermore, when we take into account the additional books found in the Septuagint and those used by the various Orthodox churches, the definition becomes even more complex. These larger canons not only include works with which some biblical scholars are quite unfamiliar (e.g., the Prayer of Manasseh), they also have differing names for the same books (e.g., the 1 Esdras of English Bibles is known as 3 Ezra in the Latin Vulgate and 2 Esdras in the Slavonic Bible). Further confusion may arise when we find the term Apocrypha used in an entirely different sense for names of certain books found at Qumran, such as the *Genesis Apocryphon* or the *Apocryphal Psalms*.

The term Pseudepigrapha is also complex. For one thing, what Jews and Protestants term Pseudepigrapha are traditionally known in Catholicism as the Apocrypha. But the most general sense denotes virtually all the ancient Jewish works outside of the Old Testament, the Apocrypha and a few other writings that were known to us prior to the discovery of the Dead Sea Scrolls (notably Philo and Josephus).[19] A most useful definition of Pseudepigrapha in this sense has

---

[19] The two most familiar collections are that of R.H. Charles, which was published in 1913, *The Apocrypha and Pseudepigrapha of the Old Testament* (2 vols.; Oxford, 1913); and the collection edited by James Charlesworth that appeared in the 1980s, *The Old Testament Pseudepigrapha* (2 vols.; Garden City, 1983-1985).

been proposed by Moshe Bernstein: "Jewish and Christian writings dating from the last centuries B.C.E. to the first centuries C.E. which did not become part of the canon in either religion."[20]

However, when we consider the literature of the Dead Sea Scrolls, a quite different sense emerges: Pseudepigrapha as a literary genre or group of falsely-attributed writings. Biblical scholars, of course, are familiar with this category in the Hebrew Bible/Old Testament itself, where the primary example is Daniel. So when discussion extends, for example, to the *Pseudo-Daniel* documents at Qumran, this is no great surprise; but the reader needs to be aware that a shift in meaning has taken place: Pseudepigrapha no longer as "previously known writings" but now as the genre or group of "falsely-attributed writings."

It should be pointed out that the categories Apocrypha and Pseudepigrapha share several elements in common. First, both terms have arisen in western scholarship, not from Hebrew tradition;[21] Jewish writers refer to all this literature as the *sefarim ḥitzonim* or "exterior books."[22] Second, virtually all the compositions involved have been transmitted by Christian sources, since they were not accepted into the Rabbinic canon finalized in the second century C.E. Third, in view of this means of transmission, we should not be surprised that the surviving forms of most or all even of these Jewish books have been altered or interpolated by later Christian editors.[23]

1.3 *Defining the Apocrypha*

Apocrypha originally denoted "hidden" or "secret" writings that were to be read only by initiates into a given Christian group. The

---

[20] M.J. Bernstein, "Pseudepigraphy in the Qumran Scrolls: Categories and Functions," in E.G. Chazon and M. Stone, eds., with the Collaboration of A. Pinnick, *Pseudepigraphic Perspectives: The Apocrypha and Pseudepigrapha in Light of the Dead Sea Scrolls. Proceedings of the International Symposium of the Orion Center for the Study of the Dead Sea Scrolls and Associated Literature, 12–14 January, 1997* (Leiden, 1999), pp. 1-26.

[21] Cf., M.E. Stone, "Categorization and Classification of the Apocrypha and Pseudepigrapha," in *AbrN* 24, 1986, pp. 167-177, esp. p. 167.

[22] I.e., books that are exterior to the canon of the Hebrew Bible; see M.E. Stone, "The Dead Sea Scrolls and the Pseudepigrapha," in *DSD* 3, 1996, pp. 270-295, esp. p. 270.

[23] With reference to the *Pseudepigrapha*, Stone, "Categorization and Classification," p. 172, comments: "There is scarcely a book without some Christian touch."

term was eventually used, however, for works similar to biblical books in content, form, or title, although not accepted into a particular canon of Scripture.[24] Some writers accordingly define Apocrypha in a rather negative manner as "quasi-scriptural" or "non-canonical" books of doubtful authorship and authority.[25] But such a pejorative sense seems to betray a degree of bias or one-sidedness on the part of the definers, since the books involved are included in the Bibles of Roman Catholics and Orthodox Christians for whom they qualify as Scripture.

The term Apocrypha should be understood in relation to the canonical process. Since the Apocrypha feature in the canons of some churches, it is clear that the pejorative definition suggested above is unacceptable. A more neutral and accurate definition is offered by Michael Stone, who describes them as "Jewish works of the period of the Second Temple not included in the Hebrew Bible but which are to be found in the Greek and Latin Old Testaments."[26] This definition is certainly an improvement but needs one major qualification: even confining the Apocrypha to the Greek and Latin Bibles may be too restrictive. It is true, of course, that virtually all the Apocrypha are to be found in these Bibles—yet the possibility of additional such works in other ancient Christian Bibles cannot automatically be ruled out. When we take into account the entire ancient church, not just the Western and Greek Orthodox churches, different streams of Christianity and somewhat different canons may emerge. Two traditions that come to mind are the Syriac and Ethiopic churches, which do not use the Greek or Latin Bible; if distinctive Second Temple Jewish writings are to be found in their Scriptures there seems to be no sound reason for not including these among the Apocrypha.

Some of the Apocrypha are accepted by all Christian groups, excluding Protestants,[27] as Scripture. As detailed in Table 1, seven of these are entire books (Tobit, Judith, the Wisdom of Solomon, 1 and 2 Maccabees, Ecclesiasticus, and Baruch [with the Letter of Jeremiah

---

[24] See Brown and Collins, "Canonicity," pp. 1035-1036 (§66.9-10).
[25] See A. Oepke, "κρύπτω,... ἀπόκρυφω," in *TDNT*, vol. 3, pp. 957-978; and *Webster's Dictionary*, 100c.
[26] "Dead Sea Scrolls and the Pseudepigrapha," p. 270.
[27] Even this statement requires qualification, since some Anglicans (mainly Anglo-Catholics) may dispute that the *Apocrypha* are excluded from the Anglican canon of Scripture.

= Baruch 6]).[28] Two more Apocrypha constitute longer endings to other canonical books (the Additions to Esther and the Additions to Daniel). However, several other works are included in the canons of some orthodox churches but not of others:

Greek Orthodox Canon	Slavonic Orthodox Canon	Ethiopian Narrower Canon
Prayer of Manasseh	Prayer of Manasseh	Prayer of Manasseh[29]
Psalm 151	Psalm 151	Psalm 151[30]
1 Esdras	2 Esdras (=1 Esdras)	1 Esdras
3 Maccabees	3 Esdras (=2 Esdras)	2 Esdras 3–14[31]
4 Maccabees (in appendix)	3 Maccabees	3 Maccabees
		1 Enoch
		Jubilees

Each of these lists represents the end of a process that took centuries to complete, and each has a prehistory. In the case of the Ethiopian canon, for example, R.W. Cowley distinguishes between the two modern forms of the canon, which he terms the "broader" and "narrower" ones.[32] Roger Beckwith has attempted to identify the probable form of the most ancient Ethiopian canon[33] and arrives at some interesting conclusions: that the book of Jubilees was most likely included, that several Old Testament books were regarded as "disputed/doubtful,"[34] and that several other books were deemed "uncanonical."[35]

---

[28] In its Ethiopian form, this book consists of Bar. 1–5 plus the *Sāqoqawä Ēremyas*, comprising Lam. 1:1–7:5 and "the rest of the words of Baruch" (i.e., 4 Bar. and Lam. 7:6–11:63). See R.W. Cowley's short but important study, "The Biblical Canon of the Ethiopian Orthodox Church Today," in *Ostkirchlichen Studien* 23, 1974, pp. 318-323, esp. p. 321.

[29] The Prayer of Manasseh appears in this Ethiopian canon as thirteen numbered verses following 2 Chron. 33:12 (Cowley, "Biblical Canon," p. 321).

[30] The sources (Cowley, "Biblical Canon;" Beckwith, *Old Testament Canon* [see n. 33 below]) do not specify whether Ps. 151 was included, but it most likely was since the Ethiopic Psalter was translated from the Septuagint.

[31] I.e., the Ezra Apocalypse as in some editions of the Vulgate, where chaps. 3–14 are known as 4 Ezra. In these editions, chaps. 1–2 are then designated as 5 Ezra and chaps. 15–16 as 6 Ezra.

[32] Cowley, "Biblical Canon," pp. 319-320.

[33] *The Old Testament Canon of the New Testament Church and Its Background in Early Judaism* (Grand Rapids, 1985), pp. 494-500, 504-505.

[34] Chronicles, Esther, Job, Proverbs, Ecclesiastes, Song of Songs.

[35] Ezra-Nehemiah, 1 Esdras, 2 Esdras (= 4 Ezra), Tobit, Judith, Wisdom, Ecclesiasticus, Baruch, 1 Enoch, the *Ascension of Isaiah*, *4 Baruch*.

Such a truncated Old Testament canon, which lacks several standard books such as Job and Proverbs, makes it clear that the concept of Apocrypha is not primarily concerned with books that were excluded from the most ancient forms of the canon in various churches nor with the prehistory of these canons. Instead, we may offer the following definition that builds upon, but is at the same time broader than, the one offered earlier by Michael Stone: *The Apocrypha are Jewish works of the Second Temple period that are excluded from the Hebrew Bible but included in the Old Testaments of some but not all churches.*

This definition allows for a list of Apocrypha that is longer than the one familiar to most scholars by including works found in Bibles other than Greek or Latin ones. One important stipulation, however, is necessary to exclude later esoteric or exotic books from being added to the list: that the Apocrypha must be Jewish works of the Second Temple period and thus of ancient origin. Even if these works were later altered or interpolated by Christian editors, this proviso prevents originally Christian or other late writings from being included among the Old Testament Apocrypha. For example, the broader Ethiopian canon includes Joseph ben Gorion's (or Pseudo-Josephus') *History of the Jews and Other Nations*, which was only composed in the tenth century C.E.[36] According to our definition, this work must be excluded from the Apocrypha. The full list of Apocrypha, then, may be given in two parts, the first of which includes works common to all Catholic and Orthodox Bibles (with their approximate dates of composition):[37]

Book	*Date*
Tobit	4th or 3rd century B.C.E.
Judith	2nd or 1st century B.C.E.
Wisdom of Solomon	Ca. 40 C.E. or earlier
1 Maccabees	Late 2nd or early 1st century B.C.E.
2 Maccabees	124 B.C.E.
Ecclesiasticus	Ca. 180 B.C.E.; prologue ca. 132 B.C.E.
Baruch	Between 200 and 60 B.C.E.
Letter of Jeremiah [= Bar 6]	4th to late 2nd centuries B.C.E.
Additions to Esther	2nd or 1st century B.C.E.
Additions to Daniel	3rd to 2nd centuries B.C.E.

---

[36] Beckwith, *Old Testament Canon*, p. 495.

[37] For dates, see the introductions to the various books in W. Meeks, et al., eds., *The HarperCollins Study Bible. New Revised Standard Version, With the Apocryphal/Deuterocanonical Books* (New York, 1993).

The list is completed with any other books that were included in one or another of the historic Christian canons (with approximate dates of composition):

Book	Date
Prayer of Manasseh	Probably 1st century B.C.E.
Psalm 151	Hellenistic period
1 Esdras	Probably 2nd century B.C.E.
2 Esdras	Late 1st to 3rd centuries B.C.E.[38]
3 Maccabees	Roman period (30 B.C.E. to 70 C.E.)
4 Maccabees	1st century B.C.E. to late 1st century C.E.[39]
1 Enoch	1st century B.C.E. to late 1st century C.E.
Jubilees	2nd century B.C.E.

Since each of these works became part of an historic Christian canon through the canonical process, none should be deemed superior or less valid than others; in at least one branch of the Christian church each came to be regarded and used as Scripture. From a scholarly point of view, all these books (or parts of books) qualify as Apocrypha as long as they are Jewish works of the Second Temple period, even if it is difficult to recover their original form or if their present form has been altered by subsequent Christian editors. As will become clear in sections 2 and 3, several of the "apocryphal" books listed above were viewed as Scripture by the Qumran community.

1.4 *Defining the Pseudepigrapha*

As detailed above,[40] scholarly and more popular writings indicate that the term Pseudepigrapha is being used in two very different senses. First, it denotes ancient Jewish works—apart from the Old Testament, the Apocrypha, and writers such as Philo and Josephus—that were known to us prior to the discovery of the Dead Sea Scrolls. Second, there is an increasing tendency in literature on this topic to view pseudepigrapha as a literary genre or group of falsely-attributed writings and accordingly to include among these writings material such as the Pseudo-Daniel or Pseudo-Ezekiel documents found in Cave 4 at Qumran.

---

[38] Although the Hebrew original of *2 Esdras* was only completed ca. 100-120 C.E., it may loosely be classified as Second Temple literature in view of its focus on the Temple and its destruction.

[39] There is disagreement among scholars as to the precise date of *4 Maccabees*.

[40] Section 1.2.

With respect to the Dead Sea Scrolls, I have suggested elsewhere[41] that the first sense of pseudepigrapha be eliminated altogether by substituting "other previously-known writings." This liberates the term to denote a literary genre or (more appropriately) a group of falsely-attributed writings. The term pseudepigrapha may accordingly be defined narrowly or broadly. In the narrow sense, as Moshe Bernstein has stated, it denotes "texts falsely ascribed to an author (usually of great antiquity) in order to enhance their authority and validity."[42] His broader definition has three categories:

- "Authoritative pseudepigraphy," in which the speaker of the work is a purported ancient figure.
- "Convenient pseudepigraphy," where the work is anonymous but individual pseudepigraphic voices are heard within it.
- "Decorative pseudepigraphy," where the work is associated with a name without particular regard for content or to achieve a certain effect.[43]

Under this broader definition of pseudepigraphy, Bernstein proceeds to offer a wide-ranging list of literary forms, including: rewritten Bible (both narrative and legal, such as in Jubilees), expansions of biblical stories (as in 1 Enoch and similar books), testaments, prophetic visions, sapiential literature, prayer, and poetry.

This approach offers a comprehensive view that takes seriously pseudepigraphy as a type of writing among all the compositions found at Qumran, including the Apocrypha, other previously known works, and compositions that were previously unknown. It should also be noted that this classification effectively incorporates into the category Apocrypha several works that scholars have traditionally grouped as Pseudepigrapha. It is for this reason that books such as 1 Enoch and Jubilees have not been italicized (which would otherwise classified them as Pseudepigrapha) in the present essay.

1.5 *Appropriate Terminology: Scripture and Scriptures*

It is clear that Canon and canonical should not be used with refer-

---

[41] P.W. Flint, "'Apocrypha,' Other Previously-Known Writings, and 'Pseudepigrapha' in the Dead Sea Scrolls," in P. Flint and J. VanderKam, eds., *The Dead Sea Scrolls after Fifty Years: A Comprehensive Assessment* (Leiden, 1998-1999), vol. 2, pp. 24-66, esp. pp. 32–33.

[42] M. Bernstein, "Pseudepigraphy in the Qumran Scrolls," p. 1.

[43] Ibid., p. 3.

ence to Qumran and other Second Temple literature, since these are clearly post-biblical terms (although it is possible to speak of the "canonical process" or "canon consciousness").[44] Of course, "canon" and "canonical" are perfectly legitimate in discourse about the Dead Sea Scrolls if the retrospective aspect of such terms remains evident (for example, in the question: "Which of our canonical books are represented at Qumran?"). In this essay "Bible" and "biblical" will also be avoided as far as possible, except with reference to the modern distinction between "biblical" and "non-biblical" books from Qumran for purposes of classification. While this distinction is not always ideal, it remains the best practical one, especially for purposes of relating the Dead Sea Scrolls to the Scriptures of Judaism and Christianity.[45] Apocrypha (along with apocryphal) will likewise be eschewed, since this category is not indicated among the Qumran writings. Such terminology may, however, be retained when it is used retrospectively ("Which apocryphal books are represented at Qumran?"), or in titles (e.g. the *Genesis Apocryphon*).

Identifying appropriate terminology for describing the sacred or authoritative status of certain writings in the Second Temple period is no simple task. The ancient sources suggest several possibilities:[46]

(1) *ha-miqra'* ("What is read," cf., Neh. 8:8). The form *miqra'* is also found in the Qumran Scrolls, but usually in the sense of "gathering."[47]

(2) *'asher katub* or *ka-'asher katub* ("As it is written"): 1QS 5:17; 8:14; 4QFlor frg. 1.2, 12, 15, 16; 4QCatena A frgs. 5–6.11; frg. 7.3; frgs. 10–11.1.

---

[44] For further comment, see P.W. Flint, *The Dead Sea Psalms Scrolls and The Book of Psalms* (Leiden, 1997), chap. 1 ("Appropriate Terminology"), pp. 13–26, esp. pp. 16–17.

[45] This statement requires further nuancing. While all Jews and Christians accept the books of the *Tanakh* as Scripture, Roman Catholics, Orthodox, and some other Christian groups include additional books in their canons. From a Roman Catholic viewpoint, for example, the Ben Sira scroll from Masada belongs to the "biblical" category of scrolls. The Ethiopian Church, with its even wider canon, would also regard the Enoch fragments as "biblical."

[46] For a survey of terminology denoting Scripture, see R.T. Beckwith, "Formation of the Hebrew Bible," in *Mikra. Text, Translation, Reading and Interpretation of the Hebrew Bible in Ancient Judaism and Early Christianity* (Assen, Maastricht, and Philadelphia, 1988), pp. 39–86, esp. pp. 39–40.

[47] The combination *miqra' qodesh* ("holy gathering") appears twice in the Temple Scroll (11QTa 17:10 and 25:3).

(3) *ha-katub* ("What is written"), 11QMelch 2:19.
(4) *kitbei ha-qodesh* ("The Holy Writings"), M. Yad. 4:6; cf. *hai hierai graphai* (1 Clem. 53:1); *ta hiera grammata* (2 Tim. 3:15); *graphai hagiai* (Rom. 1:2).
(5) *ha-sefarim* ("the Books," Dan. 9:2) or *ha-sefer* (1QS 7:2). Cf., *ta biblia ta hagia* ("the Holy Books"), 1 Macc. 12:9; *hai hierai biblio*, Alexander Polyhistor (according to Eusebius, *Preparatio Evangelica* 9.24).

These terms suggest that sacred material is contained in three loci or activities: reading, writing, and books. At Qumran, "writing" features most often with respect to sacred truth or teaching, with passages from holy and authoritative works regularly introduced by *ca-'asher katub* or a similar phrase. Accordingly, "Scripture" (and "scriptural") seems most fitting for conveying many aspects of the term "Bible," but without the accompanying later connotations. Other terms to be considered are *miqra'* ("reading") and *ha-sefarim* ("the Books)." However, the first is not really appropriate, at least at Qumran, where *qara'* does not have the sense of "Bible" found in later Rabbinic writings. The second term is somewhat more fitting, since it is frequently used for "biblical" books at Qumran.[48] Yet I shall avoid using *ha-sefarim* since it can also denote book(s) whose authority differed from that of scriptural ones.[49] So in this essay I shall use *Scripture(s)* for works that were regarded at Qumran as ancient and especially authoritative or sacred.

2. *The Shape of the Scriptures at Qumran*[50]

2.1 *The Canonical Process*

Although we cannot speak of a closed canon or Bible at Qumran, the Scrolls do offer firm evidence of the canonical process. Important information is provided by the halakhic manifesto *Miqsat Ma'asei Ha-Torah* from Cave 4 (abbreviated 4QMMT):

---

[48] For example, *sefer ha-torah* (CD 5:2); *sefer yehesqel* (4Q174 frg. 1.16); *sefer daniel* (4Q474 frg. 2.3); and *sefer ha-tehillim* (4Q491 frg. 17.4)

[49] For example, *sefer serek ha-yahad* (4Q255 frg. 1.1); *sefer zikaron* (CD 20:19 and 4Q417 frg. 2.15–16); *sefer ha-hayyim* (4Q504 frgs. 1–2 recto vi.14). Such works were authoritative for the Qumran community, but not in the same sense as the Torah, Isaiah, Daniel, or the Psalms.

[50] For further details on much of this section, see M. Abegg, P. Flint and E. Ulrich, *The Dead Sea Scrolls Bible* (San Francisco, 1999).

[And] we have [also written] to you that you should examine the book of Moses [and] the book[s of the Pr]ophets and Davi[d] ... (4Q397 14–21 C, lines 9–10)[51]

This passage indicates that three groupings of Scripture were envisaged at Qumran by the time 4QMMT was compiled (in the second century B.C.E.):[52] the "Book of Moses," the "Prophets," and "David." Four points needs be made before we proceed further. First, this reference suggests that the Hebrew Bible was completed in stages and that one or more of these stages were complete when 4QMMT was compiled; hence we may speak of the canonical process or a "Bible-in-the-making." Second, this tripartite division corresponds with the overall shape of the Hebrew (Jewish) canon, not the four divisions of Christian canons that derive from the Septuagint or Greek Bible. Third, while the first division is equivalent to the Torah or Pentateuch, the second does not exactly signify the Prophets found in modern Bibles (see 2.3). Fourth, "David" seems to denote the third division of the Hebrew Scriptures by the Psalms as the foremost Davidic book (see 2.4).[53]

The material that follows focuses on the overall shape and contents of the Scriptures at Qumran. As indicated in the introduction, I will occasionally comment on the textual form and other characteristics of specific books, but not in a systematic or comprehensive manner.

2.2 *The Torah*

There can be no doubt that this grouping contained the same five books found in the Torah or Pentateuch of modern Bibles. All five are well-represented among the Dead Sea Scrolls, which also show the Torah was well-established as a collection by the second century B.C.E.

---

[51] See E. Qimron and J. Strugnell, *Qumran Cave 4.V: Miqṣat Maʿaśe Ha-Torah* (DJD 10; Oxford: Clarendon Press, 1994) 58–59.

[52] According to the editors (DJD 10.109), the oldest manuscript was copied about 75 B.C.E. and the youngest about 50 C.E., but the archetype must have been older still.

[53] It is interesting to note that Jesus uses virtually the same terminology in Luke 24:44: "... that everything written about me in the Law of Moses and the Prophets and the Psalms must be fulfilled."

Genesis. The remains of some twenty manuscripts were discovered at Qumran itself: one in Cave 1, one in Cave 2, perhaps as many as sixteen in Cave 4, one in Cave 6, and one in Cave 8.[54] Remains of other Genesis Scrolls were found to the south at Masada and perhaps as many as three in a cave in the cliffs of Wadi Murabbaʿat which had been used as a hideout by rebels of the Bar Kokhba revolt.[55] Moreover, two of the listed manuscripts are actually pieces of the same scroll that were obtained at different times from the Bedouin.[56] Three scrolls present Genesis in the ancient Hebrew script known as paleo-Hebrew;[57] one of these, 4QpaleoGen^m, is the oldest manuscript of Genesis, dating from the mid-second century B.C.E. Despite the large number of Genesis scrolls that were found, all are relatively fragmentary, with only thirty-four of the book's fifty chapters represented.[58] A manuscript containing all the books of Moses (Genesis-Deuteronomy) would have been both large and unusual at Qumran, but at least two contain portions of both Genesis and Exodus,[59] thus confirming an ancient order for these two books.

Exodus. The eighteen manuscripts of Exodus attest to the popularity of this book among the Qumran community. Seventeen were discovered in the vicinity of Wadi Qumran: one in Cave 1, three in Cave 2, twelve in Cave 4, and one in Cave 7.[60] The final scroll was found near Wadi Murabbaʿat.[61] Two manuscripts are written in the paleo-Hebrew script,[62] and one in Greek.[63] Between them, these eighteen scrolls attest to all forty chapters of the book of Exodus. As also occurs for Genesis, some Exodus manuscripts indicate that the five books of the Torah were sometimes copied together in the same

---

[54] 1QGen, 2QGen, 4QGen-Exod^a, 4QGen^b-4QGen^g, 4QGen^{h1}, 4QGen^{h2}, 4QGen^h-title, 4QGen^j, 4QGen^k, 4QpaleoGen-Exod^l, 4QpaleoGen^m, 4QGen^n, and pap4QGen [4Q483], 6QGen, 8QGen.

[55] MasGen, MurGen 1, MurGen (origin questionable), and Sdeir 1.

[56] MurGen (origin questionable) and Sdeir 1.

[57] 4QpaleoGen-Exod^l, 4QpaleoGen^m, 6QpaleoGen.

[58] Those no longer preserved are chapters 7, 9, 11, 13-16, 20, 21, 25, 28-31, 38, and 44.

[59] 4QGen-Exod^a and 4QpaleoGen-Exod^l.

[60] 1QExod, 2QExod^a, 2QExod^c, 2QExod^c, 4QGen-Exod^a, 4QExod^b-4QExod^e, 4QExod-Lev^f, 4QExod^g, 4QExod^h, 4QExod^j, 4QExod^k, 4QpaleoGen-Exod^l, 4QpaleoExod^m, and pap7QLXXExod.

[61] MurExod.

[62] 4QpaleoGen-Exod^l and 4QpaleoExod^m.

[63] pap7QLXXExod.

scroll. Two also preserve portions of Genesis,[64] one shows Exodus to have been followed by Leviticus,[65] and the scroll from Wadi Murabbaʿat includes fragments of Genesis and Numbers in addition to Exodus.

Leviticus. Sixteen manuscripts of Leviticus were found in the Judaean desert, fourteen at Qumran: one in Cave 1, one in Cave 2, nine in Cave 4, one in Cave 6, and two in Cave 11.[66] The remaining two scrolls were discovered in the ruins on Masada.[67] Two Leviticus scrolls were copied in the paleo-Hebrew script,[68] and two in Greek.[69] Of the twenty-seven chapters of Leviticus, at least portions of twenty-six are preserved; nothing of chapter 12 remains. As already observed for Genesis and Exodus, two scrolls[70] suggest that the five books of the Torah were sometimes copied together by preserving portions of both Exodus-Leviticus and Leviticus-Numbers, respectively.

Numbers. A total of eleven Numbers scrolls were found in the Judaean Desert. Eight of these were discovered at Qumran: one in Cave 1, four in Cave 2, and three in Cave 4.[71] Three more were found at sites further to the south: two at Naḥal Ḥever, and one at Murabbaʿat.[72] One of these manuscripts was copied in the paleo-Hebrew script[73] and another in Greek.[74] Of the thirty-two chapters of Numbers, only chapters 6 and 14 are not represented in at least one of these scrolls. For comment on the scroll[75] that preserves portions of both Leviticus and Numbers, see under Leviticus above.

Deuteronomy. Of the thirty-three Deuteronomy scrolls, thirty were discovered at Qumran: two in Cave 1 and three in Cave 2,[76] twenty-

---

[64] 4QGen-Exod^a and 4QpaleoGen-Exod^l.
[65] 4QExod-Lev^f.
[66] 1QpaleoLev, 2QpaleoLev, 4QExod-Lev^f, 4QLev-Num^a, 4QLev^b-4QLev^e, 4QLev^g, 4QLXXLev^a, pap4QLXXLev^b, 6QpaleoLev, 11QpaleoLev^a, and 11QLev^b.
[67] MasLev^a and MasLev^b.
[68] 1QpaleoLev, 2QpaleoLev, 6QpaleoLev, and 11QpaleoLev^a.
[69] 4QLXXLev^a and pap4QLXXLev^b.
[70] 4QExod-Lev^f and 4QLev-Num^a.
[71] 1QpaleoLev, 2QNum^a, 2QNum^b, 2QNum^c, 2QNum$^{d?}$, 4QLev-Num^a, 4QNum^b, and 4QLXXNum.
[72] 5/6HevNum, XHev/SeNum, and MurNum.
[73] 1QpaleoLev.
[74] 4QLXXNum.
[75] 4QLev-Num^a.
[76] 1QDeut^a, 1QDeut^b, 2QDeut^a, 2QDeut^b, and 2QDeut^c.

two in Cave 4,[77] and one each in Caves 5, 6 and 11.[78] Three more manuscripts were found at sites further to the south: one at Masada, one at Naḥal Ḥever, and one at Murabbaʿat.[79] Two of the Deuteronomy scrolls were copied in the paleo-Hebrew script,[80] and another in Greek.[81] Although none of these scrolls is complete, at least part of all twenty-four chapters of Deuteronomy is represented in them.

An interesting note on abbreviations: The confusing symbols 4QDeut^{k1}, 4QDeut^{k2}, and 4QDeut^{k3} remind us just how difficult it is to categorize fragments of ancient writing, to piece them together, and to identify the scroll to which each belongs. When earlier editors first identified these fragments as belonging to Deuteronomy, they believed them all to be part of a single scroll that they termed "4QDeut^k." Later, when it was discovered that the fragments actually belong to three different scrolls, it was too late to assign the next symbols, "l" and "m," to the second and third pieces, since these had already been allocated to other scrolls. For this reason the symbol "k" is now shared by three different manuscripts of Deuteronomy!

2.3 *The Prophets*

This contains the same general grouping as the Prophets found in modern Bibles but with two important exceptions. First, Daniel was most likely included here, and not in the Writings, since Dan. 12:10 is quoted in frgs. 1–3 ii.3–4^a of the *Florilegium* (4Q174), which tells us that it is written in the Book of Daniel the Prophet. Second, it is possible—though not assured—that the Epistle of Jeremiah was included among the Prophets at Qumran; as shown in Table 1, Catholic and Orthodox canons place it in this grouping as part (chapter 6) of Baruch. In this essay, the Epistle is accordingly discussed immediately after Jeremiah. In addition, it could be argued that the Psalms should also be classed among the Prophets at Qumran, since the Great Psalms Scroll (11QPs^a) tells us that David composed his Psalms

---

[77] 4QDeut^a, 4QDeut^b, 4QDeut^c, 4QDeut^d, 4QDeut^e, 4QDeut^f, 4QDeut^g, 4QDeut^h, 4QDeut^i, 4QDeut^j, 4QDeut^{k1}, 4QDeut^{k2}, 4QDeut^{k3}, 4QDeut^l, 4QDeut^m, 4QDeut^n, 4QDeut^o, 4QDeut^p, 4QDeut^q, 4QpaleoDeut^r, 4QpaleoDeut^s, and 4QLXXDeut.

[78] 5QDeut, pap6QDeut?, and 11QDeut.

[79] MasDeut, XHev/SeDeut, and MurDeut.

[80] 4QpaleoDeut^r and 4QpaleoDeut^s.

[81] 4QLXXDeut.

"through prophecy" (col. 27:2-11). However, this suggestion is discounted in that 4QMMT refers to "David" as a grouping of Scriptures distinct from the Prophets. The following ten books belong to this section:

Joshua. Surprisingly, perhaps, only two scrolls of the book of Joshua were recovered in the Judaean Desert, both of them at Qumran.[82] The first of these is 4QJosh^a, which was copied about 100 B.C.E. and is the oldest witness to the text of Joshua in any language. Of the twenty-four chapters of this book, only chapters 2–8, 10, and 17 are represented in the remains from Qumran.

Judges. Three manuscripts of the Judges, none of them complete, were discovered at Qumran: one in Cave 1 and two in cave 4.[83] Only five (6, 8, 9, 19, 21) of this book's twenty-one chapters are represented in the Scrolls.

Samuel. A total of four Samuel manuscripts were found at Qumran, one in Cave 1 and three in Cave 4.[84] As 1QSam—of which only eight pieces remain—lay rolled, a fragment roughly the size of a quarter was preserved at the same position on each of eight successive layers of leather. 4QSam^a, which dates from the mid-first century B.C.E., is one of the most extensively preserved and important biblical manuscripts, with 2 Samuel directly following 1 Samuel. The oldest of all the Samuel manuscripts is 4QSam^b, which was copied in about 250 B.C.E. 4QSam^c, dating roughly 100-75 B.C.E., was inscribed by the same idiosyncratic scribe who copied two other manuscripts—the main copy of the *Rule of the Community* (1QS) and a collection of scriptural quotations entitled the *Testimonia* (4Q175)—and who is also responsible for a correction in the great Isaiah scroll (1QIsa^a).

Kings. Only three manuscripts of 1 and 2 Kings were discovered in the Judaean Desert: one each written on leather in Caves 4 and 5 at Qumran, and one on papyrus in Cave 6.[85] About ninety-four fragments that presumably belong to the Cave 6 scroll were found, but only seventeen of these can be identified and placed, since most preserve only a few letters each. Between them, the Scrolls preserve portions of only six (1, 3, 7, 8, 12, 22) of the twenty-two chapters in

---

[82] 4QJosh^a and 4QJosh^b.
[83] 1QJudges, 4QJudges^a, and 4QJudges^b.
[84] 1QSam, 4QSam^a, 4QSam^b, and 4QSam^c.
[85] 4QKings, 5QKings, and pap6QKings.

1 Kings, and parts of only six more (5–10) of the twenty-five chapters in 2 Kings.

Isaiah. Isaiah was one of the three most popular books at Qumran (the others being Psalms and Deuteronomy), with twenty-one manuscripts recovered. Two Isaiah scrolls were found in Cave 1,[86] eighteen in Cave 4,[87] and one in Cave 5;[88] one more was discovered further south at Wadi Murabba'at.[89] One of the most important Dead Sea Scrolls is 1QIsa^a, the "Great Isaiah Scroll," which is almost totally intact and was among the first group of discovered by a Bedouin shepherd-boy in 1947. A few others are also quite substantial, notably 1QIsa^b, 4QIsa^b, and 4QIsa^c. The Isaiah manuscripts were copied over the course of nearly two centuries, ranging from about 125 B.C.E. (1QIsa^a) to about 60 C.E. (4QIsa^c).

Jeremiah. Six Jeremiah scrolls were found at Qumran: one in Cave 2, and five more in Cave 4.[90] Although much of the book's fifty-two chapters are preserved in these manuscripts, all are so badly damaged and fragmentary that no trace of twenty-one chapters is preserved.[91] The Jeremiah scrolls were copied over approximately two hundred years, ranging from about 200 B.C.E. (4QJer^a) to the latter part of the first century B.C.E. (4QJer^e). It is interesting to note that 4QJer^b and 4QJer^d (before they were damaged) and the Septuagint contain a version of Jeremiah that is about thirteen per cent shorter than the longer version found in the Masoretic Text and in modern Bibles!

The Epistle of Jeremiah. The Epistle of Jeremiah, which is addressed to the Jews deported to Babylon by King Nebuchadnezzar, is normally printed in modern translations as the sixth chapter of Baruch. Only one tiny piece—written on papyrus and no bigger than a postage stamp—was discovered in Cave 7 at Qumran. Although the Epistle was most likely composed in Hebrew, the fragment is inscribed in Greek, hence its designation 7QpapEpJer gr.

Ezekiel. Small fragments from five manuscripts of Ezekiel were found at Qumran: one each in Caves 1, 3 and 11,[92] and two in Cave

---

[86] 1QIsa^a and 1QIsa^b.
[87] 4QIsa^a, 4QIsa^b, 4QIsa^c, 4QIsa^d, 4QIsa^e, 4QIsa^f, 4QIsa^g, 4QIsa^h, 4QIsa^i, 4QIsa^j, 4QIsa^k, 4QIsa^l, 4QIsa^m, 4QIsa^n, 4QIsa^o, pap4QIsa^p, and 4QIsa^q.
[88] 5QIsa.
[89] MurIsa.
[90] 2QJer, 4QJer^a, 4QJer^b, 4QJer^c, 4QJer^d, and 4QJer^e.
[91] I.e. chapters 1-3, 5-6, 16, 23-24, 28-29, 34-41, 45, and 51–52.
[92] 1QEzek, 3QEzek, and 11QEzek.

4.[93] Portions of one more scroll were discovered atop Masada.[94] Some of these manuscripts are very fragmentary; for example, the single fragment of 4QEzek[c]—measuring about a half inch in diameter—contains only three complete words and a few letters from six other words. The extant pieces span the course of the entire book, from chapter 1 to chapter 41, but only twelve chapters are represented: 1, 4, 5, 7, 10, 11, 13, 16, 23, 24, 31, and 41.

The Book of the Twelve (Minor) Prophets (Hosea, Joel, Amos, Obadiah, Jonah, Micah, Nahum, Habakkuk, Zephaniah, Haggai, Zechariah, Malachi). Of the ten manuscripts discovered, eight were from the caves at Qumran: seven from Cave 4 and one from Cave 5.[95] The oldest of these scrolls was copied in about 150 B.C.E. (4QXII[a]), and the youngest in about 25 B.C.E. (4QXII[g]). The two remaining scrolls were found in caves at Nahal Hever and Murabbaʿat, which were occupied by Jewish rebels during the Bar Kokhba revolt;[96] they were respectively copied in about 50 B.C.E.-50C.E. (8HevXII gr) and 75 - 100C.E. (MurXII). Portions of all twelve Minor Prophets are preserved, but none in its entirety.

One interesting question is whether the Scrolls witness to the order found in the Greek Septuagint (LXX) or to that preserved in Hebrew (MT) tradition. All of the Minor Prophets scrolls but one appear to follow the traditional Hebrew order; this includes 8HevXII gr, which—despite being a Greek manuscript—displays the order of the Hebrew tradition (Joel, Amos, Obadiah, Jonah, Micah), rather than that of the Greek (Amos, Micah, Joel, Obadiah, Jonah). However, the one odd scroll, 4QXII[a] (the oldest of all these manuscripts), suggests a third order in which Jonah follows Malachi and is probably the last booklet in the collection. The manuscript evidence thus suggests that there was more fluidity in this ancient collection than was previously recognized.

Daniel. Eight Daniel manuscripts were discovered, all of them at Qumran: two in Cave 1, five in Cave 4, and one in Cave 6.[97] None is complete due to the ravages of time, but between them these scrolls

---

[93] 4QEzek[a] and 4QEzek[b].
[94] MasEzek.
[95] 4QXII[a], 4QXII[b], 4QXII[c], 4QXII[d], 4QXII[e], 4QXII[f], 4QXII[g], and 5QAmos.
[96] 8HevXII gr and MurXII.
[97] 1QDan[a], 1QDan[b], 4QDan[a], 4QDan[b], 4QDan[c], 4QDan[d], 4QDan[e], and 6QDan.

preserve material from eleven of the twelve chapters of the book.[98] All eight manuscripts were copied in the space of one hundred and seventy-five years, ranging from 125 B.C.E.[99] to 50 C.E.[100] Between them every chapter of Daniel is represented, except for chapter 12. Yet this does not mean that the book lacked the final chapter at Qumran, since the *Florilegium* (4Q174) quotes Dan. 12:10 as written in the "Book of Daniel the Prophet."[101]

What form(s) of this book are found in the Scrolls? This is an important question since Jewish and Protestant Bibles contain Daniel in twelve chapters, whereas Roman Catholic and Orthodox Bibles have a longer version that includes the Prayer of Azariah, the Song of the Three Young Men, Susanna, and Bel and the Dragon (see Table 1). Seven of the Daniel scrolls contained the book in its shorter form, not the longer one, featuring none of the "apocryphal" texts. One scroll (4QDan^e), however, only preserves material from Daniel's Prayer in chapter 9, which suggests that it may have contained this prayer alone.

2.4 *"David" or the Writings*

This third division should not automatically be equated with the Writings (*Kethubim*) found in modern Hebrew Bibles, since it was not yet complete during the Qumran period. The evidence from the Scrolls suggests that it loosely contained most of the books now found in the Writings, as well as some others that were listed among the Apocrypha in section 1.3 above. Among the books profiled below, the most interesting features are the Qumran community's acceptance of Tobit, 1 Enoch, Jubilees, and possibly Ben Sira as Scripture, and their rejection of Esther.

Psalms. The Judaean Desert yielded no fewer than forty Psalms scrolls or manuscripts incorporating Psalms, ranging in date from the mid-second century B.C.E. (4QPs^a) to about 50–68 C.E. (e.g., 4QPs^c

---

[98] Chapters 1–11.
[99] 4QDan^a.
[100] 4QDan^c.
[101] See J.M. Allegro, *Qumrân Cave 4.I* [4Q158–4Q186] (DJD 5; Oxford, 1968), p. 54. Daniel was apparently included among the Prophets by Josephus (*Ant.* 10 §§249, 266–267), and in the New Testament (Matt. 24:15; Mark 13:14A). See also Ulrich, "Canonical Process," p. 8.

and 11QapocPs). Thirty-seven were found at Qumran: three in Cave 1,[102] one each in the Minor Caves 2, 3, 5, 6 and 8,[103] twenty-three in Cave 4,[104] and six in Cave 11.[105] Three more scrolls were discovered further south along the Dead Sea: two at Masada and one at Naḥal Ḥever.[106] Although none of these manuscripts is complete, several are very substantial, notably the Great Psalms Scroll (11QPs^a), followed (in descending order of contents) by 4QPs^a, 5/6HevPs, 4QPs^b, 4QPs^c and 4QPs^e.

Some of the Psalms scrolls differ significantly from the Psalter found in the traditional Masoretic Text;[107] for example, 4QPs^b and 11QPs^a contain a different order (arrangement) of Psalms. Of Psalms 1–89, nineteen no longer survive,[108] but of Psalms 90–150 only five are not represented,[109] since the beginnings of scrolls are usually on the outside and are thus more prone to deterioration. In addition to these Psalms that are found in modern Bibles, at least fifteen "apocryphal" Psalms or similar compositions are also distributed among four manuscripts.[110] Six of these compositions were previously familiar to scholars: Psalms 151A, 151B, 154, 155, David's Last Words (= 2 Sam 23:1-7), and Sirach 51:13-30. However, the other nine were completely unknown prior to the discovery of the Dead Sea Scrolls: the Apostrophe to Judah, the Apostrophe to Zion, David's Compositions, the Eschatological Hymn, the Hymn to the Creator, the Plea for Deliverance, and three Songs Against Demons.[111]

Job. The remains of only four scrolls were unearthed at Qumran, one in Cave 2 and the other three in Cave 4.[112] Only one of these manuscripts (4QJob^a) has more than six small fragments preserved;

---

[102] 1QPs^a, 1QPs^b, and 1QPs^c.
[103] 2QPs, 3QPs, 5QPs, pap6QPs, and 8QPs.
[104] 4QPs^a, 4QPs^b, 4QPs^c, 4QPs^d, 4QPs^e, 4QPs^f, 4QPs^g, 4QPs^h, 4QPs^j, 4QPs^k, 4QPs^l, 4QPs^m, 4QPs^n, 4QPs^o, 4QPs^p, 4QPs^q, 4QPs^r, 4QPs^s, 4QPs^t, 4QPs^u, 4QPs^v, 4QPs^w, and 4QPs^x.
[105] 11QPs^a, 11QPs^b, 11QPs^c, 11QPs^d, 11QPs^e, and 11QapocPs.
[106] MasPs^a, MasPs^b, and 5/6HevPs.
[107] For further details and discussion of these differences, see Flint, *Dead Sea Psalms Scrolls*, 135–227.
[108] Psalms 3–4, 20–21, 32, 41, 46, 55, 58, 61, 64–65, 70, 72–75, 80, and 87.
[109] Psalms 90, 108?, 110, 111, and 117.
[110] 11QPs^a, 4QPs^f, 11QPs^b, and 11QapocPs.
[111] For an English translation of all fifteen compositions, see Flint, *Dead Sea Psalms Scrolls*, pp. 243–251.
[112] 2QJob, 4QJob^a, 4QJob^b, and 4QpaleoJob^c.

the smallest is 2QJob, comprising only a single fragment with one complete word and letters from four others. One of the earliest Qumran manuscripts is 4QpaleoJob^c (copied in about 225-150 B.C.E.), which was inscribed in the archaic Hebrew script that was common before the Exile. Of the book's forty-two chapters, only eleven (8, 9, 13, 14, and 31–37) are represented among the four Job scrolls. In addition to the four Hebrew manuscripts, two copies of an Aramaic translation (targum) of Job were found at Qumran.[113]

Tobit. This fascinating book tells the story of Tobit, a Jewish exile who lived in Nineveh, capital of ancient Assyria, in the eighth century B.C.E. Five scrolls were discovered in Cave 4, four written in Aramaic[114] and one in Hebrew.[115] The best preserved manuscript is 4QpapTobit^a ar, whose nineteen identified fragments contain portions of chapters 1–7 and 12–14. The oldest is 4QTobit^d ar, copied in about 100 B.C.E.; the composition itself likely dates to the late third century. Because of damage and deterioration, none of these scrolls is fully extant, but all fourteen chapters of Tobit are represented.

Before the discovery of these copies of Tobit among the Scrolls, scholars debated whether the tale was originally written in Greek or a Semitic language (Hebrew or Aramaic). Many authorities now regard it as Aramaic; J.T. Milik, for instance, points to the tendency at Qumran—as part of a literary and nationalist renaissance—of translating works that were originally composed in Aramaic into Hebrew, but not vice versa.[116] Another indication that the Aramaic text of Tobit was most likely earlier and that the Hebrew was translated from it is that the earliest Aramaic text (4QTobit^d ar) was copied about 100 B.C.E., whereas the only Hebrew copy (4QTobit^e) is dated about 30 B.C.E. at the earliest. An Aramaic original is also supported by apparent Aramaic influences in the Hebrew copy, which seems to suggest that the Hebrew translator was using an Aramaic base text.[117]

Proverbs. The book of Proverbs was significant in Israel for gaining wisdom and insight and for training in prudent behavior and moral

---

[113] 4QtgJob and 11QtgJob.

[114] 4QpapTobit^a ar, 4QTobit^b ar, 4QTobit^c ar, and Tobit^d ar.

[115] 4QTobit^e.

[116] *Ten Years of Discovery in the Wilderness of Judaea* (SBT 26; London, 1959) 139-40.

[117] See Flint, "'Apocrypha,' Other Previously-Known Writings, and 'Pseudepigrapha'," p. 35.

character. The remnants from two scrolls of Proverbs were found in Cave 4 at Qumran,[118] one of which (4QProv^a) comprises only two fragments. Of the book's thirty-one chapters, portions of chapters 1–2, 7, and 13–15 are preserved. One verse of Proverbs is explicitly cited in one of the Qumran community's principle books, the Damascus Document, where the command is given not to send an "offering to the altar through anyone impure...; for it is written, 'The sacrifice of the wicked is disgusting; but the prayer of the righteous is like a proper offering'" (CD 11:19-21, quoting a variant form of Prov 15:8).[119]

Ben Sira. Jesus ben Sira was a Jewish teacher who compiled a book of wise sayings and instructions in Hebrew in about 190 B.C.E. This work was later translated into Greek by the author's grandson, who also added a preface of his own. The book is known as *Sirach* or *Eccleiasticus* among Catholic and Orthodox Christians, who include it in the Old Testament, and also among Protestants and some Jews who group it among the Apocrypha. This traditional form is based on the Greek translation made by Ben Sira's grandson, which is found in the Septuagint. Although the Hebrew text was known for several centuries of the Common Era, since it is discussed in some Rabbinic writings, it fell into disuse and was not recopied for very long. The Hebrew version is known as the *Wisdom of Jesus Ben Sira*, or simply *Ben Sira*, a name increasingly preferred by Jewish scholars and others working with the Hebrew text.

In view of its size (fifty-one chapters) and comparative prominence in later Christianity, it is surprising that so little of this book was found in the Dead Sea Scrolls: just portions of three chapters at Qumran and parts of six more at Masada. The most substantial manuscript was discovered at Masada,[120] and preserves portions of chapters 39-44. The only Ben Sira scroll found at Qumran was in Cave 2,[121] and preserves parts of chapters 1 and 6. One manuscript from Cave 11, the Great Psalms Scroll,[122] preserves about two thirds of a poem found in chapter 51: i.e., the second "canticle" (Sir 51:13-

---

[118] 4QProv^a and 4QProv^b.
[119] For the translation, see M. Wise, M. Abegg, and E. Cook, *The Dead Sea Scrolls* (San Francisco, 1996), p. 69.
[120] MasSir.
[121] 2QSir.
[122] 11QPs^a.

30) that follows the Epilogue written by Ben Sira. With respect to dates, the earliest of the three scrolls containing material from Ben Sira (MasSir) was copied in the first half of the first century B.C.E., and the latest (11QPs^a) about 30 to 50 C.E.

Ruth. Four manuscripts were found, two each in Caves 2 and 4 at Qumran.[123] The earliest of these scrolls was copied in the mid-first century B.C.E.[124] and the latest in the mid-first century C.E.[125] Portions of all four chapters of Ruth are preserved.

Song of Songs. Four scrolls of the Song of Songs (or Canticles) were discovered at Qumran, three in Cave 4,[126] and the fourth in Cave 6.[127] At least three of these were copied in the Herodian period (30 B.C.E. to 68 C.E.),[128] the latest being 6QCant (about 50 C.E.). Of the book's eight chapters, at least a portion of seven is preserved. 4QCant^b features several scribal errors and, although written in Hebrew, contains several Aramaic word forms that reveal Aramaic influence on the scribe. This scroll also contains several unusual scribal markings that seem to represent letters in either the Paleo-Hebrew script, the Cryptic A script, or a combination of several scripts including Greek. Since the Cryptic A script was used in Qumran sectarian writings, these letters in 4QCant^b may indicate a sectarian scribal background or a special function of this manuscript within the Qumran community. The purpose of the unusual letters is not clear. Since they appear in lines that are shorter than the surrounding ones, they possibly served as line-fillers written in the spaces at the end of the lines to prevent such lines from being mistaken as "open sections."

Ecclesiastes. Only two manuscripts of Ecclesiastes (Qoheleth) were found in Cave 4 at Qumran.[129] The older of these is 4QQoh^a (copied in about 175-150 B.C.E.), now housed at the Amman Museum in Jordan. The scribe of this manuscript made several copying mistakes, for example, skipping from one occurrence of a word to a repeated occurrence; after noticing the error he wrote the missing text supralinearly.[130] 4QQoh^b, copied in the middle or latter half of the

---

[123] 2QRuth^a, 2QRuth^b, 4QRuth^a, and 4QRuth^b.
[124] 2QRuth^b.
[125] 2QRuth^a.
[126] 4Cant^a, 4Cant^b, and 4Cant^c.
[127] 6QCant.
[128] 4Cant^c contains too little text on which to base a firm conclusion.
[129] 4QQoh^a and 4QQoh^b.
[130] I.e., above the line.

first century B.C.E., is kept with the vast majority of the Dead Sea Scrolls in the Rockefeller Museum in Jerusalem. Of the thirteen chapters of Ecclesiastes, portions of chapters 1, 5, 6, and 7 are preserved in these two scrolls.

Lamentations. Three of the Qumran caves yielded four scrolls of Lamentations,[131] and between them they preserve portions of all five chapters of the book. Scholars and students are aware that chapters 1-4 of Lamentations were originally written in acrostic form, with each line or group of lines beginning with a successive letter of the Hebrew alphabet. It is interesting to note that that the scribe of 3QLam copied Lamentations in this format, but that the scribes of 4QLam, 5QLam^a and 5QLam^b did not do so.

Esther. Many readers are aware that the book of Esther has not been found among the Dead Sea Scrolls. This could be due to mere chance: note the relatively small size of the book and the fact that several other books composed in the period following the Babylonian exile are hardly represented among the Scrolls (Joshua, Ben Sira, Chronicles, Ezra-Nehemiah). A better explanation, however, is that the Qumran community deliberately rejected Esther, for three possible reasons. First, this book makes no mention of God, which would be problematic for a religious group. Second, the emphasis on retaliation that emerges in the later chapters (7–9) of Esther is in opposition to the teachings of the Community Rule: "To no man shall I return evil for evil, I shall pursue a man only for good; for with God resides the judgment of all the living, and He shall pay each man his recompense" (1QS 10:17-18).[132] Third, Esther introduces the feast of Purim, which is not mentioned in books of Moses and not included among the Qumran community's festivals and holy days in their three hundred and sixty-four day year.[133]

Chronicles. Of the sixty-five chapters of 1 and 2 Chronicles, only one tiny fragment from Cave 4 remains.[134] Copied in about 50–25 B.C.E., this piece preserves parts of 2 Chr. 28:27 and 29:1-3. No portion of 1 Chronicles remains, but in its entirety 4QChron prob-

---

[131] 3QLam, 4QLam, 5QLam^a, and 5QLam^b.

[132] Translation by Wise, Abegg, and Cook, *The Dead Sea Scrolls*, p. 141.

[133] Alongside the article in this volume, for details of the Qumran calendar, see ibid., pp. 296–301; and S. Talmon, "Calendars and Mishmarot," in L.H. Schiffman and J.C. VanderKam, eds., *Encyclopedia of the Dead Sea Scrolls* (New York, 2000), pp. 108–117.

[134] 4QChron.

ably also contained this book, since in Jewish tradition 1 and 2 Chronicles comprise a single scroll. One possible explanation for the scarcity of Chronicles at Qumran is that the covenanters did not favor the book in view of its focus on Jerusalem and the Temple, from which they had removed themselves.

Ezra–Nehemiah. The only surviving scroll is 4QEzra, found in three small fragments, which was copied around the middle of the first century B.C.E. Of the ten chapters of Ezra, this manuscript preserves parts of chapters 4, 5, and 6. Although no portion of Nehemiah was found in the Judean Desert, 4QEzra probably contained that book as well since in Jewish tradition Ezra–Nehemiah comprise a single scroll. Taken from this book is one of the biblical terms that the Qumran community appropriated for itself, *yaḥad* or "the community" (Ezra 4:3), although the word itself is not preserved on the fragment.[135]

1 Enoch. We are told in Genesis that Enoch "walked with God; then was no more, for God took him away" (Gen. 5:24), and the New Testament interprets: "Enoch was taken (to heaven) by faith, so that he would not see death" (Heb. 11:5). The writer of 1 Enoch reports the many insights and revelations given to the biblical hero during his heavenly journeys, on topics such as of angels, the universe, calendar issues, and the future of Israel. Also known as Ethiopic Enoch, this book survives in full only in Ethiopic, and some Greek fragments are cited by ancient authors or known from papyri. Material from 1 Enoch is found in twelve scrolls, eleven from Cave 4 (all written in Aramaic)[136] and one from Cave 7 (in Greek).[137] The fact that all except one of these manuscripts are in Aramaic suggests that this, not Hebrew or Greek, was the original language of 1 Enoch.

Jubilees. The Book of Jubilees is a fascinating Jewish work that is unfamiliar to most modern readers. Containing an account of things

---

[135] See S. Talmon, *The World of Qumran from Within* (Jerusalem and Leiden, 1989), pp. 55–56.

[136] 4QEn^a ar, 4QEn^b ar, 4QEn^c ar, 4QEn^d ar, 4QEn^e ar, 4QEn^f ar, 4QEn^g ar, 4QEnastr^a ar, 4QEnastr^b ar, 4QEnastr^c ar, and 4QEnastr^d ar.

[137] pap7QEn gr. A recently identified addition to Enochic corpus is this Greek scroll, which some scholars had erroneously identified as a New Testament text. It now seems assured that 7Q4.1, 7Q8 and 7Q12 are from *1 Enoch* 103:3-4, 7-8; that 7Q11 is part of 100:12; and that 7Q13 is part of 103:15. The text of 7Q4.2 is less certain, but this scrap appears to come from *1 Enoch* 98:11 or 105:17. For further details, see Flint, "'Apocrypha,' Other Previously-Known Writings, and 'Pseudepigrapha'," pp. 42–43.

revealed to Moses during his forty days on Mount Sinai (Exod. 24:18), Jubilees presents an overview of the history of humankind and of God's chosen people until the time of Moses, which is revealed to him by an angel. Usually categorized as "rewritten Bible," Jubilees may be divided into seven main sections. Before the discovery of the Scrolls, the book was known to scholars in Greek, Syriac, Latin, and Ethiopic translations and was part of the most ancient canon of the Ethiopic church. Most scholars were surprised at the recovery of a large number of Jubilees manuscripts at Qumran, with approximately fifteen scrolls found in five caves: two each in Caves 1 and 2,[138] one in Cave 3,[139] nine in Cave 4,[140] and one in Cave 11.[141] The actual total of these manuscripts is not certain and may be as low as thirteen or as high as sixteen.[142] All were written in Hebrew, and one on papyrus.

3. *Were the above Writings Viewed as Scripture at Qumran?*

3.1 *Criteria for Identifying Scripture at Qumran*

The previous section profiled twenty-eight writings that in my estimation were viewed as Scripture at Qumran. Five of these were in the Torah (Genesis–Deuteronomy); ten among the Prophets (Joshua, Judges, Samuel, Kings, Isaiah, Jeremiah, the Epistle of Jeremiah, Ezekiel, the Twelve Minor Prophets, and Daniel); and thirteen loosely grouped under "David" or the Writings (Psalms, Job, Tobit, Proverbs, Ben Sira, Ruth, Song of Songs, Ecclesiastes, Lamentations, Chronicles, Ezra–Nehemiah, 1 Enoch, and Jubilees). But was each of these books in fact regarded or used as Scripture by the Qumran covenanters?

While it is relatively easy to prove that well-established books such as Genesis, Deuteronomy, or Isaiah were viewed as Scripture at

---

[138] 1QJub^a, 1QJub^b, 2QJub^a, and 2QJub^b.
[139] 3QJub.
[140] 4QTanh frgs. 19-21, 4QJub^a, pap4QJub^b(?), 4QJub^c, 4QJub^d, 4QJub^e, 4QJub^f, 4QJub^g, and pap4QJub^h.
[141] 11QJub.
[142] 1QJub^a and 1QJub^b may belong to the same scroll, the Cave 3 fragments may represent more than one manuscript, and the precise identification of pap4QJub^b(?) is uncertain.

Qumran, the same cannot be said for all the books listed above. So if we are not merely to assume in retrospect which books were so regarded, what criteria are to be used for determining the scriptural status of specific books by the Qumran community? The quotation from 4QMMT that appeared earlier[143] offers sufficient evidence that its author and recipients regarded the Torah ("the book of Moses") and the Prophets ("the book[s of the Pr]ophets")[144] as authoritative Scripture; however, evidence is more difficult to find for books that were listed under "David" or the Writings. In this section, therefore, I will pay particular attention to the status held by these later books at Qumran. Since no single approach is sufficient for assessing the scriptural status of individual books or groups of books, the following eight categories are proposed:

3.1.1 *Formal Indications of Scriptural status*[145]
This category involves explicit terms or statements in the Qumran community's writings which show that they regarded particular writings as authoritative or sacred Scripture. Examples include "the Torah," in which all things are strictly defined (CD 16:2), and "Moses and all [God's] servants the Prophets" (1QS 1:3). Among the Prophets, Ezekiel 44:15 is specified in the Damascus Document: "as God promised (*hekim*) them by Ezekiel the prophet, saying…" (CD 3:20–4:2). Daniel is formally indicated as Scripture in the *Florilegium*, which quotes Dan 12:3 and states: "As it is written in the Book of Daniel the Prophet" (4Q174 2:3). Two other relevant passages are in *4QText with a Citation of Jubilees* (4Q228), although the text is very fragmentary. Frg. 1 i.1 seems to denote the Book of Jubilees by its Hebrew title "[in the Divisi]ons of the Times," and frg. 1 i.9 appears to introduce the first word of the title by a citation formula: "For thus it is written in the Divisions [of the Times]."[146] Finally, Jubilees is also denoted as the source of information (the precise passage is not clear)

---

[143] At the beginning of section 2.

[144] On the books included in this grouping, see section 2.3 above.

[145] For several additional examples, see J.C. VanderKam, "Authoritative Literature in the Dead Sea Scrolls," in *DSD* 5 (Ulrich dedication, 1999), pp. 382–402, esp. pp. 391–394.

[146] See J.C. VanderKam and J.T. Milik, "4Q228. Text with a Citation of *Jubilees*," in J.C. VanderKam, Consulting Editor, *Qumran Cave 4.VIII: Parabiblical Texts, Part 1* (DJD 13; Oxford, 1994), pp. 177-185 + pl. XII.

in CD 16:2-4, concerning the times when Israel would be blind to the law of Moses:

> ²... But the specification of the times during which all Israel is blind to ³all these rules is laid out in detail in the "Book of Time Divisions by ⁴Jubilees and Weeks" (*bmhlqwt h'tym lywblyhm wbsbw'wtyhm*).¹⁴⁷

3.1.2 *The Appeal to Prophecy*

Associating a book or writing with prophecy points to authoritative or scriptural status. An important New Testament example occurs in Jude 14-15, which tells us that Enoch "prophesied" and then quotes from 1 Enoch:

> ¹⁴It was also about these [false teachers] that Enoch, in the seventh generation from Adam, prophesied, saying, "See, the Lord is coming with ten thousands of his holy ones, ¹⁵to execute judgment on all, and to convict everyone of all the deeds of ungodliness that they have committed in such an ungodly way, and of all the harsh things that ungodly sinners have spoken against him" (1 Enoch 1:9).

A comparable case occurs in David's Compositions, the extended prose "epilogue" found in col. 27:2-11 of 11QPsª:

> ²And David, the son of Jesse, was wise, and a light like the light of the sun, and literate, ³and discerning and perfect in all his ways before God and men. And the LORD gave ⁴him a discerning and enlightened spirit. And he wrote ⁵3,600 psalms; and songs to sing before the altar over the whole-burnt ⁶perpetual offering every day, for all the days of the year, 364; ... ¹¹All these he composed through prophecy which was given him from before the Most High.¹⁴⁸

The key statement "all these he composed through prophecy which was given him from before the Most High" clearly implies that all the compositions found in 11QPsª, including the canticle in Sir. 51:13-30 and Pss. 151A, 151B, 154 and 155, and even the nine previously unknown compositions,¹⁴⁹ are products of Davidic prophecy. This passage provides striking evidence that its compiler and (most likely) its readers viewed the Psalter represented by 11QPsª as sacred Scripture.

---

¹⁴⁷ Translation in Wise, Abegg, and Cook, *The Dead Sea Scrolls*, p. 66.
¹⁴⁸ Translation by J. Sanders, *The Dead Sea Psalms Scroll* (Ithaca, 1967), p. 87.
¹⁴⁹ See the full listing under "Psalms" in section 2.4 above.

3.1.3 *Claims of Divine Authority and Davidic Superscriptions*

Several of the works that were surveyed are attributed to biblical figures and/or claim their message to be from God or from an angel (e.g., 1 Enoch 1:2; 10:1–11:2; Jub. 1:5-18, 22-28, 26-29; 2:1) or from heavenly tablets (e.g., 1 Enoch 81:1-2; 93:1; Jub. 3:8-14, 31).[150] However, since such claims are often characteristic of pseudepigraphal writings, they may not be not a reliable indicator of a composition's scriptural or authoritative status among those who used it.

But Davidic superscriptions form a separate category, since one of their functions in the Book of Psalms is to associate particular pieces with David, the Psalmist *par excellence*. Moreover, there are very few instances among the Scrolls of Psalms not found in our Psalter that contain Davidic titles, which indicates that adding such titles for purposes of lending authority was not practiced among the compilers of the different Psalters found at Qumran. Two rare examples are the autobiographical Psalms 151A and 151B, whose superscriptions are clearly Davidic and thus denote the scriptural status of the two psalms:

> A Hallelujah of David the Son of Jesse (Ps. 151A:0).
> At the beginning of David's power after the prophet of God had anointed him (Ps, 151B:1).

3.1.4 *Quantity of Manuscripts*

Works represented by a large number of manuscripts were extensively used at Qumran, which is indicative of their popularity and most likely their authoritative status. Of the books discussed above, the foremost at Qumran are—in descending order—the Psalms (thirty-seven scrolls), Deuteronomy (thirty), Isaiah (twenty-one), Genesis (twenty), Exodus (eighteen), Jubilees (about fifteen), Leviticus (fourteen), 1 Enoch (twelve), and Daniel (eight).

3.1.5 *Translation into Greek or Aramaic*

Comparatively few Qumran Scrolls are written in Greek, but the translation of a Hebrew work into Greek seems indicative of its im-

---

[150] On Jubilees, for instance, James VanderKam writes: "Jubilees... advertises itself as divine revelation" ("The Jubilees Fragments from Qumran Cave 4," in J. Trebolle Barrera and L. Vegas Montaner, eds., *The Madrid Qumran Congress. Proceedings of the International Congress on the Dead Sea Scrolls, Madrid. 18–21 March 1991* [Leiden and Madrid], vol. 2, pp. 635-648, esp. p. 648).

portance and authoritative status for its scribe or users. The same appears true for a biblical book that has been translated or paraphrased into Aramaic. Of the books detailed in section 2 above, the following appear in Greek: Exodus (pap7QLXXExod), Leviticus (4QLXXLev^a, pap4QLXXLev^b), Numbers (4QLXXNum), Deuteronomy (4QLXXDeut), and 1 Enoch (pap7QEn gr). There is also a large Greek scroll containing the Book of the Twelve (Minor) Prophets, which was discovered at Naḥal Ḥever. One book (Job) was translated into Aramaic, with one targum found in Cave 4 (4QtgJob) and another in Cave 11 (11QtgJob).

3.1.6 *Pesharim and Other Commentaries*

Books on which commentaries were written must have been viewed as Scripture by the commentators and most likely their audiences. This category includes the *pesharim*, in the form of textual citation followed by interpretation (*pesher*). Fifteen "continuous" *pesharim* are found among the Scrolls: five on Isaiah (4QpIsa^{a-e}), two each on Hosea and Zephaniah (4QpHos^a, 4QpHos^b, 1QpZeph, 4QpZeph^a), one each on Micah, Nahum and Habakkuk (1QpMic, 4QpNah, 1QpHab), and three on the Psalms (1QpPs, 4QpPs^a, 4QpPs^b).[151]

Other types of commentary were found at Qumran: for example, *A Commentary on Genesis and Exodus* (4Q422), which may be classified as "rewritten Bible." A further example is *A Commentary on the Law of Moses* (4Q251), which features passages concerning the law of damages (Exod. 21:19, 28-29), firstfruits (Exod. 22:29), and proper sacrifice. It has been suggested[152] that 4Q247 may comprise a commentary on a section of 1 Enoch, the Apocalypse of Weeks. Caution is advised, however, since 4Q247 is very fragmentary.[153]

3.1.7 *Quotations and Allusions*

With respect to identifying authoritative writings,[154] ways in which a book was used in later writings are frequently (though not inva-

---

[151] For a recent discussion of *pesharim*, see Shani L. Berrin, "Pesharim," in Schiffman and VanderKam, eds., *Encyclopedia of the Dead Sea Scrolls*, pp. 644–647.

[152] J.T. Milik, *The Books of Enoch: Aramaic Fragments of Qumrân Cave 4* (Oxford, 1976), p. 256.

[153] Cf., J. VanderKam, "Authoritative Literature," p. 398; Flint, "'Apocrypha,' Other Previously-Known Writings, and 'Pseudepigrapha'," p. 64.

[154] A most useful study from the late 1990s is J. VanderKam, "Authoritative Literature in the Dead Sea Scrolls," pp. 382-402.

riably)¹⁵⁵ indicative of its special authority or scriptural status.¹⁵⁶ This extensive category, whose components are sometimes difficult to determine since definite allusion and general scriptural imagery are often hard to distinguish,¹⁵⁷ includes the following:

(a) Midrashic texts. Two examples are the *Florilegium* (4QFlor), which includes Ps. 1:1 and Ps. 2:1 as base texts,¹⁵⁸ and 4QCatena A (4Q177), which contains quotations from several Psalms.¹⁵⁹

(b) Quotations with introductory formulae. Three examples are in *4QCatena A* (4Q177), where Ps. 6:2-5 is introduced by *asher 'amar david* ("as David said," frgs. 12–13 i.2); in the *Florilegium* (4Q174), where 2 Sam. 7:11 is signaled by the similar *'asher 'amar* (col. 3:7); and in 4Q163, where a passage apparently from Jeremiah is introduced by *ka'asher katub* ("as it is written," frg. 1.4). Three others are found in the *Damascus Document*, where *'asher 'amar* ("he said") refers to Ezek. 9:4, with God as the subject (CD 19:11-12); *'asher 'amar 'el* ("as God said") refers to Mal. 1:10 (CD 6:13-14);¹⁶⁰ and *katub* ("it is written") intro-

---

¹⁵⁵ Writers can also use earlier texts in illustration or to buttress their own views.

¹⁵⁶ An important early study is I.H. Eybers, "Some Light on the Canon of the Qumran Sect," in S. Leiman, ed., *The Canon and Masorah of the Hebrew Bible. An Introductory Reader* (New York, 1974), pp. 23-36.

¹⁵⁷ For example, with reference to the *Hodayot*, Bonnie Kittel, *The Hymns of Qumran: Translation and Commentary* (Chico, 1981), pp. 48-55, posits four degrees of the use of scriptural language, ranging from definite quotations to the "free use of biblical idiom and vocabulary."

¹⁵⁸ Annette Steudel defines the *Gattung* of 4Q174 (and 4Q177) as "ein thematischer Midrasch mit Parallelen zu den (frühen) Pescharim" (*Der Midrasch zur Eschatologie aus der Qumrangemeinde [4QMidrEschat^{a,b}]. Materielle Rekonstruktion, Textbestand, Gattung und traditionsgeschichtliche Einordnung des durch 4Q174 ['Florilegium'] und 4Q177 ['Catena A'] repräsentierten Werkes aus den Qumranfunden* [Leiden, 1994], p. 191). 4QFlor is a midrash on 2 Sam. 7 and Ps. 1–2; see Y. Yadin, "Midrash on 2 Sam. vii and Ps. i–ii," in *IEJ* 9, 1959, pp. 95–98; G. Brooke, *Exegesis at Qumran. 4QFlorilgeum in Its Jewish Context* (Sheffield, 1985), p. 82; É. Puech, *La croyance des Esséniens en la vie future: immortalité, resurrection, vie éternelle* (Paris, 1993), pp. 572–591; G. Vermes, *The Dead Sea Scrolls. Qumran in Perspective* (Philadelphia, 1981), p. 293.

¹⁵⁹ This "thematic midrash" quotes from the Prophets and also Pss. 11:1-2; 12:1, 7; 5:10(?); 13:2-3, 5; 6:2-5, 6; 16:3; 17:1, apparently in that order (cf., Allegro, DJD 5, pp. 67–74 + pls. XXIV–XXVa; J. Strugnell, "Notes en marge du Volume V des «Discoveries in the Judaean Desert of Jordan»," in *RevQ* 26, 1970, pp. 163–276, esp. pp. 236–248; Steudel, *Midrasch zur Eschatologie*, pp. 190–192.

¹⁶⁰ Further examples are *kemo she-katub* ("as it is written"), *she-ne'emar* ("as it is said"), *magid ha-katub* ("Scripture tells"), and *talmud lo'mar* ("Scripture [literally, 'the Teaching'] says"); cf., M. Fishbane, "Use, Authority and Interpretation of Mikra at Qumran," in M.J. Mulder, ed., *Mikra. Text, Translation, Reading and Interpretation of the Hebrew Bible in Ancient Judaism and Early Christianity* (Assen, Maastricht, and Philadelphia, 1988), pp. 339–377, esp. pp. 347–348.

duces a variant form of Prov. 15:8 (CD 11:19-21). Another important passage occurs in the *Community Rule*, where Is. 40:3 is quoted in relation to the self-identity and mission of the Qumran desert community:

> ... they shall separate from the session of perverse men to go to the wilderness, there to prepare the way of truth, as it is written (Is. 40:3): "In the wilderness prepare the way of the Lord, make straight in the desert a highway for our God" (1QS 8:13-14).

(c) Definite allusions or quotations without introductory formulae. Examples of base-texts include the following books:

Genesis. In an obvious polemic against the polygamy of the Pharisees, the *Damascus Document* argues on the basis of Gen. 1:27 ("male and female he created them") and Gen. 7:9 ("went into the ark two by two") that one wife was the biblical norm (CD 4:19–5:1).

Leviticus. The key to understanding the Qumran community's emphasis on purity is found in Lev. 15:31, "You must keep the people of Israel separate from their uncleanness, so that they might not die in their uncleanness by defiling my tabernacle which is in their midst" (cf., 4Q512 frg. 69.2; 11QT^a 51:4b-10).

Psalms. The *Hodayot* cite Ps. 26:12 with some modification (1QH^a 2:30).

Isaiah. The *Community Rule* refers to the "precious corner-stone" of Is. 28:16 (1QS 8:7).

Proverbs. Prov. 1:1-6 is echoed in 4Q525 ("[to kno]w wisdom and disc[ipline], to understand [...]," frg. 1.2). Two texts that treat the biblical figures of Lady Wisdom and Dame Folly at Qumran are 4Q184 (*Wiles of the Wicked Woman*) and 4Q185 (*Sapiential Work*). For example, Prov. 7:12 seems to be quoted in 4Q184 where Lady Folly "lies secretly in wait [...] in the city streets" (frg. 1.11-12).[161]

Lamentations. A *Lament for Zion* (4Q179), which appears to be patterned after Lamentations, cites Lam. 1:1 (frg. 2.4).

Jeremiah. The first column (1:1-11) of *4QApocryphon of Jeremiah C* (4Q385b) draws on Jer. 40 to 44, although lines 4-6 recall the fall of Jerusalem as found in Jer. 52:12-13.

Jubilees. The *Damascus Covenant* quotes Jub. 23:11 (CD 10:9-10); Jub. 3:8-14—which grounds the legislation of Lev. 12 (concerning a

---

[161] For fuller details, see John I. Kampen, "The Diverse Aspects of Wisdom in the Qumran Texts," in Flint and VanderKam, eds., *The Dead Sea Scrolls after Fifty Years*, vol. 1, pp. 211–243, esp. pp. 223–225.

woman's impurity) in the story of Adam and Eve—may be the source for the same material in the *Miscellaneous Rules* (4Q265 frg. 7 ii.11-17);[162] and CD 10:7-10 may well be based on Jub. 23:11, which refers to people's loss of knowledge in their old age:[163]

> [7]... No one above the age [8]of sixty shall hold the office of judge of the nation, because when Adam broke faith, [9]his life was shortened, and in the heat of anger against the earth's inhabitants, God commanded [10]their minds to regress before their life was over.

3.1.8 *Dependence*

Several Qumranic texts show a more general dependence on particular earlier works:

Genesis. Retelling portions of Genesis occupied more than one Qumran scribe. For example, the Genesis Apocryphon, in Aramaic, rehearses the lives of Enoch, Lamech, Noah and his sons, and Abraham.

Exodus and Leviticus. Exod. 22-35 and Leviticus, as well as Numbers and Deuteronomy, form the foundation of the largest non-biblical manuscript, the *Temple Scroll*, which purports to be a new Torah for the Last Days in which God speaks to Israel—evidently through Moses—in the first person.

Leviticus. Of the approximately two dozen rulings found in 4QMMT, more than half are based on legal issues concerning ritual purity from the text of Leviticus. Furthermore, most of the Laws in the *Damascus Document* are rehearsals of various Levitical commands, and the assorted legal discussions in *A Commentary on the Law of Moses* (4Q251) are largely Levitical in origin.

Kings. At least one of the Dead Sea Scrolls contains a narrative retelling of some Elijah stories and other events that are described in 1 Kings: *4Qpap paraKings et al.* (4Q382), which was copied in the first half of the first century B.C.E. Another relevant scroll is the *Apocryphon of Elisha* (4Q481a), which presents a version of 2 Kgs. 2:14-16 and other material.

Ezekiel. At least five scrolls, probably representing three separate compositions, contain rewritten versions of the book of Ezekiel: *4QPseudo-Ezekiel^{a-e}* (4Q385–88, 5Q391).[164]

---

[162] Cf., VanderKam, "Authoritative Literature," p. 399.

[163] Translation by E. Cook, in *The Dead Sea Scrolls*, p. 68.

[164] For a description and further details, see G. Brooke, "Parabiblical Prophetic Biblical Narratives," in Flint and VanderKam, op. cit., vol. 1, pp. 271–301, esp. pp. 285–290.

Psalms. The *Hodayot* and some other collections of hymns found among the Dead Sea Scrolls are largely modeled on the Psalms.

1 Enoch. This book details a luni-solar calendar that combines a three hundred and sixty-four day solar year with a schematic three hundred and fifty-four day one and which served as the model for the Qumran calendars.[165]

Jubilees. This work may well be the source for dating covenants to the third month, especially the fifteenth day, as well as the Qumranic idea that the covenant was to be renewed on the Festival of Weeks.[166]

3.2 Summary

Of the list of writings presented in section 1.1, many may be regarded as definitely viewed as Scripture by the Qumran community.[167] In the Torah: Genesis, Exodus, Leviticus, Numbers, and Deuteronomy; in the Prophets: Isaiah, Jeremiah, Ezekiel, the Twelve Minor Prophets, and Daniel; and in "David" or the Writings: Psalms, Job, 1 Enoch, and Jubilees.

It is more difficult to show that certain other books were viewed as Scripture by the Qumran community. As already discussed,[168] Esther is noted by its absence and was almost certainly rejected by the covenanters. Several more books are represented by comparatively few manuscripts at Qumran: Joshua (two scrolls), Judges (three), Kings (three), the Epistle of Jeremiah (one), Proverbs (two), Ben Sira (one), Ecclesiastes (two), Lamentations (three), Chronicles (one), and Ezra-Nehemiah (one). The types of writing they contain lead to the reasonable conclusion that the community was less concerned with Israel's later history and with wisdom traditions than it was with the covenant (e.g., Exodus), legal traditions (e.g., Leviticus), prophecy (e.g., Isaiah), and liturgy (especially Psalms). Nevertheless, the evidence presented earlier in section 2 suggests that the following books were regarded as Scripture by the Qumran community: Samuel, Kings, Tobit, Proverbs, and Lamentations.

---

[165] See J. VanderKam, "Authoritative Literature," p. 398; idem, *Calendars in the Dead Sea Scrolls: Measuring Time* (London, 1998), pp. 17-27; 71-90; Stone, "Dead Sea Scrolls and the Pseudepigrapha," pp. 277-278.

[166] See J. VanderKam, "Apocrypha and Pseudepigrapha at Qumran" (in press); "Authoritative Literature," p. 399.

[167] For an early assessment and listing, see Eybers, "Some Light on the Canon of the Qumran Sect" (note 156 above).

[168] Section 2.3 above.

The remaining books—all represented by very few scrolls—were probably viewed as Scripture at Qumran, but this statement is made with less assurance than those already listed. They are Joshua, Judges, the Epistle of Jeremiah, Ben Sira, Ruth, the Song of Songs, Ecclesiastes, Chronicles, and Ezra–Nehemiah. Further research, however, may detail the use of several or all these writings in the sectarian literature of the community and thus affirm their scriptural status at Qumran.

4. *Conclusion*

This study opened with a quest for appropriate terminology for discussing authoritative literature among the Qumran community. Since it is all too easy to decide retrospectively which books were regarded as Scripture in antiquity, terms such as *canon* and *Bible* were rejected in favor of *Scripture*. Moreover, full cognizance was taken of several different ancient canons of the Hebrew Bible/Old Testament, including those containing what are now termed "apocryphal" or "pseudepigraphical" books. The employment of appropriate terminology and an awareness of the different ancient canons was most necessary because the following two sections made it clear that some books now termed "apocryphal" were viewed as Scripture by the Qumran community

The second section explored the shape of the Scriptures at Qumran, and the third considered eight criteria for determining the scriptural status of specific books among the Qumran covenanters. Results include the following:

(a) While we cannot speak of a *canon* at Qumran, the Scrolls provide evidence of the *canonical process* or *canon consciousness.*
(b) Since some Torah scrolls originally contained more than one book or possibly all five, the Torah was well-established as a collection by the second century B.C.E.
(c) All five books of the Pentateuch were accepted as Scripture by the Qumran community.
(d) Daniel and possibly the Epistle of Jeremiah were included among the Prophets.
(e) Almost all the Prophets, including Daniel, were viewed as Scripture; however, the status of Joshua, Judges, and the Epistle of Jeremiah are not fully assured.

(f) The third division, "David" or the Writings, contained several books but was not closed by the end of the Qumran period (68 C.E.).
(g) The Psalms, Job, Tobit, 1 Enoch, and Jubilees were all regarded as Scripture by the Qumran covenanters.
(h) The scriptural status of Ben Sira, Ruth, the Song of Songs, Ecclesiastes, Chronicles, and Ezra–Nehemiah is less assured.
(i) The book of Esther was deliberately rejected by the Qumran community on religious and cultic grounds.

Selected Bibliography

The Bibliography consists of three parts: 1. Editions of Biblical and Apocryphal Scrolls in the series "Discoveries in the Judaean Desert;" 2. Other editions and translations; 3. Secondary Literature.

1. Editions of the Biblical and Apocryphal Scrolls in the Series "Discoveries in the Judaean Desert"

Barthélemy, D., and J.T. Milik, *Qumran Cave I* (DJD 1; Oxford: Clarendon Press, 1955).
Benoit, P., J.T. Milik, and R. de Vaux, *Les grottes de Murabbaʿât* (DJD 2; Oxford: Clarendon Press, 1961).
Baillet, M., J.T. Milik, and R. de Vaux, *Les 'Petites Grottes' de Qumran: Exploration de la falaise Les grottes 2Q, 3Q, 5Q, 6Q, 7Q, à 10Q, Le rouleau de cuivre* (DJD 3; Oxford: Clarendon Press, 1962), 1. Texts 2. Plates.
Sanders, J.A., *The Psalms Scroll of Qumrân Cave 11* [11QPs^a] (DJD 4; Oxford: Clarendon Press, 1965).
Allegro, J.M., *Qumrân Cave 4:I* [4Q158–4Q186] (DJD 5; Oxford: Clarendon Press, 1968).
Baillet, M., *Qumrân Grotte 4.III (4Q482–4Q520)* (DJD 7; Oxford: Clarendon Press, 1982).
Tov, E., *The Greek Minor Prophets Scroll from Naḥal Ḥever (8ḤevXII gr) [The Seiyâl Collection I]* (DJD 8; Oxford: Clarendon Press, 1990).
Skehan, P.W., E. Ulrich, and J.E. Sanderson, *Qumran Cave 4.IV: Palaeo-Hebrew and Greek Biblical Manuscripts* (DJD 9; Oxford: Clarendon Press, 1992).
Ulrich, E., F.M. Cross, et al., *Qumran Cave 4.VII: Genesis to Numbers* (DJD 12; Oxford: Clarendon Press, 1994).
VanderKam, J., consulting editor, *Qumran Cave 4.VIII: Parabiblical Texts, Part 1* (DJD 13; Oxford: Clarendon Press, 1994).
Ulrich, E., F.M. Cross, et al., *Qumran Cave 4.IX: Deuteronomy, Joshua, Judges, Kings* (DJD 14; Oxford: Clarendon Press, 1995).
Ulrich, E., et al., *Qumrân Cave 4.X: The Prophets* (DJD 15; Oxford: Clarendon Press, 1997).

Ulrich, E., et al., *Qumran Cave 4.XI: The Writings* (DJD 16; Oxford: Clarendon Press, 2000).
Cross, F.M., with D. Parry; E. Ulrich, *Qumran Cave 4.XII: Samuel* (DJD 17; Oxford: Clarendon Press [forthcoming]).
VanderKam, J. (consulting editor), *Qumran Cave 4.XVII: Parabiblical Texts*, Part 3 (DJD 22; Oxford: Clarendon Press, 1998).
García Martínez, F., E.J.C. Tigchelaar, and A.S. van der Woude, *Qumran Cave 11.II: 11Q2-18, 11Q20-31* (DJD 23; Oxford: Clarendon Press, 1998).
Flint, P.W., E. Ulrich, and M.G. Abegg, *Qumran Cave 1: The Isaiah Texts* (DJD 32; Oxford: Clarendon Press [forthcoming]).
Alexander, P., et al., *Miscellaneous Texts from Qumran and Other Sites* (DJD 36; Oxford: Clarendon Press [forthcoming]).

2. *Other Editions and Translations*

Abegg, M.G., P.W. Flint and E. Ulrich, *The Dead Sea Scrolls Bible* (San Francisco: Harper Collins, 1999).
Burrows, M., with J. C. Trever and W. H. Brownlee, *The Dead Sea Scrolls of St. Mark's Monastery*, Vol. 1: *The Isaiah Manuscript and the Habakkuk Commentary* (New Haven: American Schools of Oriental Research, 1950).
Cross, F.M., D.N. Freedman, and J.A. Sanders, *Scrolls from Qumran Cave 1: The Great Isaiah Scroll, the Order of the Community, the Pesher to Habakkuk, from Photographs by J. C. Trever* (Jerusalem: Albright Institute of Archaeological Research and Shrine of the Book, 1972).
Milik, J.T, *The Books of Enoch: Aramaic Fragments of Qumrân Cave 4* (Oxford: Clarendon Press, 1976).
Nebe, G. Wilhelm, "Die Masada-Psalmen-Handschrift M1039-160 nach einem jüngst veröffentlichen Photo mit Text von *Psalm* 81,2–85,6," in *RevQ* 14/53, 1989, pp. 89–97.
Parry, D.W., and E. Qimron, *The Great Isaiah Scroll (1QIsa^a): A New Edition* (Studies on the Texts of the Desert of Judah 32; Leiden: Brill, 1999).
Sanders, J.A., *The Dead Sea Psalms Scroll* (Ithaca: Cornell University Press, 1967).
Sukenik, E.L., *The Dead Sea Scrolls of the Hebrew University* (Jerusalem: Hebrew University and Magnes Press, 1955).
Talmon, S., "Fragments of Writings Written in Hebrew at Masada" [Hebrew], in *ErIsr* 20 (Yadin Memorial, 1989), pp. 287–286, esp. pp. 281–283.
Talmon, S., "Fragments of a Psalms Scroll from Masada, MPs^b (Masada 1103–1742)," in Brettler, M., and M. Fishbane, eds., *Minhah le-Nahum: Biblical and Other Studies Presented to Nahum M. Sarna in Honour of His 70th Birthday* (Sheffield, 1993), pp. 318–327.
Talmon, S., "Fragments of Hebrew Writings without Identifying Sigla of Provenance from the Literary Legacy of Yigael Yadin," in *Dead Sea Discoveries* 5, 1998, pp. 149–157.
Yadin, Y., *The Ben Sira Scroll from Masada. With Introduction, Emendations and Commentary* (Jerusalem: Israel Exploration Society and the Hebrew University of Jerusalem, 1965).
Yadin, Y., S. Talmon, et al., *Masada, The Yigael Yadin Excavations 1963-1965. Final Reports* (Jerusalem: Israel Exploration Society and the Hebrew University of Jerusalem, 1989–).

3. Secondary Literature

Barr, James, *Holy Scripture: Canon, Authority, Criticism* (Philadelphia: Westminster, 1983).

Beckwith, R., *The Old Testament Canon of the New Testament Church and Its Background in Early Judaism* (Grand Rapids: Eerdmans, 1985).

Bernstein, M., "Pseudepigraphy in the Qumran Scrolls: Categories and Functions," in Chazon, E.G., and M. Stone, eds., with the Collaboration of A. Pinnick, *Pseudepigraphic Perspectives: The Apocrypha and Pseudepigrapha in Light of the Dead Sea Scrolls. Proceedings of the International Symposium of the Orion Center for the Study of the Dead Sea Scrolls and Associated Literature, 12–14 January, 1997* (STDJ 36; Leiden: Brill, 1999) 1–26.

Cowley, R.W., "The Biblical Canon of the Ethiopian Orthodox Church Today," in *Ostkirchlichen Studien* 23, 1974, pp. 318–323.

Cross, Frank. M., and S. Talmon, eds., *Qumran and the History of the Biblical Text* (Cambridge, MA, and London: Harvard University Press, 1975).

Fitzmyer, J.A., *The Dead Sea Scrolls. Major Publications and Tools for Study* (rev. ed., SBLRBS 20; Atlanta: Scholars Press, 1990).

Flint, P.W., *The Dead Sea Psalms Scrolls and The Book of Psalms* (STDJ 17; Leiden: Brill, 1997).

Flint, P.W., "The Prophet Daniel at Qumran," in Evans, C.A., and P.W. Flint, eds., *Eschatology, Messianism, and the Dead Sea Scrolls* (SDSRL 1; Grand Rapids: Eerdmans, 1997), pp. 41–60.

Flint, P.W., "The Book of Psalms in the Light of the Dead Sea Scrolls," in *VT* 48, 1998, pp. 453–472.

Flint, P.W., "'Apocrypha,' Other Previously-Known Writings, and 'Pseudepigrapha' in the Dead Sea Scrolls," in Flint, P.W., and J.C. VanderKam, eds., *The Dead Sea Scrolls after Fifty Years: A Comprehensive Assessment* (2 vols., Leiden: Brill, 1999), vol. 2, pp. 24–66.

García Martínez, F., and E.J.C. Tigchelaar, "The Books of Enoch (1 Enoch) and the Aramaic Fragments from Qumran," in *RevQ* 14/53, 1989, pp. 131–146.

Gooding, D.W., "An Appeal for Stricter Terminology in the Textual Criticism of the Old Testament," in *JSS* 21, 1976, pp. 15–25.

Hoffman, T.A., "Inspiration, Normativeness, Canonicity, and the Unique Sacred Character of the Bible," in *CBQ* 44, 1982, pp. 447–469.

Leiman, Sid Z., *The Canonization of Hebrew Scripture* (Transactions of the American Academy of Arts and Sciences 47; Hamden: Anchor Books, 1976).

Mulder, Martin J., ed., *Mikra. Text, Translation, Reading and Interpretation of the Hebrew Bible in Ancient Judaism and Early Christianity* (CRINT 2.1; Assen and Maastricht: Van Gorcum; Philadelphia: Fortress, 1988).

Puech, É., *La croyance des Esséniens en la vie future: immortalité, résurrection, vie éternelle* (Paris: Gabalda, 1993).

Sanders, James A., *The Dead Sea Psalms Scroll* (Ithaca: Cornell University Press, 1967).

Sanders, James A., "Variorum in the Psalms Scroll (11QPs^a)," in *HTR* 59, 1966, pp. 83–94.

Sanders, James A., "The Qumran Psalms Scroll (11QPs^a) Reviewed," in Black, M., and W.A. Smalley, eds., *On Language, Culture, and Religion: In Honor of Eugene A. Nida* (The Hague and Paris: Mouton, 1974), pp. 79–99.

Skehan, Patrick W., "Qumran and Old Testament Criticism," in Delcor, M., ed., *Qumrân. Sa piété, sa théologie et son milieu* (BETL 46; Paris: Éditions Duculot; Leuven: Leuven University Press, 1978), pp. 163–182.

Stone, M., "Categorization and Classification of the Apocrypha and Pseudepigrapha," in *AbrN* 24, 1986, pp. 167–177.

Stone, M., "The Dead Sea Scrolls and the Pseudepigrapha," in *DSD* 3, 1996, pp. 270–295.

Stuckenbruck, L.T., *The Book of Giants from Qumran* (TSAJ 63; Tübingen: Mohr-Siebeck, 1997).

Tov, Emanuel, *Textual Criticism of the Hebrew Bible* (Assen and Maastricht: Van Gorcum; Minneapolis: Fortress, 1992).

Ulrich, Eugene, "The Canonical Process, Textual Criticism, and Latter Stages in the Composition of the Bible," in Fishbane, M., and E. Tov, eds., *"Sha'arei Talmon." Studies in the Bible, Qumran, and the Ancient Near East Presented to Shemaryahu Talmon* (Winona Lake: Eisenbrauns, 1992), pp. 267–291.

VanderKam, J.C., "The Jubilees Fragments from Qumran Cave 4," in Barrera, J. Trebolle, and L. Vegas Montaner, eds., *The Madrid Qumran Congress. Proceedings of the International Congress on the Dead Sea Scrolls, Madrid. 18–21 March 1991* (2 vols., STDJ 11; Leiden: Brill; Madrid: Universidad Complutense, 1992), vol. 2, pp. 635-648.

VanderKam, J.C., "The Scrolls, the Apocrypha, and the Pseudepigrapha," in *Hebrew Studies* 34, 1993, pp. 35-47.

VanderKam, J.C., "Authoritative Literature in the Dead Sea Scrolls," in *DSD* 5 (Ulrich dedication, 1998), pp. 382-402.

Wilson, Gerald H., *The Editing of the Hebrew Psalter* (SBLDS 76; Chico, CA: Scholars Press, 1985).

APPENDIX[1]

Index of Passages in the Biblical, Apocryphal, and "Pseudepigraphal" Scrolls

1. Index of Passages in the Biblical Scrolls

For previous indices of the Biblical Scrolls, see E. Ulrich, "An Index of the Passages in the Biblical Manuscripts from the Judean Desert (Genesis to Kings)," in *DSD* 1, 1994, pp. 113–129; "Part 2: (Isaiah to Chronicles)," in *DSD* 2, 1995, pp. 86–107; and idem, "Appendix 1: Index of Passages in the Biblical Scrolls," in P.W. Flint and J.C. VanderKam, eds., *The Dead Sea Scrolls after Fifty Years: A Comprehensive Assessment* (2 vols., Leiden: Brill, 1998-1999), vol. 2, pp. 649–665.

Verses marked with a supralinear 'a' or 'b' (e.g., Exod 7:29^b) indicate a verse in which there is additional text, usually from the Samaritan Pentateuch as numbered by A. von Gall (*Die hebraïsche Pentateuch der Samaritaner* [Gießen: Töpelmann, 1918; repr. 1966). Occasionally, however, the numbering is based on the Greek or on another source.

Genesis		17:12-19	8QGen
1:1-28	4QGen^b	18:20-25	8QGen
1:1-11, 13-22	4QGen^g	19:27-28	2QGen
1:8-10	4QGen^{h1}	22:13-15	1QGen
1:9, 14-16, 27-28	4QGen^k	22:14	4QGen-Exod^a
1:18-27	4QGen^d	23:17-19	1QGen
1:18-21	1QGen	24:22-24	1QGen
1:28	pap4QGen?	26:21-28	4QpaleoGen^m
2:1-3	4QGen^k	27:38-39, 42-43	4QGen-Exod^a
2:6-7 or 18-19	4QGen^g	32:4-5, 30, 33	MurGen
2:14-19	4QGen^b	33:1	MurGen
2:17-18	4QGen^{h2}	33:18-20	Mur(?)Gen
2:18-19 or 6-7	4QGen^g	34:1-3	Mur(?)Gen
3:1-2	4QGen^k	34:5-7, 30-31	MurGen
3:11-14	1QGen	34:7-10	4QGen^n
4:2-11	4QGen^b	34:17-21	4QGen-Exod^a
5:13 or 14	4QGen^b	35:1, 4-7	MurGen
6:13-21	6QpaleoGen	35:6-10, 25-29	SdeirGen
8:20-21(?)	4QGen-Exod^a	35:17-29	4QGen-Exod^a
10:6, 20?	6QGen? ar	36:1-13, 19-27	4QGen-Exod^a
12:4-5	4QGen$^{h\,para}$	36:1-2, 5-17	SdeirGen

---

[1] Appendix © 2000 by Peter W. Flint.

36:6, 35-37	2QGen	7:17-23, 26-29	4QExod^c
36:43	4QGen^e	7:29^b (28-29?)	4QExod^j
37:1-2, 27-30	4QGen^e	8:1^{a-b} (1-2?)	4QExod^j
37:5-6, 22-27	4QGen-Exod^a	8:1, 5-14, 16-18, 22	4QExod^c
39:11-23	4QGen-Exod^a	8:1[𝕲 5], 12-18[16-22], 19^b-22[24-26]	
40:1	4QGen-Exod^a		4QpaleoExod^m
40:12-13, 18-23	4QGen^c	8:13-15, 19-21	4QpaleoGen-Exod^l
40:18?/19?-23	4QGen^e	8:20-22	4QGen-Exod^a
41:1-11	4QGen^c	9:5^b-16, 19^b-21, 35	4QpaleoExod^m
41:1-8, 35-44	4QGen^e	9:8?	4QGen-Exod^a
41:15-18, 23-27, 29-36, 38-43	4QGen^j	9:10-12, 15-20, 22-25, 27-35	4QExod^c
42:15-22, 38	4QGen^j	9:25-29, 33-35	4QpaleoGen-Exod^l
42:17-19	4QGen^e	9:27-29	2QExod^a
43:1-2, 5-8	4QGen^j	10:1-5, 7-9, 12-19, 23-24	4QExod^c
43:8-14	4QGen^e	10:1, 2^b-12, 19-28	4QpaleoGen-Exod^l
45:14-22, 26-28	4QGen^j	10:1-5	4QpaleoGen-Exod^l
45:23	4QGen-Exod^a	11:3-7	2QExod^a
46:7-11(?)	MasGen?	11:4-10	4QpaleoGen-Exod^l
47:13-14	4QGen-Exod^a	11:8-10	4QpaleoExod^m
48:1-11	4QGen^f	11:9-10	4QExod^c
48:2-4, 15-17, 18-22	4QGen-Exod^a	12:1-12, 42-46	4QpaleoGen-Exod^l
49:1-5	4QGen-Exod^a	12:1-2, 6-8, 13-15, 17-22, 31-32, 34-39	
49:6-8	4QGen^e		4QpaleoExod^m
50:3	4QGen^n	12:12-16, 31-48	4QExod^c
50:26?	4QpaleoGen-Exod^l	12:26-27(?)	2QExod^b
		12:32-41	2QExod^a
Exodus		12:43-44, 46-51	4QDeut^j
1:1-6, 16-21	4QExod^b	13:1-5	4QDeut^j
1:1-5 (bis?)	4QpaleoGen-Exod^l	13:3-7, 12-13	4QpaleoExod^m
1:3-17, 22	4QGen-Exod^a	13:3-5	4QExod^e
1:11-14	2QExod^a	13:15-16	4QExod^d
2:2-18	4QExod^b	13:18-22	4QExod^c
2:1-5	4QGen-Exod^a	14:1-13	4QExod^c
2:10, 22-25	4QpaleoGen-Exod^l	14:3-5, 8-9, 25-26	4QpaleoExod^m
3:1-4, 17-21	4QpaleoGen-Exod^l	14:15-24	4QpaleoGen-Exod^l
3:8-16, 18-21	4QGen-Exod^a	14:21-27	4QExod^g
3:13-21	4QExod^b	15:1	4QExod^d
4:1-8	4QExod^b	15:9-21	4QExod^c
4:4-9, 26-31	4QGen-Exod^a	15:23-27	4QpaleoExod^m
4:28-31	MurExod	16:1, 4-5, 7-8, 31-36	4QpaleoExod^m
4:31	2QExod^b	16:2-7, 13-14, 18-20, 23-31, 33-36	
5:1, 3-17	4QGen-Exod^a		4QpaleoGen-Exod^l
5:3-14	4QExod^b	16:12-16	1QExod
5:3-5	2QExod^c	17:1-16	4QExod^c
5:3	MurExod	17:1-16	4QpaleoGen-Exod^l
6:3-6	4QExod^h	17:1-3, 5-11	4QpaleoGen-Exod^l
6:4-21, 25	4QGen-Exod^a	18:1-27	4QpaleoExod^m
6:5-11	MurExod	18:1-12	4QExod^c
6:25-30	4QpaleoExod^m	18:17-24	4QpaleoGen-Exod^l
7:1-19, 29^b	4QpaleoExod^m	18:21-22	2QExod^b
7:1-4	2QExod^a	19:1, 7-17, 23-25	4QpaleoExod^m
7:5-13, 15-20	4QGen-Exod^a	19:9	2QExod^b

19:24-25	1QExod
19:24-25	4QpaleoGen-Exod^l
20:1, 5-6, 25-26	1QExod
20:1-2	4QpaleoGen-Exod^l
20:1, 18-19^a	4QpaleoExod^m
21:1, 4-5	1QExod
21:5-6, 13-14, 22-32	4QpaleoExod^m
21:18-20(?)	2QExod^a
21:37	2QExod^b
22:1-2, 15-19	2QExod^b
22:3-4, 6-7, 11-13, 16-30	4QpaleoExod^m
22:23-24	4QpaleoGen-Exod^l
23:5-16	4QpaleoGen-Exod^l
23:15-16, 29-31	4QpaleoExod^m
24:1-4, 6-11	4QpaleoExod^m
25:7-20	4QpaleoGen-Exod^l
25:11-12, 20-29, 31-34	4QpaleoExod^m
26:8-15, 21-30	4QpaleoExod^m
26:11-13	2QExod^a
26:29-37	4QpaleoGen-Exod^l
27:1-3, 9-14, 18-19^b	4QpaleoExod^m
27:1, 4?, 6-14	4QpaleoGen-Exod^l
27:17-19	2QExod^b
28:3-4, 8-12, 22-24, 26-28, 30-43	4QpaleoExod^m
28:4-7	pap7QLXXExod
28:33-35, 40-42	4QpaleoGen-Exod^l
29:1-5, 20, 22-25, 31-41	4QpaleoExod^m
30:10	4QpaleoExod^m
30:12-18, 29-31, 34-38	4QpaleoExod^m
30:21?, 23-25	2QExod^a
31:1-8, 13-15	4QpaleoExod^m
31:16-17	2QExod^b
32:2-19, 25-30	4QpaleoExod^m
32:32-34	2QExod^a
33:12-23	4QpaleoExod^m
34:1-3, 10-13, 15-18, 20-24, 27-28	4QpaleoExod^m
34:10	2QExod^b
35:1	4QpaleoExod^m
36:9-10	4QExod^k
36:21-24	4QpaleoExod^m
36:34-36	4QpaleoGen-Exod^l
37:9-16	4QpaleoExod^m
38:18-22	4QExod-Lev^f
39:3-24	4QExod-Lev^f
40:8-27	4QExod-Lev^f
40:15?	4QpaleoGen-Exod^l

Leviticus

1:1-7	4QLev^c
1:11-17	4QLev^b
1:11	pap4QLXXLev^b
1:13-15, 17	4QExod-Lev^f
2:1	4QExod-Lev^f
2:1-16	4QLev^b
2:3-5, 7-8?	pap4QLXXLev^b
3:1, 8-14	4QLev^b
3:2-8	4QLev^e
3:4, 7, 9-14	pap4QLXXLev^b
3:16-17	4QLev^c
4:1-6, 12-14, 23-28	4QLev^c
4:3-4, 6-8, 10-11, 18-19, 26-28, 30	pap4QLXXLev^b
4:3-9	MasLev^a
4:24-26	11QpaleoLev^a
5:6, 8-10, 16-19	pap4QLXXLev^b
5:12-13	4QLev^c
6:1-5[~ 5:20-24]	pap4QLXXLev^b
7:19-26	4QLev^g
8:12-13	6QpaleoLev
8:26-28	4QLev^c
8:31, 33-34	MasLev^b
9:1-10, 12-13, 15, 22-24	MasLev^b
9:23-24	11QLev^b
10:1-2	11QLev^b
10:1, 9-20	MasLev^b
10:4-7	11QpaleoLev^a
11:1-21, 24-40	MasLev^b
11:10-11	1QpaleoLev
11:22-29	2QpaleoLev
11:27-32	11QpaleoLev^a
13:3-9, 39-43	11QpaleoLev^a
13:32-33	4QLev-Num^a
13:58-59	11QLev^b
14:16-21, 52-57	11QpaleoLev^a
14:22-34, 40-54	4QLev-Num^a
14:27-29, 33-36	4QLev^d
15:1-5	11QpaleoLev^a
15:10-11, 19-24	4QLev-Num^a
15:20-24	4QLev^d
16:1-6, 34	11QpaleoLev^a
16:15-29	4QLev-Num^a
17:1-5	11QpaleoLev^a
17:2-11	4QLev^d
18:16-21	4QLev-Num^a
18:27-30	11QpaleoLev^a
19:1-4	11QpaleoLev^a
19:3-8	4QLev-Num^a
19:30-34	1QpaleoLev
19:34-37	4QLev^e
20:1-6	11QpaleoLev^a
20:1-3, 27	4QLev^e

20:20-24	1QpaleoLev	19:2-4	XHev/SeNum[a]
21:1-4, 9-12, 21-24	4QLev[e]	20:7-8	5/6HevNum
21:6-12	11QpaleoLev[a]	20:12-13[b], 16-17, 19-29	4QNum[b]
21:17-20, 24	4QLev[b]	21:1-2, 12[a]-13[a], 20-21[a]	4QNum[b]
21:24	1QpaleoLev	22:5-21, 31-34, 37-38, 41	4QNum[b]
22:1-6	1QpaleoLev	22:5-6, 22-24	4QLev-Num[a]
22:2-33	4QLev[b]	23:1-4, 6, 13-15, 21-22, 27-30	4QNum[b]
22:4-6, 11-17	4QLev[e]	24:1-10	4QNum[b]
22:21-27	11QpaleoLev[a]	25:4-8, 16-18	4QNum[b]
23:1-8, 10-25, 40	4QLev[b]	26:1-5, 7-10, 12, 14-34, 62-65	4QNum[b]
23:1-3? (or Num 18:8-9?)	2QNum[d?]	26:5-7	4QLev-Num[a]
23:4-8	1QpaleoLev	27:1-5, 7-8, 10, 18-19, 21-23[b]	4QNum[b]
23:22-29	11QpaleoLev[a]	27:2-13	XHev/SeNum[b]
24:2-23	4QLev[b]	28:11-12	XHev/SeNum[b]
24:9-14	11QpaleoLev[a]	28:13-17, 28, 30-31	4QNum[b]
24:11-12	4QLev-Num[a]	29:10-13, 16-18, 26-30	4QNum[b]
25:28-36	11QpaleoLev[a]	30:1-3, 5-9, 15-17	4QNum[b]
25:28-29, 45-49, 51-52	4QLev[b]	30:3?, 7? (9?, 13?)	4QLev-Num[a]
26:2-16	4QLXXLev	31:2-6, 21[b]-25, 30-33, 35-36, 38, 43-44, 46-54	4QNum[b]
26:17-26	11QpaleoLev[a]		
26:26-33	4QLev-Num[a]	32:1, 4-5, 7-10, 13-17, 19, 21-30, 35, 37-39, 41	4QNum[b]
27:5-22	4QLev-Num[a]		
27:11-19	11QpaleoLev[a]	32:8-15, 23-42	4QLev-Num[a]
27:30-31(?)	1QpaleoLev	33:1-4, 23, 25, 28, 31, 45, 47-48, 50-52	4QNum[b]
Numbers		33:5-9, 22-34, 52-54	4QLev-Num[a]
1:1-5, 21-22, 36-40	4QLev-Num[a]	33:47-53	2QNum[b]
1:48-50	1QpaleoLev	34:4-9, 19-21, 23	4QNum[b]
2:18-20, 31-32	4QLev-Num[a]	34:10	MurNum
3:3-19, 51	4QLev-Num[a]	35:3-5, 11-12, 14-15, 18-25, 27-28, 33-34	4QNum[b]
3:38-41, 51	2QNum[a]		
3:39?, 40-43, 50-51?	4QLXXNum	35:4-5	4QLev-Num[a]
4:1-12, 40-49	4QLev-Num[a]	36:1-2[a], 4[a]-7	4QNum[b]
4:1?, 5-9, 11-16	4QLXXNum	36:7-11	MurNum
4:1-3	2QNum[a]	36:7-8(?)	1QpaleoLev
5:1-9	4QLev-Num[a]		
7:88	2QNum[c]	*Deuteronomy*	
8:7-12, 21-22	4QLev-Num[a]	1:1-17, 22-23, 29-39, 41, 43-46	4QDeut[h]
9:3-10, 19-20	4QLev-Num[a]		
10:13-23	4QLev-Num[a]	1:4-5	11QDeut
11:4-5, 16-22	4QLev-Num[a]	1:7-9	2QDeut[a]
11:31-35	4QNum[b]	1:8?	4QpaleoDeut[r]
12:1-6, 8-11	4QNum[b]	1:9-13	1QDeut[b]
12:3-11	4QLev-Num[a]	1:22-25	1QDeut[a]
13:7, 10-13, 15-24	4QNum[b]	1:45?	4QpaleoDeut[r]
13:21	4QLev-Num[a]	2:1-6, 28-30	4QDeut[h]
15:41	4QNum[b]	2:8	4QDeut[o]
16:1-11, 14-16	4QNum[b]	2:24-36	4QDeut[d]
17:12-17	4QNum[b]	3:14-29	4QDeut[d]
18:8-9 (or Lev 23:1-3?)	2QNum[d?]	3:18-22	4QDeut[m]
18:25-32	4QNum[b]	3:24	4QDeut[e]
19:1-6	4QNum[b]	3:25-26	4QDeut[c]

4:1	4QDeut^d	13:1-6, 13-14	1QDeut^a
4:13-17, 31-32	4QDeut^c	13:5, 7, 11-12, 16	4QDeut^c
4:24-26	4QDeut^f	13:7-11	11QDeut?
4:30-34	4QDeut^o	13:19	4QpaleoDeut^r
4:31-34	4QDeut^h	14:1-4, 19-22, 26-29	4QpaleoDeut^r
4:32-33	4QDeut^m	14:21, 24-25	1QDeut^a
4:47-49	1QDeut^a	14:29	MurDeut
5:1-33	4QDeut^n	15:1 or 2	MurDeut
5:1-11, 13-15, 21-33	4QDeut^j	15:1-4, 15-19	4QDeut^c
5:1-5, 8-9	4QDeut^o	15:5-6, 8-10	4QpaleoDeut^r
5:28-32	4QDeut^{k1}	15:14-15	1QDeut^b
6:1-3	4QDeut^j	16:2-3, 6-11, 21-22	4QDeut^c
6:1	4QDeut^n	16:4, 6-7	1QDeut^a
6:4-11	4QDeut^p	17:1-5, 7, 15-20	4QDeut^c
7:2-7, 16-25	4QpaleoDeut^r	17:5-6?	4QpaleoDeut^r
7:3-4	4QDeut^c	17:12-15	2QDeut^b
7:12-16, 21-26	4QDeut^e	17:16	1QDeut^b
7:15-24	5QDeut	17:17-18	4QDeut^f
7:18-22	4QDeut^m	18:1	4QDeut^c
7:19? or 29:2-4?	4QpaleoDeut^r	18:6-10, 18-22	4QDeut^f
7:22-25	4QDeut^f	19:2-3	4QpaleoDeut^r
8:1-7, 10-11, 15-16	4QDeut^c	19:8-16	4QDeut^{k2}
8:1-5	4QDeut^c	19:17-21	4QDeut^f
8:2-14	4QDeut^f	19:21	4QDeut^h
8:5-20	5QDeut	20:1-6	4QDeut^f
8:5-10	4QDeut$^{j, n}$	20:6-19	4QDeut^{k2}
8:8-9	1QDeut^b	20:9-13	4QDeut^i
8:18-19	1QDeut^a	21:4-12	4QDeut^f
9:1-2	5QDeut	21:8-9	1QDeut^b
9:5-6, 21-23	XHev/SeDeut	21:8-9? or 30:7-8?	4QpaleoDeut^r
9:6-7	4QDeut^f	21:16?	4QDeut^{k2}
9:10	1QDeut^b	21:23	4QDeut^i
9:11-12, 17-19, 29	4QDeut^c	22:1-9	4QDeut^c
9:12-14	4QDeut^g	22:3-6	4QpaleoDeut^r
9:27-28	1QDeut^a	22:12-19	4QDeut^f
10:1-2, 5-8	4QDeut^c	23:6-8, 12-16, 22-26	4QDeut^i
10:1-3	MurDeut	23:7, 12-15	4QpaleoDeut^r
10:6? or 28:23? or 32:22?	4QpaleoDeut^r	23:18-20	4QDeut^g
10:8-12	2QDeut^c	23:21-26	4QDeut^f
10:11-12	4QpaleoDeut^r	23:22-26	4QDeut^{k2}
10:12, 14-15	4QDeut^l	23:26	4QDeut^a
11:2-3	MurDeut	24:1-8	4QDeut^a
11:3, 9-13, 18	4QDeut^c	24:1-3	4QDeut^{k2}
11:4	4QLXXDeut	24:1	4QDeut^i
11:6-13	4QDeut^{k1}	24:2-7	4QDeut^f
11:6-10, 12-13, 21?	4QDeut^j	24:10-16	1QDeut^b
11:27-30	1QDeut^a	24:16-22	4QDeut^g
11:28, 30-32	4QpaleoDeut^r	25:1-5, 14-19	4QDeut^g
11:30-31	1QDeut^b	25:3-9	4QDeut^f
12:1-5, 11-12, 22	4QpaleoDeut^r	25:13-18	1QDeut^b
12:18-19, 26, 31	4QDeut^c	25:19	4QDeut^{k2}
12:25-26	MurDeut	26:1-5, 18-19(?)	4QDeut^{k2}

26:1-5	4QDeut^g	*Joshua*	
26:14-15	4QpaleoDeut^s	2:11-12	4QJosh^b
26:18-19	4QDeut^f	3:15-17	4QJosh^b
26:19	4QDeut^c	4:1-3	4QJosh^b
26:19?	pap6QDeut?	5:X, 2-7	4QJosh^a
27:1-2, 24-26	4QDeut^c	6:5-10	4QJosh^a
27:1-10	4QDeut^f	7:12-17	4QJosh^a
27:1?	4QDeut^k2	8:3-14, 18?, 34-35	4QJosh^a
28:1-14, 20, 22-25, 29-30, 48-50, 61	4QDeut^c	10:2-5, 8-11	4QJosh^a
28:15-18, 20	4QpaleoDeut^r	17:1-5, 11-15	4QJosh^b
28:15-18, 33-36, 47-52, 58-62	4QDeut^o	*Judges*	
28:21-25, 27-29	4QDeut^g	6:2-6, 11-13	4QJudg^a
28:23? or 10:6? or 32:22?	4QpaleoDeut^r	6:20-22	1QJudg
		8:1?	1QJudg
28:44-48	1QDeut^b	9:1-6, 28-31, 40-43, 48-49	1QJudg
28:67-68	4QDeut^l	19:5-7	4QJudg^b
29:2-4? or 7:19?	4QpaleoDeut^r	21:12-25	4QJudg^b
29:2-5	4QDeut^l		
29:9-20	1QDeut^b	*Samuel*	
29:17-19	4QDeut^c	1 Samuel	
29:22-25	4QDeut^o	1:11-13, 22-28	4QSam^a
29:24-27	4QDeut^b	2:1-6, 8-11, 13-36	4QSam^a
30:3-14	4QDeut^b	3:1-4, 18-20	4QSam^a
30:7-8? or 21:8-9?	4QpaleoDeut^r	4:9-12	4QSam^a
30:16-18	4QDeut^k3	5:8-12	4QSam^a
30:19-20	1QDeut^b	6:1-7, 12-13, 16-18, 20-21	4QSam^a
31:1-10, 12-13	1QDeut^b	7:1	4QSam^a
31:9-11	4QDeut^h	8:9-20	4QSam^a
31:9-17, 24-30	4QDeut^b	9:6-8, 11-12, 16-24	4QSam^a
31:12	4QDeut^l	10:3-18, 25-27	4QSam^a
31:16-19	4QDeut^c	11:1, 7-12	4QSam^a
31:29	4QpaleoDeut^r	12:7-8, 14-19	4QSam^a
32:1-3	4QDeut^b	14:24-25, 28-34, 47-51	4QSam^a
32:3	4QDeut^c	15:24-32	4QSam^a
32:6-8, 10-11, 13-14, 33-35	4QpaleoDeut^r	16:1-11	4QSam^b
		17:3-6	4QSam^a
32:7-8	4QDeut^j	18:17-18	1QSam
32:9-10?, 37-43	4QDeut^q	19:10-17	4QSam^b
32:17-18, 22-23, 25-27	4QDeut^k1	20:26-42	4QSam^b
32:17-29	1QDeut^b	21:1-10(?)	4QSam^b
32:22? or 28:23? or 10:6?	4QpaleoDeut^r	23:9-17	4QSam^b
33:1-2	1QDeut^l	24:4-5, 8-9, 14-23	4QSam^a
33:2-8, 29	4QpaleoDeut^r	25:3-12, 20-21, 25-26, 39-40	4QSam^a
33:8-22	4QDeut^h	25:30-32	4QSam^c
33:12-19, 21-24	1QDeut^b	26:10-12, 21-23	4QSam^a
33:17-21	MasDeut	27:8-12	4QSam^a
34:1	4QpaleoDeut^r	28:1-2, 22-25	4QSam^a
34:2-6	MasDeut	30:28-31	4QSam^a
34:4-6, 8?	4QDeut^l	31:2-4	4QSam^a

Reference	Scroll
2 Samuel	
2:5-16, 25-27, 29-32	4QSam^a
3:1-8, 23-29	4QSam^a
4:1-4, 9-12	4QSam^a
5:1-16 [omitted 5:4-5]	4QSam^a
6:2-9, 12-18	4QSam^a
7:23-29	4QSam^a
8:2-8	4QSam^a
10:4-7, 18-19	4QSam^a
11:2-12, 16-20	4QSam^a
12:4-5, 8-9, 13-20, 30-31	4QSam^a
13:1-6, 13-34, 36-39	4QSam^a
14:1-3, 18-19	4QSam^a
14:7-33	4QSam^c
15:1-15	4QSam^c
15:1-6, 27-31	4QSam^a
16:1-2, 11-13, 17-18, 21-23	4QSam^a
18:2-7, 9-11	4QSam^a
19:7-12	4QSam^a
20:2-3, 9-14, 23-26	4QSam^a
20:6-10	1QSam
21:1-2, 4-6, 15-17	4QSam^a
21:16-18	1QSam
22:30-51	4QSam^a
23:1-6	4QSam^a
23:7	11QPs^a
23:9-12	1QSam
24:16-20	4QSam^a

Kings

Reference	Scroll
1 Kings	
1:1, 16-17, 27-37	5QKgs
3:12-14	pap6QKgs
7:20-21, 25-27, 29-42, 51	4QKgs
8:1-9, 16-18	4QKgs
12:28-31	pap6QKgs
22:28-31	pap6QKgs
2 Kings	
5:26	pap6QKgs
6:32	pap6QKgs
7:8-10, 20	pap6QKgs
8:1-5	pap6QKgs
9:1-2	pap6QKgs
10:19-21	pap6QKgs

Isaiah

Reference	Scroll
1:1–66:24	1QIsa^a
1:1-6	4QIsa^b
1:1-6	4QIsa^j
1:1-3	4QIsa^a
1:4-8, 11-14	MurIsa
1:10-16, 18-31	4QIsa^f
2:1-4	4QIsa^e
2:1-3	4QIsa^f
2:3-16	4QIsa^b
2:7-10	4QIsa^a
3:14-22	4QIsa^b
4:5-6	4QIsa^a
5:1	4QIsa^a
5:13-14, 25	4QIsa^f
5:15-28	4QIsa^b
5:28-30	pap4QIsa^p
6:3-8, 10-13	4QIsa^f
6:4-8	4QIsa^a
7:14-15	4QIsa^l
7:16-18, 23-25	4QIsa^f
7:17-20	4QIsa^e
7:22-25	1QIsa^b
8:1, 4-11	4QIsa^f
8:1	1QIsa^b
8:2-14	4QIsa^e
8:11-14	4QIsa^l
9:3-12	4QIsa^c
9:10-11	4QIsa^b
9:17-20	4QIsa^e
10:1-10	4QIsa^e
10:16-19	1QIsa^b
10:23-33	4QIsa^c
11:4-11, 14-16	4QIsa^c
11:7-9	4QIsa^b
11:11-15	4QIsa^a
11:14-15	4QIsa^e
12:1-6	4QIsa^e
12:1	4QIsa^c
12:2	4QIsa^b
12:3-6	1QIsa^b
12:4-6	4QIsa^a
13:1-16	4QIsa^a
13:1-8, 16-19	1QIsa^b
13:1-4	4QIsa^e
13:3-18	4QIsa^b
14:1-13, 20-24	4QIsa^e
14:1-5, 13?	4QIsa^c
14:28-32	4QIsa^o
15:1-2	4QIsa^o
15:3-9	1QIsa^b
16:1-2, 7-12	1QIsa^b
17:8-14	4QIsa^b
17:9-14	4QIsa^a
18:1, 5-7	4QIsa^b
19:1-25	4QIsa^b
19:7-17, 20-25	1QIsa^b
19:24-25	4QIsa^a

20:1-6	4QIsa^a	42:4-11	4QIsa^h
20:1-4	4QIsa^b	42:14-25	4QIsa^g
20:1	1QIsa^b	43:1-13, 23-27	1QIsa^b
20:4-6	4QIsa^f	43:1-4, 16-24	4QIsa^g
21:1-16	4QIsa^a	43:12-15	4QIsa^b
21:11-14	4QIsa^b	44:3-7, 23	4QIsa^c
22:10-14, 23	4QIsa^c	44:19-28	4QIsa^b
22:11-18, 24-25	1QIsa^b	44:21-28	1QIsa^b
22:13-25	4QIsa^a	45:1-13	1QIsa^b
22:14-22, 25	4QIsa^f	45:1-4, 6-8	4QIsa^c
22:24-25	4QIsa^b	45:20-25	4QIsa^b
23:1-12	4QIsa^a	45:20	4QIsa^d
23:1-4	1QIsa^b	46:1-3	4QIsa^b
23:8-18	4QIsa^c	46:3-13	1QIsa^b
24:1-15, 19-23	4QIsa^c	46:8-13	4QIsa^c
24:1-3	4QIsa^f	46:10-13	4QIsa^d
24:2, 4	4QIsa^b	47:1-14	1QIsa^b
24:18-23	1QIsa^b	47:1-6, 8-9	4QIsa^d
25:1-8	1QIsa^b	48:6-8	4QIsa^b
25:1-2, 8-12	4QIsa^c	48:8-22	4QIsa^d
26:1-9	4QIsa^c	48:10-15, 17-19	4QIsa^c
26:1-5, 7-19	4QIsa^b	48:17-22	1QIsa^b
26:1-5	1QIsa^b	49:1-15	1QIsa^b
27:1, 5-6, 8-12	4QIsa^f	49:1-15	4QIsa^d
28:6-14	4QIsa^c	49:21-23	4QIsa^b
28:6-9, 16-18(?), 22, 24?	4QIsa^f	49:22	4QIsa^c
28:15-20	1QIsa^b	50:7-11	1QIsa^b
28:26-29	4QIsa^k	51:1-10	1QIsa^b
29:1-9	4QIsa^k	51:1-2, 14-16	4QIsa^b
29:1-8	1QIsa^b	51:8-16	4QIsa^c
29:8?	4QIsa^f	52:2, 7	4QIsa^b
30:8-17	4QIsa^c	52:4-7	4QIsa^d
30:10-14, 21-26	1QIsa^b	52:7-15	1QIsa^b
30:23	4QIsa^r	52:10-15	4QIsa^c
33:2-8, 16-23	4QIsa^c	53:1-12	1QIsa^b
33:16-17(?)	4QIsa^a	53:1-3, 6-8	4QIsa^c
35:4-6	1QIsa^b	53:8-12	4QIsa^d
35:9-10	4QIsa^b	53:11-12	4QIsa^b
36:1-2	4QIsa^b	54:1-11	4QIsa^d
37:8-12	1QIsa^b	54:1-6	1QIsa^b
37:29-32	4QIsa^b	54:3-5, 7-17	4QIsa^c
38:12-22	1QIsa^b	54:10-13	4QIsa^q
39:1-8	1QIsa^b	55:1-7	4QIsa^c
39:1-8	4QIsa^b	55:2-13	1QIsa^b
39:3? (or 41:25?)	5QIsa	56:1-12	1QIsa^b
40:1-4, 22-26	4QIsa^b	56:7-8	4QIsaⁱ
40:2-3	1QIsa^b	57:1-4, 17-21	1QIsa^b
40:16, 18-19	5QIsa	57:5-8	4QIsaⁱ
41:3-23	1QIsa^b	57:9-21	4QIsa^d
41:8-11	4QIsa^b	58:1-14	1QIsa^b
41:25? (or 39:3?)	5QIsa	58:1-3, 5-7	4QIsa^d
42:2-7, 9-12	4QIsa^b	58:13-14	4QIsaⁿ

59:1-8, 20-21	1QIsa^b	42:7-11, 14	2QJer
59:15-16	4QIsa^e	43:2-10	4QJer^d
60:1-22	1QIsa^b	43:8-11	2QJer
60:20-22	4QIsa^m	44:1-3, 12-14	2QJer
61:1-3	4QIsa^b	46:27-28	2QJer
61:1-2	1QIsa^b	47:1-7	2QJer
61:1, 3-6	4QIsa^m	48:2-4(?), 7, 25-39, 41-42(?), 43-45	
62:2-12	1QIsa^b		2QJer
63:1-19	1QIsa^b	49:10?	2QJer
64:1, 6-8	1QIsa^b	50:4-6	4QJer^e
64:5-11	4QIsa^b		
65:1	4QIsa^b	*Ezekiel*	
65:17-25	1QIsa^b	1:10-13, 16-17, 19-24	4QEzek^b
66:1-24	1QIsa^b	4:3-6	11QEzek
66:20-24	4QIsa^c	4:16-17	1QEzek
66:24	4QIsa^b	5:1	1QEzek
		5:11-17	11QEzek
Jeremiah		7:9, 11-12	11QEzek
4:5, 13-16	4QJer^c	10:6-22	4QEzek^a
7:1-2, 15-19, 28-34	4QJer^a	10:11	11QEzek
8:1-12, 18-19, 23	4QJer^a	11:1-11	4QEzek^a
8:1-3, 21-23	4QJer^c	13:17	11QEzek
9:1-5	4QJer^c	16:31, 33	3QEzek
9:1-2, 7-15	4QJer^a	23:14-18, 44-47	4QEzek^a
9:22-25	4QJer^b	24:2-3	4QEzek^c
10:1-5a, 9, 5b, 11-21	4QJer^b	31:11–37:15 (frgs. only)	MasEzek
10:9-14, 23	4QJer^a	41:3-6	4QEzek^a
10:12-13	4QJer^c		
11:3-6, 19-20	4QJer^a	*XII Prophets*	
12:3-7, 13-17	4QJer^a	Hosea	
13:1-7, 22? (or 22:3?), 27	4QJer^a	1:6-9	4QXII^d
13:22?	2QJer	2:1-5, 14-19, 22-25	4QXII^g
14:4-7	4QJer^a	2:1-5	4QXII^d
15:1-2	4QJer^a	2:13-15	4QXII^c
17:8-26	4QJer^a	3:1-5	4QXII^g
18:15-23	4QJer^a	3:2-4	4QXII^c
19:1	4QJer^a	4:1-19	4QXII^c
19:8-9	4QJer^c	4:1, 10-11, 13-14	4QXII^g
20:2-5, 7-9, 13-15	4QJer^c	5:1	4QXII^c
20:14-18	4QJer^a	6:3-4, 8-11	4QXII^g
21:1?	4QJer^a	7:1, 13-16	4QXII^g
21:7-10	4QJer^c	7:12-13	4QXII^c
22:3? (or 13:22?), 3-16	4QJer^a	8:1	4QXII^g
22:4-6, 10-28, 28-30(?)	4QJer^c	9:1-4, 9-17	4QXII^g
25:7-8, 15-17, 24-26	4QJer^c	10:1-14	4QXII^g
26:10-13	4QJer^c	11:2-11	4QXII^g
26:10?	4QJer^a	12:1-15	4QXII^g
27:1-3, 13-15	4QJer^c	13:1, 6-8(?), 11-13	4QXII^g
30:6-9, 17-24	4QJer^c	13:3-10, 15	4QXII^c
31:1-9, 11-14, 19-23, 25-26	4QJer^c	14:1-6	4QXII^c
32:24-25(?)	2QJer	14:9-10	4QXII^g
33:?, 16-20	4QJer^c		

Joel		4:1-11	MurXII
1:10-20	4QXII^c	4:1-2, 5	8HevXII gr
1:12-14	4QXII^g	4:5-11	4QXII^g
2:1, 8-23	4QXII^c		
2:2-13	4QXII^g	Micah	
2:20, 26-27	MurXII	1:1-16	MurXII
3:1-5	MurXII	1:1-8	8HevXII gr
4:1-16	MurXII	1:7, 12-15	4QXII^g
4:4-9, 11-14, 17, 19-20	4QXII^g	2:1-13	MurXII
4:6-21	4QXII^c	2:3-4	4QXII^g
		2:7-8	8HevXII gr
Amos		3:1-12	MurXII
1:3-15	4QXII^g	3:5-6	8HevXII gr
1:3-5	5QAmos	3:12	4QXII^g
1:5-15	MurXII	4:1-14	MurXII
2:1, 7-9, 15-16	4QXII^g	4:1-2	4QXII^g
2:1	MurXII	4:3-10	8HevXII gr
2:11-16	4QXII^c	5:1-6 [𝔊 2-7]	8HevXII gr
3:1-15	4QXII^c	5:1-2	4QXII^f
3:1-2	4QXII^g	5:1, 5-14	MurXII
4:1-2	4QXII^c	5:6-7	4QXII^g
4:4-9	4QXII^g	6:1-7, 11-16	MurXII
5:1-2, 9-18	4QXII^g	7:1-20	MurXII
6:1-4, 6-14	4QXII^g	7:2-3, 20	4QXII^g
6:1?	MurXII		
6:13-14	4QXII^c	Nahum	
7:1-4, 7-9, 12-16	4QXII^c	1:1-14	MurXII
7:1, 7-12, 14-17	4QXII^g	1:7-9	4QXII^g
7:3-17	MurXII	1:13-14	8HevXII gr
8:1-5, 11-14	4QXII^g	2:1-14	MurXII
8:3-7, 11-14	MurXII	2:5-10, 13-14	8HevXII gr
9:1-15	MurXII	2:9-11	4QXII^g
9:1, 6, 14-15	4QXII^g	3:1-19	MurXII
		3:3, 6-17	8HevXII gr
Obadiah		3:1-3, 17	4QXII^g
1-21	MurXII		
1-5, 8-12, 14-15	4QXII^g	Habakkuk	
		1:3-13, 15	MurXII
Jonah		1:5-11, 14-17	8HevXII gr
1:1-16	MurXII	2:1-8, 13-20	8HevXII gr
1:1-9	4QXII^g	2:2-3, 5-11, 18-20	MurXII
1:1-5, 7-10, 15-16	4QXII^a	2:4?	4QXII^g
1:6-8, 10-16	4QXII^f	3:1-19	MurXII
1:14-16	8HevXII gr	3:9-15	8HevXII gr
2:1-11	MurXII		
2:1-7	8HevXII gr	Zephaniah	
2:1, 7	4QXII^a	1:1-6, 13-18	8HevXII gr
2:3-11	4QXII^g	1:1-2	4QXII^b
3:1-10	MurXII	1:1, 11-18	MurXII
3:1-3	4QXII^g	2:1-15	MurXII
3:2-5, 7-10	8HevXII gr	2:9-10	8HevXII gr
3:2	4QXII^a	2:13-15	4QXII^b

APPENDIX

2:15	4QXII^c	9:12-21	5/6HevPs
3:1-6, 8-20	MurXII	10:1-6, 8-9, 18	5/6HevPs
3:1-2	4QXII^c	11:1-4	5/6HevPs
3:3-5	4QXII^g	12:5-9	11QPs^c
3:6-7	8HevXII gr	12:6-9	5/6HevPs
3:19-20	4QXII^b	13:1-3	5/6HevPs
		13:2-3, 5-6	11QPs^c
Haggai		14:1-6	11QPs^c
1:1-2	4QXII^b	14:3?	5/6HevPs
1:1, 12-15	MurXII	15:1-5	5/6HevPs
2:1-8, 10, 12-23	MurXII	16:1	5/6HevPs
2:2-4	4QXII^b	16:7-9	4QPs^c
2:18-21	4QXII^e	17:1?	4QPs^c
		17:5-9, 14	8QPs
Zechariah		17:9-15	11QPs^c
1:1-4, 12-14	8HevXII gr	18:1-12, 15-17?	11QPs^c
1:1-4	MurXII	18:3-14, 16-17, 32-36, 39-42	4QPs^c
1:4-6, 9-10, 13-14	4QXII^e	18:6-11, 18-36, 38-43	5/6HevPs
2:2-4, 7-9, 11-12, 16-17 [= 𝔊 1:19-21; 2:3-5, 7-8, 12-13]	8HevXII gr	18:6-13 [= 2 Sam 22:6-13]	8QPs
2:10-14	4QXII^e	18:26-29, 39-42	11QPs^d
3:1-2, 4-7	8HevXII gr	18:26-29	MasPs^a
3:2-10	4QXII^e	19:3? or 60:9?	11QPs^d
4:1-4	4QXII^e	19:4-8	11QPs^c
5:8-11	4QXII^e	22:4-9, 15-21	5/6HevPs
6:1-5	4QXII^e	22:14-17	4QPs^f
8:2-4, 6-7	4QXII^e	23:2-6	5/6HevPs
8:19-21, 23	8HevXII gr	24:1-2	5/6HevPs
9:1-5	8HevXII gr	25:2-7	11QPs^c
10:11-12	4QXII^g	25:4-6	5/6HevPs
11:1-2	4QXII^g	25:15	4QPs^a
12:1-3	4QXII^g	26:7-12	4QPs^r
12:7-12	4QXII^e	27:1	4QPs^r
14:18	4QXII^a	27:12-14	4QPs^c
		28:1-4	4QPs^c
Malachi		29:1-2	5/6HevPs
2:10-17	4QXII^a	30:9-13	4QPs^r
3:1-24	4QXII^a	31:3-22	5/6HevPs
3:6-7(?)	4QXII^c	31:23-24	4QPs^a
		31:24-25	4QPs^q
		33:1-7, X, 8-14, 16-18	4QPs^q
Psalms		33:2, 4-6, 8, 10, 12	4QPs^a
2:2-8	11QPs^c	34:21-22	4QPs^a
2:6-7	3QPs	35:2, 13-18, 20, 26-27	4QPs^a
5:8-13	4QPs^s	35:4-5, 8, 10, 12, 14-15, 17, 19-20	4QPs^q
5:9-13	4QPs^a	35:27-28	4QPs^c
6:1	4QPs^s	36:1, 3, 5-7, 9	4QPs^a
6:2, 4	4QPs^a	36:13	11QPs^d
9:3-6	11QPs^d	37:1-4, 5?	11QPs^d
7:13-18	5/6HevPs	37:18-19	4QPs^c
8:1, 4-10	5/6HevPs	38:2, 4-6, 8-10, 12, 16-23	4QPs^a
9:3-6	11QPs^d	39:13-14	11QPs^d
9:3-7	11QPs^c		

40:1-2	11QPs^d	89:44-48, 50-53	4QPs^e
42:5	4QPs^c	91:1-14, 16	11QapocPs
42:5	4QPs^u	91:5-8, 12-15	4QPs^b
43:1-3	11QPs^d	92:4-8, 13-15	4QPs^b
44:3-5, 7, 9, 23-25	1QPs^c	92:12-14	1QPs^a
44:8-9?	4QPs^c	93:1-3	11QPs^a
45:6-8	11QPs^d	93:3-5	4QPs^m
45:8-11	4QPs^c	93:5	4QPs^b
47:2	4QPs^a	94:1-4, 8-14, 17-18, 21-22	4QPs^b
48:1-3, 5, 7, 9	4QPs^j	94:16	1QPs^a
45:15	4QPs^c	95:3-7	4QPs^m
49:1-17	4QPs^c	95:11	1QPs^a
49:6?, 9-12, 15, 17?	4QPs^j	96:1-2	1QPs^a
50:3-7?	11QPs^e?	96:2	4QPs^b
50:14-23	4QPs^c	97:6-9	4QPs^m
51:1-5	4QPs^c	98:4	4QPs^b
51:2-6	4QPs^j	98:4-8	4QPs^m
52:6-11	4QPs^c	99:1-2, 5	4QPs^k
53:1	4QPs^c	99:1	4QPs^v
53:4-5, 7	4QPs^a	99:5-6	4QPs^b
54:2-3, 5-6	4QPs^a	100:1-2	4QPs^b
56:4	4QPs^a	101:1-8	11QPs^a
59:5-6, 8	11QPs^d	102:1-2, 18-29	11QPs^a
60:9? or 19:3?	11QPs^d	102:5, 10-29	4QPs^b
62:13	4QPs^a	103:1	11QPs^a
63:2, 4	4QPs^a	103:1-6, 9-14, 20-21	4QPs^b
66:16, 18-20	4QPs^a	103:2, 4-6, 8-11	2QPs
67:1-2, 4-8	4QPs^a	104:1-6, 21-35	11QPs^a
68:1-5, 16-18	11QPs^d	104:1-5, 8-11, 14-15, 22-25, 33-35	
69:1-19	4QPs^a		4QPs^d
71:1-14	4QPs^a	104:1-3, 20-22	4QPs^e
76:10-12	4QPs^e	104:3-5, 11-12	4QPs^l
77:1	4QPs^e	104:6, 8-9, 11	2QPs
77:18-21	11QPs^b	105:X, 1-11, 25-26, 28-29(?), 30-31,	
78:1	11QPs^b	33-35, 37-39, 41-42, 44-45	11QPs^a
78:5-12	11QPs^d	105:1-3, 23-25, 36-45	4QPs^e
78:6-7, 31-33	4QPs^e	106:1?	4QPs^e
78:36-37	pap6QPs	106:48?	4QPs^d
78:36-37?	11QPs^e?	107:2-5, 8-16, 18-19, 22-30, 35-42	
81:2-3	4QPs^e		4QPs^f
81:2-3, 5-17	MasPs^a	109:1?, 8?, 13	4QPs^e
81:4-9	11QPs^d	109:4-7, 24-28	4QPs^f
82:1-8	MasPs^a	109:21-22, 24-31	11QPs^a
83:1-19	MasPs^a	112:1, 3, 5, 7, 9	4QPs^w
84:1-13	MasPs^a	112:4-5	4QPs^b
85:1-6	MasPs^a	113:1	4QPs^b
86:5-6, 8	1QPs^a	114:5?	4QPs^e
86:10-11	4QPs^e	114:7	4QPs^o
86:11-14	11QPs^d	115:1-2, 4	4QPs^o
88:1-2, 4-5	4QPs^e	115:2-3	4QPs^b
88:15-17	4QPs^t	115:15-18	4QPs^e
89:20-22, 26, 23, 27-28, 31	4QPs^x	116:1	11QPs^d

APPENDIX

116:1-3	4QPs^e
116:5, 7-10	4QPs^o
116:17-19	4QPs^b
118:1-3, 6-10, 12, 18-20, 23-26, 29	4QPs^b
118:1, 15-16, 8-9, X, 29	11QPs^a
118:1, 15-16	11QPs^b
118:25-29	11QPs^a
118:29?	4QPs^e
119:1-6, 15-28, 37-49, 59-73, 82-96, 105-120, 128-142, 150-164, 171-176	11QPs^a
119:10-21	4QPs^h
119:31-34, 43-48, 77-80	1QPs^a
119:37-46, 49-50, 73-74, 81-83, 89-92	4QPs^g
119:99-101, 104, 113-120, 138-142	5QPs
119:163-65	11QPs^b
120:6-7	4QPs^e
121:1-8	11QPs^a
122:1-9	4QProphecy of Joshua
122:1-9	11QPs^a
123:1-2	11QPs^a
124:7-8	11QPs^a
125:1-5	11QPs^a
125:2-5	4QPs^e
126:1-6	11QPs^a
126:1-5	4QPs^e
126:6	1QPs^b
127:1-5	1QPs^b
127:1	11QPs^a
128:3-6	11QPs^a
128:3	1QPs^b
129:1-8	11QPs^a
129:8	4QPs^e
130:1-8	11QPs^a
130:1-3, 6	4QPs^e
131:1	11QPs^a
132:8-18	11QPs^a
133:1-3, X	11QPs^a
133:1-3, X	11QPs^b
134:1-3	11QPs^a
135:1-6, X, 7, 9, 17-21	11QPs^a
135:6-8, 10-13, 15-16	4QPs^k
135:6-8, 11-12	4QPs^n
136:1-7, X, 8-16, 26	11QPs^a
136:22-24	4QPs^n
137:1, 9	11QPs^a
138:1-8	11QPs^a
139:8-24	11QPs^a
140:1-5	11QPs^a
141:5-10	11QPs^a
141:10	11QPs^b
142:4-8	11QPs^a
143:1-8	11QPs^a
143:3-4, 6-8	4QPs^p
144:1-7, 15	11QPs^a
144:1-2	11QPs^b
145:1-7, 13, X, 14-21, X	11QPs^a
146:1?	4QPs^e
146:9, X, 10	11QPs^a
147:1-4, 13-17, 20	4QPs^d
147:1-3, 18-20	11QPs^a
147:18-19	MasPs^b
148:1-12	11QPs^a
149:7-9, X	11QPs^a
150:1-6	11QPs^a
150:1-6	MasPs^b
151A:1-7	11QPs^a
151B:1-2	11QPs^a
154:3-19	11QPs^a
155:1-19	11QPs^a
Apocryphal Psalms I-III	11QapocPs
Apostrophe to Judah	4QPs^f
Apostrophe to Zion 1-18	11QPs^a
Apostrophe to Zion 1-2, 11-18	4QPs^f
Apostrophe to Zion 4-5	11QPs^b
David's Compositions	11QPs^a
David's Last Words 7 (= 2 Sam 23:7)	11QPs^a
Eschatological Hymn	4QPs^f
Hymn to Creator 1-9	11QPs^a
Plea for Deliverance	11QPs^a
Plea for Deliverance	11QPs^b

Job

8:15-17	4QJob^b
9:27	4QJob^b
13:4	4QJob^b
13:19-20, 24-27	4QpaleoJob^c
14:4-6	4QJob^b
14:13-17	4QpaleoJob^c
31:14-19	4QJob^a
31:20-21	4QJob^b
32:3-4	4QJob^a
33:10-11, 24-26, 28-30	4QJob^a
33:28-30	2QJob
34:28-31	4QJob^a
35:16	4QJob^a
36:7-11, 13-27, 32-33	4QJob^a
37:1-5, 14-15	4QJob^a

Proverbs
1:27-33	4QProv^a
2:1	4QProv^a
7:9-11(?)	4QProv^b
13:6-9	4QProv^b
14:5-10, 12-13, 31-35	4QProv^b
15:1-8, 19-31	4QProv^b

Ruth
1:1-12	4QRuth^a
1:1-6, 12-15	4QRuth^b
2:13-23	2QRuth^a
3:1-8	2QRuth^a
3:13-18	2QRuth^b
4:3-4	2QRuth^a

Canticles
1:1-7	6QCant
2:9-17	4QCant^b
3:1-2, 5, 9-11	4QCant^b
3:4-5, 7-11	4QCant^a
3:7-8	4QCant^c
4:1-7	4QCant^a
4:1-3, 8-11, 14-16	4QCant^b
5:1	4QCant^b
6:11?-12	4QCant^a
7:1-7	4QCant^a

Qoheleth
1:10-14 (15?)	4QQoh^b
5:13-17	4QQoh^a
6:1, 3-8, 12	4QQoh^a
7:1-10, 19-20	4QQoh^a

Lamentations
1:1-18	4QLam
1:10-12	3QLam
2:5	4QLam
3:53-62	3QLam
4:5-8, 11-16, 19-22	5QLam^a
4:17-20	5QLam^b
5:1-13, 16-17	5QLam^a

Esther
[not represented]

Daniel
1:10-17	1QDan^a
1:16-20	4QDan^a
2:2-6	1QDan^a
2:9-11, 19-49	4QDan^a
3:1-2	4QDan^a
3:22-30	1QDan^b
3:23-25	4QDan^d
4:5?-9, 12-14	4QDan^d
4:29-30	4QDan^a
5:5-7, 12-14, 16-19	4QDan^a
5:10-12, 14-16, 19-22	4QDan^b
6:8-22, 27-29	4QDan^b
7:1-6, 11?, 26-28	4QDan^b
7:5-7, 25-28	4QDan^a
7:15-19, 21-23?	4QDan^d
8:1-8, 13-16	4QDan^b
8:1-5	4QDan^a
8:16-17(?), 20-21(?)	pap6QDan
9:12-14, 15-16(?), 17?	4QDan^e
10:5-9, 11-16, 21	4QDan^c
10:8-16	pap6QDan
10:16-20	4QDan^a
11:1-2, 13-17, 25-29	4QDan^c
11:13-16	4QDan^a
11:33-36, 38	pap6QDan

Ezra
4:2-6, 9-11	4QEzra
5:17	4QEzra
6:1-5	4QEzra

Nehemiah
[not represented]

Chronicles
2 Chron 28:27	4QChr
29:1-3	1QChr

2. Index of Passages in the Apocryphal and "Pseudepigraphal" Scrolls

For previous indices of the Apoctyphal and "Pseudepigraphical" Scrolls, see U. Gleßmer, "Liste der Biblischen Texte aus Qumran," in *RevQ* 16/62, 1993, pp. 153–192, esp. 189–192; and P.W. Flint, "Appendix II: Index of Passages from the Apocrypha and Previously-Known Writings ("Pseudepigrapha") in the Scrolls," in P.W. Flint and J.C. VanderKam, eds., *The Dead Sea Scrolls after Fifty Years*, vol. 2, pp. 666–668. Some passages relating to the Testaments are listed with the understanding that the *Aramaic Levi Document* et al. are not Vorlagen (i.e., Hebrew texts used by the translator) of the T12P, but Hebrew or Aramaic compositions that were extensively reworked by later Christian editors.

Tobit			6:20-31	2QSir
1:17, 19-22	pap4QTobit^a ar		39:27-28c, 29-32	MasSir
2:1-3, 10-11	pap4QTobit^a ar		40:10-19, 28-30	MasSir
3:5, 9-15, 17	pap4QTobit^a ar		41:1-22	MasSir
3:6-8	4QTobit^b ar		42:1-25	MasSir
3:3-4?, 6, 10-11	4QTobit^e		43:1-25 (>26-28), 29-30	MasSir
4:2, 5, 7	pap4QTobit^a ar		44:1-17	MasSir
4:3-9	4QTobit^e		51:1-11, 23 [𝔊 13-20, 30]	11QPs^a
4:21	pap4QTobit^a ar			
4:21	4QTobit^b ar		*Epistle of Jeremiah*	
5:1, 9	pap4QTobit^a ar		43-44	papEpJer gr
5:1, 12-14, 19-22	4QTobit^b ar			
5:2	4QTobit^e		*"Apocryphal" Psalms*	
6:1-18	4QTobit^b ar		Psalm 151A	
6:6-8, 13, 15-19	pap4QTobit^a ar		151A:0-7	11QPs^a
7:?	pap4QTobit^a ar			
7:1-6, 13	pap4QTobit^a ar		Psalm 151B	
7:1-10	4QTobit^b ar		151B:1-2	11QPs^a
7:11	4QTobit^d ar			
8:17-19, 21	4QTobit^b ar		Psalm 154	
9:1-4	4QTobit^b ar		154:3-19	11QPs^a
10:7-9	4QTobit^e			
11:10-14	4QTobit^e		Psalm 155	
12:1, 18-22	pap4QTobit^a ar		155:1-19	11QPs^a
12:20-22	4QTobit^e			
13:1-4, 13-14, 18	4QTobit^e		*1 Enoch*	
13:3-18	pap4QTobit^a ar		1:1-6	4QEn^a ar
14:1-2	4QTobit^e		1:9	4QEn^c ar
14:2-6, 10?	4QTobit^e		2:1-3	4QEn^a ar
14:1-3, 7	pap4QTobit^a ar		2:1-3	4QEn^c ar
14:10	4QTobit^d ar		3:1	4QEn^a ar
			3:1	4QEn^c ar
Ben Sira (Sirach)			4:1	4QEn^a ar
1:19-20(?) or 6:14-15(?)	2QSir		4:1	4QEn^c ar

5:1	4QEn^c ar	82:9-13	4QEnastr^b ar
5:1-6	4QEn^a ar	after 82:20	4QEnastr^d ar
5:9	4QEn^b ar	86:1-3	4QEn^f ar
6:1-4, 7-8	4QEn^b ar	88:3	4QEn^e ar
6:4-8	4QEn^a ar	89:1-16, 26-30	4QEn^e ar
6:7	4QEn^c ar	89:11-14, 29-31, 43-44	4QEn^d ar
7:1-6	4QEn^a ar	89:31-37	4QEn^c ar
7:1-6	4QEn^b ar	91:10?, 11-17, 18-19	4QEn^g ar
8:1, 3-4	4QEn^a ar	92:1-2, 5	4QEn^g ar
8:1-4	4QEn^b ar	93:1-4, 9-11	4QEn^g ar
9:1-3, 6-8	4QEn^a ar	94:1-2	4QEn^g ar
9:1-4	4QEn^b ar	98:11?	pap7QEn gr
10:3-4, 21-22	4QEn^a ar	100:12	pap7QEn gr
10:8-12	4QEn^b ar	103:3-4, 7-8, 15	pap7QEn gr
10:13-19	4QEn^c ar	104:13	4QEn^c ar
11:1	4QEn^a ar	105:1-2	4QEn^c ar
12:3	4QEn^c ar	105:17?	pap7QEn gr
12:4-6	4QEn^a ar	106:1-2, 13-19	4QEn^c ar
13:6-10	4QEn^c ar	107:1-2	4QEn^c ar
14:1-16, 18-20	4QEn^c ar		
14:4-6	4QEn^b ar	*Jubilees*	
15:11?	4QEn^c ar	Prologue	4QJub^a
18:8-12	4QEn^c ar	1:1-2, 4-15, 26-28	4QJub^a
18:15?	4QEn^e ar	1:26-29(?)	pap4QJub^b(?)
21:2-4	4QEn^e ar	2:1-4, 7-24	4QJub^a
22:3-7	4QEn^e ar	2:14? or Gen 1:28?	
22:13-14	4QEn^d ar		pap4QJub? (4Q483)
23:1-4	4QEn^d ar	2:26-27	4QJub^c
24:1	4QEn^d ar	3:25-27? or 14:4-6?	11QJub
25:7	4QEn^d ar	4:6-11, 11-12 (or 16-17), 13-14, 17-18?,	
26:1-6	4QEn^d ar	29-30, 31	11QJub
27:1	4QEn^d ar	4:17-24 (similar)	4QpseudoJub^c
28:3	4QEn^e ar	5:1-2	11QJub
29:1-2	4QEn^e ar	12:15-17, 28-29	11QJub
30:1-3	4QEn^c ar	13:29? or Gen 14:22-23?	
31:1-3	4QEn^c ar		pap4QJub? (4Q482)
31:2-3	4QEn^e ar	14:4-6? or 3:25-27?	11QJub
32:1	4QEn^c ar	21:1-2, 7-10, 12-16, 18-26	4QJub^d
32:1-3, 6	4QEn^e ar	21:5-10	4QJub^e
33:3-4	4QEn^e ar	21:22-24	4QJub^f
34:1	4QEn^e ar	22:1	4QJub^d
35:1	4QEn^c ar	22:22, 30?	4QJub^f
36:1-4	4QEn^c ar	23:6-7, 10, 12-13, 23a	3QJub
73:1–74:9 (similar)	4QEnastr^a ar	23:7-8	2QJub^a
73:1–74:9 (similar)	4QEnastr^b ar	23:21-23	4QTanḥ
76:3-10, 13-14	4QEnastr^c ar	23:30-31	4QTanḥ or 4QJub^f
76:13-14	4QEnastr^b ar	23:10-13	4QJub^f
77:1-4	4QEnastr^b ar	25:9-12	4QJub^g
77:1-4	4QEnastr^c ar	27:6-7	4QJub^g
78:6-8	4QEnastr^c ar	27:19-21	1QJub^a
78:9-12, 17	4QEnastr^b ar	32:18-21	pap4QJub^h
79:1, 3-5	4QEnastr^b ar	33:12-15	4QJub^f

34:4-5	pap4QJub^h	38:6-8	4QJub^f
35:7-22	pap4QJub^h	39:4-9	4QJub^f
35:8-10	1QJub^b	39:9-18	pap4QJub^h
36:7-23	pap4QJub^h	40:1-7	pap4QJub^h
36:12?	1QJub^b	41:7-10, 28?	pap4QJub^h
37:11-15	4QJub^f	46:1-3	2QJub^b
37:17-25	pap4QJub^h	48:5?	4QJub^g
38:1-13	pap4QJub^h		

Material Related to the Testaments of the 12 Patriarchs

To the Testament of Levi
2:4 (similar)	4QLevi^b ar
8:11?	1QLevi ar
9:4 et passim	1QLevi ar
chap. 8 (similarities)	4QLevi^b ar
12:7	4QLevi^a ar
13:1-4, 6, 8-9	4QLevi^a ar
19:1 (alleged)	Visions of Amram^f? ar

To the Testament of Judah
12:2 (similar)	pap4QTJudah?
25:1-2 (similar)	3QTJudah?
25:2 (similar)	pap4QTJudah?

To the Testament of Naphtali
1:6-8	4QTNaph

To the Testament of Joseph
17:1	4QAJo ar

12. BIBLICAL INTERPRETATION AT QUMRAN

Craig A. Evans
Trinity Western University

Virtually every document at Qumran engages in or presupposes biblical interpretation. The most obvious examples are the so-called *pesharim*, or interpretations of Scripture. But even the Bible Scrolls themselves give evidence of interpretive tendencies[1] (as seen, for example, in the "Great Isaiah Scroll" of cave 1).[2] There are examples of "rewritten Bible" (such as the *Genesis Apocryphon*), liturgical materials, apocalyptic, wisdom, and didactic writings that in various ways interpret Scripture, either explicitly or implicitly.[3] In the present essay most of the attention will be given to the *pesharim*, but examples of biblical interpretation in other writings will also be taken into account. We shall explore (1) the origin and definition of *pesher*, (2) the types of *pesher* found in the Dead Sea Scrolls, and (3) biblical interpretation in other Scrolls.

Before probing the origin and definition of *pesher*, it must be emphasized that Scripture played a defining and life-giving role for the Jewish society that left behind the Scrolls near the Dead Sea. Not only is Scripture appealed to, as one would expect, in order to discover and defend Jewish law and therefore a lifestyle both sacred and mundane, and not only is Scripture appealed to in order to find the

---

[1] For a discussion of this phenomenon, see G.J. Brooke, "The Biblical Texts in the Qumran Commentaries: Scribal Errors or Exegetical Variants?" in C.A. Evans and W.F. Stinespring, eds., *Early Jewish and Christian Exegesis: Studies in Memory of William Hugh Brownlee* (Atlanta, 1987), pp. 85-100; J. Trebolle Barrera, "The Authoritative Functions of Scriptural Works at Qumran," in E. Ulrich and J.C. VanderKam, eds., *The Community of the Renewed Covenant: The Notre Dame Symposium on the Dead Sea Scrolls* (Notre Dame, 1994), pp. 95-110.

[2] See W.H. Brownlee, *The Meaning of the Qumrân Scrolls for the Bible: With Special Attention to the Book of Isaiah* (New York, 1964), pp. 155-246; J.R. Rosenbloom, *The Dead Sea Isaiah Scroll: A Literary Analysis. A Comparison with the Masoretic Text and the Biblia Hebraica* (Grand Rapids, 1970); E. Tov, "The Text of Isaiah at Qumran," in C.C. Broyles and C.A. Evans, eds., *Writing and Reading the Scroll of Isaiah: Studies of an Interpretive Tradition* (Leiden, 1997), vol. 2, pp. 491-511.

[3] Illustrative is the recently published M.E. Stone and E.G. Chazon, eds., *Biblical Perspectives: Early Use and Interpretation of the Bible in Light of the Dead Sea Scrolls* (Leiden, 1998).

community's origin and destiny—again, something that is not unusual in a Jewish context—Scripture informs the collectors and authors of the Dead Sea Scrolls as to how they differ from other Jews, especially from those who maintain the Temple in Jerusalem and also from those who belong to the other various religious-political parties (such as the Pharisees). *Pesher* interpretation permits the Scripture scholars of Qumran to find themselves—in contrast to and in distinction from other Jews—and their story in the sacred text, foretold by the prophets of old. This story involves the past, present, and future. Members of the sect (probably the Essenes, or a branch of the Essenes) can know why and when their movement arose, who are the faithful who belong to it and how they may remain in it, and what the future holds for them, for other Israelites, and for the gentiles, particularly the Romans. *Pesher* interpretation is, therefore, of vital importance for this community, equaling, perhaps even exceeding, the importance of midrash for later expressions of Rabbinic Judaism.

Origin and Definition of Pesher *at Qumran*

Pesher interpretation has its roots in Scripture itself. The overwhelming majority of occurrences are found in Aramaic Daniel, but one Hebrew example is found in Ecc. 8:1: "Who is like the wise man? And who knows the interpretation [*pesher*] of a thing [*dabar*]?" The Preacher's rhetorical question has in mind the interpretation of a saying, problem, riddle, or any matter (*dabar*, lit., "word") put before the wise man. But the explicit association of interpretation (*pesher*) and mystery (*raz*)—the essential vocabulary of *pesher* interpretation as it was pursued at Qumran—particularly a mystery of divine origin, is found in the book of Daniel. In this writing we find four major instances: in chapter 2, where Nebuchadnezzar wishes to know the significance of the image seen in his dream; in chapter 4, where Nebuchadnezzar wishes to know the meaning of his dream of the tree; in chapter 5, where Belshazzar wishes to know the meaning of the writing on the wall; and in chapter 7, where Daniel himself wishes to know the meaning of his heavenly vision.

In Dan. 2:4 the Chaldean magicians say to Nebuchadnezzar, "O king, live for ever! Tell your servants the dream, and we will show the interpretation [*pesher*]" (also Dan. 2:5-7, 9, 16, 24-26, 30, 36, 45). The troubled monarch views his dream of the human image as a "mystery" (*raz*; cf., 2:18-19, 27-30, 47) in need of solution. He dreams again in chapter 4 and again is in need of an interpretation: "Therefore I made a decree that all the wise men of Babylon should be brought before me, that they might make known to me the interpretation of the dream" (4:6; also 4:7, 9, 18-19, 24). In chapter 5, the frightened Belshazzar requests to know the interpretation of the mysterious writing on the wall (5:7: "Whoever reads this writing and shows me its interpretation [*pesher*]..." cf., 5:8, 12, 15-17, 26). In 7:16, Daniel asks an angel for the interpretation of the vision he has had: "I approached one of those who stood there and asked him the truth concerning all this. So he told me and made known to me the interpretation [*pesher*] of the things."

Because the words *pesher* (or *pishro*, "its *pesher*") and *raz* also occur in Qumran's commentaries, scholars think that either Daniel was the inspiration for this interpretive method or that the book of Daniel itself has its origins in the early stages of the Qumran community. In my view, Daniel predates the Qumran community (by a generation or so), and the *pesher* exegesis of Qumran is a later, more Scripture-oriented development of the *pesher*-mystery dream interpretation of Daniel.[4]

Pesher functions similarly at Qumran and in Daniel. Its use at Qumran is easily illustrated from the best preserved and best known *pesher*, the commentary on Habakkuk. Two passages are especially important:

> 2:5...it refers [to the trai]tors in the Last ⁶Days. They are the cru[el Israel]ites who will not believe ⁷when they hear everything that [is to come upon] the latter generation that will be spoken by ⁸the Priest in whose [heart] God has put [the ability] to explain all ⁹the words of his servants the prophets, through [whom] God has foretold ¹⁰everything that is to come upon his people....

---

[4] On Daniel's relationship to Qumran, see K. Elliger, *Studien zum Habakuk-Kommentar* (Tübingen, 1953), pp. 164-167; A. Szorényi, "Das Buch Daniel, ein kanonisierte Pescher?" in *Volume du Congrès: Genève 1965* (Leiden, 1966), pp. 278-294; A. Mertens, *Das Buch Daniel im Lichte der Texte vom Toten Meer* (Stuttgart, 1971); I. Fröhlich, "*Pesher*, Apocalyptical Literature and Qumran," in J. Trebolle Barrera and L. Vegas Montaner, eds., *The Madrid Qumran Congress: Proceedings of the International Congress on the Dead Sea Scrolls Madrid 18–21 March, 1991* (Leiden, 1992), vol. 1, pp. 295-305. Fröhlich concludes: "The authors of the Qumran literary works were...heirs of the Danielic *pishra* (interpretation)-tradition, which they improved and elaborated into a sophisticated system in their commentaries of prophetical and other Biblical texts, the *Pesharim* and Florilegia" (p. 305).

> 6:14...Then the Lord answered me ¹⁵[and said, Write down the vision plainly] on tablets, so that with ease ¹⁶[someone can read it" (Hab. 2:1-2). Its interpretation is...] (7:1) then God told Habakkuk to write down what is going to happen to ²the generation to come; but when that period would be complete He did not make known to him. ³When it says, "so that with ease someone can read it." ⁴Its interpretation is (*pishro*) the Teacher of Righteousness to whom God made known ⁵all the mysteries (*razim*) of his servants the prophets. "For a prophecy testifies ⁶of a specific period; it speaks of that time and does not deceive" (Hab. 2:3a). ⁷Its interpretation is (*pishro*) that the Last Days will be long, much longer than ⁸the prophets had said; for the mysteries (*razim*) of God are wonderful. ⁹"If it tarries, be patient, it will surely come true and not ¹⁰be delayed" (Hab. 2:3b). Its interpretation refers (*pishro*) to those loyal ones, ¹¹obedient to the Law, whose hands will not cease from ¹²loyal service even when the Last Days seems long to them, for ¹³all the times fixed by God will come about in due course as He ordained ¹⁴that they should by his inscrutable insight.[5]

These passages illustrate clearly the eschatological orientation of *pesher* exegesis (i.e., what was foretold in the prophets of old is now taking place), its one-to-one correspondence (i.e., this element in Scripture refers to that person or event in our time), and its revelatory, even inspired nature. Habakkuk is understood to have foretold the coming of the Teacher of Righteousness, "to whom God made known all the mysteries." These mysteries, inscrutable to others, are found in the prophets, who spoke of the Last Days. But the Teacher of Righteousness is able to find the *pesher*, the interpretation, of these mysteries. In a certain sense, *pesher* exegesis understands itself as an inspired exegesis.[6] Given this exalted view of the Teacher's exegesis, the *pesharim* should be regarded as having an authority for Qumran that equals, perhaps even exceeds, the authority of the Rule Scrolls.[7]

---

[5] Adapted from E.M. Cook, "A Commentary on Habakkuk," in M.O. Wise, M.G. Abegg Jr., and E.M. Cook, *The Dead Sea Scrolls. A New Translation* (San Francisco, 1996), pp. 116, 119.

[6] See D.E. Aune, "Charismatic Exegesis in Early Judaism and Early Christianity," in J.H. Charlesworth and C.A. Evans, eds., *The Pseudepigrapha and Early Biblical Interpretation* (Sheffield, 1993), pp. 126-150, esp. pp. 133-137 (on the *pesharim*).

[7] For a selection of critical literature, see W.H. Brownlee, "Biblical Interpretation among the Sectaries of the Dead Sea Scrolls," in *BA* 14, 1951, pp. 54-76; F.F. Bruce, *Biblical Exegesis in the Qumran Texts* (London, 1960); E. Slomovic, "Towards an Understanding of the Exegesis in the Dead Sea Scrolls," in *RevQ* 7, 1969-1971, pp. 3-15; G.J. Brooke, *Exegesis at Qumran: 4QFlorilegium in its Jewish Context* (Sheffield, 1985); D. Dimant, "The Bible Explained (Prophecies)," in R.A. Kraft and G.W.E. Nickelsburg, eds., *Early Judaism and Its Modern Interpreters* (Atlanta, 1986), pp. 247-253; M.

Types of Pesharim

Devorah Dimant divides the *pesharim* into four classifications: (1) continuous *pesharim*, (2) thematic *pesharim*, (3) isolated *pesharim*, and (4) other forms of *pesharim*.[8] Although not all are happy with these categories, they provide a reasonable overview. Only the first two categories will be treated below.

Continuous Pesharim

Most of the *pesharim* belong to this category. In canonical order, they include 4QpIsa^a (= 4Q161, on Is. 10:22-27, 33-34; 11:1-5), 4QpIsa^b (= 4Q162, on Is. 5:5-30), 4QpIsa^c (= 4Q163, on Is. 8:7-8; 9:11-20; 10:24; 14:8, 26-30; 29:10-23; 30:1-21; 31:1), 4QpIsa^d (= 4Q164, on Is. 54:11-12), 4QpIsa^e (= 4Q165, on Is. 40:11-12; 14:19; 15:4-5; 21:10-15; 32:5-7; 11:11-12), 4QpHos^a (= 4Q166, on Hos 2:8-14), 4QpHos^b (= 4Q167, on Hos 5:13-15; 6:4-11; 8:6-14), 1QpMic (= 1Q14, on Mic. 1:2-9; 6:15-16), 4QpNah (= 4Q169, on Nah 1:3-6; 2:12-14; 3:1-14), 1QpHab (on Hab. 1:1–2:20),[9] 1QpZeph (= 1Q15, on Zeph. 1:18–2:2), 4QpZeph (= 4Q170, on Zeph. 1:12-13), 1QpPs (= 1Q16, on Ps 68:13, 30), 4QpPs^a (= 4Q171, on Ps 37:2-39; 45:1-2; 60:8-9), and 4QpPs^b (= 4Q173, on Ps 129:7-8).[10] It will be useful to

---

Fishbane, "Use, Authority and Interpretation of Mikra at Qumran," in M.J. Mulder, ed., *Mikra: Text, Translation, Reading and Interpretation of the Hebrew Bible in Ancient Judaism and Early Christianity* (Assen and Philadelphia, 1988), pp. 339-377; D. Dimant, "*Pesharim*, Qumran," in *ABD*, vol. 5, pp. 244-251; D.I. Brewer, *Techniques and Assumptions in Jewish Exegesis before 70 CE* (Tübingen, 1992), pp. 187-198; G.J. Brooke, "The *Pesharim* and the Origins of the Dead Sea Scrolls," in M.O. Wise, N. Golb, J.J. Collins, and D.G. Pardee, eds., *Methods of Investigation of the Dead Sea Scrolls and the Khirbet Qumran Site: Present Realities and Future Prospects* (New York, 1994), pp. 339-352; M.J. Bernstein, "Introductory Formulas for Citation and Re-Citation of Biblical Verses in the Qumran *Pesharim*: Observations on a *Pesher* Technique," in *DSD* 1, 1994, pp. 30-70.

[8] Dimant, "*Pesharim*," p. 245. See also J. Carmignac, "Le document de Qumran sur Melkisédeq," in *RevQ* 7, 1969-1971, pp. 360-361; D. Dimant, "Qumran Sectarian Literature," in M.E. Stone, ed., *Jewish Writings of the Second Temple Period* (Assen and Philadelphia, 1984), pp. 504-505.

[9] The Habakkuk *pesher* does not have an inventory number.

[10] There are a few other scrolls that at one time were tentatively identified as *pesharim*. For various reasons, such as insufficient extant text, we cannot be sure that these texts really are *pesharim*. They include 3Q4 (possibly on Isaiah; Is. 1:1-2 is quoted), 4Q168 (possibly on Micah; Mic. 4:8-12 is quoted), 4Q172 (no biblical text is cited), 4Q173 frg. 5 (which does not belong to the four [other] frgs. of 4Q173; Ps. 118:20 may be quoted: "this is] the gate to the God; the right[eous will enter into it").

treat briefly the principal themes of these *pesharim*. Emphasis falls on the larger and better preserved fragments.

Rivaled only by the well preserved Habakkuk *pesher* from cave 1, the Isaiah *pesharim* are the most extensive of the *pesharim*.[11] Pesher A, which treats portions of Is. 10–11, provides important insight into Qumran's messianic and eschatological expectations. The first six fragments make up the remains of cols. 1 and 2, in which the remnant of Is. 10 appears to be identified with the Qumran community, though the fragmentary condition of these columns makes certainty impossible. Mention of the "Prince of the Congregation" (*nasi ha'edah*) and "end of days" (*aharit hayyomim*) gives the *pesher* an unmistakably eschatological orientation (1Q161 2–6 ii 15 and 22; a similar interpretation is found in *Pesher* C col. 2, also commenting on Is. 10).

Column 3, made up of fragments 7-10, comments on Is. 10:34–11:5. The trees of Lebanon that will be felled is understood to refer to the Kittim, almost universally understood to be the Romans. The Romans will be routed before Israel and the shoot of David will arise, he who will execute Israel's enemies and rule Israel wisely and justly. Reference to Magog in line 21 heightens the eschatological orientation, but again the text is quite fragmentary. The parallel in 4Q285 fills in some of the lacunae:

> [6][... the P]rince of the Congregation to the[Mediterranean] Sea[...] [7][... And they shall flee] from Israel at that time[...] [8][...And the High Priest]shall stand before them and they shall arrange themselves against them[in battle array...] [9][...] and they shall return back to the land at that time[...] [10][...]then they shall bring him before the Prince of[the congregation...] (frgs. 6 + 4)

> [1][...just as it is written in the book of]Isaiah the prophet, "And [the thickets of the forest] shall be cut down [2][with an ax, and Lebanon with its majestic trees w]ill fall. A shoot shall come out from the stump of

---

[11] For critical study of the Isaiah *pesharim*, see J. Carmignac, "Notes sur les Peshârîm," in *RevQ* 3, 1961-1962, pp. 503-558, esp. pp. 511-515; J.M. Allegro, *Qumrân Cave 4. I (4Q158–4Q186)* (Oxford, 1968), pp. 11-30 [NB: this work is marred by numerous errors and must be used with J. Strugnell, "Notes en marge du volume V des 'Discoveries in the Judaean Desert of Jordan," in *RevQ* 7, 1969-1971, pp. 163-276]; J.M. Rosenthal, "Biblical Exegesis of 4QpIs," in *JQR* 60, 1969-1970, pp. 27-36; J.D. Amoussine, "The Reflection of Historical Events of the First Century B.C. in Qumran Commentaries (4Q161, 4Q169, 4Q166)," in *HUCA* 48, 1977, pp. 123-152; M.P. Horgan, *Pesharim: Qumran Interpretations of Biblical Books* (Washington, 1979), pp. 70-138; R.J. Bauckham, "Messianic Interpretation of Is. 10:34 in the Dead Sea Scrolls: 2 Baruch and the Preaching of John the Baptist," in *DSD* 2, 1995, pp. 202-216.

Jesse ³[and a branch shall grow out of his roots" (Is. 10:34). This is the]Branch of David. Then [all forces of Belial] shall be judged, ⁴[and the king of the Kittim shall stand for judgment]and the Prince of the community—the Bra[nch of David]—will have him put to death. ⁵[Then all Israel shall come out with timbrel]s and dancers, and the [High] Priest shall order ⁶[them to cleanse their bodies from the guilty blood of the c]orpse[s of] the Kittim,[and all the people shall] (frg. 5)[12]

4Q285 provides an important link between the War Scroll (1QM) and *Pesher* A of Isaiah. The extant fragments of the War Scroll's poorly preserved conclusion make no mention of the messiah. The priests, however, are conspicuous in their role of organizing and sanctifying Israel for the great battle (reflecting the holy war legislation of Deut 20:1-4). This aspect of their task is alluded to in 4Q285 6 + 4 line 8 and in frg. 5 lines 5-6. The missing messiah appears in frg. 5 lines 3-4, thus strongly supporting the assumption that he played a role in 1QM's original final columns of text. Not only does the messiah play a role in the final eschatological battle, he evidently slays "the king of the Kittim," that is, the Roman emperor himself.[13]

Pesher B of Isaiah comments on Is. 5 and is chiefly concerned with the judgments that will befall sinful Israel, particularly the "arrogant men who are in Jerusalem" (col. 2, lines 6-7, 10). These things will happen "in the last days" and "at the time of visitation" (lines 1-2). A similar judgmental interpretation is found in *Pesher* C. Frg. 23, col. 2, lines 10-11, refers to the "congregation of those seeking smooth things, who are in Jerusalem." Judgment will come upon them in "the last days." *Pesher* D promises the founding of the "Council of the Community, the priests and the people...an assembly of the elect" (frg. 1, lines 1-3). Isaiah 54:12 is said to concern the "chiefs of the tribes of Israel in the last days" (line 7). *Pesher* E comments on other portions of Isaiah, but seems to be concerned with the same theme and may refer to the expectation of the coming of the Teacher of Righteousness (cf., frgs. 1–2, line 3), though this reading has to be restored.

The Hosea *pesharim* pursue themes quite similar to those found in

---

[12] Adapted from M.G. Abegg, Jr., "The War of the Messiah," in Wise, Abegg, and Cook, *The Dead Sea Scrolls*, p. 293.

[13] The implausible reading of the Hebrew to the effect that the messiah, the Branch of David, is slain by the king of the Kittim has been put to rest by M.G. Abegg, Jr., "Messianic Hope and 4Q285: A Reassessment," in *JBL* 113, 1994, pp. 81-91.

the Isaiah *pesharim*.[14] Columns 1 and 2 of *Pesher* A preserve the only substantial portions of commentary in the Hosea *pesharim*. In col. 1 we hear words of judgment upon the wicked of Israel (commenting on Hos. 2:8, "she cannot find her paths"), who will be struck "with blindness and madness" (line 8, alluding to Deut. 28:28). They are "the generation of the visitation...gathered in the times of wrath" (lines 10 and 12). According to col. 2, which begins with a quotation of Hos. 2:10, which complains of Israel's idolatry, the wicked "forgot God" and "cast behind them all his commandments" (lines 3-4). Hosea 2:11-12 and 2:13 are then quoted, with commentary appended to each quotation. The allusions could be historical, that is, what Israel did in the distant past, or the allusions could be to the recent past, as part of the beginning of the final period of judgment. Given the eschatological orientation in col. 1, the latter alternative is the more likely. The second fragment of *Pesher* B quotes Hos. 5:13-14, which includes reference to the "young lion." We are told that this refers to the "last priest, who will stretch out his hand to strike Ephraim" (line 3). This "last priest" may be the expected faithful priest of the last days, who will judge apostate Ephraim. But it is also possible, perhaps even probable, that this priest is none other than the Hasmonean priest-king Alexander Janneus. In the *pesher* on Nahum he is called the "lion of wrath" who "hanged men up alive (crucified?)" (4QpHab 3–4 i 5, 7). If so, then from the perspective of the *pesher*, Alexander may have been viewed as the final wicked priest (on the "Wicked Priest," see below).

The Micah *pesher* consists of twenty-three fragments, mostly very small, with very little interpretation preserved.[15] The eschatological orientation seems plain enough, however. In frg. 10, line 4, we hear of the Teacher of Righteousness. Then we hear of the "chosen ones" and the "council of the community, who will be saved from the day" of judgment (lines 5-6, with "judgment" in line 7 restored). Someone

---

[14] For critical study of the Hosea *pesharim*, see Allegro, *Qumrân Cave 4*, pp. 33-36; J.D. Amoussine, "Observatiunculae qumraneae," in *RevQ* 7, 1969-1971, pp. 533-552, esp. pp. 545-552; Horgan, *Pesharim*, pp. 138-158; D.C. Carson, "An Alternative Reading of 4QpHosa II 3-6," in *RevQ* 11, 1983, pp. 417-421; M.J. Bernstein, "'Walking in the Festivals of the Gentiles': 4QpHosea^a 2:15-17 and Jubilees 6:34-38," in *JSP* 9, 1991, pp. 21-31.

[15] For critical study of the Micah *pesher*, see D. Barthélemy and J.T. Milik, eds., *Qumran Cave I* (Oxford, 1955), pp. 77-80; Carmignac, "Notes sur les Pesharîm," pp. 515-519; Horgan, *Pesharim*, pp. 55-63.

"will judge his enemies" in frg. 11, line 4. The "last generation" is referred to in frgs. 17–18, line 5.

The *pesher* on Nahum consists of five fragments.[16] Fragments 1 and 2 constitute most of one column, while frgs. 3 and 4 constitute most of four columns. The fifth fragment preserves portions of only four lines. The *pesher* offers a mix of historical interpretation, applying the biblical text to recent events in history, and of eschatological interpretation, particularly as it pertains to judgment on the Kittim. The plainest historical allusion is found in 3–4 i 2-3, after commenting on Nah. 2:12b, "Its interpretation concerns Demetrius, king of Greece (lit., Yavan), who sought to enter Jerusalem on the advice of those who seek after smooth things, [but God did not give Jerusalem] into the hands of the kings of Greece, from Antiochus until the rise of the rulers of the Kittim. But later it will be trampled." This Demetrius is probably the Seleucid ruler Demetrius III Eukairos (95–88 B.C.E.). Antiochus is the notorious Antiochus IV Epiphanes (175–163 B.C.E.), against whom the Maccabean struggle began.[17] Those "who seek after smooth things" (*dor°shei hah°laqoth*), that is, who seek less demanding legal interpretations of Scripture, are probably the Pharisees. Most interpreters suspect this because the vocalization of "smooth things" closely resembles "legal things" (*halakoth*). Thus, the author of this *pesher* is making a sarcastic allusion to the legal interpretations of the Pharisees, that is, those who seek (the verb is *darash*, from which *midrash* is derived) halakhot—legal rulings—are in fact seeking halaqoth—easy, convenient rulings. The incident referred to in this *pesher* is probably the struggle between the Pharisees and Alexander Janneus (103–76 B.C.E.; cf., Josephus, *Ant*. 13.13.5–14.1 §372-378). The aftermath of this failed effort resulted in Alexander's having some eight hundred Jews crucified (*Ant*. 13.14.2 §380-383), a grisly event also alluded to in the Nahum *Pesher* (on Nah. 2:13b): "Its interpretation concerns the Lion of Wrath [who...to]ok revenge against those seeking smooth things, who hanged living men [from

---

[16] For critical study of the Nahum *pesher*, see Allegro, *Qumrân Cave 4*, pp. 37-42; Y. Yadin, "*Pesher* Nahum (4QpNah) Reconsiderd," in *IEJ* 21, 1971, pp. 1-12; Horgan, *Pesharim*, pp. 158-191; A. Palumbo, "A New Interpretation of the Nahum Commentary," in *FO* 29, 1992-1993, pp. 153-162; L.H. Schiffman, "Pharisees and Sadducees in Pesher *Nahum*," in M. Brettler and M. Fishbane, eds., *Minhah le-Nahum: Biblical and Other Studies Presented to Nahum M. Sarna in Honour of his 70th Birthday* (Sheffield, 1993), pp. 272-290.

[17] The specificity of this interpretation encourages us to assume similar degrees of specificity in the other *pesharim*, even when personal names are not provided.

the tree, a deed that had not been done] in Israel since ancient times" (3–4 i 6-8). The Pharisees may again be mentioned in 3–4 ii 7-9 where they are accused of misleading nations and misguiding Ephraim "with their false teaching [$b^e talmûd$]." We have here the earliest attestation of "Talmud," which may lend a measure of support for identifying the "seekers of smooth things" (also mentioned in 4QpNah 3–4 ii 2; iii 3, 7) with the Pharisees.[18] At this point in the *pesher*, we seem to be moving beyond recent history to prophecy of events soon to transpire. The false teaching and immorality of the seekers after smooth things will lead to destruction (line 9: "cities and tribes will perish on account of their advice"), but "they will die" and their council will dissolve (3–4 iii 7). The remainder of the *pesher*, commenting on much of Nah. 3:6-14, speaks of warfare and destruction.

The best preserved *pesher*, which enjoyed its long period of storage in an earthen jar, is the one on Habakkuk found in Cave 1. This scroll comprises thirteen columns of text, quoting and commenting on Hab. 1–2.[19] Because the thirteenth column has only four lines of text at the top, with rest of the column blank, it is almost certain that this column is the final column of the *pesher*. Because of deterioration, about two lines of text are lost at the bottom of each column. This *pesher* presents an interpretive framework and an eschatological scenario that are very much consistent with those found in the *pesharim* already surveyed. We again have a blend of relatively recent events in the life of the community and the anticipated eschatological events expected to unfold soon. Major players include the "Teacher of Righteousness" (1:13; 2:2; 5:9-12; 8:3; 9:9-12; 11:4-8), the "Man of the Lie" (2:1-2), the "House of Absalom" (5:9-12), the "Wicked Priest" (8:8-13; 8:16; 9:2, 9-12; 11:4-8, 12-15; 12:2-10), and the "One who Spouts the Lie" (10:9-13). These identifications chiefly concern the Community's recent history. The principal eschatological elements concern the coming of the Kittim, or Romans (2:12-15; 2:17–

---

[18] See Horgan, *Pesharim*, p. 184, for comments and bibliography against S. Zietlin's theory that the references to talmud, darash, and halakhah constitute weighty evidence that the Scrolls originated in the Middle Ages.

[19] For critical study of the Habakkuk *pesher*, see K. Elliger, *Studien zum Habakuk-Kommentar vom Toten Meer* (Tübingen, 1953); L.H. Silberman, "Unriddling the Riddle: A Study in the Structure and Language of the Habakkuk *Pesher* (1QpHab)," in *RevQ* 3, 1961-1962, pp. 323-364; W.H. Brownlee, *The Midrash Pesher of Habakkuk* (Missoula, 1979); Horgan, *Pesharim*, pp. 10-55.

3:1; 3:4-6, 9-13; 4:1-3, 5-13; 6:1-2, 6-12; 9:6-7), the final judgment (5:3-6; 8:1-3; 10:3-5; 12:12-14; 13:1-4), and the downfall of the last priest in Jerusalem (9:4-7).

The prophecy of Habakkuk conveniently accommodates Qumran's self-understanding and eschatological expectations. The prophecy begins with a description of violence, strife, and lawlessness (Hab. 1:1-4a), which the interpreter of Qumran saw fulfilled in the tumultuous transition from Seleucid to Hasmonean rule and the ongoing strife during the Hasmonean period. When Hab. 1:4b speaks of the wicked surrounding the righteous, it takes little interpretive imagination to "*pesher*" the main antagonist (the "Wicked Priest") and protagonist (the "Teacher of Righteousness") from the text. Reference to the "traitors" in Hab. 1:5 prompts the interpretive reference to the "Man of the Lie," who persuades Israel not to "believe the words of the Teacher of Righteousness, (words which were) from the mouth of God" (1QpHab 2:1-3). The claim that the words of the Teacher were "from the mouth of God" attests the great respect with which this founding teacher's instruction was held. The reference in Hab. 1:13 to those who remain silent when the wicked swallow up the righteous leads to the identification of the "House of Absalom" and their confederates, who remained silent when the Teacher of Righteousness was wrongly rebuked and opposed by the Man of the Lie (5:9-12). Anticipation of the coming of the Kittim is sourced in Hab. 1:6, which speaks of the "Chaldeans, that bitter and hasty nation" (1QpHab 2:11-12). What is said of the Chaldeans throughout Hab. 1–2 is applied to the Kittim, or Romans. The commentator anticipates a judgment of his people Israel but victory for the elect within Israel, who will themselves judge the nations (1QpHab 5:3-6, commenting on Hab. 1:12b-13a). Habakkuk's famous dictum, "the righteous person will live by his faithfulness" (Hab. 2:4b), is applied to "all those who observe the Torah in the house of Judah, whom God will save from the house of judgment on account of their tribulation and fidelity to the Teacher of Righteousness" (1QpHab 8:1-3). The Wicked Priest and the other corrupt, avaricious priests in Jerusalem will be plundered by the Kittim and brought low by disease and calamity (cols. 8–12).[20]

---

[20] Although it is disputed, many scholars identify the Wicked Priest as either Jonathan (ruled 160–143 B.C.E.) and/or Simon (ruled 142-134 B.C.E.), the brothers of Judas Maccabeus (see Horgan, *Pesharim*, p. 7 and notes).

The *pesher* on Zephaniah comprises only two fragments of one column, quoting and commenting on Zeph. 1:12-13.[21] Not one complete sentence of interpretation has survived. *Pesher* B, on Ps. 129, is hardly better preserved. The "Teacher of Righteousness" appears twice (frg. 1, line 4; frg. 2, line 2). A "priest at the end of time" is mentioned (frg. 1, line 5). *Pesharim* B on the Psalms is much better preserved, presenting familiar themes.[22] The "Man of the Lie" (1–10 i 26; 1–10 iv 14) appears, as well as the "Teacher of Righteousness" (1–10 iii 15), who is probably the same person as the "Interpreter of Knowledge" (1–10 i 27; cf. 1QH 10:13 [*olim* 2:13]). The Teacher is identified as "Priest" (1–10 iii 15) and is probably "the Priest," who along with his "partisans" must be rescued from the "wicked ones of Ephraim and Manasseh" (1–10 ii 18-20). The "Wicked Priest" has attempted to murder the Teacher of Righteousness (1–10 iv 8). We also find the "congregation of the chosen" (1–10 ii 5; 1–10 iii 5; cf. 1QpHab 5:4), who are probably to be identified with the "congregation of the poor" (1–10 ii 10; 1–10 iii 10), that is, the members of the Qumran community.

Psalm 37 is the principal text commented upon in *Pesher* A, but there are also quotations of and comments on portions of Pss. 45 and 60. Psalm 37 is particularly suited to Qumran's exegetical framework of the righteous being persecuted by the wicked. The enemy are described as the "ruthless ones of the covenant who are in the house of Judah; they will plot to destroy completely those who observed the law, who are in the council of the Community. But God will not abandon them" (1–10 ii 14-15).

These several *pesharim* present us with a coherent interpretive method and a coherent interpretation of recent history and anticipated eschatological events. That they came out of the same school of thought seems undeniable. Prophetic Scriptures that contain themes and images resembling (either somewhat literally or symbolically) the Qumran Community's recent history (from the Maccabean struggle down to the time of Alexander Janneus) are unpacked, as

---

[21] For critical study of the Zephaniah *pesher*, see Allegro, *Qumrân Cave 4*, pp. 42-53; Horgan, *Pesharim*, pp. 191-92.

[22] For critical study of the Psalms *pesharim*, see Allegro, *Qumrân Cave 4*, pp. 42-53; R.B. Coote, "MW'D HT'NYT in 4Q171 (*Pesher* Psalm 37) fragments 1-2, col. II, line 9," in *RevQ* 8, 1972, pp. 81-85; D. Pardee, "A Restudy of the Commentary on Psalm 37 from Qumran Cave 4," in *RevQ* 8, 1972-1975, pp. 163-194; Horgan, *Pesharim*, pp. 192-228.

though containing "mysteries" (*razim*), through charismatic *pesher* interpretation. Israel's false teachers, especially the Wicked Priest, will lead the nation into disaster at the hands of the nations (principally the Romans). The Teacher of Righteousness and his following (the "congregation of the chosen") will be vindicated in the last days, when God will raise up the Branch of David and will annihilate the Romans. The balance of the *pesharim* elaborates this basic theme.

Thematic Pesharim

Thematic *pesharim* constitute collections of key biblical passages that focus on a given theme. In 4Q174 (4QFlorilegium) + 4Q177 (4QCatena[a]) we have two significant fragments of a *pesher* devoted to eschatology.[23] In this document we find a cluster of Scriptures with which the author clarifies 2 Sam. 7. The seed promised David in 2 Sam. 7:12-14 is the "Branch of David, who will arise with the Interpreter of the Law who will arise in Zion in the last days, as it is written, 'I will raise up the hut of David which has fallen' [Amos 9:11], who will arise to save Israel" (4Q174 3:11-13). 4Q177, which is quite fragmentary, describes the struggle of the last days between the forces of darkness and the "sons of light."

One could perhaps classify 4Q252 (4QPatriarchal Blessings) as another example of a thematic *pesher*. Somewhat like the *Testaments of the Twelve Patriarchs* 4Q252 and the related 4Q254, both commentaries on selected passages and topics in Genesis, offer eschatological interpretations of the blessings of the Patriarchs.[24] Judah's blessing (col. 5, commenting on Gen. 49:8-12) is given an explicit messianic cast:

---

[23] For critical study of the eschatological *pesher*, see D. Dimant, "4QFlorilegium and the Idea of the Community as Temple," in A. Caquot, et al., eds., *Hellenica et Judaica: Hommage à V. Nikiprovetzky* (Leuven, 1986), pp. 165-189; M.O. Wise, "4QFlorilegium and the Temple of Adam," in *RevQ* 15, 1991, pp. 103-132. For a persuasive argument that 4Q174 and 4Q177 are actually portions of a single *pesher*, see A. Steudel, *Der Midrasch zur Eschatologie aus der Qumrangemeinde* (Leiden, 1994).

[24] For critical study of the Genesis *pesharim*, see G.J. Brooke, "The Thematic Content of 4Q252," in *JQR* 85, 1994, pp. 33-59; idem, "4Q254 Fragments 1 and 4, and 4Q254a: Some Preliminary Comments," in *Proceedings of the Eleventh World Congress of Jewish Studies* (Jerusalem, 1994), pp. 185-192; idem, "4Q252 as Early Jewish Commentary," in *RevQ* 17, 1996, pp. 385-401; C.A. Evans, "'The Two Sons of Oil': Early Evidence of Messianic Interpretation of Zechariah 4:14 in 4Q254 4 2," in D.W. Parry and E. Ulrich, eds., *The Provo International Conference on the Dead Sea Scrolls: Technological Innovations, New Texts, and Reformulated Issues* (Leiden, 1998), pp. 566-575.

> ¹A ruler shall [no]t depart from the tribe of Judah when Israel has dominion. ²[And] the one who sits on the throne of David [shall never]be cut off, because the "ruler's staff" is the covenant of the kingdom ³[and the thous]ands of Israel are "the feet," until the Righteous Messiah, the Branch of David, has come. ⁴For to him and to his seed the covenant of the kingdom of his people has been given for the eternal generations, because ⁵he has kept [...] the Law with the men of the Community. For ⁶[... the "obedience of the people]s" is the assembly of the men of ⁷[...]²⁵

In 4Q254 4 2 we encounter the curious phrase, "two sons of oil," which has been taken from Zech. 4:14. This Hebrew phrase is attested no where else apart from Zechariah. Although uncertain because of the fragmentary condition of this document, this brief quotation probably appears in the *pesher* on Gen. 49:8-12, Jacob's blessing on Judah (or on Levi, as has been also suggested). If so, then we may have here important attestation of Qumran's diarchic messianism, wherein two messiahs, one of Aaron and one of Israel, were expected to arise in the last days (e.g., 1QS 9:11; CD 14:19 = 4Q266 10 i 12). 4Q254 may provide evidence that this diarchic messianism was rooted in Zechariah.²⁶

The Melchizedek *pesher*, which revolves around the jubilee legislation of Lev. 25 and the eschatological promises of Is. 61, offers several points of interest.²⁷ Almost nothing of cols. 1 and 3 has survived. Most of col. 2 has been pieced together. It reads:

> ²[...] And concerning what Scripture says, "In [this] year of jubilee [you shall return, every one of you, to your property" (Lev. 25:13) and what is also written, "And this] ³is the [ma]nner of [the remission:] every creditor shall remit the claim that is held [against a neighbor, not exacting it of a neighbor who is a member of the community, because God's] remission [has been proclaimed" (Deut. 15:2) ⁴[the interpretation] is that it applies [to the L]ast Days and concerns the captives, just as [Isaiah said: "To proclaim the jubilee to the captives" (Is. 61:1)... just] as ⁵[...] and from the inheritance of Melchizedek, f[or... Melchize]dek, who ⁶will

---

²⁵ Adapted from M.G. Abegg, Jr., "Commentaries on Genesis," in Wise, Abegg, and Cook, *The Dead Sea Scrolls*, p. 277.

²⁶ *Sifra* §97 and *Num. Rab.* 14.13 (on Num. 7:84) interpret Zech. 4:14 as referring to Aaron and David.

²⁷ For critical study of the Melchizedek *pesher*, see M. de Jonge and A.S. van der Woude, "11Q Melchizedek and the New Testament," in *NTS* 12, 1965-1966, pp. 301-326; P.J. Kobelski, *Melchizedek and Melchirešaʿ* (Washington, 1981); E. Puech, "Notes sur le Manuscrit de XIQMelkîsédeq," in *RevQ* 12, 1985-1987, pp. 483-513; A. Aschim, "The Genre of 11QMelchizedek," in F.H. Cryer and T.L. Thompson, eds., *Qumran between the Old and New Testament* (Sheffield, 1998), pp. 17-31.

return them to what is rightfully theirs. He will proclaim to them the jubilee, thereby releasing th[em from the debt of a]ll their sins.

[He shall pro]claim this decree ⁷in the fir[s]t [wee]k of the jubilee period that foll[ows nine j]ubilee periods. Then the "D[ay of Atone]ment" shall follow af[ter] the [te]nth [ju]bilee period, ⁸when he shall atone for all the Sons of [Light] and the peopl[e who are pre]destined to Mel[chi]zedek. [...] upo[n the]m [...] For ⁹this is the time decreed for "the year of Melchiz[edek]'s favor" (Is. 61:2, modified) [and] by his might he w[i]ll judge God's holy ones and so establish a righteous ki[n]gdom, as it is written ¹⁰about him in the Songs of David, "A godlike being has taken his place in the council of God; in the midst of the divine beings he holds judgment" (Ps. 82:1). Scripture also s[ays] about him, "Over [it] ¹¹take your seat in the highest heaven; a divine being will judge the peoples" (Ps. 7:7-8). Concerning what scripture s[ays, "How long will y]ou judge unjustly, and sh[ow] partiality to the wick[e]d? [S]el[ah]" (Ps. 82:2), ¹²the interpretation applies to Belial and the spirits predestined to him, becau[se all of them have rebe]lled, turn[ing] from God's precepts [and so becoming utterly wicked.] ¹³Therefore Melchizedek will thoroughly prosecute the veng[ea]nce required by Go[d's] statu[te]s. [Also, he will deliver all the captives from the power of B]elial, and from the power of all [the spirits predestined to him.] ¹⁴Allied with him will be all the ["righteous] divine beings" (Is. 61:3). [The...] is that wh[ich...al]l the divine beings.

This vi[sitation] ¹⁵is the Day of [Salvation] that He has decreed [through Isai]ah the prophet [concerning all the captives,] inasmuch as Scripture sa[ys, "How] beautiful ¹⁶upon the mountains are the fee[t of] the messeng[er] who [an]nounces peace, who brings [good] news, [who announces salvat]ion, who [sa]ys to Zion, 'Your [di]vine being [reigns]'" (Is. 52:7). ¹⁷This Scripture's interpretation: "the mounta[ins" are the] prophet[s,] they w[ho were sent to proclaim God's truth and to] proph[esy] to all I[srael.] ¹⁸"The messenger" is the [An]ointed of the spir[it,] of whom Dan[iel] spoke, ["After the sixty-two weeks, an Anointed one shall be cut off" (Dan. 9:26). The "messenger who brings" ¹⁹good news, who announ[ces salvation"] is the one of whom it is wri[tt]en, ["to proclaim the year of the Lord's favor, the day of vengeance of our God;] ²⁰[to comfo[rt all who mourn" (Is. 61:2). This Scripture's interpretation:] he is to inst[r]uct them about all the periods of history for eter[nity... and in the statutes of] ²¹[the] truth. [...] ²²[...dominion] that passes from Belial and ret[urns to the Sons of Light...] ²³[...] by the judgment of God, just as it is written concerning him, ["who says to Zi]on 'Your divine being reigns.'" ["Zi]on" is ²⁴[the congregation of all the sons of righteousness, who] uphold the covenant and turn from walking [in the way] of the people. "Your di[vi]ne being" is ²⁵[Melchizedek, who will del]iv[er them from the po]wer of Belial.²⁸

---

²⁸ Adapted by M.O. Wise, "The Coming of Melchizedek," in Wise, Abegg, and Cook, *The Dead Sea Scrolls*, pp. 456-457.

The eschatological scenario envisioned in 11QMelchizedek is consistent in general terms with that we have observed in the other *pesharim*. But the mysterious figure Melchizedek does not easily fit into the drama of the last days. He seems to play the role of the prophetic herald, who announces the jubilee and releases Israel "from the debt of all their sins" (lines 5-6). In due course he will "atone for all the Sons of Light and the people who are predestined" to him (line 8). This will take place in fulfillment of Is. 61:2, but instead of "the year of the Lord's favor," it is "the year of Melchizedek's favor." What is implied by this substitution for the Divine Name? Is Melchizedek the Lord himself? or his representative? Applying Pss. 82:1 and 7:7-8 to him (in lines 10-11) suggests that Melchizedek was viewed as a divine being (as also in line 25), perhaps as the Qumran Community's own protective archangel. This being will exact vengeance in the Community's behalf and will deliver it from the power of Belial.

Biblical Interpretation in Other Scrolls

Isolated *pesharim* are found throughout other Scrolls in order to buttress or illustrate points that are being made. Important examples occur in the Damascus Document, the Serek Scrolls, and the Halakhic Letter, which were among the most authoritative of the sectarian writings.

Damascus Document

The Damascus Document was discovered at the end of the nineteenth century in a genizah of the old synagogue in Cairo (hence its abbreviation CD—"Cairo Damascus" Document).[29] Several fragments have been found in caves 4, 5, and 6. This text is punctuated throughout with Scripture. In col. 6, Num. 21:18 ("the well the princes dug, the nobility of the people dug it with a rod") is quoted and then *pesher*ed:

---

[29] For critical study of the Damascus Document, see C. Rabin, *The Zadokite Documents* (rev. ed., Oxford, 1958); P.R. Davies, *The Damascus Covenant: An Interpretation of the "Damascus Document"* (Sheffield, 1982); C. Hempel, *The Laws of the Damascus Document: Sources, Traditions, and Redaction* (Leiden, 1998).

The well is the Law, and its "diggers" are ⁵the captives of Israel who went out the land of Judah and dwelt in the land of Damascus...⁶...and the "rod" is the Interpreter of the Law... ⁸... and the "nobility of the people" are ⁹those who come to "dig the well" by following rules that the Rod made ¹⁰to live by during the whole era of wickedness, and without these rules they shall obtain nothing until the appearance of ¹¹one who teaches righteousness in the Last Days.[30]

One passage of Scripture after another is *pesher*ed to explain the community's experience and expectations of what soon will come to pass. The imagery of Num. 24:17 is explained: the "star" is the Interpreter of the Law who comes to Damascus, while the "staff" is the Prince of all the congregation (7:18-21). The retreat to Damascus, it would seem, has resulted in the establishment of the New Covenant, which the "Men of Mockery" have rejected and defamed (20:11-12). However, in the end those who heed the Teacher of Righteousness will rejoice "and will rule over all the inhabitants of the earth. Then God will make atonement for them and they will experience his deliverance because they have trusted in his holy Name" (20:27-34).

Rule of the Community

Whereas the history of the community is explained in terms of *pesher*ed Scripture in the Damascus Document, the rules of the Community are laid out in the Rule Scrolls. Among the best preserved of these scrolls is 1QS.[31] In 1QS 8:12-16 we learn that the community of the covenant is to separate from perverse men, "to go into the wilderness, there to prepare the way of truth, as it is written, 'In the wilderness prepare the way of the Lord, make straight in the desert a highway for our God'" (Is. 40:3). In col. 9 the doctrine of the community is summarized simply as "the Way" (lines 18-20), which finds a parallel in early Christianity (cf., Acts 9:2; 19:9, 23; 24:14, 22). Recent criticism of the textual history of the Rule Scrolls has ob-

---

[30] Adapted from E.M. Cook, "The Damascus Document," in Wise, Abegg, and Cook, *The Dead Sea Scrolls*, p. 56.

[31] For critical study of the Rule Scrolls, see W.H. Brownlee, *Dead Sea Manual of Discipline: Translation and Notes* (New Haven, 1951); P. Wernberg-Møller, *The Manual of Discipline: Translated and Annotated with an Introduction* (Leiden, 1957); A.R.C. Leaney, *The Rule of Qumran and Its Meaning* (London, 1966); M. Weinfeld, *The Organizational Pattern and Penal Code of the Qumran Sect* (Göttingen, 1986); S. Metso, *The Textual Development of the Qumran Community Rule* (Leiden, 1997).

served that in the later editions, scriptural citations are added to provide a firmer rationale for the community's strict rules. It has been suggested that we may have a parallel in Matthew's tendency to supplement Mark with citations of Scripture.[32]

Halakhic Letter

The Halakhic Letter, or 4QMMT, is apparently addressed to a somewhat sympathetic group that stands outside of the Qumran community.[33] The letter attempts to persuade them of the correctness of the community's views, especially with regard to issues of mixing the pure with the impure. Two dozen halakhic rulings are laid down. These rulings are then followed by a series of warnings and exhortations, which like the halakhot, are rooted in Scripture. The following passage gives us an important glimpse into the community's self-understanding:

> [But you know that]we have separated from the council of the con[gregation (or majority of the peo[ple) and from all their uncleanness] ⁸[and]from being party to or going along wi[th them] in these matters. And you k[now that no] ⁹unfaithfulness, deception, or evil are found in our hands, for we have given [some thought (?)] to [these issues.]
>
> [Indeed,] ¹⁰we [have written] to you so that you might understand the book of Moses, the book[s of the Pr]ophets, and Davi[d...] ¹¹[...all] the generations. In the book of Moses it is written [...] not ¹²[to] you and days of old [...]. It is also written that you[will turn] from the pa[t]h and evil will befall you (Deut. 31:29). And it is writ[ten] ¹³that when ¹⁴[al]l these thing[s happ]en to you in the Latter Days, the blessing ¹⁵[and] the curse, [that you call them]to m[ind] and return to Him with all your heart ¹⁶and with [al]l [your] soul (Deut. 30:1-2) [...] at the end of [the age,] then [you] shall l[ive...][34]

The final exhortation, with which the letter concludes, contains an important allusion to Ps. 106:31 and may clarify the background of Paul's comments about works of the Law and being reckoned as righteous:

---

[32] S. Metso, "The Use of Old Testament Quotations in the Qumran Community Rule," in F.H. Cryer and T.L. Thompson, eds., *Qumran between the Old and New Testament* (Sheffield, 1998), pp. 217-231.

[33] For text and critical study, see E. Qimron and J. Strugnell, eds., *Qumran Cave 4.V: Miqsat Ma'ase Ha-Torah* (Oxford, 1994).

[34] Adapted from M.G. Abegg, Jr., "A Sectarian Manifesto," in Wise, Abegg, and Cook, *The Dead Sea Scrolls*, pp. 363-364.

Now, we have written to you ²⁷some of the works of the Law, those which we determined would be beneficial for you and your people, because we have seen [that] ²⁸you possess insight and knowledge of the Law. Understand all these things and beseech Him to set ²⁹your counsel straight and so keep you away from evil thoughts and the counsel of Belial. ³⁰The you shall rejoice at the end time when you find the essence of our words to be true. ³¹And it will be reckoned to you as righteousness, in that you have done what is right and good before Him, to your own benefit ³²and to that of Israel. (reconstruction C)

The words, "works of the Law" (*miqṣat maʿase ha-torah*) may very well lie behind Paul's "works of the Law" (*erga nomou*) in Rom. 3:20, 28; Gal. 2:16 [*tris*]; 3:2, 5, 20. Probability of conceptual overlap is significantly increased with the phrase, "it will be reckoned to you as righteousness," which meaningfully parallels Paul's statement, "it was reckoned to him as righteousness" (Gal. 3:6). Of course, Paul is paraphrasing Gen. 15:6. The author of the Halakhic Letter is probably alluding to the similar language found in Ps. 106:31: "that has been reckoned to him as righteousness." The author of Ps. 106 has referred to Phineas (cf., Num. 25:1-8), whose zeal for the Lord averted divine wrath. Because of his righteous *deeds*, it was reckoned to him as righteousness. But Paul, appealing to Abraham's example, says that because of his *faith*, it was reckoned to him as righteousness. In recent studies, Martin Abegg has argued convincingly that 4QMMT and Paul are disputing two sides of a theological issue and hold to opposing views.[35] Recall above the interpretation of Hab. 2:4b in 1QpHab 8:1-3, and compare to Paul's understanding of the passage in Rom. 1:17 and Gal. 3:11.

Conclusion

It is difficult to exaggerate the importance of Scripture and its interpretation for the Qumran community. The community finds within Scripture its self-understanding, its reason for being, that is, for separating from the rest of Israel, which has been misled and deceived by

---

[35] M.J. Abegg, Jr., "Paul, Works of the Law, and the MMT," in *BARev* 20.6, 1994, pp. 52-55, 82; idem, "4QMMT C 27, p. 31, and "'Works of Righteousness,'" in *DSD* 6, 1999, pp. 139-147. See also the similar view advanced in J.D.G. Dunn, "4QMMT and Galatians," in *NTS* 43, 1997, pp. 147-153. Neither Abegg nor Dunn thinks Paul had direct contact with 4QMMT.

priests and politicians who lie and violently oppress the Teacher of Righteousness and his followers. Scripture has foretold all of these recent, disturbing events. It also foretells further struggle and eventual triumph. The community therefore takes great comfort from Scripture, knowing that its cause is not futile and will not fail. They know that in the last days God will raise up his Messiah of righteousness, the Branch of David, the Prince of the congregation. He will slay the Roman emperor and will rule the remnant of Israel with truth and justice. The righteous High Priest will take his rightful place, and the messiah will respect his authority. A time of unprecedented blessing will be ushered in. What makes these associations and predictions possible is *pesher* exegesis, and what makes *pesher* exegesis possible is divine illumination.

Scripture also clarifies every point of doctrine (the Halakhic Letter and the Temple Scrolls are very instructive in this regard). Exegesis in this context, which has only been touched upon briefly in this essay, is not as daring or charismatic. This exegesis is more akin to Rabbinic midrash, at least in its earlier and simpler forms. It is just as important as *pesher* exegesis, if less dramatic.

It is therefore no exaggeration to say that biblical interpretation was central to Qumran's community identity, supplying answers to who, what, why, where, when, and how. It is therefore not surprising that such an abundance of manuscripts was discovered near the community's Dead Sea wilderness retreat: some two hundred and twenty Bible scrolls and another six hundred and fifty scrolls, most of which interpret Scripture or at least allude to and presuppose it. Biblical language, imagery, and motifs have shaped the world view(s) found in these scrolls. But the interpretation of Scripture at Qumran was also conditioned by experience and recent historical events. It is through this confluence of Scripture and experience that the distinctiveness of Qumran biblical interpretation emerged.

13. HISTORY AND ESCHATOLOGY AT QUMRAN: MESSIAH

Todd S. Beall
Capital Bible Seminary

Any discussion of history and eschatology at Qumran must be approached with a healthy dose of uncertainty. For one thing, to understand how the group at Qumran looked at history, it would surely be advantageous to have a clear view of the origin and history of the group itself. Yet, even after half a century of Qumran studies, there is still no consensus on this point. Especially as we are concerned with Qumran theology vis à vis other Judaisms, knowing the precise reasons for the group's separation from more established Jewish groups would aid immeasurably in our comparison. But despite numerous attempts, such precision has proved elusive. The Scrolls themselves contain a number of hints and clues but not a clear blueprint. Second, while approximate dates for the Scrolls may be obtained from paleography and other means, firm dates of composition for each of the Scrolls is lacking. In addition, some documents undoubtedly had a complex history of development, further complicating efforts to put the data in some sort of chronological framework.[1] And, finally, it is not entirely certain which of the Scrolls found at Qumran were actually written by the community members and which were brought into the community from other sources (for example, it is doubtful that the previously known pseudepigraphical texts of Jubilees or Enoch were written by the group, though both were found there in abundance).[2]

While we can not be certain of every detail, a relatively clear outline of the group's approach to history and eschatology may be

---

[1] For only one example of the complexity of this problem, see the discussion of the development of the Rule of the Community (1QS, 4QS$^{a\text{-}j}$, and 5QS) in S. Metso, *The Textual Development of the Qumran Community Rule* (Leiden, 1997).

[2] Similarly, a number of scholars believe that some Aramaic texts were not written by the group. See E. Puech, "Messianism, Resurrection, and Eschatology at Qumran and in the New Testament," in E. Ulrich and J. VanderKam, eds., *The Community of the Renewed Covenant* (Notre Dame, 1994) 236; also in the same volume, D. Dimant, "Apocalyptic Texts at Qumran," p. 187.

constructed from the documents of Qumran. Our brief discussion will begin with an overview of the group's view of God and the periods of history, their perception of themselves as the true Israel who could interpret the Scriptures, and their beliefs about the Teacher of Righteousness and his enemies. Then we will consider their understanding of the end of days, their messianic hopes, and their view of the afterlife.

Periods of History

The primary starting point for reflection on the Qumran community's view of history and eschatology is to understand its view about God and his workings in the world. In brief, God is sovereign and has determined the events of history from beginning to end. This teaching is stated clearly in the Rule of the Community: "From the God of knowledge stems all there is and all there shall be. Before they existed he made all their plans and when they came into being they will execute all their works in compliance with his instructions, according to his glorious design without altering anything" (1QS 3:15-16).[3] The same thought is echoed by the writer of the Thanksgiving Hymns (1QH 9:16-20):

> You have divided their tasks in all their generations [17]and the regulation at predetermined times to ru[le] generation after generation just like the visitation of this punishment [18]with all its agonies. [] you divide it out among all their descendants according to the number of their eternal generations [19]for all the endless years. [] And in the wisdom of your knowledge you have determined their course before they came to exist. [20]And with [your approval] everything happens, and without you nothing occurs.

Parallel with this idea is the belief that God divided history into fixed periods. This concept is seen in the opening lines of the fragmentary text 4Q180 (4QagesCreat 4Q180 1 i 1-5):

> Interpretation concerning the ages which God has made: An age to achieve [all that there is] [2]and all that will be. Before creating them he determined their operations [according to the precise sequence of the

---

[3] Except where otherwise noted, translations of the Dead Sea Scrolls in this chapter are from F. García Martínez, *The Dead Sea Scrolls Translated* (Leiden, 1994), with occasional slight modifications.

ages,] ³one age after another age. And this is engraved on the [heavenly] tablets [for the sons of men,] ⁴[for] /all/ the ages of their dominion. This is the sequence of the so[ns of Noah, from Shem to Abraham,] ⁵[unt]il he sired Isaac; the ten ge[nerations].

Similarly, the Damascus Document speaks of "the exact interpretation of their ages about the blindness of Israel in all these matters, behold, it is defined in the book 'of the divisions of the periods according to their jubilees and their weeks'" (CD 16:2-4). It is possible that the work referenced is Jubilees. In any event, the concept is reinforced that God divided all of history into set periods.

Certainly this belief is not new within Judaism. In Dan. 9:24, the angel Gabriel speaks of a period of seventy sevens or four hundred and ninety years that have been determined for Israel and Jerusalem "to finish transgression, to put an end to sin, to atone for wickedness, to bring in everlasting righteousness, to seal up vision and prophecy and to anoint the most holy." This text probably forms the basis of the ten jubilees (i.e., four hundred and ninety years) enumerated in 11QMelchizedek (where Daniel is specifically mentioned in 11QMelch 2:18).[4]

Sons of Light

But the Qumran community not only believed that God ordered the periods of history; they also were convinced that they were a part of that history in a vital, personal way. In their thinking, the world was divided into two groups, the righteous and the wicked, and they were the righteous, true Israel who would stand fast for God to the end. The famous section on the two spirits in the Rule of the Community demonstrates the community's division of mankind into good and evil (1QS 3:17-4:1; 4:23-26):

> He created man to rule ¹⁸the world and placed within him two spirits so that he would walk with them until the moment of his visitation: they are the spirits of truth and of deceit. ²⁰In the hand of the Prince of Lights is dominion over all the sons of justice; they walk on paths of light. And in the hand of the Angel ²¹of Darkness is total dominion over the sons of deceit; they walk on paths of darkness. Due to the Angel of Darkness

---

[4] See the discussion of this text in A. Steudel, "'*aharit hayyamim* in the Texts from Qumran," in *RevQ* 16, 1993, pp. 233-234.

> [22]all the sons of justice stray, and all their sins, their iniquities, their failings and their mutinous deeds are under his dominion [23]in compliance with the mysteries of God, until his moment; and all their punishments and their periods of grief are caused by the dominion of his enmity; [24]and all the spirits of their lot cause the sons of light to fall. However, the God of Israel and the angel of his truth assist all [25]the sons of light. He created the spirits of light and of darkness and on them established all his deeds [26][on their p]aths all his labors ‹and on their paths [all] his [labors.]›. God loved one of them for all [4:1]eternal ages and in all his deeds he takes pleasure for ever; of the other one he detests his advice and hates all his paths forever.... [4:23]Until now the spirits of truth and of injustice feud in the heart of man [24]and they walk in wisdom or in folly. In agreement with man's birthright in justice and in truth, so he abhors injustice; and according to his share in the lot of injustice he acts irreverently in it and so [25]abhors the truth. For God has sorted them into equal parts until the appointed end and the new creation. He knows the result of his deeds for all times [26][everlas]ting and has given them as a legacy to the sons of men so that they know good [and evil], so they decide the lot of every living being in compliance with the spirit there is in him [at the time of] the visitation.

Similarly, the battle described in the War Scroll is between the "sons of light" and the "sons of darkness" (1QM 1:1)—in fact the term "sons of light" is a common designation for the group (used twenty-seven times in the Scrolls).

As the sons of light, the Qumran community believed that God gave them a unique ability to understand the truth about history and eschatology. According to the Rule of the Community, the "man of understanding" was to "inform and teach all the sons of light about the history of all the sons of man, concerning all the ranks of their spirits, in accordance with their signs, concerning their deeds and their generations, and concerning the visitation of their punishment and the moment of their reward" (1QS 3:13-15). This understanding came from a proper interpretation of Scripture.

Inspired Interpretation

It is important to reaffirm that the Qumranians' view of history and eschatology is continually supported by appeals to Scripture. They believed that they themselves were to play an important role in the fulfillment of scriptural prophecies and in particular that they were living in the times right before the end of the age. So they had no difficulty interpreting some passages as referring to their own recent and current history, while at the same time interpreting other portions of the same text eschatologically.

This dual interpretation can be seen in the Nahum Pesher, which contains some of the clearest references to historical personages that we have in any of the Scrolls. In commenting on Nah. 2:12 (a prophecy against Nineveh), the pesher states (4QpNah 3-4 i 2-3):

> Its interpretation concerns Deme]trius, king of Yavan (i.e., Greece), who wanted to enter Jerusalem on the advice of the those looking for easy interpretations, ³[but he did not go in because God did not deliver Jerusalem] into the hand of the kings of Yavan from Antiochus up to the appearance of the chiefs of the Kittim. But later, it will be trampled.

Similarly, a few lines later, the pesher explains that Nah. 2:13 "concerns the Angry Lion [who filled his den with a mass of corpses, carrying out rev]enge against those looking for easy interpretations, who hanged living men [from the tree, committing an atrocity which had not been committed] in Israel since ancient times, for it is horrible for the one hanged alive from the tree" (4QpNah 3-4 i 6-8).

Most scholars believe that Demetrius is Demetrius III Eukerus (95-88 B.C.E.); Antiochus is Antiochus IV Epiphanes (175-164 B.C.E.); "those looking for easy interpretations" are the Pharisees; the Angry Lion is Alexander Jannaeus (103-76 B.C.E.); and the Kittim are the Romans.[5] The scroll relates how the Pharisees were opposed to Alexander Jannaeus and sought help from the Seleucid ruler Demetrius, who was unable to take Jerusalem. When Alexander Jannaeus regained his authority, he had eight hundred Pharisees crucified. All of these recent events the writer of the scroll saw in what would appear to be a fairly straightforward prophecy against Nineveh.

But mixed in with this interpretation of recent history is an eschatological understanding of the same text. The opening verses of Nah. 1 (which speak of God's power over nature) are seen as describing the fate of the Kittim: "He roars against the sea and dries it up. Its interpretation: the sea are all the Kit[tim], since [ ] to carry out judgment against them and to eliminate them from the face of [the earth. And dries up all the rivers.] [Its interpretation concerns the Kittim] with [all their chi]efs, since his rule will end" (4QpNah 1-2 i 3-5). Similarly, in commenting on Nah. 3, the pesher later describes

---

[5] See M. Horgan, *Pesharim: Qumran Interpretations of Biblical Books* (Washington, 1979), pp. 161-162; and S. Berrin, "Pesher Nahum," in L. Schiffman and J. VanderKam, eds., *Encyclopedia of the Dead Sea Scrolls* (New York, 2000), vol. 2, pp. 653-655.

the fate both of those who listen to the Pharisees ("Cities and clans will perish through his advice, nobles and le[aders] will fall [due to the fero]city of their tongues" [4QpNah 3-4 ii 9-10]) and of the Pharisees themselves ("Its interpretation concerns those looking for easy interpretations, whose council will die and whose society will be disbanded" [4QpNah 3-4 iii 6-7]). The scroll writer hoped that both the Romans and the Pharisees would be defeated and found in Nahum's prophecy evidence of these future fates.

The Teacher of Righteousness and the End of Days

The Habakkuk Pesher contains the same mix of historical and eschatological interpretation. Here the Teacher of Righteousness, a key figure in the early history of the Qumran group, is mentioned frequently,[6] as well as his chief opponent, the Wicked Priest. While many scholars believe the Wicked Priest is the high priest Jonathan Maccabee (ruling from 160-143 B.C.E.) or his brother Simon (142-134 B.C.E.), the identification is not certain.[7]

The pesher provides a number of details about the Teacher of Righteousness. He was an inspired interpreter of Scripture, "to whom God has disclosed all the mysteries of the words of his servants, the prophets" (1QpHab 7:4-5). Those who opposed the Teacher had "rejected the Law of God" and were "traitors," since "they do not [believe in the words of the] Teacher of Righteousness from the mouth of God" (1QpHab 1:11; 2:1-3). The Teacher had various enemies, including the Man of Lies, the House of Absalom, who kept silent when the Man of Lies attacked the Teacher (1QpHab 5:9-11), and the Wicked Priest, who relentlessly persecuted the Teacher, even to exile (1QpHab 9:9-11; 11:4-8).

The Teacher was himself a priest (1QpHab 2:7-8), as is also stated

---

[6] Surprisingly the Teacher of Righteousness is only mentioned in the Damascus Document, Pesher Habakkuk, Pesher Psalms^a (4Q171), Pesher Psalms^b (4Q173), and Pesher Micah (1Q14).

[7] A. Dupont-Sommer believes that Hyrcanus II was the Wicked Priest (76-40 B.C.E.), but the chronology seems too late for his rivalry with the Teacher (*The Essene Writings from Qumran* [Gloucester, 1973], p. 263, n. 5). Other scholars believe that there were a multiplicity of Wicked Priests (so F. García Martínez, *The Dead Sea Scrolls Translated*, pp. lv-lvi). See further, T. Lim, "Wicked Priest," in Schiffman and VanderKam, op. cit., vol. 2, pp. 973-976.

in Pesher Psalms^a.[8] But the Teacher was no ordinary priest. He was a priest who could foretell the events of the last days, as the Habakkuk Pesher makes clear (1QpHab 2:5-10):

> The interpretation of the word [concerns the trai]tors in the ⁶last days. They shall be violators of [the coven]ant who will not believe ⁷when they hear all that is going [to happen to] the final generation, from the mouth of the ⁸Priest whom God has placed wi[thin the Community,] to foretell the fulfillment of all ⁹the words of his servants, the prophets, [by] means of whom God has declared ¹⁰all that is going to happen to his people [Israel].

This passage indicates that the Teacher lived in the beginning of the period of the "last days," since he is depicted as contemporaneous with the traitors; and yet, he prophesied of what was going to happen to the "final generation."

Much of the Habakkuk Pesher deals with the Kittim (the Scroll's interpretation of the Chaldeans of Habakkuk), i.e., the Romans,[9] who were raised up by God to judge the false leaders of Israel. But while the Kittim were clearly on the scene at the time the pesher was written (probably ca. 50 B.C.E.[10]), they will also take part of the events of the last days. 1QpHab 9:4-7 speaks of "...the last priests of Jerusalem, who will accumulate riches and loot from plundering the peoples. However, in the last days their riches and their loot will fall into the hands of the army of the Kittim." The War Scroll details a forty-year struggle between the "sons of light" and the "sons of darkness" and speaks vividly of the defeat of the Kittim: "And on the day on which the Kittim fall, there will be a battle, and savage destruction before the God of Israel, for this will be the day determined by him since ancient times for the war of extermination against the sons of darkness" (1QM 1:9-10). The Kittim are also mentioned in 4Q285

---

[8] "Its interpretation concerns the Priest, the Teacher of [Righteousness, whom] God chose to stand [in front of him, for] he installed him to found the congregation [of his chosen ones] for him, [and stra]ightened out his path, in truth" (4QpPs^a 1-10 iii 15-17).

[9] The view that the Kittim are the Romans is substantiated by 1QpHab 6:4-5, which indicates that the Kittim "offer sacrifices to their standards and their weapons are the object of their worship," a practice true of the Roman army (see Josephus, *Jewish War* 6.6.1 §316).

[10] So A. Steudel, op. cit., p. 231; H. Stegemann, *The Library of Qumran* (Grand Rapids, 1998), p. 131; and J. Collins, "Eschatology," in Schiffman and VanderKam, op. cit., vol. 1, p. 258.

5 i 4, where the leader of the Kittim will be killed by the Prince of the Congregation.

So, in brief, the Scrolls speak of the historical struggles of the group, especially the Teacher of Righteousness' struggle with some of the religious leaders of Israel, who rejected his inspired teachings and persecuted him and his followers. These false teachers (the "last priests of Jerusalem") would themselves fall prey to the Romans, but, in the end, after a prolonged struggle, the "sons of light" would be victorious over the Romans and all their enemies, and true Israel would be restored.

Calculation of the End of Days

The scrolls use the term *'aḥarit hayyamim* ("the last days" or "the end of days") thirty-three times, mainly in the pesharim and in midrashic texts such as the Melchizedek Scroll, the Florilegium (4Q174), and the Catena (4Q177).[11] Two primary emphases are indicated by the term. First, it refers to a time of testing and refining for the faithful. This may be seen in 4QFlorilegium, which interprets Ps. 2:1 ("why do the nations become agitated?") as a time of trial and purification for "the elect of Israel in the last days" (4QFlor 1-3 i 19; 1-3 ii 1-4). 4QCatena[a] contains a similar statement: "The interpretation of the word concerns the purification of the heart of the men of [the Community] in the last days [] to test them and refine them" (4QCatena[a] 2:10-11).[12]

Second, "the end of days" refers to the time of the inauguration of the salvation of Israel.[13] In commenting on 2 Sam. 7:12-14, 4QFlorilegium states that it refers to "'the branch of David,' who will arise with the Interpreter of the law who [will rise up] in Zi[on in] the last days, as it is written: 'I will raise up the hut of David which has

---

[11] For a detailed study of *'aḥarit hayyamim*, see Steudel, op. cit., pp. 225-246.

[12] Some scholars believe that 4QFlorilegium and 4QCatena[a] are actually part of the same document, called Eschatological Midrash (see A. Steudel, *Der Midrash zur Eschatologie aus der Qumrangemeinde (4QMidrEschat[a,b])* [Leiden, 1994]), but this is uncertain.

[13] Here I differ slightly from Steudel, who concludes that *'aḥarit hayyamim* indicates "the last period of time directly before the time of salvation" ("*'aḥarit hayyamim* in the Texts from Qumran," p. 231); rather, as J. Collins, *Apocalypticism in the Dead Sea Scrolls* (London, 1997), p. 57, states, "it is a time of at least incipient salvation."

fallen,' This (refers to) 'the hut of David which has fallen', who will arise to save Israel" (4QFlor 1-3 i 11-13). Similarly, the Rule of the Congregation, set in the "end of days" (1QSa 1:1), describes a banquet in which the messiah of Israel is present (1QSa 2:17-22). The end of days, then, is a time when the messiah(s) will come to save Israel.

As already noted, the Scrolls depict the Teacher and the current sufferings of the community as part of the end of days, especially in the first sense of testing and refining. But the second aspect, that of the return of the messiah(s) and the beginning of the salvation of Israel, was still in the future. As L. Schiffman well states, "the sect lived on the verge of the End of Days, with one foot, as it were, in the present age and one foot in the future."[14] But when would this second aspect of the end of days commence? Since God ordered the periods of history, the writers of the Scrolls believed that they could calculate the time of the end through their inspired interpretation of Scripture. Apparently the scriptures used were Ezek. 4:4-6 and Dan. 9:24-27. In the former, the prophet is commanded to lie on his left side

> ...and place the punishment of the house of Israel upon it; you shall bear their punishment for the number of the days that you lie there. For I assign to you a number of days, three hundred ninety days, equal to the number of the years of their punishment; and so you shall bear the punishment of the house of Israel. When you have completed these, you shall lie down a second time, but on your right side, and bear the punishment of the house of Judah; forty days I assign you, one day for each year.

The beginning of the Damascus Document (CD 1:5-11) mentions the three hundred and ninety-year period of Ezekiel:

> ...And at the moment of wrath, three hundred and ⁶ninety years after having delivered them up into the hands of Nebuchadnezzar, king of Babylon, ⁷he visited them and caused to sprout from Israel and from Aaron a shoot of the planting, in order to possess ⁸his land and to become fat with the good things of his soil. And they realized their sin and knew that ⁹they were guilty men; but they were like blind persons and like those who grope for the path ¹⁰over twenty years. And God appraised their deeds, because they sought him with a perfect heart ¹¹and raised up for them a Teacher of Righteousness, in order to direct them in the path of his heart.

---

[14] L. Schiffman, *Reclaiming the Dead Sea Scrolls* (Philadelphia, 1994), p. 136.

Similarly, the end of the Damascus Document (CD 20:13-19) apparently refers to the forty-year period of Ezekiel:

> ...And from the day ¹⁴of the gathering in of the unique teacher, until the destruction of all the men of war who turned back ¹⁵with the man of lies, there shall be about forty years. *Blank* And in this age the wrath ¹⁶of God will be kindled against Israel, as he says: 'There shall be no king, no prince, no judge, no-one [who] ¹⁷reproaches in justice.' But the converts from the sin of [Ja]cob, those keeping the covenant of God, shall then speak, each ¹⁸to his fellow, each one to make his brother holy, so that their steps become steady in the path of God, and God pays attention to 19their words."

So the Damascus Document speaks of a three hundred and ninety-year period following the Babylonian captivity, then twenty years of groping, then the Teacher of Righteousness, and finally, forty years after the Teacher's death ("gathering in") until the final destruction of the wicked. If the ministry of the Teacher of Righteousness was viewed as a generation (another forty years), then the period from the Babylonian Captivity to the end of days would be equivalent to the four hundred and ninety years of the prophecy of Dan. 9:24.[15] Assuming a date of 586 B.C.E. for the fall of Jerusalem, subtracting three hundred and ninety years from that would yield a date of ca. 196 B.C.E. for the beginnings of the group, with the Teacher emerging twenty years later, around 176 B.C.E. The Teacher's death would have been around forty years later (ca. 136 B.C.E.), and forty years after his death would put the time of the end at 96 B.C.E.

Modifications to this chronology have been proposed. A. Laato suggests that some ancient Jewish histographers, such as Demetrius, calculated a chronology of the intertestamental period twenty-six years shorter than the actual figure. If the writer of the Damascus Document was following this chronology, it would place the beginning of the group's wanderings ca. 170 B.C.E. and the Teacher's beginning ca. 150 B.C.E.[16] If his death was around forty years later, the final forty years would make the time of the end ca. 70 B.C.E.[17]

---

[15] So J. Collins, *Apocalypticism in the Dead Sea Scrolls*, pp. 55-56. Cf., S. Talmon, "Waiting for the Messiah at Qumran," in J. Neusner, W. Green, and E. Frerichs, eds., *Judaisms and Their Messiahs at the Turn of the Christian Era* (Cambridge, 1987), pp. 117-119.

[16] A. Laato, "The Chronology in the *Damascus Document* of Qumran," in *RevQ* 15, 1992, pp. 605-607.

[17] So H. Stegemann, *The Library of Qumran*, pp. 123-124.

Others have come up with similar conclusions, suggesting that the Damascus Document author took his chronology from 2 Bar. 1:1, which dates the siege of Jerusalem to the twenty-fifth year of Jehoiachin (i.e., 572 B.C.E.) instead of 597 B.C.E., and the final siege ten years later, in 562 B.C.E. That would place the foundation of the group in 172 B.C.E., the Teacher's emergence in 152 B.C.E., and the time of the end in 72 B.C.E.[18]

A Delay in the Time of the End

We can never be certain that the Qumranians were following such exact calculations, though the suggestions are intriguing. Given their view of history as predetermined by God's plan, it would be surprising if they had not attempted to work out the time frame with some precision.

Assuming for the moment that the above calculations are roughly correct, what happened when the time of the end did not occur as the community had anticipated? As Talmon states, "they did not live to see their hopes materialize and thus were suspended in limbo between the real and the visionary stage of history. They present to us a prime example of stumped millenarianism."[19] Once again we may turn to the Habakkuk Pesher for a clear textual indication of a delay in the group's expectations for the time of the end (1QpHab 7:1-14; emphasis mine):

> And God told Habakkuk to write what was going to happen ²to the last generation, but he did not let him know the end of the age. ³*Blank* And as for what he says: 'So that the one who reads it /may run/.' ⁴Its interpretation concerns the Teacher of Righteousness, to whom God has disclosed ⁵all the mysteries of the words of his servants, the prophets. For the vision has ⁶an appointed time, it will have an end and not fail. *Blank* ⁷Its interpretation: *the final age will be extended and go beyond all that* ⁸*the prophets say, because the mysteries of God are wonderful.* ⁹Though it might delay, wait for it; it definitely has to come and will not ¹⁰delay. *Blank* Its interpretation concerns the men of truth, ¹¹those who observe the Law, whose hands will not desert the service ¹²of truth *when the final age is extended beyond them, because* ¹³*all the ages of God will come at the right time, as he established* ¹⁴*for them in the mysteries of his prudence.*

---

[18] So E. Puech, *La Croyance des Esséniens en la vie future: immortalité, résurrection, vie éternelle* (Paris, 1993), p. 506; Steudel, op. cit., pp. 237-238.
[19] S. Talmon, op cit., p. 115.

This section shows that by the time the Habakkuk Pesher was written (ca. 50 B.C.E.), the expected time of the "end of the age" had been delayed by at least twenty years. Once again, the writer of the scroll turns to a biblical text to unlock the mystery, in this case Hab. 2:3: "For there is still a vision for the appointed time; it speaks of the end, and does not lie. If it seems to tarry, wait for it; it will surely come, it will not delay."[20] There is thus a frank admission in this pesher that the final age has been "extended" but will come at exactly the right time.

What was the group to do in the meantime? The citation above gives the answer: "men of truth" will "observe the Law" and their hands "will not desert the service of truth" (1QpHab 7:10-12). The Rule of the Community, in commenting on Is. 40:3, says the same thing (1QS 8:13-16):

> ...they are to be segregated from within the dwelling of the men of sin to walk to the desert in order to open there His path. [14]As it is written: 'In the desert, prepare the way of ****, straighten in the steppe a roadway for our God.' [15]This is the study of the law which he commanded through the hand of Moses, in order to act in compliance with all that has been revealed from age to age, 16 and according to what the prophets have revealed through his holy spirit.

As the true Israel, the community was to study and observe the Law until the coming of the messiah(s) and the final restoration of Israel.[21]

In a very real sense, then, there was to be a continuity between the group's current obedience to the Law and their behavior in the end of days. As Schiffman observes, "In the messianic vision of the Dead Sea sect, the approaching End of Days would inaugurate an era of perfection and engender the fulfillment of the rituals and regulations the sect was currently practicing. The resulting eschatological community would reflect the perfection of the present community at Qumran."[22] This may be seen in the Rule of the Congregation (1QSa), which gives ordinances for the messianic community at the end of days that bear a striking resemblance to those given in the Rule of the Community (1QS).[23] Whether this constitutes a true "re-

---

[20] See also Dan. 12:12.
[21] Similar to exhortations in the NT for believers to remain pure before Jesus' second coming (2 Peter 3:10-14).
[22] L. Schiffman, *Reclaiming the Dead Sea Scrolls*, p. 329.
[23] Schiffman, ibid., p. 133, states that 1QSa "provides an eschatological mirror image of *Rule of the Community*."

alized eschatology" at Qumran, as some claim,[24] is debatable; but there is definitely a continuum between present holiness in the community and future purity in restored Israel.

Messianic Hopes

Central to the group's understanding of the end of days was their messianic expectation. At least two and possibly three different messianic figures were expected.[25] The Rule of the Community speaks of three eschatological figures: "They should not depart from any counsel of the law in order to walk in complete stubbornness of their heart, but instead shall be ruled by the first directives which the men of the Community began to be taught until the prophet comes, and the messiahs of Aaron and Israel" (1QS 9:9-11).[26] The Scrolls frequently speak of a royal Davidic messiah (here called the "messiah of Israel"), but occasionally present a priestly messiah ("messiah of Aaron") as well as a possibly messianic eschatological prophet.

Davidic Messiah

The most frequently mentioned messianic figure in the Scrolls is the Davidic messiah. Scriptures such as Gen. 49:10 and Is. 11:1-5 were interpreted messianically by the community. For example, the fifth column of 4Q252 (4QpGen^a) provides a messianic commentary on Gen. 49:10 (4Q252 5:1-5):

---

[24] So J. Collins, "Apocalypticism and Literary Genre in the Dead Sea Scrolls," in P. Flint and J. VanderKam, *The Dead Sea Scrolls after Fifty Years* (Leiden, 1999), vol. 2, p. 426.

[25] M. Abegg, "The Messiah at Qumran: Are We Still Seeing Double? in" *Dead Sea Discoveries* 2, 1995, pp. 143-144, argues that "the dual messiah that we have come to accept as dogma in discussions of the DSS must be tempered," yet even he acknowledges that messianic hopes were not "only or always singular," and that there is at the very least a "dual nature" evident in some texts. He rightly emphasizes that most of the messianic references in the Scrolls are to the Davidic messiah.

[26] It is true that an older copy of the Rule of the Congregation (4QS^e) omits this section, leading some to conclude that it is not original (so M. Wise and J. Tabor, "The Messiah at Qumran," in *BRev* 18, 1992, p. 60; J. Starcky, "Les quatres étapes du messianism à Qumrân," in *RB* 70, 1963, pp. 481-505). However, 4QS^e omits twenty-four lines of text at this point, and it is more likely a copyist's error. See M. Abegg, "Messiah at Qumran," p. 131.

> A sovereign shall [not] be removed from the tribe of Judah. While Israel has the dominion, ²there will [not] lack someone who sits on the throne of David. For "the staff" is the covenant of royalty, ³[the thou]sands of Israel are "the feet." Until the messiah of justice comes, the branch ⁴of David. For to him and to his descendants has been given the covenant of royalty over his people for all everlasting generations, which ⁵he has observed [] the Law with the men of the Community.

Here Jacob's blessing of Judah is seen as a messianic promise, with the notoriously difficult "Shiloh" of Gen. 49:10 being replaced by "the messiah of justice" in the pesher. This messiah will be from the line of David: the designation "branch of David" comes from Jer. 23:5 ("The days are surely coming, says the Lord, when I will raise up for David a righteous Branch, and he shall reign as king and deal wisely, and shall execute justice and righteousness in the land."). While fragmentary, this pesher indicates that the Davidic monarchy will be restored, and the messiah will be concerned with justice and execution of the Law.

Three scrolls interpret Is. 11 messianically. The first of these is Pesher Isaiahᵃ (4Q161), which cites Is. 11:1-5 and then provides the interpretation (4QpIsaᵃ 8-10 iii 18-25):

> [The interpretation of the word concerns the shoot] of David which will sprout [in the final days, since] ¹⁹[with the breath of his lips he will execute] his enemies and God will support him with [the spirit of] courage [] ²⁰[] throne of glory, [holy] crown and hemmed vestments ²¹[] in his hand. He will rule over all the peoples and Magog ²²[] his sword will judge all the peoples. And as for what he says: 'He will not ²³[judge by appearances] or give verdicts on hearsay', its interpretation: ²⁴[] according to what they teach him, he will judge, and upon his mouth ²⁵[] with him will go out one of the priests of renown, holding clothes in his hand.

The Davidic leader is not explicitly called messiah but, given the equation in 4Q252 of the messiah with the "branch of David," undoubtedly the "shoot of David" in this pesher is messianic as well. He has a glorious throne, a crown, and royal garments. His tasks are to rule the peoples (not merely Israel) and to execute judgment against his enemies (presumably including Magog, described in Ezek. 38 and 39). His judgments are just, and he is aided by the instruction of the priests. This is a unique twist to the Davidic messiah, similar to the rules for the king in the Temple Scroll. There the king "will have twelve princes of his people with him and twelve priests and twelve Levites who shall sit next to him for judgment and for the law. He shall not divert his heart from them or do anything in all his councils without relying on them" (11QTemple^a 57:11-15; see also 11QTemple^a 58:18-19, where the king is not to go to war without the High Priest's blessing).[27]

Two other scrolls that use Is. 11:1-5 messianically are the Rule of the Blessings (1QSb) and 4Q285. Both of these texts refer to the messiah as the "Prince of the Congregation." In the Rule of the Blessings, the role of the "Prince of the Congregation" is to establish the kingdom of his people forever, to judge righteously, to trample his enemies, and to renew the covenant. The fact that the messiah is called the "Prince of the Congregation" clearly links him with the community in the end times.

In 4Q285 frag. 5 (the so-called "Pierced Messiah" text), the "bud of David" is equated with the Prince of the Congregation (4Q285 5 i 1-6):

> [as] the Prophet Isaiah [said]: '[The most massive of the] ²[forest] shall be cut [with iron and Lebanon, with its magnificence,] will fall. A shoot will emerge from the stump of Jesse [ ] ³[ ] the bud of David will go into battle with [ ] ⁴[ ] and the Prince of the Congregation will kill him, the bu[d of David] ⁵[ ] and with wounds. And a priest will command [ ] ⁶[ ] the destruction of the Kittim [ ].

This text emphasizes the military prowess of the Davidic messiah, who kills his enemy (presumably the head of the Kittim).[28] Interestingly, the priest also has an important leadership role. Unfortunately, the text is too fragmentary to learn anything more about the priest.

It is possible that 4Q246 2:1-7 (the Aramaic "Son of God" text) also speaks of the Davidic messiah:

> He will be called son of God, and they will call him son of the Most High. Like the sparks ²of a vision, so will their kingdom be; they will rule several years over ³the earth and crush everything; a people will crush another people, and a city another city. ⁴*Blank* Until the people of God arises and makes everyone rest from the sword. ⁵His kingdom will be an eternal kingdom, and all his paths in truth and uprigh[tness]. ⁶The earth (will be) in truth and all will make peace. The sword will cease in the earth, ⁷and all the cities will pay him homage.

---

[27] Compare Deut. 17:18-20, where the king is to write out a copy of the Law and read it every day.

[28] R. Eisenman and M. Wise, *The Dead Sea Scrolls Uncovered* (New York, 1992), pp. 24-29, originally proposed that it was the Prince of the Congregation that was put to death by his enemies, but most scholars have concluded the opposite (see for example, L. Schiffman, *Reclaiming the Dead Sea Scrolls*, p. 346).

The interpretation of this passage, however, is disputed. García Martínez believes that the reference is to a "heavenly messiah," similar to the "Son of Man" of Dan. 7:13.[29] Others believe that the designation is given to an evil ruler.[30]

Multiple Messiahs (Davidic and Priestly)

But the Qumran scrolls do not speak only of a Davidic messiah, who would conquer and rule with justice in the end time. A number of texts mention a priestly messiah (messiah of Aaron) alongside the Davidic. Mention has already been made of 1QS 9:9-11. In addition, the Damascus Document contains four references to the "messiah of Aaron and Israel" (CD 12:23-13:1; 14:19; 19:10-11; and 20:1). While this phrase could refer to only one messiah, it seems odd that one person would be called a messiah of both Aaron and Israel (why not simply, "messiah of Aaron" or "messiah of Israel"?).[31] In these texts, the coming of the messiahs is immediately after a time of great wickedness and distress, and their coming follows the Teacher of Righteousness (thus differentiating clearly between the Teacher and the messiahs). As in 1QSb, the messiahs participate in the life of the community. Little else is said about the work of the messiahs, except for CD 14:18-19: "And this is the exact interpretation of the regulations by which [they shall be ruled] [19][until there arises the messiah] of Aaron and Israel. He shall atone for their sins." Unfortunately the text is fragmentary, but presumably the phrase "he shall atone for their sins" refers to the work of the Aaronic messiah. Another text with a similar phrase is 4Q541 (4QAaronA):

> And he will atone for all the children of his generation, and he will be sent to all the children of [3]his people. His word is like the word of the heavens, and his teaching, according to the will of God. His eternal sun

---

[29] F. García Martínez, "Messianic Hopes in the Qumran Writings," in F. García Martínez and J. Barrera, *The People of the Dead Sea Scrolls* (Leiden, 1995), pp. 173-77. Compare Dan. 7:14, 27 with 4Q246 2:5, 9.

[30] So J. VanderKam, *The Dead Sea Scrolls Today* (Grand Rapids, 1994), p. 179; see also VanderKam, "Messianism in the Scrolls," in E. Ulrich and J. VanderKam, eds., *The Community of the Renewed Covenant* (Notre Dame, 1994), pp. 219- 220. Cf., J. Collins, *Apocalypticism in the Dead Sea Scrolls*, pp. 82-85, who believes that 4Q246 refers to the Davidic messiah.

[31] So Collins, ibid., p. 77; J. VanderKam, "Messianism in the Scrolls," p. 230. Cf., G. Brooke, "The Messiah of Aaron in the *Damascus Document*," in *RevQ* 15, 1992, pp. 215-230.

will shine ⁴and his fire will burn in all the ends of the earth; above the darkness his sun will shine. Then, darkness will vanish ⁵from the earth, and gloom from the globe. (4Q541 9 i 2-5)

If this text refers to the Aaronic messiah, then it emphasizes his role as teacher as well.[32]

An important text that mentions the messiah of Israel along with a priest in the end of days is the Rule of the Congregation (1QSa 2:11-22):

> This is the assembly of famous men, [those summoned to] the gathering of the community council, when [God] begets ¹²the messiah with them. [The] chief [priest] of all the congregation of Israel shall enter, and all ¹³his brothers, the sons] of Aaron, the priests [summoned] to the assembly, the famous men, and they shall sit ¹⁴befo[re him, each one] according to his dignity. After, [the Me]ssiah of Israel shall ent[er] and before him shall sit the chiefs ¹⁵[of the clans of Israel, each] one according to his dignity, according to their [positions] in their camps and in their marches. And all ¹⁶the chiefs of the cl[ans of the congre]gation with the wise [men and the learned] shall sit before them, each one according ¹⁷to his dignity. And [when] they gather at the table of community [or to drink] the new wine, and the table of ¹⁸community is prepared [and] the new wine [is mixed] for drinking, [no-one should stretch out] his hand to the first-fruit of the bread ¹⁹and of the [new wine] before the priest, for [he is the one who bl]esses the first-fruit of bread ²⁰and of the new wine [and stretches out] his hand towards the bread before them. Afterwards, the messiah of Israel shall stretch out his hand ²¹towards the bread. [And afterwards, shall] bless all the congregation of the community, each [one according to] his dignity. And in accordance with this regulation they shall act ²²at each mea[l, when] at least ten m[en are gat]hered.

Given the other texts at Qumran, it seems clear that the priest mentioned here is the priestly messiah, the messiah of Aaron. The most striking thing about this text is the priority of the priestly messiah over the Davidic. He is the head of "all the congregation of Israel;" he enters the assembly first before the other priests and before the messiah of Israel; and he blesses the bread and wine before the messiah of Israel. The superiority of the Aaronic messiah over the Davidic is also evident in the designation "messiah of Aaron and Israel" used in the Damascus Document, but it is even clearer in this text.

---

[32] So J. Collins, *The Scepter and the Star* (New York, 1995), p. 115. Elsewhere he describes the figure as "a 'teacher of righteousness' for the end of days" (Collins, *Apocalypticism in the Dead Sea Scrolls*, p. 86).

Two Qumran texts speak of the Davidic messiah plus an eschatological "Interpreter of the law." The first is CD 7:18-21, which provides a messianic interpretation of the Balaam oracle in Num. 24:17: "And the star is the Interpreter of the law, who will come to Damascus, as is written: 'A star moves out of Jacob, and a scepter arises out of Israel.' The scepter is the prince of the whole congregation, and when he rises he will destroy all the sons of Seth." The second is 4QFlorilegium (4Q174 1-3 i 10-13), in which 2 Sam. 7:12-14 is explained:

> And "yhwh de[clares] to you that he will build you a house. I will raise up your seed after you and establish the throne of his kingdom ¹¹[for ev]er. I will be a father to him and he will be a son to me." This (refers to the) "branch of David," who will arise with the Interpreter of the law who ¹²[will rise up] in Zi[on in] the last days, as it is written: "I will raise up the hut of David which has fallen" (Amos 9:11). This (refers to) "the hut of ¹³David which has fallen," who will arise to save Israel.

In both these texts, the Davidic messiah is clear (the "scepter" and "prince of the congregation" in CD 7 and the "branch of David" in 4QFlorilegium), but who is the "Interpreter of the law" (the "star" of CD 7:18)? Some have identified the Interpreter as the eschatological prophet, since the reference in CD 7:19 to "Damascus" may be an allusion to the prophet Elijah (told in 1 Kgs. 19:15 to come to Damascus to anoint two kings and a prophet).[33] The prophet Elijah was expected in the end time according to Mal. 4:5. It seems more likely, however, in harmony with other Qumran texts, that the Interpreter of the law is the priestly messiah.[34] The Teacher of Righteousness himself is given the title of "Interpreter of the law" in CD 6:7. Similar to the Teacher, the "Interpreter of the law" is both a teacher and a priest (see discussion of 4Q541 above for the priest/teacher).

Messianic Prophet?

Since 1QS 9:9-11 mentions a "prophet" who is to come in the same context as the "messiahs of Aaron and Israel," the Qumran commu-

---

[33] So F. García Martínez, "Messianic Hopes in the Qumran Writings," pp. 183-184.

[34] So M. Knibb, "Eschatology and Messianism in the Dead Sea Scrolls," in Flint and VanderKam, op. cit., vol. 2, pp. 388-389; J. Collins, *Apocalypticism in the Dead Sea Scrolls*, 86. Note as well that the "star" imagery is used to refer to a future priest in *T. Levi* 18:2-3.

nity may have expected a messianic prophet (probably taken from Deut. 18:15, 18—a prophet like Moses). As mentioned above, some take the Interpreter of the law to be a reference to this eschatological prophet. It is also possible that 4Q521 (4QMessianic Apocalypse) refers to the messianic prophet. The first two lines read: "[for the heav]ens and the earth will listen to his messiah, [and all] that is in them will not turn away from the holy precepts" (4Q521 2 ii 1-2). A few lines later, the text reads: "the Lord will perform marvelous acts such as have not existed, just as he sa[id] for he will heal the badly wounded and will make the dead live, he will proclaim good news to the meek" (4Q521 2 ii 11- 12). Since this messiah is a prophetic herald (proclaiming good news) and is raising the dead similar to the prophet Elijah, Collins believes that he is a messianic prophet.[35] Unfortunately, it is not clear from the text whether the messiah or the Lord is the one who is performing these feats.

A more likely text in which three messianic figures are presented (similar to 1QS 9:9-11) is 4QTestimonia (4Q175). This work consists of four quotations, the first three of which are biblical texts that the community apparently interpreted messianically. It begins by combining Deut. 5:28- 29 and 18:18-19, the "prophet" passage. It continues with the Balaam oracle in Num. 24:15-17, speaking of the star (priestly messiah) and the scepter (Davidic messiah). The third citation is the blessing of Levi in Deut. 33:8-11 (priestly messiah). Finally, it concludes with a citation from the *Psalms of Joshua*, which speaks of a curse on the man who rebuilds Jericho. If the first three citations are all meant to be messianic texts, it would be evidence that the "prophet" should be understood messianically in the same sense as the priest and the Davidic king.[36]

Summary of Messianism in the Scrolls

Though there may indeed be a development of messianic thought reflected in the Qumran scrolls, the expectation of multiple messianic figures seems to have been an integral part of the community's un-

---

[35] J. Collins, ibid., 87-89.
[36] See F. García Martínez, "Messianic Hopes in the Qumran Writings," pp. 186-188. H. Stegemann, *The Library of Qumran*, p. 208, even goes so far as to say that the eschatological prophet would be "above" the Aaronic and Davidic messiahs, but the texts he cites do not clearly support his contention.

derstanding.³⁷ It is possible that this expectation goes back to OT texts such as Zech. 4:14, which speaks of two "anointed ones," and Zech. 6:11-13, where the High Priest Joshua is given a crown.³⁸ Talmon suggests that the post-exilic political situation (where the king's position was weaker, and the priesthood was enhanced) may have given rise to the expectation of dual messiahs in the Qumran community.³⁹ More intriguing is Collins' hypothesis that the bifurcation arose because of the group's objection to the Hasmonean combination of the royal and priestly offices into one man. In the ideal restored kingdom, the royal and priestly roles would again be separated, just as they should have been all along.⁴⁰

Also unusual in the community's view of the messiah(s) is that the priestly messiah is clearly elevated over the Davidic one. The royal messiah has an important role in establishing the kingdom and winning the battle against the sons of darkness. But the priestly messiah has an even more important function as the one who would lead in sacrifice and ritual and instruct the people in the Law. In some texts this latter function seems to be shared with the eschatological prophet. Once again, it appears that the messianic expectations were an outgrowth of the current experiences and practices of the community.

Last Judgment and Resurrection

While the chronology is not always clear, the coming of the messiah(s) in the end time seems to coincide with the eschatological war. In particular, the Davidic messiah appears to play an important

---

³⁷ As J. VanderKam, *The Dead Sea Scrolls Today*, p. 117, observes, "this pattern of both a secular and a priestly leader of the end time is repeated in a relatively large number of Qumran texts of diverse types."

³⁸ Interestingly, Zech. 6:13 may be translated to indicate either two different figures (ruler and priest) or one ruler with priestly and royal functions.

³⁹ S. Talmon, "Waiting for the Messiah at Qumran," pp. 123-125.

⁴⁰ J. Collins, *Apocalypticism in the Dead Sea Scrolls*, pp. 78-80. Collins notes that the last reference in 4QTestimonia (a curse on the one who rebuilds Jericho and his sons) may refer to John Hyrcanus, who apparently rebuilt Jericho and whose sons died in 103 B.C.E., a year after their father. If so, the Testimonia would be a reaction to Hyrcanus' efforts to combine the offices into one. See H. Eshel, "The Historical Background of the Pesher Interpreting Joshua's Curse on the Rebuilder of Jericho," in *RevQ* 15, 1992, pp. 409-420.

part in this war, participating in the final defeat of Belial and the sons of darkness (see discussion of 4Q285 and 4QpIsa^a above). The War Scroll describes a forty-year long battle resulting in the destruction of the sons of darkness (1QM 1:16). There is also a cosmic dimension to this final battle, as the archangel Michael (also apparently called Melchizedek in 11QMelchizedek) defeats Belial and "the spirits of his lot" (11QMelch 2:12-13; 1QM 17:6-7; 18:1-3). On that day Melchizedek "will carry out the vengeance of God's judgments" (11QMelch 2:13). The effects of judgment upon the earth are dramatically depicted in the Hodayot (1QH 11:29-36):

> Then the torrents of Belial shall go up over all the high banks...so as to destroy every green tree ^{30}and dry tree alongside their tributaries.... ^{31}It devours right down to the great deep. ^{32}The torrents of Belial burst through into Abaddon, and the plotters from the deep make an uproar with the noise of those who belch forth slime. The earth ^{33}shouts out, because of the disaster which comes about in the world, and all its plotters scream. All who are upon it behave as if mad, ^{34}and they melt away in the great disaster. For God thunders with the roar of His strength and His holy dwelling roars forth in His glorious truth. ^{35}Then the heavenly hosts shall raise their voice and the everlasting foundations shall melt and quake. The war of the heroes ^{36}of heaven shall spread over the world and shall not return until an annihilation that has been determined from eternity is completed. Nothing like this has ever occurred.[41]

The Rule of the Community presents a stark contrast between the rewards for the righteous and the punishment of the wicked (1QS 4:6-8, 11-14; words in brackets added from context):

> And the visitation of those who walk in {truth} will be for healing, ^{7}plentiful peace in a long life, fruitful offspring with all everlasting blessings, eternal enjoyment with endless life, and a crown of glory 8with majestic raiment in eternal light.... ^{11}And the visitation ^{12}of those who walk in {the paths of darkness} will be for a glut of punishments at the hands of all the angels of destruction, for eternal damnation for the scorching wrath of the God of revenge, for permanent error and shame ^{13}without end with the humiliation of destruction by the fire of the dark regions. And all the ages of their generations they shall spend in bitter weeping and harsh evils in the abysses of darkness until ^{14}their destruction, without there being a remnant or a survivor among them.

---

[41] Translation from M. Wise, M. Abegg, Jr., and E. Cook, *The Dead Sea Scrolls: A New Translation* (San Francisco, 1996), p. 95.

So the sons of light will have everlasting blessings, but the sons of darkness will experience eternal damnation.

Did these "everlasting blessings" include a physical resurrection? Some texts indicate that the community hoped for fellowship with the angels (see 1QH 11:19-23; 19:10-14), but this does not necessitate a bodily resurrection. Several texts, however, do speak of physical resurrection. In 4Q385 (4QPseudo-Ezekiel^a) the parable of the dry bones (Ezek. 37) is used to comfort those who are loyal to God with the hope of resurrection in the end time. The clearest affirmation of resurrection is in 4Q521 (4QMessianic Apocalypse), which states, "the Lord will perform marvelous acts such as have not existed, just as he sa[id] for he will heal the badly wounded and will make the dead live" (4Q521 2 ii 11-12). If this text was written by the community, it provides strong evidence of a belief in resurrection.[42] Interestingly, two ancient sources on the Essenes differ in their views here. Josephus states that the Essenes believe only the souls are immortal (*Jewish War* 2.8.5 §154-55), while Hippolytus states that "the doctrine of resurrection is firmly established among them. They declare, in fact, that flesh will rise again and be immortal, just as the soul is already immortal" (*Refutation of All Heresies* 9.27). If the Qumran group was Essene, then Hippolytus' presentation may on this point be closer to the truth.

While not every aspect of the Qumran community's eschatology is certain, enough is known to say that it is entirely Jewish. In God's sovereignty he has determined the course of all history, right up to the end. An understanding of these mysteries of God comes through an inspired interpretation of the biblical texts. These scriptures make clear that the sons of light, who follow the Law and obey him, will ultimately triumph over the sons of darkness. As a community of priests, the Qumran group was living in a manner that would enable a smooth transition to the last period of history, when the messiahs would come and true Israel would be restored forevermore.

---

[42] It is possible, too, that the archaeological evidence from the cemeteries of Qumran, where the bodies face north (towards paradise?), may indicate a belief in resurrection (so E. Puech, "Messianism, Resurrection, and Eschatology at Qumran and in the New Testament," p. 254). Cf., J. Collins, *Apocalypticism in the Dead Sea Scrolls*, pp. 123-124, who remains properly cautious.

14. WISDOM AT QUMRAN

Torleif Elgvin
Lutheran Theological Seminary, Oslo

The Qumranites' view of wisdom was not only formed by their own teachers. To a large degree it was formed by literature the Community had inherited, including the Bible. We will therefore survey biblical and post-biblical texts that may have influenced their Qumran readers. Among post-biblical texts we will give attention to 1 Enoch and some texts that may derive from the precursors of the *Yahad*.

The men of the *Yahad* heeded the admonition of the sapiential Pss. 1 and 119 to meditate upon God's Torah. They searched Scripture and other writings they held in esteem for clues to wisdom and to attain knowledge, to understand the times and the challenges facing their community. Passages dealing with wisdom and revelation or with the restoration of Israel in the end-time were of particular interest to this community of "latter day saints."

The Wisdom of God

Biblical texts dealing with the image of divine wisdom would be of central importance for Qumran readers. In the discourses in Prov. 1-9, they encountered "Lady Wisdom," who is contrasted by "Lady Folly," portrayed as the frivolous woman who seduces the simpleton (9:13-18). Lady Wisdom calls out to men and offers true knowledge and understanding to those who listen to her. Wisdom is intimately connected to the Lord; she is God's voice and teacher on earth. The discourses admonish man to seek Wisdom and listen to her teaching. He who seeks shall find her; "he will understand the fear of the Lord and find the knowledge of God" (2:5). Wisdom "is a tree of life to those who embrace her" (Prov. 3:18). Second Temple readers, including those of the *Yahad*, would heed the call to seek the attractive Lady Wisdom and to embrace her (see below on Ben Sira 51:13-19).

According to Prov. 1–9, people can obtain the wisdom needed to master the challenges of life and to understand the ways of God. Wisdom is reasonable, achieved by listening to parents and teachers, by taking to one's heart the life experience reflected in the Book of Proverbs, including the sentential part, chaps. 10–31. The admonition to seek the knowledge of the Lord in the post-exilic chaps. 1–9 relates to non-sapiential parts of the Israelite tradition as well, such as Deuteronomistic and prophetic teaching (the wisdom speech in Prov. 1:20-33 is modeled as a prophetic admonition speech and uses Deuteronomistic language). A similar message on the accessibility of wisdom from above is found in Deut. 30:11-14. The word and the commandments are near at hand and can be understood by the men of Israel.

Creation and the creator are important themes in the Hodayot. When Qumran readers searched biblical texts dealing with creation, they would note that the figure of Wisdom had an essential role in the act of creation. Late biblical texts reflect on God's agents in the creation of the world and rephrase the roles of God's creative word and his breath/spirit in Gen. 1. The opening word of Gen. 1:1 (*bereshit*) is probably interpreted instrumentally ("By the Beginning/Origin") rather than temporarily ("In the beginning"). The "Origin" (*reshit*) is thus another designation for a creative agent of God.

While Ps. 33:6 asserts that the heavens were made "by the word of the Lord" and "by the breath of his mouth," the wisdom tradition turns to sapiential terms to describe these agents of God. According to Prov. 3:19, God laid the foundations of the earth by (his) Wisdom, set the heavens in place by Understanding (*tevunah*), and divided the deeps by his Knowledge (*da'at*). These words recur in a sapiential addition to Jer. 10, which contrasts the idols and the so-called wisdom of the gentiles with God, who "made the earth by his power (*koah*); founded the world by his wisdom (*hokhmah*), and stretched out the heavens by his understanding (*tevunah*)" [v. 12]. In Prov. 8:23-31, Wisdom is described as the preexistent partner of God in the act of creation, that was brought forth as the beginning (*reshit*) of all God's works.

The people of Qumran affirmed this view of God's act of creation when they sung the Hymn to the Creator in the psalm scroll from Cave 11, in its origin probably a pre-Qumranic hymn (11QPs^a 26:11-15):

> He separated light from darkness,
> By the knowledge of his mind he established the dawn....
> Blessed be he who made the earth by his power,
> establishing the world by his wisdom.

> By his understanding he stretched out the heavens,
> and brought out [the wind] from [his] sto[rehouses.[1]

The question would inevitably be raised: what is the relation between this creative wisdom of God and the wisdom humans can attain?

The men of the *Yahad* also encountered biblical texts with a view of wisdom different from that of Proverbs. They found texts proclaiming that the wisdom of God is inaccessible. Ecclesiastes and texts in Job assert that man cannot obtain understanding of the order of creation and the wisdom of God. God alone possesses divine wisdom. This theme they found elaborated in the poem on Wisdom in Job 28, an addition to the original composition: "Wisdom is hidden from the eyes of every living thing, concealed even from the birds of the air.... God understands the way to it, he alone knows where it dwells" (vv. 21, 23). The only wisdom for humans is to fear the Lord and shun evil (v. 28). The speech of God in Job 38-41 describes how God's wisdom penetrates creation. After his encounter with God, Job acknowledges that he cannot attain full understanding of the ways of God (42:2-6).

In (the exilic framework of) Deuteronomy the Qumranites found a similar proclamation: "The hidden things belong to YHWH our God, but the things revealed (*haniglot*, i.e., the words of this Torah) belong to us and to our children forever" (29:28—we will return to the *Yahad*'s view of this verse). The sapiential Ps. 73 was probably meaningful for Qumran readers: he who is poor and pious cannot fully understand God's ways when he sees the success of the ungodly, but the encounter with God can nevertheless give him existential satisfaction (vv. 16-17, 23-26).

For Second Temple readers, the Book of Job contained more than chaps. 28 and 38–42. Job is convinced that God is the one who "reveals the deep things of darkness" (12:22). Job 5:1 and 6:10 (cf., 33:14-16) refer to supernatural revelation Job received from "holy ones" (angels). Eliphaz refers to this claim of Job, which in his eyes distorts true fear of God, in 15:2-16: "Did you listen in on God's council (*sod*), did you (only) seize wisdom?" (v. 8)—the council is probably identical with God's "holy ones" (v. 15). According to these traditions, Job *did* experience direct revelation from the heavenly council; he had access to wisdom from above. Thus, in a biblical

---

[1] Translation based on Sanders, *DJD* IV.

wisdom book, the people of Qumran would learn that God may provide revelation from the angelic council on high. Prov. 30:2-4 reflects the same tradition of the heavenly wisdom of the angels; cf., especially v. 3: "I have not learned wisdom, and I lack the knowledge of the holy ones (da'at qodashim)" [translation: *The Jerusalem Bible*]. The Qumranites would also note biblical prophets who based their prophecies upon revelations from the heavenly council (Amos 3:7; 1 Kgs. 22:19-23; Is. 6; Jer. 23:18, 22, cf., Gen. 18:16-33).

Some fragments of the wisdom book Ben Sira were found at Qumran (2Q18). Ben Sira 51 contains a poem on searching out the attractive Lady Wisdom, probably not composed by Ben Sira himself. The first half of this acrostic (vv. 13-19) is included in the great Psalms scroll from Cave 11 (col. 21), in a version more sensual than the existing Greek version of Ben Sira:

> When I was still young, before I had gone astray, I searched for her.
> She came to me in her beauty, and up to the end I kept investigating her.
> Even when the blossom falls, when the grapes are ripening, they make the heart happy.
> My foot tread on a straight path, for since my youth I have known her.
> I had hardly bent my ear, when I found much teaching.
> A wet-nurse she became to me, to my teacher I give my honor.
> I determined to enjoy myself, I was zealous for (her) good things, incessantly.
> I became ablaze for her and could not avert my face.
> I stirred my soul for her and on her heights I was not calm.
> My "hand"[2] opened [her bosom], I gazed upon her nakedness.
> My hands I purified, and into[..., I found her while she was pure.][3]

We concur with those scholars who think that for the *Yahad*, 11QPs^a was a community hymnal, not a biblical scroll. When reading or singing this imaginative psalm, the male members were certainly reminded of the need to embrace Lady Wisdom (they may have been reminded of other things too...).

---

[2] "Foot" and "hand" are euphemisms for the sexual organ; cf., the double meaning of "foot" in the fourth line of the poem. See Carl R. Holladay, "Euphemism and Dysphemism in the Bible," in *ABD*, vol. 1, pp. 720-722.

[3] Our translations of Qumran texts usually follow F. García Martínez and E.J.C. Tigchelaar, *The Dead Sea Scrolls Study Edition* (2 vols., Leiden, 1997-1998). However, in a number of occasions (including the text quoted here) we depart from this translation. Emendations above are according to Geniza MS. b, which is close to, but not identical with, the Qumran text.

We don't know how Ben Sira was evaluated in the *Yahad*. Ben Sira himself attributes some kind of divine inspiration to his book (24:30-34). 1:1-20 and 24:1-29 continue and elaborate the tradition of Wisdom from Prov. 1–9. Gen. 1 and Prov. 8:23-31 play particularly in the background. Wisdom was created first, she penetrates the universe and found her abode among Israel in Zion. While the (pre-Sirachide?) hymn of 24:1-22 stresses the presence of God's Wisdom in Zion (in tabernacle and Temple), in vv. 23-28 Ben Sira equates Wisdom with the Torah, the Books of Moses: the Torah is the pre-existent order of creation which is given solely to Israel as inheritance.[4] The connection of Wisdom and Torah in Ben Sira and Baruch draws upon Deut. 4:6-8, which equates wisdom and understanding with the commandments of the Law.

In summary, readers at Qumran would find two contrasting views of wisdom and revelation in the sapiential tradition. According to Prov. 1-9, some passages in Job, and the younger Ben Sira, God reveals his wisdom, and man can attain the wisdom he needs. In contrast, Ecclesiastes and other passages in Job assert that humans cannot achieve full understanding of creation, the conditions of life and the wisdom of God. Some texts (biblical and post-biblical) stress that ultimate wisdom only can be attained through revelation from the divine council to elect ones on earth (such as Noah, Joseph,[5] Moses, David,[6] Job, and the prophets).

Divine Wisdom in the Sapiential-Apocalyptic Tradition

The Qumran library contained a number of Hebrew sapiential compositions. Most of these do not display identity markers of the *Yahad*.[7]

---

[4] We do not deal with the related poem on Wisdom in Baruch 3:9-4:4, as the book of Baruch was not found in Qumran.

[5] Joseph is seen as a model sage in the Geniza Levi fragments, closely related to 4QLevi ar. See R.A. Kugler, *From Patriarch to Priest. The Levi-Priestly Tradition from Aramaic Levi to Testament of Levi* (Atlanta, 1996), pp. 119-121.

[6] 11QPsa David's Compositions (col. 27) attributes divine inspiration to David, seen as the author of biblical Psalms as well as liturgical ones used in the Community.

[7] On the characteristics of sectarian documents, see C. Newsom, "'Sectually Explicit' Literature from Qumran," in W.H. Propp, B. Halpern, and D.N. Freedman, eds., *The Hebrew Bible and Its Interpreters* (Winona Lake, 1990), pp. 167-187; E.G. Chazon, "Is *Divrei ha-me'orot* a Sectarian Prayer?" in D. Dimant and U. Rappaport, eds., *The Dead Sea Scrolls. Forty Years of Research* (Leiden and Jerusalem, 1992), pp. 3-17;

Among such non-sectarian writings we can mention Ben Sira, 4Q184 and 4Q185, 4Q525 (4QWisdom Text with Beatitudes), 4Q302 (4QpapAdmonitory Parable), the proverbial composition 4Q424, and some of the non-biblical hymns in the great psalm scroll from Cave 11. We suggest that most of these compositions predate the *Yahad* and perhaps were preserved at Qumran due to their sapiential language, which had affinities with that of the Community.

Hypostatic Wisdom occurs in a number of these scrolls. 4Q184 (4QWiles of the Wicked Woman) and 4Q185 (4Qsap. work) portray Lady Folly and Lady Wisdom and elaborate these motifs from Prov. 1-9 and Job 28. Readers are exhorted to keep away from Lady Folly and hearken to Lady Wisdom and follow her ways. Wisdom has been revealed and given to all the people of Israel: "for God gave her] to Israel, and like a [g]ood gift, gives her. He has saved all his people" (4Q185 1-2 ii 10). We encounter hypostatic Wisdom also in 4Q525 (4QBeat) 2 ii 2-9; 4 6-13; 11QPs^a 154:5-15; 11QPs^a Creat; 11QPs^a Sirach, and 4Q420/421 (4QWays of Righteousness). With one exception, none of these compositions reveal signs of sectarian authorship. Similar to Sirach 24 and Baruch, 4Q525 and 11QPs^a 154 explicitly connect Wisdom and Torah:

> Blessed are those who search for her with pure hands, and do not pursue her with a treacherous heart. Blessed is the man who attains Wisdom and walks in the torah of the Most High, and directs his heart to her way, is constrained by her discipline and alwa[ys] takes pleasure in her punishments, and does not forsake her in the hardship of [his] wrongs (4Q525 2 ii 2-5).
>
> For to make known the glory of YHWH is wisdom given. And for recounting his many deeds she has been taught to man... Her voice is heard from the gates of just ones, and from the assembly of devout ones her song; when they eat to bursting they speak about it; and when they drink in unison with one another, their meditation is on the torah of the Most High, their words make his power known. (11QPs^a 154:5)

The revelation of God's wisdom is here presented in a non-apocalyptic manner; "For to make known the glory of the Lord is Wisdom

---

D. Dimant, "The Qumran Manuscripts: Contents and Significance," in D. Dimant and L.H. Schiffman, eds., *Time to Prepare the Way in the Wilderness. Papers on the Qumran Scrolls by Fellows of the Institute for Advanced Studies of the Hebrew University, Jerusalem, 1989-90* (Leiden, 1995), pp. 23-68. We see the *Yahad* as an elite group within a wider Essene movement. The *Yahad* was in some way connected to the center at Qumran but was probably not restricted to this geographical location.

given, and for recounting his many deeds she is revealed to man" (11QPs^a 154 5-6).

Only one sectarian scroll, 4QWays of Righteousness, refers to Lady Wisdom. 4Q421 1 ii 9-10 exhorts man to "carry the yoke of Wisd[om" (*la-se't 'ol ḥokhmah*)[8] before it continues with an elaboration of the virtues of the righteous (4Q421 1 ii 9-17, par. 4Q420 1 ii 1-6, italics):

>] to carry the yoke of Wisd[om... A man of virtue will re]ceive the admonition of the knowledgeable. A man of [prudence will know]to walk in the ways of God, to do righteousness [*as follows: he will not answer before he hea]rs*, and not speak before he understands. *In great pa[tience will he give answer, and by studying rig]hteousness he will understand* their consequences. A m[an *who is humble and meek in mind will not tur]n away until* [...A man *who is trustworthy will not turn aside from ways of righteousness.*] He will set [his heart to truth (?), and *his* bo*nes and his hands* to righteousness(?)

4QWays of Righteousness is a composite work: the first section deals with the organization of the Community, the second consists of wisdom sayings on the righteous man, while the third provides *Yahad*-halakhah with regard to Temple and Sabbath. The wisdom sayings of this composition represent older sapiential traditions reworked by a sectarian editor. The yoke of Wisdom probably represents the older, inherited tradition. Among these wisdom sayings adopted by the *Yahad*, those on a humble and responsible attitude in discussions gave meaningful advice for the sessions and meals of the Community (cf., 1QS 6:4, 8-13). In their adaptation of such wisdom sayings, the *Yahad* shows itself an heir of the old wisdom tradition of biblical and post-biblical times (similar sayings form a large part of the presectarian 4QInstruction; see below).

In contrast to the sapiential works surveyed above, "Lady Wisdom" does not figure clearly in 4QInstruction or the writings of the *Yahad*. For the *Yahad* God's wisdom and power are intrinsically connected to God himself and not related to any derived hypostatic figure: "there is no power to compare with your mig[ht]. There is no [bound] to your glory, and to your wisdom, no measure" (1QH^a

---

[8] E. Tigchelaar has questioned the reading *lase'et* in "Sabbath Halakha and Worship in *4QWays of Righteousness*: *4Q421* 11 and 13+2+8 par *4Q264a* 1-2," in *RevQ* 18, 1998, pp. 359-372. Our reading is based upon examination of the original with microscope.

17:16-17).[9] When the Hodayot state "by your wisdom you de[signed the generations] of history" (1QH^a 9:7), wisdom is only a characteristic of God himself. It is our suggestion that in the presectarian 4QInstruction (see below) and sectarian writings "Lady Wisdom" has been replaced by the apocalyptic concept *raz* or *raz nihyeh*, the unfolding mystery of God. Through books they had inherited and copied, the *Yahad* knew the tradition of hypostatic Wisdom as a means of revelation. In their own writings, however, they reinterpreted this concept.

The Qumran library contained some sapiential books of more apocalyptic flavor, which stress revelation of divine mysteries, viz., the Enochic books (authored between the late third and mid-second century), Daniel (finalized c. 164 B.C.E.), and 4QInstruction (mid-second century?). These books were held in high esteem in the Qumran commune: seven copies of Enochic books were found in the caves (apart from the Book of Giants), seven copies of 4QInstruction (1Q26/4Q415/416/417/418/418a/423), and six copies of Daniel. The latter had obtained authoritative status at Qumran (cf., the reference to the words of Daniel in 11QMelch 1 ii 18). The concepts of wisdom and revelation in these writings influenced the *Yahad* and are therefore worth scrutiny.

Sages and wise men are highly esteemed in these books. Daniel is educated as a sage (1:3-10), while Enoch is designated as scribe (1 Enoch 12:4; 15:1; 92:1). The Book of Daniel concludes by praising the wise ones who have lead many to righteousness (12:1-3). Interpretation of dreams and visions belonged to the office of the sage (Gen. 40–41; Dan. 2–5). The sapiential Joseph cycle in Genesis ascribes the wisdom of Joseph to a God-given charisma; the same is true of the apocalyptic heroes Enoch and Daniel. Further, the content of the Enochic books is described as "wisdom" (5:6; 92:1; 93:10). And both Enoch and Daniel were privileged with special revelation from the divine realms. We will return to 4QInstruction below.

From the early Enochic books onwards, apocalyptic writers, including those in Qumran, interpret and transform the tradition of divine wisdom. In contrast to the views of Sirach and Baruch 3-4, for the apocalyptists the ultimate wisdom of God is not what is revealed

---

[9] In the numbering of the columns of 1QHa, we follow the *Study Edition* not the earlier Sukenik edition.

to all Israel through the Torah.[10] Seen in eschatological light, the statements of Job 28:20-21, that wisdom is concealed (*nistar*) and "hidden (*ne'elmah*) from the eyes of every living thing," and Deut. 29:28, that "the hidden things (*hanistarot*) belong to the Lord our God, but the things revealed (*haniglot*) belong to us," are not sufficient any more. They may be true for Israel at large but not for the elect community. The apocalyptists found support in late biblical texts that proclaim that God reveals hidden and deep matters (Job 12:22 "He reveals the deep things of darkness;" cf., Dan. 2:22: "He reveals deep and hidden things"). Thus, there are secrets that were made known to pre-Mosaic sages—to Adam, Enoch, Noah, and Abraham —and are again revealed to the elect of the end-time community. For the *Yahad*, *haniglot* are biblical laws known to all Israel, while *hanistarot* are truths made known only to the Teacher and his Community, through revelation and inspired exegesis. Writings of the *Yahad* praise God who reveals *nistarot*: CD 3:11; 1QS 5:11-12; 4QH^a 7 i 18-19 (quoted on p. 166).

The expectation of the approaching end[11] and the perception of Israel at large as disobedient caused apocalyptic circles, including the *Yahad*, to reinterpret biblical promises about God's end-time renewal of his people: the promised renewal would be for the elect circles only (identified with the "remnant" expected by the prophets; cf., e.g., Mic. 4:7; 5:6-7; Jer. 23:3; 31:7). The apocalyptists connected these promises with the tradition of divine wisdom: wisdom from on high is now revealed to the elect remnant and is a condition of eschatological salvation.

4QInstruction is a large sapiential-didactic composition that probably derives from precursors of the *Yahad*. It was highly esteemed in the Community and was influential for the development of sectarian thinking. According to Strugnell, it "almost attained "canonical" sta-

---

[10] G.W.E. Nickelsburg, "Wisdom and Apocalypticism in Early Judaism," in *Society of Biblical Literature Seminar Papers* 33, 1994, p. 720, comments on 1 Enoch: "The relationship of Enoch's wisdom to the Mosaic Torah is ambiguous. His revelations preceded those of Moses by millennia. At least in the Animal Vision, the giving of the Torah is deleted from the account of the Sinai experience (89:28-35).... Especially striking is the use of the wisdom myth in 81:1-82:4, where, in contrast to Sirach 24 and Baruch 4:1, it is Enoch's books rather than the Mosaic Torah that are the earthly repository of heavenly wisdom."

[11] Jer. 23:20 probably functioned as a source of inspiration for this end-time reinterpretation of Scripture: "in days to come/in the last days you shall clearly perceive it."

tus at Qumran."¹² We shall see that 4QInstruction to a large degree prefigures the sapiential-apocalyptic theology of the *Yahad*.

Large sections of 4QInstruction consist of wisdom admonitions (a command or prohibition followed by a motive clause) that convey traditional sapiential advice based on reason in their advocating of life wisdom (4Q416 2 ii 15-21):

> Do not humble yourself before someone who is not your equal, then you will b[e] for him as a […] father. Do not strike someone who does not have your strength, lest you stumble and be put greatly to shame …. Do not fill yourself with bread when you lack clothing. Do not drink wine when there is no food. Do not request luxury when you lack bread. Do not boast about your lowly estate—you who are poor—lest you bring your life into contempt.¹³

The book further includes sections dealing with eschatology and revelation to the elect ones. A trial speech discerns sharply between the "foolish of heart," who can expect destruction and damnation, and the "elect of truth," who will inherit glory and honor (the same dichotomy recurs in the Hodayot) (4Q418 69 ii 7-14):

> The seekers of truth will wake up to the judgements[of God(?).] And then all the foolish of heart will be destroyed, the sons of iniquity will not be found any more, and all those who support evil will be asham[ed] at your judgement….
> But you are the elect of truth, those who pursue [righteousness according to the] judgme[nt of God(?),…] watchfu[l] according to all knowledge. How can you say, "We toiled for understanding and have been awake to pursue knowledge." F[or he is…] in all [his deed]s (?) and he has not tired during all the years of eternity. Does he not delight in truth forever? Knowledge [and Understanding] will minister to him. And even the s[ons] of heaven, whose inheritance is eternal life, will they <not> say, "We toiled in the deeds of truth and have ti[red] during all the ages"?—will they not wal[k] in eternal light? […] also you [will inherit g]lory and abundant honor.

The "elect of truth" are the addressees of this work, designated "knowledgeable one," "understanding one" [*(ben) mevin; (ben) maskil*]. The men of the *Yahad* knew they were among the knowledgeable ones. This text reassured them of their ultimate salvation. It also reminded them of their fellowship with the angels ("the sons of heaven"), the guardians of heavenly knowledge.

---

¹² *DJD* XXXIV, pp. 31, 36.
¹³ Translations from 4QInstruction are our own.

Raz nihyeh—the mystery to come—is the central revelatory concept in 4QInstruction, occurring twenty-three times. Not the Torah (cf., Sirach and Baruch) but the mystery to come is the center of God's revelation. In contrast to Josh. 1:8 and Pss. 1:2 and 119, which urge meditation on God's Torah and the book of Torah, 4QInstruction instructs the addressee to meditate on *raz nihyeh* to attain knowledge: "Meditate on] the mystery to come and grasp the nature [of m]an...then you will understand the judgment on mankind and the weighing[of their deeds(?)" (4Q418 77 2-3). *Raz nihyeh* is related to God's redemptive plan. "Gaze upon the mystery to come, understand the birth-times of salvation and know who will inherit glory and corruption. Will it not be[a garland for the poor ones(?)] and eternal joy for their sorrow?" (4Q417 2 i 10-12). When you study God's mysterious plan of redemption you will understand the pangs of salvation—the secrets about the end-time—and thereby know who will inherit glory (viz., the elect, including the addressee) and who corruption (viz., the sons of the pit).

A long wisdom instruction (4Q417 1 i 1-27) deals with the mysteries of creation, history and the ways of every creature. *Raz nihyeh* is related to God's act of creation (4Q417 1 i 2-8, par. 4Q418 43, italics):

> Loo[k] at [His won]drous mysteries,[for *He is God of the awesome angels. Get knowledge about the beginnings of*] your ... Look[at the mystery to come and the deeds of *old, to what was and what comes into being and to wh*at will be, and at al]l eternal myster[ies] with the [everlasting] se[crets(?)]..., then you will see(?) *what was and what comes into being with what* will b]e, in all [the periods of eternity(?)]... look upon]deed and d[eed, day and *night meditate on the mystery to c]ome*, and search always. Then you will know truth and evil, wisdom [and simplici]ty. ...[ ] understand(?) the creatures [of God(?)] in all their ways with their destiny in all the periods of eternity as well as the eternal visitation. Then you will discern between [go]od and [evil in their]deed[s,] for the God of knowledge is the foundation of truth

Especially revealing are lines 8-10: "By the mystery to come he designed its foundation, <and> its creatures with a[ll wis]dom. According to all[cun]ning he fashioned it, and the domain of its creatures according to a[l]l [under]standing (?)."

A comparison with the Hymn to the Creator in 11QPs^a is illuminating (see above). 11QPs^a Creat 4-8 combines Jer. 10:12-13 with Gen. 1:1; Prov. 3:19; Prov. 8:22-31; and Ps. 33:6, and states that God created the world "by the knowledge of his mind" (*da'at libo*), "by his power" (*koḥo*), "by his wisdom" (*ḥokhmato*), and "by his understanding" (*tevunato*). The Hymn to the Creator does not reveal apocalyptic or sectarian characteristics. Various synonyms (knowledge, power, wisdom, understanding) are used to describe the wisdom of God, the agent by which he created the world. The preposition *b*ᵉ is used in an instrumental meaning. However, according to 4QInstruction, God's agent in creation is not Wisdom, but *raz nihyeh*:: "By the mystery to come he designed its foundation." While "wisdom," "cunning" (*ʿor[mah]*) and "understanding" (*[bi]nah*) are portrayed as accompanying attributes of God, *raz nihyeh* is the plan by which he designed the world and its foundations: only *raz nihyeh* is preceded by the instrumental *b*ᵉ.

The role in creation that biblical texts and 11QPsª Creat attribute to God's Wisdom is in 4QInstruction ascribed to *raz nihyeh*, which conveys divine revelation and provides the means for the right relation to God and fellow man. Thus, *raz nihyeh* represents an apocalyptic reinterpretation of the concept of divine Wisdom, which stresses the esoteric nature of God's revelation. In the apocalyptic setting "the mystery to come" has a wider meaning than its biblical predecessor: *raz nihyeh* is a comprehensive word for God's mysterious plan for creation and history, his plan for man and for redemption of the elect. Different from Sirach 1 and 24, Bar 3:9-4:4, 4Q525 and 11QPsª 154, true wisdom and earthly blessings have their source in (studying) *raz nihyeh*, not in (following) Torah.

The Remnant Community

A wisdom instruction describes the portion of the elect and the idea of the remnant community, of which the addressee is a partaker (4Q418 81 1, 3-6, 9-14:

> For he] opened your lips as a fountain to bless the holy ones.
> And you, as an everflowing fountain praise [His] n[ame.... And ⁴honor him in this, by sanctifying yourself to him. As he set you to sanctify the holy ones[over all]the earth, cast your lot among all the [god]l[y ones] and greatly increased your glory, he has set you as his firstborn am[ong the sons of Israe]l(?),[and said "My riches(?)] and my favor I will give you." Is not his goodness yours? <So> walk always faithful to him[...
> ⁹And for you he opened insig[ht], gave you authority over his storehouse and entrusted[you] with an accurate ephah [...] are with you. It is in your hands to turn aside wrath from the men of <his> favor and

punish[the men of Belial(?)...] are ¹¹with you. Before you take your portion from his hand, honor his holy ones, and be[fore you ...] ¹²He opened[a foun]tain <for> all the ho[ly] ones, all who by his name are called holy o[nes,...they will be] for all the eras the splendors of his sprout, an [ete]rnal planting [...] will co[me,] for thus will walk all those who inherit the land, for by [his] nam[e are they called(?)

A number of phrases in this text refer to the end-time community, of which the addressee is a member. The elect are "the men of God's favor," the community is the "sprout" as well as the "eternal plant" promised by Trito-Isaiah, the members of the community are the group that will "inherit the land." These designations would be inherited by the *Yahad* and provide clues for its self-understanding.[14]

In biblical (Is. 60:21; 61:3) and post-biblical literature, the "planting" is a metaphor for the righteous community, the true descendants of the patriarchs—either national Israel of the end-time or a more narrowly defined ecclesia. A plant requires soil to grow. The "planting" concept is therefore connected to the end-time inheriting of the land. The portion of the elect is described with the words inherit (*yarash*), "inheritance" (*nahalah*), "portion" (*heleq*), and "lot" (*goral*). These terms denote the spiritual-eschatological inheritance of the elect community, an inheritance they share with the angels.[15]

The elect is admonished to praise the holy ones, i.e., the angels (ls. 1, 4 , 11). However, according to l. 12, God has opened a fountain for the "holy ones" on earth. As in later sectarian writings there seems to be a fellowship of the saints that includes both the angels and the earthly community. God has opened a fountain of insight for the elect (ls. 9, 12), and has opened his lips as a fountain praising the angels (l. 1). This praise is described as *maqor 'olam*, "an everflowing fountain." *Patah maqor* (ls. 1, 12) is not used verbally in the Bible.

---

[14] For "men of favor," see 1QHa 4:32-33; 11:9: "the sons of His/Your favor;" 1QS 8:6: "the elect of favor;" 4Q298 (4QcrA Words of the Maskil to All Sons of Dawn) 1:3-4: "O m[en of]His fa[vor and] eternal [peace without] end." For "eternal planting," see 1 Enoch 84:6; 93:5; 93:10; 1QS 8:5, 9, 20, 21; 11:8; 1QHa 6:15; 8:4-26; CD 1:7. For "inherit the land," see Ps. 37:9, 11; Is. 60:21; 1 Enoch 5:7-9; Jub. 22:14; 32:19; 4Q385 (4QpsEzeka) 3:3; 5:1 ; CD 1:7-8; 8:14-15 (= Deut. 9:5); 4Q171 (4QpPsa) 1 iii 9-11.

[15] For sectarian usage, see 1QS 2:2: "the men of God's lot;" 11:7-8: "He gave them inheritance in the lot of the holy ones;" 1QHa 11:11-12: "have portion with Your holy ones;" 1QM 12:12: "Fill Your land with glory and Your inheritance with blessing: herds of flocks in your fields, gold, silver and precious stones in Your palaces!"

However, a similar construction occurs once: according to Zech. 13:1, God will at Zion open a fountain for repentant Israel of the end-time. When this phrase recurs in 4QInstruction and the Hodayot[16] it is clearly an eschatological term with Temple connotations. Revelation of esoteric wisdom has been given to the elect fellowship that stands on the threshold to the eschatological time.

Enochic writings preserve similar traditions. The *Epistle of Enoch* and *Apocalypse of Weeks* foresee the emergence of an elect group at the end of the seventh week of history. By the completion of the seventh week of history "there shall be chosen the e[lect] ones as witnesses of righteousness from the eter[n]al p[lanting] of righteousness, [to whom] shall be give[n] sevenf[ol]d wisdom and knowledge" (1 Enoch 93:10, 4QEnoch^g; cf., 91:10: "Wisdom shall arise and be given to them"). They shall receive books conveying knowledge (104:12-13). The Enochic tradition reflects a group of scribes and wise men (5:8; cf., the description of Enoch as scribe, 12:4; 15:1; 92:1). They see themselves as the end-time group that has received sevenfold wisdom, and the Enochic books are the books that convey knowledge and salvation. According to the *Epistle*, only those who listen to the words of these wise ones will be saved (99:10; 105:1), while the others will be destroyed (98:9).

The *Yahad* would find support for its understanding of its own fellowship as the enlightened community of the last days also in Jubilees. According to CD 16:3, Jubilees (found in fourteen copies at Qumran) was considered a book of authority. Jubilees purports to be special revelation, received in ancient times and now presented for Israel when the end-time is close at hand. Jub. 23:26-31 envisages a group that searches the scriptures differently from their fathers and discovers the right halakhah.

Similar to 4QInstruction, 4QTime of Righteousness employs sapiential terminology and sees the time of redemption close at hand. The main fragment runs as follows:

---

[16] God is likened to a fountain, e.g., 1QHa 9:4: *ke'e['atah eli maqor dJe'ah* [Stegemann's reconstruction, quoted from S. Tanzer, *The Sages at Qumran: Wisdom in the Hodayot* (Ph.D. diss.; Harvard University, 1987), p. 28]. For the subject matter, cf., Jer. 2:13; 17:13; Ps. 36:10. *Patah maqor* is used to express God opening a fountain in the believer in 1QHa 10:18; 18:31; 23:10 ("You have opened a [foun]tain in the mouth of Your servant," 12, 13. The phrase *maqor 'olam* recurs in 1QHa 14:17-18; 16:8; 18:31; 1QSb 1:3, 6. 4Q286 (4QBera) 1 ii 6 speaks of the heavenly realms as *maqor binah* and *maqor 'ormah*.

> For the age of wickedness has been completed and all injustice shall p[ass awa]y.
>
> [For] the time of righteousness has come, and the earth has been filled of knowledge and praise of God.
>
> For [ ] the age of peace has come, and of true laws and [r]ighteous testimony, to instruct[the sons of men] in the ways of God[and] in his mighty deeds[and the strength of his power f]or ever.
>
> Every t[ongu]e shall bless him and every man shall prostrate bef[ore him, and their he[arts] will be on[e.]
>
> For he [knew] their deeds before they were created, and the deeds of righteousness he portioned out in their divisions [and orders] for their generations.
>
> For the dominion of good has come, and he will highly raise up the throne of [his reign].
>
> Knowledge, prudence and sound insight are proved by the h[o]ly pla[n (4Q215a 1)

This text is filled with wisdom terminology: to instruct (*lehaskil*), knowledge (*sekel*), prudence (*'ormah*), insight (*toshiah*), plan (*mahshevah*). The ultimate redemption is described in sapiential language. Thus the text suggests that living according to sapiential admonition may bring forth redemption. A community that now "instructs the sons of men in the ways of God" paves the way for the final consummation. To live in harmony with God's plans according to "knowledge, prudence and insight" may push the world towards the age of peace and righteousness, of knowledge and praise of God. This text may be more universal in its outlook than texts authored in the *Yahad*, as it expects a general renewal of mankind. It may nevertheless have given the members of the Community encouragement and hope as they continued walking "in the ways of God."

1Q/4QMysteries is a "relative" of 4QInstruction. The number of copies found in Qumran, three or four (1Q27, 4Q299, 4Q300, possibly 4Q301), points to its importance for the *Yahad*. The mysteries of God is a main theme. Similar to 4QInstruction, 1Q/4QMysteries discerns sharply between those who have insight in the mysteries and the ungodly who lack understanding.[17] *Raz nihyeh*, the central revela-

---

[17] 1Q27 1 i 2-7; 4Q299 2 2-5; 6 ii 4; 8 2-7; 4Q300 1 ii 2-5: "you have not considered the eternal mysteries, and you have not come to understand wisdom;" 4Q300 9 1.

tory concept in 4QInstruction, occurs twice in 1Q/4QMysteries, and *raz* another eleven times.[18] One passage relates salvation and judgment to knowledge of "the mystery to come" (1Q27 1 i 3-7):

> But they did not know *the mystery to come*, and the former things they did not consider. And they did not know what shall befall them. And they did not save their lives by *the mystery to come*. And this shall be the sign to you that it is taking place: when the begotten of unrighteousness are delivered up, and wickedness is removed from before righteousness, as darkness is removed from before light. Then, just as smoke wholly ceases and is no more, so shall wickedness cease forever, and righteousness shall be revealed as the sun (throughout) the full measure of the world. And all the adherents of the mysteries of wickedness are to be no more. But knowledge shall fill the world, nor shall folly evermore be there.

Wisdom in the Yahad

Some of the writings that surely originated in the *Yahad* show distinct sapiential terminology, a characteristic that is particularly true of the Hodayot and also the Community Rule.[19] The fact that only some writings demonstrate sapiential characteristics is probably related to the different genres represented in this collection. In some literary types sectarian writers found it natural to utilize sapiential vocabulary, in other types they did not. The biblical commentaries of the Community (the *pesharim*), as one example, had no need of a sapiential vocabulary.

The Two-Spirit Treatise (1QS 3:13-4:26) abounds with sapiential terms and motifs: the two ways, "knowledge, understanding and powerful wisdom," "the God of knowledge,"[20] "spirit of knowledge."

---

[18] *Raz nihyeh* in 1Q27 1 i 3, 4 (=4 Q300 3 4), *raz* further in 1Q27 2, 7; 13 3; 4Q299 3a ii 11, 15; 3c 5; 5 2; 43 2; 4Q300 1 ii 2; 8 5, 7.

[19] See J.E. Worrell, *Concepts of Wisdom in the Dead Sea Scrolls* (Ph.D. diss., Claremont, 1968); Tanzer, *The Sages at Qumran*. Sapiential biblical terms common in these works: fool, wicked, righteous, blameless, way, understand, knowledge, insight, wisdom, investigate, council/counsel, advice, rebuke, discipline, measure.

[20] The designation "God of knowledge" is based on 1 Sam. 2:3, and used by 4QInstruction (4Q417 1 i 8; 4Q418 55 5) and 1Q/4QMysteries (4Q299 35 1; 73 3) before it is adopted by the *Yahad* [1QS 3:15; 1QHa 9:26; 20:10; 22:33 (frg. 4 15)]. Similar phrases occur in the Songs of the Sabbath Sacrifice (4Q400 2 8, 4Q401 11 2; 4Q401 4 12; 4Q405 23 ii 12) and 4QCant (4Q510 1 2; 4Q511 1 7-8).

The Community Rule may be seen as the handbook of "the Instructor" (*ha-maskil*, 3:13; 9:12; CD 12:21; 13:22), a typical sapiential term.

At the same time, sectarian writings reflect a community with an apocalyptic world-view. Eschatology, angelology and revelation to the community of the last days are important themes. In this, the *Yahad* continues and interprets themes from the earlier sapiential-apocalyptic tradition.[21]

Teacher Hymns

In our discussion of wisdom in the *Yahad* we will concentrate on the testimony of the Hodayot. Cols. 10–17 (previously numbered 2–9) of 1QH^a preserve a collection of hymns often ascribed to the Righteous Teacher.[22] In the final edition of the Hodayot (preserved by 1QH^a and 4QH^b), the Teacher hymns are surrounded by two large sections of "community hymns."[23]

The Teacher hymns reflect an elect individual to whom has been revealed divine wisdom. God has made him a source of knowledge for those who listen to him.

> Like perfect dawn you have revealed yourself to me with per[fect] light (12:6).

> Through me you have enlightened the face of the Many, you have increased them so that they are uncountable, for you have shown me your wondrous mysteries (12:27).

---

[21] J.J. Collins, *Apocalypticism in the Dead Sea Scrolls* (London, 1997), p. 11, comments, "...the books of Enoch and Daniel...exercised a profound influence on the Dead Sea Sect. Their worldview, however, is not simply adopted and reproduced in the sectarian documents. They represent a source for the ideology of the sect, not an expression of it."

[22] See, e.g., M.C. Douglas, "The Teacher Hymn Hypothesis Revisited: New Data for an Old Crux," in *DSD* 6, 1999, pp. 239-266. Tanzer counts twelve Teacher hymns and twenty-five community hymns in the scroll. She suggests that 15:27-33 is a community hymn that was redacted and included in the corpus of the Teacher hymns, and that "community material" was added to six Teacher hymns to make them more fit for community use (*The Sages at Qumran*, pp. 136-140).

[23] Stegemann's and Newsom's reconstruction of Hodayot scrolls from Cave 4 provides support for the hypothesis that the Righteous Teacher was the central figure behind the middle section of 1QHa. The scroll 4QHc contained only hymns from these eight columns, while 4QpapHf contained teacher hymns as well as the creation hymn preceding it (col. 9). On the other hand, 4QHa contained only psalms of the "community hymn" type: *DJD* XXIX, pp. 74-75.

> You have set me...as a foundation of truth and knowledge for those on the straight path.... You have set me as a banner for the elect of justice, as a knowledgeable mediator of secret wonders...the man whose mouth you have confirmed, and into whose heart you put understanding, to open a source of knowledge to all men of insight (10:9-10, 13, 17-18).

The Teacher's confidence of being imparted revelation rests on his assurance of being in fellowship with the angels, the bearers of divine wisdom.

> The depraved spirit you have purified from great offence so that he can take a place with the host of the holy ones and can enter in communion with the congregation of the sons of heaven. You cast eternal destiny for man with the spirits of knowledge, so that he praises your name in the community of jubilation (11:21-23).

> Those who walk on the path of your heart have listened to me, they have aligned themselves before you in the council of the holy ones (12:24-25).

The enlightened community is portrayed with images connected with Eden and the Temple—source, running water, planting, trees,[24] a sign of the community's self-understanding as a spiritual Temple. The Teacher is the source through whom the waters flow to the members of the community. The Eden image is here used eschatologically. The *Urzeit* prefigures the *Endzeit*, the community has access to the fountain of the end-times (Ezek. 47:1-12; Zech. 13:1; 14:8).

> For you have brought [your truth and] your [g]ory to all the men of your council, and cast their lot with the angels of presence... [Their root] will sprout like a flo[wer of the field f]or ever, to make a shoot grow in branches of the everlasting plantation... All the streams of Eden [will water] its [bra]n[ch]es.... The source of light [will] be an ever-flowing spring (14:12-17).

> I give [you] thanks, [Lord,] because you have set me at the source of streams in a dry land, at the spring of water in a parched land, in a garden watered by channels [,] a plantation of cypresses and elms together with cedars, for your glory. Trees of life in the secret source, hidden among all the trees at the water, shall make a shoot grow in the everlasting plantation, to take root before they grow. Their roots extend to the gul[ly], its trunk opens to the living waters that will be an ever-

---

[24] On the relation between Eden and Temple images, see O. Keel, *The Symbolism of the Biblical World. Ancient Near Eastern Iconography and the Book of Psalms* (New York, 1978), pp. 116-118, 140-143, 186-188; T. Elgvin, *An Analysis of 4QInstruction* (Ph.D. diss., Hebrew University of Jerusalem, 1978), pp. 128-133.

lasting spring... He who causes the h[o]ly shoot to grow in the true plantation hides, his sealed mystery is neither considered nor known... You, my God, have placed in my mouth as it were early rain and a spring of running water for all [who are thirsty]... But the plantation of fruit [will be] everlasting, a glorious garden of Eden that will bear fru[it always.] By my hand you have opened their spring with channels [of water]... When I stretch my hand to dig out its ditches, its roots pierce the rock of silex, [ ] their trunk into the earth, and in the time of heat it retains its vitality. But if I remove my hand it will be like the acac[ia in the desert,] its trunk like nettles in salt flats...it is impossible to silence the voice of [the tong]ue of my instruction, (16:4-8, 10-11, 16, 20-24, 35-36)

The creation hymn that precedes the Teacher hymn (1QH^a 9) praises the God of knowledge (9:26) for the wonders of creation: "You have established the eternal [generations] by your wisdom" (9:7); "In the wisdom of your knowledge you have determined their course before they came to exist" (9:19-20); "You have created the earth by your strength, you founded the seas and deeps [and all their] by your wisdom" (9:13-14). Also this hymn has a deep confidence in divine revelation of mysteries to the elect: "These things I know through your knowledge, for you opened my ears to wondrous mysteries although I am a creature of clay" (9:21). The hymn concludes by an exhortation: "Listen, wise men, you who meditate on knowledge and are impetuous, be of staunch purpose!" (9:34-35).

Community Hymns

The community hymns demonstrate the impact of the Teacher on his followers. The speakers of these hymns do not exalt in being mediators of revelation and knowledge to others. But they have a deep confidence of belonging to a community to whom has been imparted heavenly knowledge, angelic wisdom. The angels accompany their partners below ("the mediators of knowledge are with all my steps," 23:6). The community of the end-times has access to the everflowing spring. As was the case with the Teacher, the singers know they are unworthy of the mercies bestowed upon them:

> I flourish like a [li]ly, my heart opens to an everflowing spring (28:31).

> You have opened a [spr]ing in the mouth of your servant... You mediate these matters to dust such as me (23:10-12).

> Blessed are yo[u, Lord,] because you have given [your] ser[vant] the insight of knowledge to understand your wonders (19:27-28).

> I, the knowledgeable, have known you, my God, through the spirit which you gave in me, and I have listened loyally to your wonderful secret through your holy spirit. You have [op]ened within me knowledge of the mystery of your wisdom (20:11-13).
>
> To the sons of your truth you have given intelligence [that will last] for ever (28:27).
>
> Bless the one who does amazing wonders, and shows the might of his hand seal[ing] up mysteries and revealing hidden things" (26:14-15, 4QH^a 7 i 18-19).
>
> What is flesh to these things? And what is [man] to recount these things from period to period, and to stand in positio[n with] the sons of heaven (col. 2b bottom = 4QH^a 7 ii 16-18).
>
> [What is] the spirit of flesh to understand all these matters and to have insight in [your wonders] and great council? (5:19-20).

The members of the community shall also honor each other according to each one's level of insight. "According to his [int]elligence I bring him near, I love him in proportion to the abundance of his inheritance" (6:18-19).

Two hymns in particular (15:26-33; 19:3-14) connect the salvation of the elect with imparted knowledge.[25] These hymns refer to the community of the elect (the sons of God's truth/favor), who through purification are brought from a sinful state to salvation.

> I give [you] thanks, [Lord,] because you have taught me your truth, you have made me know your wonderful mysteries and your kindness toward [ ] man, with the abundance of your compassion with the depraved of heart.... All the sons of your truth (you bring) to forgiveness in your presence, you pu[ri]fy them from their offences by the greatness of your goodness, and by the abundance of your com[pas]sion, to make them stand in your presence for ever and ever (15:26-27, 29-31).
>
> What am I that you have [ta]ught me the basis of your truth, and have instructed me in your wonderful works? ... In your wrath are all punishing judgements, but in your goodness is abundance of forgiveness and compassion for all the sons of your favor, for you have taught them the basis of your truth, and have instructed them in your wonderful mysteries. For the sake of your glory you have purified man from offence, so that he can make himself holy for you from every impure abomination and guilt of unfaithfulness, to become united wi[th] the sons of your truth and in the lot with your holy ones, to raise the worms of the dead from the dust to an ever[lasting] community, and from a depraved

---

[25] Tanzer, *The Sages at Qumran*, pp. 37-42.

spirit to knowledge[of you], so that he can take his place in your presence with the perpetual host and the spirits of [heaven] (19:3-4, 8-13).

Revelation, Mysteries and the End-Time Community

As the community of the end-time with access to the sources of Eden, the *Yahad* has been given "as inheritance all the glory of Adam [and] abundance of days" (1QH^a 4:15; cf., 1QS 4:22-23: "For those God has chosen for an everlasting covenant and to them shall belong all the glory of Adam;" CD 3:20: "Those who remained steadfast in it will acquire eternal life, and all the glory of Adam is theirs").

The *Yahad* inherited an apocalyptically flavored tradition on revelation of wisdom from above, "the mysteries of God," drawing upon writings that perhaps belonged to groups antecedent to the Community (Enochic books, 1Q/4QMysteries, 4QInstruction). Where earlier sapiential tradition saw a close relation between God's creation and his *wisdom*, 1Q/4QMysteries, 4QInstruction, and the Hodayot relate creation to God's *mysteries*, *raze 'el*. *Raz* is the central phrase for the secrets of God.[26] It is often used about the knowledge of God and his ways, which now are revealed to the members of the community: "You have [o]pened within me knowledge of the mystery of your wisdom and the source of [your] power" (1QH^a 20:13).

The precise term "mystery to come" (known from 4QInstruction and 1Q/4QMysteries) occurs once, in the hymn that closes the Community Rule: "He let his light shine from the source of his knowledge. My eye has beheld his wonders, and the light of my heart the mystery to come" (1QS 11:3-4). A few lines below comes a parallel sentence "My eyes have gazed on what came into being from eternity (*haw'e 'olam*), on wisdom concealed from men, on knowledge and wise design (hidden) from the sons of men" (1QS 11:5-6). We encounter similar phrases in 1QS 3:15 "From the God of knowledge is everything that was and comes into being" (*kol howeh ve-hiyeh*), and CD 2:9-10: "He decided the number and length of their years and their determined periods, for the times that have been and those that ever will be" (*lekol howe 'olamim ve-nehiyot 'ad*). The evidence suggests that the meaning of "mystery to come" is close to what we found in 4QInstruction.

---

[26] See, e.g., 1QHa 11:11; 8:5-6, 11; 9:23; 12:13, 20. "Wondrous mysteries" is used in 1QS 4:6; 9:18; 11:5; 1QHa 1:21; 2:13; 7:27; 11:10.

To a large degree the Community writes about God's "mysteries" and "wondrous mysteries" in the same sense 4QInstruction and 1Q/4QMysteries use this word group. The mysteries are the secrets of God that are revealed to the elect community, and these mysteries include knowledge about the ways of history and the last days. The Habakkuk Pesher uses "mysteries" for God's secret plan for history and the last days. The mysteries have been revealed to the Teacher, and through him to the Community (1QpHab 7:1-8):

> God told Habakkuk to write down that which would happen to the final generation, but he did not make known to him when time would come to an end. And when it reads "that he who reads may read it speedily," its interpretation refers to the Righteous Teacher, to whom God made known all the mysteries of his servants the prophets... Its (Hab. 2:3a) interpretation means that the final age shall be prolonged and shall exceed all that the prophets have said, for the mysteries of God are astounding.

Knowledge is to understand the times. From the Teacher the Community has learned how to use Scripture as a key to understanding its own time and the challenges it encounters.

The eschatological community portrayed in the War Scroll enjoys fellowship with the angels, who play an important role in the battle. The Hodayot as well as the hymn concluding the Community Rule (1QS 11:7-8) portrays the sectarians as partners of the angels in God's revelation and in the heavenly praise. Also this preoccupation with the heavenly world belongs to the apocalyptic heritage of the *Yahad*. In the writings of the *Yahad*, angelology is related to ecclesiology. The community saw itself as a spiritual temple that temporarily substitutes for the defiled Temple in Jerusalem.[27] The worship in this "temple of men" (4Q174 3:6) is connected to the angelic worship in the heavenly temple.

Enochic writings and 4QInstruction presuppose a connection between revelation and the fellowship of the elect. The authors of the Enochic books belonged to circles, perhaps some kind of a community, who saw themselves as living in the end-times. In 4QInstruction the elect addressee who has knowledge of God's mysteries is related to the "eternal planting" who will inherit the land. When we encounter the *Yahad*, we find a clearly defined community with a hierarchi-

---

[27] See 1QS 5:5-7; 16:1-10; 17:3-6; CD 3:19-4:1; 1QpHab 12:1-6; 4Q164 (4QpIsad) frg. 1; 4Q174 (4QMidrEschata) 3:6-7.

cal structure. The last days have broken in, and God has established on earth a spiritual temple, a community that actively participates in the final spiritual struggle (1QS 8:5-6):

> ...the Council of the Community is founded by truth. And it shall be an eternal planting, a holy house for Israel, an assembly of supreme holiness for Aaron. They shall be witnesses to truth at the judgement, the elect of (his) goodwill that shall atone for the land.

To summarize, the sages of the *Yahad* interpreted the (biblical and post-biblical) tradition of "the wisdom of God" in an apocalyptic manner. True wisdom belongs to the mysteries of God that he has revealed to the elect community only. The revelation of these mysteries provides knowledge of God and his ways as well as understanding of history and the last days. The elect community is portrayed as a spiritual temple that enjoys fellowship with the angels. It is the "eternal planting" that will enjoy blessings in the renewed land of Israel.

PART 4

COMPARING JUDAISMS

15. PAUL'S AND QUMRAN'S JUDAISM

Heikki Räisänen
University of Helsinki

The members of the "new covenant" in Qumran were radical Jews. So was Paul of Tarsus, though his radicalism developed in a different direction. In many ways his "universalism" came to represent the opposite to the introverted piety of the Qumranites, who more or less isolated themselves from the outside world.[1] Nevertheless, certain analogies in details make a personal contact with Essenes, if not with Qumranites, at some point in Paul's life quite likely. More important, a striking structural correspondence at the very center of the respective theologies emerges. Both Paul and the Qumranites believed that they represented the true Israel who could trust on God's promises to his people, whereas the great mass of the people had forfeited this privilege.[2]

Paul started his religious life in a rather Qumran-like manner. He was a Pharisee. To be sure, even Pharisees were attacked by the Qumranites for being too liberal—"seekers of smooth things." Paul, however, belonged to a rigorous wing, surely being equal to the Qumranites as far as halakhic zeal is concerned (though of course he went astray, from the Qumranic point of view, by not observing the

---

[1] There is one very Qumran-like section in Paul's writings, 2 Cor. 6:14 - 7:1, but it is most likely an interpolation.

[2] For recent comparisons of Paul and Qumran see, e.g., H-W. Kuhn, "The Impact of the Qumran Scrolls on the Understanding of Paul," in D. Dimant and U. Rappaport, eds., *The Dead Sea Scrolls: Forty Years of Research* (Leiden, 1992), pp. 327-339; idem, "Qumran und Paulus: Unter traditionsgeschichtlichem Aspekt ausgewählte Parallelen," in U. Mell and U.B. Müller, eds., *Das Urchristentum in ihrer literarischen Geschichte, Festschrift J. Becker* (Berlin & New York, 1999), pp. 227-246; J.A. Fitzmyer, "Paul and the Dead Sea Scrolls," in P.W. Flint and J.C. VanderKam, eds., *The Dead Sea Scrolls after Fifty Years* (Leiden, 1999), vol. 2, pp. 599-621. It is customary to compare details of language and theology on one hand and to explore the issue of possible interdependence or common traditio-historical roots on the other. Structural comparisons are few and far between. E.P. Sanders, *Paul and Palestinian Judaism* (London, 1977), has a comprehensive discussion (pp. 239-328) of the "pattern" of the religion of Qumran. His brief (but perceptive) remarks on Paul and Qumran are embedded in a comparison of Paul to Palestinian Judaism at large (especially Rabbinic Judaism); see esp. pp. 544-547.

right calendar). In retrospect, Paul described his "former life" as follows (Gal 1:13-14):

> You have heard of my former life in Judaism, how I persecuted the church of God violently and tried to destroy it; and I advanced in Judaism beyond many of my own age among my people, so extremely zealous was I for the traditions of my fathers.[3]

The word *ioudaismos* indicates that Paul devoted special attention to those rulings and customs that maintained a boundary between the pure and the impure, especially between Jews and gentiles, but—as in Qumran—also between Jew and Jew. Like the author of the "Halakhic letter" (4Q MMT) he probably tried to "segregate himself from the rest of the people."[4] Unlike the Qumranites, however, he was not content with that. His loyalty to the traditions of the fathers kindled in him a sense of a mission: he had to fight for the tradition, if it was jeopardized. In his later life he similarly fought for spreading his new discovery.

Paul's zeal led him to oppose fanatically a new religious movement in Palestine. Followers of a certain Jesus of Nazareth claimed that this man was God's messiah who had suffered an ignominious death on a Roman cross but had been vindicated by God. God had raised him from the dead to his right hand. This meant that the end-time, or the great turn of history, eagerly awaited by many, had begun. Jesus the Messiah was soon to return in glory to hold judgment over the living and the dead.

There was nothing scandalous in the proclamation of an eschatological message; Paul must have been bent on end-time expectation himself. So were the Qumranites who believed that the final days had already begun. Of course, belief in a crucified messiah may have seemed ridiculous. But what made it really offensive and moved it from the sphere of private curiosity to a public issue was the fact that part of the Jesus people—a group of "Hellenists" in Jerusalem—had ceased to observe the Torah in its totality. It seems that they associated themselves with gentiles (probably "God-fearers," sympathizers from the fringes of local synagogues) whom they had welcomed to their common meals without paying proper attention to the food

---

[3] The biblical quotations follow the RSV.
[4] 4Q 397 frags. 7+8: 7. Apart from a few exceptions (to be indicated when necessary), I follow the translation and the enumeration system of F. García Martínez, *The Dead Sea Scrolls Translated* (2nd ed., Leiden, 1996).

laws. Worse, gentiles were invited to join a Jewish community without subjecting themselves to the God-given entrance rite, circumcision. Some gentiles were being made part of Israel *qua* gentiles!⁵

Such outrageous behavior could not be tolerated, and Paul tried to destroy the Jesus people by "persecuting" them—whatever the word means in this connection. At the very least, he must have been engaged in violent polemics; probably he also tried to have measures of discipline applied to them. Lashing, even stoning, may have been included.⁶

In the middle of this activity, a vision changed Paul's life. He saw what he took to be the heavenly Jesus, the messiah raised to glory. There are some indications of an ecstatic inclination in Paul's letters. His foundational vision seems akin to (later) Rabbinic visions connected with the experiences known as Merkabah (chariot) mysticism.⁷ Whatever the nature of the experience, the inference Paul drew was clear: the Jesus-believers were, after all, right in their messianic claims.

It followed that they were right even in their convictions about the Torah and the gentiles. They were right about what it meant to be heir to the promises of the God of Israel in the present. In his letter to the Galatians, Paul suggests that the Christ vision immediately made it clear to him that he had been called to work as an "apostle" to the gentiles (Gal. 1:15f). This indicates that it was the (law-free) mission to gentiles that had been the bone of contention between Paul and those he had persecuted. It is hard not to associate Paul's later ostentatious license with regard to the Torah somehow—however vaguely—with an ecstatic sense of liberation. One can speculate that in some sense the law had been a (suppressed) problem for him all along, in particular perhaps as an entity that separated Jews from other people and stood in the way of the realization of the Hellenistic ideal of universal humanity.⁸ "Why would a universal God desire and

---

⁵ For a discussion of the "Hellenists" around Stephen, mentioned in Acts 6-8, see H. Räisänen, *Jesus, Paul and Torah* (Sheffield, 1992), pp. 149-202.

⁶ Scholars disagree on the nature and setting of Paul's persecution of the Christians; many doubt Luke's account, which portrays Saul/Paul as participating in the stoning of the Hellenist Stephen, Acts 7.58, 8.1. Gal. 1, rather, suggests that Paul was not in Jerusalem shortly before his conversion experience.

⁷ See the seminal work of A. Segal, *Paul the Convert* (New Haven, 1990).

⁸ This is the thesis of D. Boyarin, *A Radical Jew* (Berkeley, 1994).

command that one people should circumcise the male members of the tribe and command food taboos that made it impossible for one people to join in table fellowship with all the rest of his children?" he may have asked himself.[9] "We can account for Paul's [later] putting everyone in the same situation by assuming that this was exactly what was bothering him about Judaism, namely that it did not 'equate the status of Jew and gentile.'"[10] Some clues indicate that ecstatic experiences had much to do with the birth of liberal "Christian" communities as a whole.[11]

The vision sparked off a colorful career. Paul first became a missionary of the Antiochian congregation and, later, after a break with the Antiochians due to a conflict over the law, an independent "apostle." His career lasted some thirty years, down to the early sixties. He traveled widely, founded communities in various cities in Greece and Asia Minor, preached a law-free message of Jesus the Christ and Lord, and encouraged Jewish and gentile believers to live together, sharing meals without regard to Jewish purity regulations. As a consequence, he faced grave opposition both from the synagogue and from more traditional Jewish Christ-believers. Most Jews regarded him as an apostate;[12] for many Christ-believers too he was a suspect heretic. But he himself never ceased to regard himself as a Jew, and one of the rather few true Jews at that.

In an eschatological fervor, Paul hurried from one city to another. He kept contact with his congregations through letters, a number of which have been preserved. The main letters are those to Corinth, Galatia, and Rome. The Corinthian correspondence bears witness to all kinds of practical problems among the new, mainly gentile, converts and to a remarkable opposition to Paul from various quarters.

---

[9] Ibid., p. 39.
[10] Ibid., p. 44.
[11] In Gal. 3:2-5, Paul asks his converts polemically: "Did you receive the Spirit by works of the law, or by hearing with faith? (...) Does he who supplies the Spirit to you and works miracles among you do so by works of the law, or by hearing with faith?" In Acts 10:44-48, Peter's decision to baptize his gentile hearers right away depends on their having begun to speak in tongues.
[12] Cf., Acts 21: "they [zealous Jews] have been told about you [Paul] that you teach all the Jews who are among the gentiles to forsake Moses, telling them not to circumcise their children or observe the customs" (v. 21). "This is the man who is teaching men everywhere against the people and the law and this place [the Temple]..." (v. 28).

The heavily polemical Galatians is a virulent attack on unknown, more conservative teachers who had recommended to Paul's converts that they take a complementary second step and become full Jews by accepting circumcision. This letter contains very negative statements on the Torah. Paul's later letter to the Romans, to a group of congregations he had not founded himself, has a more conciliatory tone, steering a middle course between the radicalism of Galatians and the conservatism of the apostle's critics.[13]

Community Life

Both in Qumran and in Paul's congregations an end-time atmosphere reigns. One can speak of an "inaugurated eschatology" in both cases: some of the blessings of the new age have already been realized. Worship in the Qumran community anticipates the eternal worship in heaven and gives a foretaste of the latter in that the cult is shared with heavenly hosts. "The corrupt spirit you have purified from great sin so that he can take his place *with the host of the holy ones*, and can enter into communion with the congregation of the *sons of heaven*." (1 QH 11:21-22)[14] The cultic meal of the community was felt to be a ritual anticipation of the messianic banquet (1QSa 2:17-22).

For Paul, the spirit of God, believed to have been poured on his congregations, amounts to a foretaste of the eschatological fulfillment. In his congregations, especially in Corinth, charismatic freedom reigns. The spirit manifests itself in frequent ecstatic outbursts—healings, visions, prophecy, glossolaly—to the extent that Paul (though claiming to speak more than anyone else in tongues) finds it necessary to counter this tendency and to attempt to keep ecstasy in check. Some prophetesses in particular seem to make him nervous (1 Cor. 14:33-36).

---

[13] The picture is rounded by an early letter to the Thessalonians, a late one to the Philippians, and a personal note to a private person, Philemon, concerning the future of his slave. The pseudonymous letters include 2 Thessalonians, Colossians, Ephesians, and the Pastorals.

[14] Cf., the cryptic reference to the presence of angels in 1 Cor. 11:10: "That is why a woman ought to have a veil on her head [in the cultic meetings], because of the angels."

In this, the life-style in Paul's mixed congregations differs markedly from that in Qumran. In Qumran, blameless *order* is everything, as the Rule of the Congregation (1 QS) makes abundantly clear. The maintenance of holiness demands strict hierarchy; everybody knows his place and rank. The adamant order was made possible through the strict rules of admission. They contrast markedly with Paul's spontaneous practice, which led to problems afterwards, especially in Corinth, where some members continued practices Paul branded as fornication and idolatry.[15]

Order reigned in the Qumran worship as well. A contribution of women would have been as unthinkable as the presence of uncircumcised gentiles. Still, as a remote analogy to the excitement in Corinth, even in Qumran some kind of ecstasy may have been the goal. The Songs of Sabbath Sacrifice seem, due to their "hypnotic" repetitive and formulaic character, "to have increased the possibility of ecstatic experience among some worshippers."[16] By such means, people are led to feel that they are indeed worshiping together with angels. This insight gives the present moment its exalted character.

The End-Time Drama

And the time is short. In Qumran, a violent eschatological war was expected, in which God would dramatically vindicate his faithful. The sect would occupy Jerusalem (1 QM) and rebuild the Temple (11QT). Paul does not expect a final war; humans do not apparently actively participate in the end-drama. But he too expects God to take control over everything. This involves the destruction of the unbelievers and the unrighteous on the earth, and of inimical powers in heaven.[17] The Qumranites and Paul agree in trusting that God's victory, and with it the final great turn of history, is close at hand. The Qumranites seem to expect a transformed new life on earth,

---

[15] "... a man is living with his father's wife" (1 Cor. 5:1); some Corinthian Christians visit prostitutes (1 Cor. 6:12-20); some must be warned against "the worship of idols" (1 Cor. 10:14).

[16] C. Newsom, *Songs of the Sabbath Sacrifice* (Atlanta, 1985), p. 17.

[17] "Then comes the end, when he [Christ] delivers the kingdom to God the Father after destroying every rule and every authority and power. For he must reign until he has put all his enemies under his feet" (1 Cor. 15:24-25).

whereas Paul apparently hopes for a transcendent life in God's heaven, though in neither case is the nature of the hope unambiguously clear.[18] In this, both share in tendencies common among Second Temple Judaisms. Yet both must be located on the more "intolerant" side of the spectrum (as no mass conversion of gentiles, but rather the destruction of God's enemies is in view).

Salvation by Grace

As characteristic representatives of Second Temple Judaisms, both Qumran and Paul, trusting on God's promises, believed themselves to be on the victorious side when the end would come. Unlike most, however, both the Qumranites and Paul thought that there were, at present at least, very few persons who (still) belonged to God's elect. They themselves were the tiny remnant. The majority of the Jewish people were outside (not to speak of the mass of the gentiles).

Both the Qumran people and Paul's converts believed that they were God's elect, destined to attain salvation, but not because of any merits of their own. The priority of God's grace is emphasized by the Qumranites and Paul alike, just as it had been emphasized in the traditional doctrine of election. The significant difference is, however, that it is not the people as a collective that has been elected (1QS 11:11-15):

> As for me, if I stumble, the mercies of God shall be my salvation always, and if I fall in the sin of the flesh, in the justice of God, which endures eternally, shall my judgment be. If my grief commences, he will free my soul from the pit and make my steps steady on the path; he will draw me near in his mercies, and by kindnesses set in motion my judgment; he will judge me in the justice of his truth, and in his plentiful goodness always atone for my sins; in his justice he will cleanse me from the uncleanness of the human being and from the sins of the sons of man.

God has given wisdom, righteousness and glory to his elect "as everlasting possession, until they inherit them in the lot of the holy ones"

---

[18] There are some traces of the expectation of an earthly fulfillment in Paul: the "eager longing of the creation" for the coming glory (Rom. 8:18-25); the expectation that the Christians will judge both the world and angels (1 Cor. 6:2-3); possibly the conviction that Christ "must reign" (1 Cor. 15:25, see previous note). And it has long been debated whether the Qumran people expected a bodily resurrection of their dead or not.

(1QS 11:7). The poet feels his sinfulness; as such he belongs to those who walk in darkness (11:9-10). A stark contrast is thus established between sinful human beings and the righteous God. The view of life is theocentric. Salvation, one's lot in the holy community, depends on God's grace alone. "*Only* by your goodness is man acquitted" (1QH 5:23).[19] A humble feeling of unworthiness and sinfulness runs through the Qumran hymns when the poets compare themselves to God, the creator.[20]

In Qumran the acknowledgement of grace leads to loyalty shown through obedience to the Torah or, in practice, to the distinctive halakhah of the community. Occasionally the deeds specifically required by the Torah are called "works of the law," an exact verbal parallel to Paul's *erga nomou*. The writer of the "Halakhic letter" summarizes (4Q398 frag. 2: 2.2-4): "We have written to you *some of the works of the Torah* which we think are good for you and for your people, for [we saw] in you intellect and knowledge of the Torah." In this phrase are summed up such rulings as have been mentioned in the earlier paragraphs, rulings that relate chiefly to the temple, priesthood, sacrifices, and purity.

Still, even correct obedience is conceived as an act of divine grace. Man himself is unable to establish his steps, so everything is established by God, which for the Psalmist is a cause of delightful confidence:

> As for me, in God is my judgment; in His hand is the perfection of my path.... (1QS 11:2)

> For to man (does not belong) his path, nor to a human being the steadying of his step; since judgment belongs to God, and from his hand is the perfection of the path. (1QS 11:10-11)

Paul states in Rom. 3:24 that the believers "are justified by [God's] grace as a gift." But in contrast to Qumran, justification by grace

---

[19] Or "justified" (*ysdq*). With Luther in mind, Kuhn notes that "apart from the polemic "not by faith alone" in James 2:24, in all ancient Jewish and Christian literature this is the only literary "only" concerning justification. "So the sola gratia is Jewish, too, while the sola fide (...), of course, is especially Pauline" ("Impact," pp. 333f).

[20] When the Qumranites compare themselves to each other, they are quite capable of detecting grades of holiness, worthiness und wisdom; indeed the correct ranking along such lines plays a decisive role in the life of the community. Cf., Sanders, *Paul*, pp. 266f.

implies for Paul that "works of the law" are not required of them. This is so, because there is only one way to salvation, which God has graciously opened and revealed in the end-time: faith in Jesus the Christ. Paul's vision had made him firm in this conviction. This is, first of all, good news to the gentiles who need not subject themselves to circumcision in order to be part of God's people. Before God there is neither Jew nor Greek. Therefore, salvation is by faith (in Jesus as the Christ) (Gal 3:27-28):

> For as many of you as were baptized into Christ, have put on Christ. There is neither Jew nor Greek, there is neither slave nor free, there is neither male nor female; for you are all one in Christ Jesus.

Nevertheless, Paul too assumes a judgment according to deeds:

> For [God] will render to every man according to his works...there will be tribulation and distress for every human being who does evil, the Jew first and also the Greek, but glory and honor and peace for every one who does good, the Jew first and also the Greek. For God shows no partiality (...) It is not the hearers of the law who are righteous before God, but the doers of the law will be justified. (Rom. 2:6-13)

> We must all appear before the judgment seat of Christ, so that each one may receive good or evil, according to what he has done in the body. (2 Cor. 5:10)

Paul, too, regards right moral action as necessary. Herein he follows the traditional structure of the Jewish religion. Only, for him the actions needed are not what he calls the works of the law, i.e., deeds specifically required by the Torah. Paul claims that right actions come forth spontaneously as the fruit of God's spirit in the life of his communities.

There is less sense of actual sinfulness in Paul than in the Qumran hymns, though he does dwell on sinfulness as a theological theory.[21] In the beginning of Romans (chap. 1-3) he seems indeed to argue that since the human condition is hopeless, God sent Christ (Rom. 3:9-12-24; note the third person, as contrasted with the first person in the Qumran hymns):

> (...) all men, both Jews and Greeks, are under the power of sin, as it is written: "None is righteous, no, not one ... all have turned aside, to-

---

[21] The interpretation of the "I" who is "sold under sin" in Rom. 7 is notoriously controversial. Most scholars would (in the light of Rom. 8) deny that Paul is speaking of sinfulness as a personal experience of Christians.

gether they have gone wrong, no one does good, not even one" (...) there is no distinction; since all have sinned and fall short of the glory of God, they are justified by his grace as a gift....

This argument is, however, undermined by Rom. 2 with its emphasis on judgment according to the deeds (see above on Rom 2:9ff.). Even good gentiles are in the position to obey God's will (Rom. 2:14):

> When gentiles who have not the law do by nature what the law requires, they are a law to themselves....

So what Paul is really aiming at is the removal of any difference between Jews and gentiles. Jews are not in a privileged position. The point of the catena of biblical quotations in Rom. 3:10ff. is the conclusion that no one is justified through works of the law. The whole world is guilty before God (Rom. 3:19-20):

> Now we know that whatever the law says it speaks to those who are under the law, so that every mouth may be stopped, and the whole world may be held accountable to God. For no human being will be justified in his sight by works of the law, since through the law comes knowledge of sin.

Paul's communities consist of Jews and gentiles; this leads him to stress the impartiality of God. He is convinced that God has made this coexistence possible by making Jesus the gateway to the community of the faithful. Since faith in Jesus is all-important in bringing humans into a right relationship to God—humans are "justified by faith in Christ"—the significance of obedience to God's law is reduced.[22] Jesus becomes the only and exclusive way to salvation.

Paul passionately defends the right of his gentile believers to belong to the group of God's chosen ones (Rom 3:27-31):

> Then what becomes of our boasting? It is excluded. On what principle/law? Through the law of works? No, but through the "law" of faith. For we hold that a man is justified by faith apart from works of law. Or is God the God of Jews only? Is he not the God of gentiles also? Yes, of gentiles also, since God is one; and he will justify the circumcised on the ground of their faith and the uncircumcised through their faith. Do we

---

[22] Logically, this might not have been inevitable; Paul's aversion to the law hangs together with the practice of his mixed congregations. The interpretation of Paul's view of the Torah is extremely controversial in scholarship. I follow the course outlined in my *Paul and the Law* (2nd ed.; Tübingen, 1987). For a fresh discussion, see now K. Kuula, *The Law, the Covenant and God's Plan. Vol. 1: Paul's Polemical Treatment of the Law in Galatians* (Helsinki, 1999).

then overthrow the law by this faith? By no means! On the contrary, we uphold the law.[23]

Paul's language of justification has often been overemphasized. It appears almost exclusively in such contexts in which Paul defends in biblical language the right of uncircumcised gentiles to be members of his communities. For Paul's own soteriology the notion of participation in Christ, or in his "body", or the spirit of God or of Christ, as an experienced power, are more central.[24] Therefore, even in Galatians, having proposed his thesis of justification by faith, Paul immediately moves to speak of salvation and the law in terms of "participation in Christ" (Gal. 2:15-21):

> [15]We ourselves, who are Jews by birth and not Gentile sinners, [16]yet who know that a man is not justified by works of the law but through faith in Jesus Christ, even we have believed in Christ Jesus, in order to be justified by faith... [17]But if, in our endeavor to be justified in Christ, we ourselves were found to be sinners, is Christ then an agent of sin? Certainly not! [18]But if I build again those things which I tore down, then I prove myself a transgressor. [19]For I through the law died to the law, that I might live to God. [20]I have been crucified with Christ; it is no longer I who live but Christ who lives in me... [21]I do not nullify the grace of God; for if justification were through the law, then Christ died to no purpose.

This can be read in the following way. The difference between Jews and gentiles (15) is removed: even "we" (Jews) have had to take a new step, for this is the way to salvation for *all* people (16). In doing this, in living out our new freedom by sharing the table with our gentile sisters and brothers, we have transgressed some requirements of the Torah. But since Christ cannot possibly serve sin, God must have meant that ours is a correct attitude to the Torah. If, on the other hand, we now return to our earlier practice (as Peter and company had done in giving up the table fellowship under pressure[25]), then we show that our freedom has indeed been arbitrary (18). But this is not the case! God himself has seen to it[26] that we have died to the law in

---

[23] The argument continues in Rom. 4, where Abraham is set up as a prototype of uncircumcised believers.

[24] The point has been forcefully made by Sanders, *Paul*, pp. 447ff.

[25] This "Antiochian incident" is described in Gal. 2:11-14.

[26] The expression "through the law" in v. 19 is unclear, but it must mean something like this: Paul's giving up full observance was not an arbitrary decision of his own, but conformed to God's will.

order to live for God (note that "law" and "God" become opposites!). And here Paul moves to celebrate his mystical participation in Christ (20-21).

The author of the "Halakhic letter" hopes that "at the end of time, you may rejoice in finding that some of our words are true. And it shall be *reckoned to you as righteousness* (cf., Gen. 15:6) when you do what is upright and good before him...."[27] Righteousness is reckoned to those who are faithful in following the practices outlined in the earlier paragraphs of the letter. For Paul (Gal. 3:6), Gen. 15:6 proves that "men of faith" (rather than those who rely on the law) are the true sons of Abraham, even if they be uncircumcised gentiles. He redefines the descendants of Abraham as those who believe (namely, in Jesus) (Gal 3:6-9):

> "Abraham believed God, and it was reckoned to him as righteousness." So you see that it is men of faith who are the sons of Abraham. And the scripture, foreseeing that God would justify the Gentiles by faith, preached the gospel beforehand to Abraham, saying: 'In you shall all the nations be blessed.' So then, those who are men of faith are blessed with Abraham who had faith.

In Rom. 4 Paul goes on to ask whether Abraham was circumcised at the time when faith was reckoned to him as righteousness. No, he was not (yet) circumcised, and therefore he is "the father of all who believe without being circumcised" (Rom. 4:10-11).[28]

A similar contrast (often noted) can be seen in the use of Hab. 2:4. Although Paul and Qumran speak of faith in Christ or loyalty to the Teacher of Righteousness respectively, for Paul observance and faith stand totally opposed to each other. On the other hand, for Qumran "loyalty" or "trust" (*emunah*, the equivalence of Paul's *pistis*) is part of law observance which leads to salvation (1QpHab 8.1-2):[29]

---

[27] 4Q398 frag. 2.2:6-7; García Martínez translates "it shall be reckoned to you as in justice."

[28] In Galatians, Paul fails to mention that two chapters later (Gen. 17) Abraham did receive the commandment of circumcision as an "everlasting covenant." In Rom. 4 he has discovered an explanation for this: Abraham "received circumcision as a seal of the righteousness which he had by faith while he was still uncircumcised" (4:11). What a marvelous weapon this argument would have been to his pro-circumcision opponents! To be sure, Paul does not deny that Abraham is "the father of the circumcised" as well—insofar as they share Abraham's faith which, for Paul, means faith in Jesus as the Christ.

[29] Kuhn, "Impact," p. 330.

Its [Hab 2:4] interpretation concerns all observing the Law in the House of Judah, whom God will deliver from the House of Judgement on account of their deeds[30] and of their loyalty to the Teacher of Righteousness.

Paul, by contrast, claims in Gal. 3:10-14 that observant Jews are under a curse:[31]

> [10]For all who rely on works of the law are under a curse; for it is written, "Cursed be every one who does not abide by all things written in the book of the law, and do them." [11]Now it is evident that no man is justified before God by the law, for "the righteous shall live by faith;" [12]but the law does not rest on faith, for "He who does them shall live by them." [13]Christ redeemed us from the curse of the law, having become a curse for us—for it is written, "Cursed be every one who hangs on a tree"[32]—[14]that in Christ Jesus the blessing of Abraham might come upon the gentiles, that we might receive the promise of the Spirit through faith.

Verse 10 could perhaps be taken as an attempt at "empirical" explanation: the law amounts to a curse, because no one is capable of fulfilling it perfectly. But this is uncertain, and in any case vss. 11 and 12 reveal Paul's main point: the way of the faith excludes by definition the way of the law. Christ redeems "us" from the curse (13), and somehow this opens for gentiles the way to the God of Abraham (14). The gentiles are never far from sight when Paul makes negative comments on the Torah of the Jews.

In the sequel (Gal. 3:15-18) Paul argues that no additions can be made to a will; therefore, the law, regarded as an "addition" to the promise to Abraham, is not valid. He then suggests (Gal. 3:19-20) that it may not even stem directly from God (though this must be regarded as an *ad hoc* argument, not a constant conviction of Paul[33]):

> The law, which came four hundred and thirty years afterwards, does not annul a covenant previously ratified by God, so as to make the promise void (...) Why then the law? It was added because of transgressions, till the offspring should come to whom the promise had been

---

[30] Or their "toil" or "suffering" (*'amal*).

[31] The fact that Jesus-believing Jews are in focus here does not make a difference, for it is precisely their traditional Jewish identity that is at stake.

[32] Paul's understanding of Deut. 21:23 as a reference to crucifixion is illuminated by 4QpNah 1.7-8 and 11QT 64.6-13, which shows that Paul depends on a Jewish tradition here after all. See, e.g., Kuhn, "Impact," p. 329.

[33] This is cogently argued by Kuula, *Law*, pp. 96-133.

made; and it was ordained by angels through an intermediary. Now an intermediary implies more than one; but God is one.

In the following verses (Gal. 3:22-25) Paul does make an attempt to find some positive purpose for the law after all ("the scripture consigned all things to sin, that what was promised to faith in Jesus Christ might be given to those who believe" v. 22; "the law was our custodian until Christ came," v. 24). Yet "no further positive theology of the law is built" on these verses in the following treatment.[34] In Gal. 4 Paul soon goes so far as to construct an analogy between the law and the demonic "elements of the world", putting observance of the Torah in parallel to pagan idolatry. He asks, "how can you [former pagans] turn back again to the weak and beggarly elemental spirits, whose slaves you want to be once more? You observe days and months, and seasons, and years!" (v. 9-10). This is how Paul might have viewed the Qumran people: they were slaves under a calendar!

On the whole, it seems that Paul is not thinking of Abraham "as an ancestor of the covenant people of God but as an exemplary *individual* who received promises that aimed far into the future." The history of Israel as God's chosen people is ignored.[35] In Gal. 4:21-31 Paul does draw a "historical" line—not from Abraham, but from Sinai—to the present, but that is a line of slavery! The Sinaitic covenant gives birth to slaves (4:24-25). Non-Christian Jews are descendants of the slave woman Hagar; it is only the Jesus-believers who are "children of the promise, like Isaac." In the context of such a letter, the talk of "God's Israel" in Gal. 6:16 can only refer metaphorically to the new community.[36] In Galatians, the Jews have been "allegorized out of real historical existence."[37]

If Paul allegorizes the Jews, he can at times allegorize the Torah as well. He speaks of circumcision of the heart (Rom. 2:25-29).

> He is a Jew who is one inwardly, and real circumcision is a matter of the heart, spiritual and not literal (Rom. 2:29).

---

[34] Ibid., p. 181.
[35] Ibid., p. 82.
[36] "For neither circumcision counts for anything, nor uncircumcision, but a new creation. Peace and mercy be upon all who walk by this rule, and upon the Israel of God" (Gal. 6:15-16).
[37] Boyarin, *A Radical Jew*, p. 156.

Look out for those who mutilate the flesh. For we are the [true] circumcision, who worship God in spirit, and glory in Christ Jesus, and put no confidence in the flesh (Phil 3:2-3).

In a sense, Paul was anticipated in this interpretation not only by Philo and the more radical allegorizers debated by him, but even by the Qumran people. They gave the Temple cult, in which they could not participate, an "internalized" interpretation (although sacrifices *should* have been performed, if only the Temple had been pure and not corrupt). Their own prayers substituted for the sacrifices of the Temple. The community consisted of "the men of his council who have kept the covenant in the midst of wickedness to atone [for the e]arth" (1QSa 1:3). They atoned "without the flesh of burnt offerings and without the fats of sacrifice," in their stead were "the offering of the lips in compliance with the decree" and "the correctness of behavior" (1 QS 9:4-5). The community was the Temple, "an everlasting plantation," "a holy house for Israel and the foundation for the holy of holies for Aaron" (1QS 8:5-6). Paul, too, regarded his community as God's temple (1 Cor. 3:16); indeed his ecclesiological temple language seems to go back to people associated with Qumran.[38] But Paul went much further in not just presenting allegorical interpretations: he gave up the demand of actual circumcision, at least as far as gentile converts were concerned.

Nor was Paul contented merely with internalizing or allegorizing commandments of the Torah (thus far he may simply have followed the teachings developed by the Hellenist Christians in Antioch). In the course of his debates, Paul was led much further, to connect the law with sin, curse, and death, as we have seen.[39] He construes an analogy between the Torah and the demonic "elements of the world" (Gal. 4). Here he parts company with almost all other Jews (including most Jewish Christ-believers).

Paul selected from the Torah what he had to observe. He certainly did recommend, especially through the model of his own behavior, that the food laws of the Torah could be relaxed when table fellowship between Jewish and gentile believers was at stake. In whatever

---

[38] Kuhn, "Qumran und Paulus," pp. 231, 244. Note that Paul, like 1QS, uses in the same context the metaphors of "plantation" and "foundation" as well (1 Cor. 3:5ff).

[39] For the law and sin, see also Paul's talk of "sinful passions *aroused* by the law" (Rom. 7:5); for the law and death see 2 Cor. 3:6: "the written code kills, but the Spirit gives life." "Written code" here refers to the "tablets of stone" of Moses (v. 3).

way it may have begun, during his mission Paul became largely indifferent to important parts of the Torah. Observing kosher laws became optional to him.

A lax practice demanded a liberal theology, critical of the Torah, for its defense. This is what we find in Paul's main letters. A passage in which Paul describes his mission (writing to his gentile converts in Corinth, which allows him to use less circumspect, and more frank, language than when addressing his Jewish compatriots) is revealing (1 Cor 9:19-22):

> To the Jews I became *as a Jew*, in order to win Jews; to those under law I became as one under the law—though *not being myself under the law*—that I might win those under the law. To those outside the law I became as one outside the law—not being without law toward God but under the law of Christ—that I might win those outside the law (...) I have become *all things to all men*, that I might by all means save some.

Paul here discloses that he acts among his kinsfolk *as if* he were committed to the Torah, implying of course that at bottom he was not committed. Although he had by no means broken all continuity with his Jewish heritage, he had become internally alienated from central parts of it. He felt free to pick and choose. Boyarin is right in thinking that Paul's flexibility regarding food laws "thoroughly undermines any argument that Paul intended Jews to remain Jewish, although Paul...would probably argue that he was redefining Jewishness in such a way that everyone could be Jewish."[40] A Qumranite would have counted Paul among those who had "chosen their whims (...) each one doing (what was) his desire" (CD 3:11-12).

Boundaries

In Qumran, humanity was divided into sons of light and sons of darkness (e.g., 1 QS 1:9-10). Such a dichotomy was not foreign to Paul. "You are not in darkness," he writes to his converts, "for you are sons of light and sons of the day" (1 Thess. 5:4-5).[41] Actually, in both cases one had to *enter* a new community into which one had not

---

[40] Boyarin, op. cit., p. 10.

[41] For the Qumranian background of the passage, see Kuhn, "Impact," pp. 328f. The closer Christian analogy to the Qumran people on this score is, however, the Johannine community.

been born. A member of a Pauline community had to leave his or her old life. The rite of baptism symbolized death to one's old self and often amounted to a break with one's former social life. A gentile had to leave the worship of the traditional gods of his city. But even Jews had to enter a new community, to undergo baptism. Even a Jew had to become a "new creation" in Christ (2 Cor. 5:17, Gal. 6:15). Gal. 2:16, discussed above, shows the logic: even "we" (Jews) have had to take a new step to find righteousness with God, for this is the way to salvation for *all* people. In Qumran, too, the poet perceives the forgiving of his sins in connection with his entering the community as a present experience of salvation which amounts to a new creation: "I know that there is hope for someone you *fashioned out of clay* to be an everlasting community" (1 QH 11:20-21).[42]

Within the community, purity had to be maintained. Strict punishments were meted out for transgressions in Qumran, exclusion from the community being the gravest of them. But Paul, too, could resort to requiring expulsion in the case of what he deemed to be heinous immorality (1 Cor. 5: a member of his congregation living with his father's wife). Paul, too, was profoundly concerned with purity.

Within both groups, mutual love and good-will were demanded. The "Inspector of the camp" in Qumran shall "have pity on them [the members] like a father on his sons and shall heal all strays like a shepherd his flock" (CD 13:9). The Qumran people were exhorted to reproach each other only "in truth, in meekness and in compassionate love," not "in anger or muttering" or with "spiteful intent" (1 QS 5:24-26). They cultivated a different attitude towards outsiders: "everlasting hatred" (1 QS 9:21). The "men of the pit" whom they were to hate were the rest of humanity, especially other Israelites. People who joined the community devoted themselves not only to "love all the sons of light" but also to "hate[43] all the sons of darkness" (1 QS 1:9-10), since this is what God himself does. The opening lines of the War Rule look forward to the destruction of other Jews before the showdown with gentiles.[44] Paul on the other hand speaks of living in

---

[42] For the interpretation of the passage in terms of a new creation in connection with the forgiving of sins, see Kuhn, "Qumran und Paulus," p. 236. In this case the similarity is due to common Jewish roots; it is not a question of direct interdependence.

[43] García Martínez translates: "detest."

[44] The Messianic Rule seems more optimistic and anticipates the conversion of other Israelites (1 QSa 1.1-2); see below.

peace with others and even praying for persecutors (Rom. 12:14-21);[45] still, while he exhorts the Galatians to "do good to all men," he adds the qualification "especially to those who are of the household of faith" (Gal. 6:10).

Predestination

Both the Qumran people and Paul were very much concerned with the limits of the community, though they drew the line differently. Who is in? For Paul, believing gentiles are in, without circumcision; by contrast, most of Israel are out. For Qumran, unfaithful Israel is out, and so are the gentiles. As for Israel, Paul thus agrees with Qumran, as we have seen in our reading of Galatians. Only, the rules of "righteousness" are defined differently. In the end both Qumran and Paul adhere to the principle *extra ecclesi(ol)am nulla salus*: there is no salvation outside (our) community. And each group resorts to a "doctrine" of *predestination*, both to explain why we are in and to explain why the great majority are out.

The War Scroll states that from the beginning God divided humankind into two parts. What is emphasized is the election of the community (1 QM 13:7ff.):

> You are the God of our fathers, we bless your name always. We are the people of your inheritance. You established a covenant with our fathers and ratified it with their offspring for times eternal (...) You [have crea]ted us for you, eternal people, and you have made us fall into the lot of light in accordance with your truth. From old you appointed the Prince of light to assist us....

By contrast, God created Belial "for the pit;" all the spirits of his lot walk in the laws of darkness. Here the historical election of the fathers (the covenant) and the eternal election in the creation melt together. The exhortatory scope of the passage is obvious: the chil-

---

[45] Kuhn, "Qumran und Paulus," pp. 233-235, compares the passages 1 QS 10.17-21 and Rom. 12:20, finding a contrast regarding the attitude to the enemy. On the other hand, G. Vermes, *The Dead Sea Scrolls in English* (2nd ed., Harmondsworth, 1976), p. 52, says concerning the Qumranites that "(t)he severity of their judgment of the wicked was more dogmatic than practical, as appears from their insistence that vengeance is for God alone." That vengeance belongs to the Lord is Paul's point in Rom. 12:19 as well.

dren of light are encouraged as they wait for the eschatological battle (13:14).

In the hymns, strictly predestinarian ideas are found in connection with the creation tradition. "Before creating them you know all their deeds for ever and ever" (1QH 9:7-8). This might be taken to mean mere foreknowledge, but line 19 points to another direction: "In the wisdom of your knowledge you have determined their course before they came to exist."

Another hymn states: "But the wicked you have created for the time of wrath, from the womb you have predestined them for the day of annihilation" (1 QH 7:21). Yet the idea of predestination is immediately relativized: "*For* they have walked on paths that are not good, they have rejected your covenant, their soul has loathed your decrees, they have taken no pleasure in what you command, instead they have *chosen* what you hate" (7:22-23).[46] It seems that the wicked have been created for wrath because of their own misdeeds. On the other hand, the just man, too, has been created as just by God (7:19-20):

> For him, from the womb, you determined the period of approval, *so that* he will keep your covenant and walk on all (your paths), to [empty] upon him your plentiful compassion, to open all the narrowness of his soul to eternal salvation and endless peace, without want.

Man's free will—or the lack of it—is, of course, not discussed as a philosophical problem. The just man, the Qumranite, finds strength in the conviction that his finding himself on the right path is due to God's eternal decision. The fact that others stay outside is accounted for with the explanation that this, too, is due to God's mysterious will, and yet the just man cannot help attributing some guilt to the wicked themselves. Divine predestination is never used as an excuse; it does not free man from culpability. We will see below that human choice and decision is also emphasized in Qumran (and, of course, by Paul).

The treatise on the spirits in 1 QS 3:13-4:26 is unique. It starts in a predestinarian vein, reminiscent of the creation tradition of the hymns: God has in advance established a design for everything (1 QS 3:15-16):

---

[46] The translation differs here from that of García Martínez in using the past tense (thus also Lohse and Vermes).

> From the God of knowledge stems all there is and all there shall be. Before they existed he made all their plans and when they came into being they will execute all their works in compliance with his instructions, according to his glorious design without altering anything.

But then dualism enters the stage. God has appointed two spirits for man, the spirits of truth and deceit (3:18-19), both created by him (3:25). This results in two classes of people, ruled by two different angels (3:20ff): "In the hands of the Prince of Light is dominion over all the sons of justice; they walk on paths of light. And in the hand of the Angel of Darkness is total dominion over the sons of deceit; they walk on paths of darkness." The next lines (21-22) break, however, the limits of rigid dualism, as the writer tackles the problem of actual evil, even within the community of the just: "Due to the Angel of Darkness all the sons of *justice* stray...." Their sins are caused by him; he brings punishment and grief on them. But this is temporary. In the course of the battle "the God of Israel and the angel of his truth assist all the sons of light" (3:24-25). The scope of the treatise is exhortatory: the children of light are encouraged to endure their hardships. Everything is in the hands of God whose secret plan is being carried out all the time.[47]

Despite the predestinarian theory found in this treatise and in many hymns, in practice the community presupposed the possibility of free choice. The members have entered the community voluntarily (1QS 6:13). They have "freely volunteered to carry out God's decrees" (1QS 1:7) or "to convert from all evil" (5:1); they can "choose the path" (9:17-18). The precise rules and minutely organized punishments also presuppose the possibility of choice. Despite the theory of predestination, no one is thought to be saved by merely belonging to the community. At some point, the theology of predestination has been felt to be problematic, for in the (later) Damascus Rule it is no longer present. CD 2:7-8 speaks of foreknowledge:

---

[47] The passage 1QS 4.15ff. has probably been added later. See P. von der Osten-Sacken, *Gott und Belial* (Göttingen, 1969), pp. 17-27; his analysis is now supported in the light of 4QSa by S. Metso, *The Textual Development of the Qumran Community Rule* (Leiden, 1997), pp. 138-140. In the later passage the dualism has been projected into the heart of an individual person. *All* men have a portion in *both* spirits (4:15). Light and darkness struggle even in the heart of every child of light (4:23f). Yet a child of light can be confident, for God has elected him. The doctrine of predestination found in the earlier text has been revised by the writer of 4:15ff who is more interested in the position of the faithful Qumranite as a battle-field of truth and falsehood than in a predetermined dichotomy between the sons of light and darkness.

> For God did not choose them [those who turn aside from the path, line 6] at the beginning of the world, and before they were established he knew their deeds, and abominated the generations on account of blood....

God saw in advance what the wicked would do, did not elect them, but chose the just. These lines are a comfort to the righteous: punishment will certainly meet their persecutors, for so it has been decreed from the beginning.

Thus the Qumran texts present a multifaceted picture. Some texts, hymns in particular, represent a strict doctrine of predestination, rooted in the notion of God found in the creation tradition. When compared to God, no one can be righteous or worthy. It follows that membership in the community must be attributed to God's choice, not to human effort or merit. Before God, gratitude is the appropriate response, accompanied by wonder at being chosen. Predestinarian thinking has also been well suited to the separatist theology of the community. It accounts for the stubbornness of the outside majority, and its comforting significance in the distress of the last days is obvious. In practice, man's responsibility is emphasized throughout. "The 'doctrine of predestination' in the Scrolls is best seen as answering the question of why the covenanters are elect, rather than whether or not there is free will."[48] The same is true of Paul's "predestinarian" statements. Paul, too, finds comfort among the eschatological woes in the notion of a positive predestination to salvation (Rom. 8:28-30):

> We know that in everything God works for good with those who love him, who are called according to his purpose. For those whom he foreknew he also predestined to be conformed to the image of his Son (...) And those whom he predestined he also called; and those whom he called he also justified; and those whom he justified he also glorified.

Negative predestination enters the picture when Paul tries to make sense of his undelightful social experience, voiced in Rom. 9:1ff.[49] We there find him struggling with the issue of continuity.

In Gal. 3-4, discussed above, he had gone a long way toward virtually denying any significant continuity between Israel as a people

---

[48] Sanders, *Paul*, p. 268.
[49] For a more comprehensive discussion of Rom. 9-11, see my *Marcion, Muhammad and the Mahatma* (London, 1997), pp. 17-32.

and his faith communities. Yet Paul could not just leave the matter there.

In Romans 9 Paul raises the worrisome question, how the gospel can be taken to represent a triumph for God, even though most Jews have rejected it. What gain will Israelites have for all their advantages (the long list of which must come as a great surprise to a reader of Galatians), if they remain outside the salvation in Christ? (Rom. 9:2-4):

> I have great sorrow and unceasing anguish in my heart. For I could wish that I myself were accursed and cut off from Christ for the sake of my brethren, my kinsmen by race. They are Israelites, and to them belong the sonship, the glory, the covenants, the giving of the law, the worship and the promises; to them belong the patriarchs, and of their race, according to the flesh, is the Christ (...).

God's integrity is at stake: has his word failed, if Israel stays outside? Paul answers by redefining "Israel:" all those who are "of Israel" (the empirical people) do not really belong to "Israel." Who belongs and who does not is freely decreed by God. He has always *freely* called some, like Jacob, and not others, like Esau, without any regard to their character or ancestry. Unlike the Damascus Document, Paul does not think of God's foreknowledge of wicked deeds; God is wholly sovereign in his decisions (Rom. 9:6-13):

> But it is not as though the word of God had failed. For not all who are descended of Israel belong to Israel, and not all are children of Abraham, because they are his descendants (...) it is not the children of the flesh who are the children of God, but the children of the promise are reckoned as descendants (...) when Rebecca had conceived children by one man, our forefather Isaac, she was told, "The elder will serve the younger," though they were not yet born and had done nothing either good or bad, in order that God's purpose of election might continue, not because of works but because of his call. As it is written, "Jacob I loved, but Esau I hated."

It follows that the initial question is falsely put. The gospel is not being rejected by the elect of God, for the majority of ethnic Israel never belonged to the elect! The gospel is being rejected by the non-elect and accepted by the true "Israel." Everything is as God meant it to be.

Paul goes to great lengths in undergirding the thesis of God's free election. God "hardens whom he wills" (Rom. 9:14-18):

> Is there injustice on God's part? By no means! For he says to Moses, "I

will have mercy on whom I have mercy, and I will have compassion on whom I have compassion." So it depends not upon man's will or exertion, but upon God's mercy (...) he has mercy upon whomever he wills, and he hardens the heart of whomever he wills.

Verse 19 shows that Paul senses that a moral problem is involved in his argument: how can humans be held responsible for their doings if everything is effected by God? All he can do is to assert that the Great Potter has the right to create what he wants (an idea with analogies in the Qumran hymns that praise the creator), even "vessels of wrath" prepared for destruction (9:22). This idea would logically imply double predestination. The unbelieving Jews of Paul's time are to be seen as such vessels of wrath. Paul then shows from Scripture that God always intended to also call gentiles to be his sons. Of Israel, only a remnant will be saved (9:24-29).

Undoubtedly Paul has Jewish *Christians* in mind all the time when he speaks of God's merciful election. The shape of his argument prevents him, however, from spelling this out; otherwise the argument which rests on God's total sovereignty would be undermined. Paul's omission of any mention of faith in this connection may indicate that somehow he sensed the tension. For in Rom. 9:6ff he speaks as if humans are saved simply by God's arbitrary action: their destinies are decreed by God before they are born. In saying this, however, he is not developing a "doctrine;" he is wrestling with a burning practical mission problem: why does Israel not accept the message?

The next section (Rom. 9:30-10:21) introduces, however, a quite different point of view. Paul explains why Israel, now seen as an ethnic entity after all, has failed to attain righteousness, whereas gentiles have found it (9:30-33). We now hear nothing about sovereign divine hardening. On the contrary, God has held out his hands toward Israel "all day long," patiently inviting her to salvation, but Israel remains "a disobedient and contrary people" (10:21). Clinging to works, she has refused to obey God and to accept his action in Christ with faith. Thus she has stumbled over the stumbling stone, Christ (9:32-33). Similarly, from Qumran's point of view, Israel had gone astray by disregarding the Teacher of Righteousness and the divine revelation given to him.

Then, however, Paul suddenly asserts that God cannot have rejected his people, ethnic Israel (11:1-2). This is rather surprising after chap. 9, but it continues the argument about the remnant. Ethnic Israel has split into the elect remnant and the hardened rest (11:7).

Paul goes on to suggest that the hardening of Israel has a positive purpose in God's plans: somehow it serves to bring salvation to the gentiles (11:11-12). He then presents a parable of an olive tree (Israel), from which some branches have been broken off, and on to which branches of a wild tree have been grafted (11:17-24). In effect he is saying that Israel basically remains God's people; some apostates have been excluded, and some believing gentiles have been included as proselytes. The present state of things is caused by the unbelief of "some" (11:17, 20): by human failure, not by a divine decree. Gentiles are admonished to remain in faith so that they will not be "broken off" as well (v. 22). Here the idea of divine hardening would be out of place. But God has the power to graft back again those Israelites who have fallen, "if they do not persist in their unbelief" (v. 23).

And indeed a miracle will happen. Paul's discloses a "mystery:" the hardening will not be final. When the "full number of the gentiles" has "come in," *all Israel*—not just a remnant—will be saved (11:25), for "the gifts and the call of God are irrevocable" (v. 29).

If Paul's predestinarian thoughts have parallels in Qumran, his hope for the salvation of the people of Israel after all also has its counterpart there. The eschatological Rule of the Congregation states (1QSa 1:1-6):

> And this is the rule of the congregation of Israel in the final days, when they gather [in community to wa]lk in accordance with the regulation of the sons of Zadok, the priests, and the men of the covenant who have turn[ed away from the pa]th of the people. These are the men of his counsel who have kept the covenant in the midst of wickedness to atone [for the e]arth. When they come, they shall assemble all those who come, including children and women, and they shall read into their ea[rs] all the regulations of the covenant....

This passage has suggested to some scholars that "the sectaries envisaged a large-scale conversion to the Community on the eve of [this] new age."[50] While such an interpretation of this particular passage may remain somewhat uncertain,[51] the Pesher of Nahum does voice the expectation that in the end-time the simple folk who have been

---

[50] Vermes, *Dead Sea Scrolls*, p. 48; Sanders, *Paul*, p. 247.
[51] The matter-of-fact style in which the joining of "the congregation of Israel" may make one think of the entrance of members of the Qumran sect rather than that of the rest of the people; this is how most scholars understand the passage.

misled by the Pharisees will reject those false teachers and, as the "glory" of the Qumran community will be revealed to them, they will join the true "Israel" (4QpNah 3.3-5):

> Its interpretation concerns those who seek smooth things, whose evil deeds will be exposed to *all Israel at the end of time*. Many will understand their iniquity and treat them with contempt (…) And when the glory of Judah is revealed the simple people of Ephraim will flee from among their assembly and abandon those who led them astray and *will join Israel*....

This is not quite the conversion of all Israel (though "all Israel" is said to recognize the falsehood of the competing party), but in any case "many" will join the community. Likewise, the author of the Halakhic letter expresses the hope that everything written in Deut. 30 will come true, including the return of the people to the law:

> "And it is written that all these things shall happen to you at the end of days, the blessing and the curse…and you shall assent in your heart and will turn to me with all your […]"[52] "And this is the end of days, when they will return in Israel to the L[aw]…"[53]

Obviously, the authors of the letter "still held out the hope that others in Israel would also return to the Lord and to his Torah."[54]

Thus the Qumran community did expect its final vindication before the majority of the people, much as Paul does in Rom. 11. Both expected an eschatological verification of their particular message in the near future. Neither clings consistently to a predestinarian doctrine: it is possible for people to be converted and to return.

From the viewpoint of a non-Christian Jew, Paul's statement of the salvation of all Israel is not nearly so generous as many Christians, often in connection with a Jewish-Christian dialogue, tend to think. In effect, Paul is saying that you will be saved, since eventually you will become like us. (The Qumran people are saying the same thing.) This salvation is for non-Christian Jews "a bitter gospel not a sweet one," because it is conditioned precisely on abandoning their separate cultural, religious identity.[55] "If the only value and promise

---

[52] 4Q397 frags. 7+8: 12-14. The text is in a poor condition. Its many small lacunae that have not been indicated above can be reasonably filled, however, since the author is paraphrasing Deuteronomy.

[53] 4Q398 frag. 1: 4-5.

[54] J.D.G. Dunn, "4QMMT and Galatians," in *NTS* 43, 1997, p. 149.

[55] Boyarin, *A Radical Jew*, p. 152.

afforded the Jews, even in Romans 11, is that in the end they will see the error of their ways, one cannot claim that there is a role for Jewish existence in Paul."[56] From a traditional Jewish perspective Paul's theology, even in Rom. 11, is "supersessionist."[57]

With all its tensions, the section Rom. 9-11 vividly illustrates how central and how difficult the questions of identity and continuity were for Paul. It shows him in a struggle to legitimate his mission and to assert his and his little group's identity in terms of traditional values. In the olive tree parable, Paul talks as if his church were a mainstream synagogue, with some new proselytes, from which a few apostates have been expelled. The social reality was quite different.

It is the tension between a novel liberal practice and the pressure toward a more conservative ideology that gets Paul into difficulty. His practice, the abandonment of circumcision and food laws, amounts to a break with sacred tradition; but his legitimating theory in Romans stresses continuity, so that he can even assert that in it, he truly "upholds the law" (Rom. 3:31). A related tension between innovation and tradition is found in Qumran.

The Judaism of Qumran and of Paul—Continuity and Discontinuity

A member of the Qumran sect, too, had to take a *new step* to enter the community; one was not born in it. The Qumranite had to *believe in the new things* revealed to the Teacher. Only the Teacher was able to decipher the secrets concealed in the Scriptures (the eschatological mysteries of the ages, as well as the special halakhah). Consequently, "only those who accepted his interpretation of the written word of God could be sure of living in conformity with His desire."[58]

Yet it is also held that the rest of the people had *fallen away*. Thus, the wicked priest was "called by the name of loyalty at the start of is office," but, "when he ruled over Israel his heart became conceited, he deserted God and betrayed the laws for the sake of riches" (1QpHab 8:8-11). By contrast, the Qumranites had remained faithful. Entering the community can be depicted as a *return* to the law of

---

[56] Ibid., p. 151.
[57] Ibid., p. 202. To be sure, the doctrine is not "anti-Judaic" (correctly Boyarin, ibid., p. 205).
[58] Vermes, *Dead Sea Scrolls*, p. 35.

Moses: the one who enters has to be enrolled "with the covenant oath which Moses established with Israel, the covenant to rev[ert to] the law of Moses with the whole heart..." (CD 15:9-10).

> [T]hose who joined the Essenes "returned" to the "law of Moses," which, however, contained secrets that they could not have known until they joined. The Essene formulation, "return," shows that the Essenes thought that God really had revealed their version of the covenant and the law to Moses; and then to the Zadokite priests. They do not explicitly explain this: how the law could have been given to Moses and yet contain secrets that were later revealed to the Zadokite priests. But, in their view, Israelites who did not seek for and discover the secret revelations broke the law, and people who joined "returned" to it.[59]

I suspect that the Qumranites did not explain the matter, because they did not have a fully consistent position here but were caught in a salvation-historical dilemma reminiscent of Paul's. In neither case does it become clear whether a member of the group in question has *remained* in the covenant from which others have turned away (as in Paul's olive tree parable in Rom. 11:17ff), or whether the one who enters takes a *new* step (as in Gal. 2:16ff).

And yet there is an enormous difference between Qumran and Paul on the practical level. Despite the innovation, Qumran stuck strictly to the central visible symbols of the old covenant. The group could speak of circumcision as a metaphor (a convert "should circumcise in the Community the foreskin of his tendency and of his stiff neck," 1QS 5:5), but it certainly did not reject the rite, and no one thought of accepting gentiles as members. Of course, no shortcomings were attributed to the Torah; its requirements were not relaxed but intensified. Therefore, the Jewish identity of the sect was not in doubt, not even in the eyes of outsiders. Paul's case was different.

In the sociological classification of R. Stark and W.S. Bainbridge, Qumran must be classified as a *sect*: a deviant religious organization with *traditional* beliefs and practices that has come into being through a schism from existing religious bodies (in this case, Temple-priesthood). By contrast, Paul's communities can be said to represent a *cult* movement: a deviant religious organization with *novel* beliefs and practices.[60] No doubt Paul in his own mind always retained a Jewish

---

[59] E.P. Sanders, *Judaism* (London, 1992), pp. 376f.

[60] I am drawing on a forthcoming article on "Jewish Christianity" by P. Luomanen, who discusses Matthew's community from the point of view of Stark's and

identity. But Donald Riddle long ago found the right formulation: "Always regarding himself as a faithful and loyal Jew, his [Paul's] definitions of values were so different from those of his contemporaries that, notwithstanding his own position within Judaism, he was, from any point of view other than his own, at best a poor Jew and at worst a renegade."[61]

Both Qumran and Paul were reacting to a cultural crisis in a time when, in Boyarin's words, the "tribe" of Israel no longer dwelt alone, as it were.[62] The Qumran people retreated to a holy isolation. Paul tried to destroy barriers, being "impelled by a vision of human unity that was born of two parents: Hebrew monotheism and Greek longing for universals."[63] But from a traditional Jewish point of view his "neither Jew nor Greek" was bound to mean: "we are all Greeks"! (Again, from a traditional Greco-Roman point of view, the required abandonment of traditional cults and sexual codes may have meant: we are all Jews! Perhaps Paul was too much of a Greek to the Jews, and too much of a Jew to the Greeks.)

There are dangers in isolationism; Essenism became extinct. Paul's universalism survived and rose to a new flourishing that, however, entailed dangers of a different kind. In a new context, the sense of universal mission (coupled with the spirit of militant biblical monotheism) was easily translated into aggressive missionizing, colonialism, and persecution. That, however, was not part of the original vision of Paul, the radical Jew.

Bainbridge's theory (R. Stark and W.S. Bainbridge, *A Theory of Religion* (New York, 1987). He concludes that even though the community has maintained many traditional beliefs, there is so much new to Jesus' role (despite the fact that it can partly be traced back to Jewish messianic expectations) that it can be regarded as religious innovation and that "Matthew's community can be best characterized as a cult movement." If this is the case with (the relatively conservative) Matthew, Paul's communities must *a fortiori* be regarded as "cults."

[61] D.W. Riddle, "The Jewishness of Paul," in *Journal of Religion* 23, 1943, p. 244.
[62] Boyarin, op. cit., p. 258.
[63] Ibid., p. 228.

16. THE GOSPEL OF JOHN AND THE COMMUNITY RULE OF QUMRAN: A COMPARISON OF SYSTEMS[1]

Adriana Destro and Mauro Pesce
University of Bologna

1. *The Method of Comparison*

Ever since the Dead Sea Scrolls were discovered, scholars have compared the Gospel of John and Qumranic literature.[2] This comparison has brought out a variety of individual features, dualism being the theme attracting most interest. Recently, P. Esler has compared John and Qumran from the social scientific perspective to discover to what extent both communities were "introverted sectarian" *vis-à-vis* Judaism.[3]

The aim of our work is to compare two texts: John and the Community Rule of Qumran (hereafter, 1QS) insofar as they provide evidence for the reconstruction of two religious systems. At the level of methodology, comparison has to be made of complete systems in their entirety and their principal features. The three fundamental features of a religious system are (a) a social group, (b) a consistent set of religious practices, and (c) a complex of cultural conceptions or visions of the world, shared by the social group in question.[4]

For a systemic comparison, it is first of all necessary that the texts analyzed provide an adequate amount of information on the three

---

[1] Translated by Charles Hindley.
[2] On the relationship between John and Johannine literature in general and Qumran, cf., the commentaries of Barrett, Brown, and Schnackenburg. See also the works listed in the bibliography of Segalla, *Giovanni. Versione. Introduzione. Note* (Cinisello, 1990), pp. 41-44; Ashton, *Understanding the Fourth Gospel* (Oxford, 1991), pp. 232-237; Bauckham; Baumbach; Benoit; Böcher; Braun; Brown, "The Qumran Scrolls and the Johannine Gospel and Epistles;" Charlesworth; Esler; Fitzmyer; Kuhn; Roloff; Schnackenburg; and Segalla.
[3] "Introverted Sectarianism at Qumran and in the Johannine Community," in *The First Christians in their Social Worlds* (London and New York, 1994), p. 7.
[4] C. Geertz, *Interpretazione di culture* (Bologna, 1998), pp. 111-159; J. Neusner, *The Systemic Analysis of Judaism* (Atlanta, 1988); and A. Destro and M. Pesce, *Come nasce una religione. Antropologia ed esegesi del Vangelo di Giovanni* (Rome, 2000), pp. vii-xi.

systemic features. The analysis will demonstrate that John and 1QS fully meet these requirements. Secondly, justification has to be found for making use of a single document for the reconstruction of the religious system of which it is the expression. Here it must be borne in mind that the Gospel of John, the three Letters of John, and the Apocalypse seem to come from a similar background. However, it is by no means clear whether these texts belong to several communities or to the same group to which John belongs.[5] Restricting oneself to only one text offers a less uncertain basis for analysis. In the case of the Qumranic literature, it has rightly been suggested that some texts reflect different kinds of Judaism. P. Davies[6] for example, has argued that the religious system of the *Document of Damascus* is substantially different from that of 1QS, and has spoken of a plurality of Judaisms at Qumran. On the other hand, it is well known that in the period of more than two hundred years presupposed by the texts discovered at Qumran, a multiplicity of evolutions took place. To reconstruct the religion of the Johannine community or the religion of Qumran on the basis of a multiplicity of *different* documents means incorrectly mixing up different religious forms and therefore presenting religious forms that never existed. Therefore we shall examine only one religious system as it appears in just one text. Further, in the case of both John and 1QS, we are faced with texts that have gone through successive redactions that have put together and reworked various texts and materials.[7] We are going to analyze only the final redaction of these works, not the previous stages. It is the religious system expressed in this final redaction that interests us.

The legitimacy of the comparison between John and 1QS is not based on the idea that the two systems were historically contempo-

---

[5] See S.E. Porter, ed., *Handbook to Exegesis of the New Testament* (Leiden, 1997), pp. 582-588; E. Lupieri, *L'apocalisse di Giovanni* (Milan, 1999), pp. lxv-lxvi.

[6] "The Dead Sea Writings, The Judaisms of," in J. Neusner, A.J. Avery-Peck, and W.S. Green, eds., *The Encyclopaedia of Judaism* (Leiden, 2000), vol. 1, pp. 186-192.

[7] On John, see M.-E. Boismard, *Synopse des Quatre Evangiles en français. Tome III. L'Evangile de Jean* (Paris, 1987); R. Schnackenburg, *Das Johannesevangelium* (Freiburg, 1965-1979); R.E. Brown, *The Gospel according to John* (Garden City and New York, 1966-1970). On 1QS, see C. Martone, *La "Regola della Comunità". Edizione critica* (Turin, 1995), pp. 32-37; S. Metso, *The Textual Development of the Qumran Community Rule* (Leiden, 1997); M. Blockmuehl, "Redaction and Ideology in the Rule of the Community," in *Revue de Qumran* 18, 1998, pp. 541-560. Bibliography and history of the research are found in these studies.

rary, a fact that can neither be proved nor entirely excluded. The probable paleographical dating of 1QS is the first half of the first century B.C.E.[8] But this does not rule out that the text was normative for a community whose final phase of existence coincided with the formation phase of the Johannine community. The comparison does not aim to discover relations of historical dependence, but to clarify the differences and similarities of the systemic structure.

2. *The Johannine System*

One characteristic of John was to project the community's order, its conceptions, and the religious practices typical of the Johannine community of its time, on the events of Jesus' life.[9] This is why it is legitimate to detect traces of the Johannine system within the Gospel.

The social group: a) For John, anyone can be a member of the Johannine community. Being a Judean (*ioudaios*) or becoming one is not a necessary pre-condition. The only required condition is believing in Jesus (9:35-36; 11:25-27; cf. 1:50), proclaiming this openly (12:42), separating oneself off from the group one previously belonged to.

b) For John the basic socio-religious form allowing the aggregation of individuals in a community is discipleship. This represents for the Gospel the central factor of cultural dynamism, because it involves a master and a guide, capable of opening up paths for, and realizing the needs felt by, a certain sector of the population. The criterion of legitimacy is simply the unquestioned authority of the master. For John, other social forms are unable to fulfil this function. A criterion of historical and genealogical legitimacy, such as we find for example in Matt. 1:1-16, is entirely absent. Family or genealogical relationships are not the dynamic factor in society.[10] The disciples are not

---

[8] C. Martone, *Testi di Qumran* a cura di Florentino García Martínez (Brescia, 1996), p. 71.

[9] J.L. Martyn, *History and Theology in the Fourth Gospel* (Nashville, 1979); Brown, op. cit.; P.F. Esler, "Introverted Sectarianism at Qumran and in the Johannine Community," in *The First Christians in Their Social Worlds* (London and New York, 1994), p. 85.

[10] It is not that he ignores family relationships, which are basic for him also within the relations of discipleship (A. Destro and M. Pesce, *Antropologia delle origini cristiane* (Rome, 1997), pp. 81-82; C. Osiek and D. Balch, *Families in the New Testament World. Households and House Churches* (Louisville, 1997), pp. 144, 162-163).

called "brothers", but "friends" (15:13-15), a term that does not evoke any kinship link even at the figurative level.[11]

c) One characteristic of the group around Jesus, in John, is the heterogeneous nature of its components. E.W. and W. Stegemann[12] have tried to represent the composition of the group of Jesus' disciples in John from the perspective of social stratification. Nicodemus, Joseph of Arimathaea, probably the beloved disciple and perhaps the family of the king's official, whose son Jesus heals (4:53), belong to the higher stratum. Other disciples seem to belong to a lower one, though not to the really poor, while Mary, Martha, and Lazarus would seem to be relatively comfortably off. Further apart socially are the ill Jesus heals (like the paralyzed man and the man born blind). From this it emerges that the group is varied and is not defined by economic or *status* criteria, nor does it imply changes of an economic kind. John is not interested in social stratification, neither defending nor criticizing it. Closeness to an ideal such as equality or the sharing of goods is not a criterion of orientation.

It is starting from the point of view of adherence to the master that a distinction appears between public followers and hidden sympathizers, like Nicodemus and Joseph of Arimathaea, or people who do not adhere because they are afraid, like those leaders who believe in Jesus but do not proclaim him to avoid being expelled from the synagogues (12:42). Because adherence to the master is difficult, differences arise among the disciples.

The religious practices: The Johannine community is autonomous by comparison to other Jewish groups also at the level of norms and religious practices, primarily because it believes it possesses the true form of the cult, the true "adoration" (*proskynein*, literally "to prostrate oneself"). This is an act that John imagines is external to the organization of the Jerusalem Temple and entirely independent of it. True adoration consists in the encounter with divinity, within and through one's own body, independent of the place in which one finds oneself. The Temple, i.e. the dwelling-place of God, is only the "body" of Jesus himself (2:21).[13] The Jesus of John maintains that in future the

---

[11] This use of "friends" can be paralleled to the use of "woman" that John makes in reference to the mother: cf., Destro and Pesce, ibid., pp. 70-72.

[12] *Storia sociale del cristianesimo primitivo* (Bologna, 1998), pp. 383-392.

[13] Cf., A. Destro and M. Pesce, "Lo spirito e il mondo vuoto. Prospettive esegetiche e antropologiche su Gv 4,21-24," in *Annali di Storia dell'esegesi* 12, 1995, pp. 9-32.

true cult of God will not have to take place on Mount Gerizim and Jerusalem, but only "in spirit and truth" (4:21-24):

> Woman, believe me, the hour comes, when you shall adore the Father neither in this mountain nor in Jerusalem.... But the hour comes, and is now, when the true adorer shall adore the Father in spirit and true. For the Father seeks such an adorer. God is spirit and they that adore him must adore in spirit and truth.[14]

The fact that "adoration" does not occur in special places means that John identifies the true cult with an inner prostration. From this derives the fact that it is no longer necessary to enter the Temple to gain contact with the highest level of holiness and meet God. That adoration takes place within each person, simply through the mediation of the Spirit, excluding from the fundamental act of the cult any kind of place and any kind of human mediator.

The autonomy of the Johannine community is also to be seen in the admission rituals that require an explicit confession of faith in Jesus (cf., 9:35-39; 11:26-27; 20:26-29). It is above all a process of initiation that introduces the members of the Johannine community to the fundamental experience. Right from the start John states that the final purpose of Jesus' mission is to confer a new condition on humanity. The mission is to give "to those who welcome him" (1:12) "the power to become sons (*tekna*) of God," i.e., to provide the condition of being generated directly by the creator. The metaphor of generating and giving life underlies the entire Gospel, and even at the end it is stressed that its purpose is to enable the believers to have "life" (20:31). Jesus explains that his aim is for his disciples to pass "from death to life" and indeed to obtain "eternal life" (5:24). Translating the Johannine language into one nearer the social sciences, the purpose of Jesus' actions is to enable access to a form of perfect life, of divine order,[15] through leaving behind ordinary, incomplete or inadequate conditions. The instrument by which the disciples can have the basic religious experience of rebirth is the ritual process of

---

[14] See ibid.
[15] The purpose of Jesus' actions is not expressed in terms of *conversion* to God (cf., T.M. Finn, *From Death to Rebirth. Ritual Conversion in Antiquity* (New York, 1997), pp. 26-27). On the relationships of the concept of life with Hellenistic Judaism and the Synoptic Gospels, cf., J. Ashton, op. cit., pp. 214-220; Brown, op. cit., pp. 182-185.

initiation. Chapters 13-17 of John function as presentation of the way in which the disciples may achieve rebirth.[16]

The first stage of initiation[17] consists of three features. (a) The first is an inversion ritual in which the traditional roles of the relationship between master and disciple are turned upside down. Jesus takes over the function of a slave (as the act of washing the disciples' feet and dressing like a slave shows),[18] and the disciples that of the master. This alludes to a relation of radical opposition between the Johannine community and the surrounding social environment. B. Malina and R. Rohrbaugh[19] have defined this relation as "antisociety."

The second feature is the master's delivery of an esoteric doctrine to his adepts; the disciples will be quite unable to follow the master in the mission he has to carry out: "Were I go, you cannot go" (13:33).

The third feature is the delivery of a new precept: "a new commandment I give you: that you love one another. As I have loved you, so you also love one another" (13:34).

The second stage of initiation consists in going more deeply into the doctrine and the commandment. The disciples are told they may follow the master only if they undergo a particular kind of union with him: "without me you can do nothing" (15:5). Also the precept of reciprocal love consists in loving in the way the master loved, i.e., in giving his life for his friends.

The third stage of initiation is not of a ritual character and lies in the impossibility of the disciples' following the master. Peter is the example of this impossibility. He tries first to defend Jesus by force, then follows him, but ends up by denying him (18:10.15-27).

---

[16] Destro and Pesce, *Come nasce una religione*, p. 25. According to the Synoptic Gospels, on special occasions Jesus explained in private and in an esoteric way to the disciples what he had previously set out in public. In John there is no lack of *individual* moments of initiation (cf., the meeting with Nicodemus or the withdrawal to Ephraim). However, esoteric initiation is presented and exalted mainly in a great ritual process in chaps. 13-17. It is this wide-ranging and detailed private instruction, absent in Synoptics, that makes John's perspective so unique. C.H. Dodd, *The Interpretation of the Fourth Gospel* (Cambridge, 1953, p. 514) already tried to make sense of chaps. 13-17 as a vast initiation process just for disciples. Our hypothesis differs on the nature, purposes, and stages of this initiation.

[17] On initiation in John, cf., Destro and Pesce, ibid., pp. 35-110.

[18] John 13:4-5. Cf., A. Destro and M. Pesce, "La lavanda dei piedi di Gv 13,1-20, il *Romanzo di Esopo* e i *Saturnalia* di Macrobio," in *Biblica* 80/2, 1999, pp. 239-249.

[19] *Social-Science Commentary on the Gospel of John* (Minneapolis, 1998), pp. 9-10.

The final stage of initiation is a complex ritual action (20:19-23) in which the disciples meet the body of the master who was killed and came back to life, i.e., experience in themselves the passage from death to life, receive (a) the supernatural power of the Holy Spirit, (b) the mission in the world, and (c) the power of forgiveness of sins.[20] The redactor, with the scene of the transmission of the spirit, seems to say that to live in the world, as envoys of Jesus and the Father, the disciples need to be invested with and impregnated by the power of the spirit. The spirit the disciples receive before being sent out into the world is defined as *haghion* (saint) (20-22) and its function is to *haghiazein* (sanctify),[21] i.e., to communicate the holy power of God (cf., 17:17-19).

The main point here is that the physical act of breathing marks the exact moment of the passage of powers from Jesus to the disciples: "As the Father has sent me, even I send you" (20:21). This is where their new *status* is concretely inaugurated, through the efficacy of the ritual act itself. This is the fundamental purpose behind the entire initiation proceedings. From now on the disciples are "sons of God" and have undergone the experience of regeneration through the work of God that John pursues. It is at this point that a community is formed, because people have a specific experience in common that unites them in a common destiny through the exclusive and indivisible gift of the spirit.

Being *sent out* into the world implies abandoning the situation of secrecy, separation, and obscurity, to face the "world" (*kosmos*) openly, with all the difficulties this leads to, and make those that accept the new message "become *sons* of God." To characterize the community, it is important that the sending out be towards an undifferentiated universe ("the world") and that the preaching of the new doctrine be not addressed only to Jews.

Initiation, with the breath of the spirit, inaugurates a new religious practice: the *forgiveness of sins*. In the official Jewish religious system of Jesus' time, the forgiveness of sins was linked to sacrificial practices

---

[20] On the connection between the breath of the spirit and the power of forgiveness of sins, cf., A. Destro and M. Pesce, *Antropologia delle origini cristiane* (Rome, 1997), p. 176, n. 72.

[21] The Holy Spirit gives the disciples the complete truth, through which they are sanctified. The truth is the word of God, that is the *logos*, which has both functions: to purify and to sanctify (John 17:17-19).

and to inner conversion on the day of expiation (*Yom ha-kippurim*).²²
This implies a set of officially recognized ritual agents. Those sent out
into the world by Jesus do not belong to the Jewish institutional
system. Their ritual procedures are different from traditional ones.
With the forgiveness of sins by the disciples, a new expiatory system
is inaugurated, independent of those that had existed up to that
time.²³ It should not be forgotten that at the time of the final
redaction of the Gospel, the Jerusalem Temple had already been
destroyed. Various Jewish communities had already developed or
were in the process of developing expiatory systems independent of
the sacrificial system. The Johannine community was going in the
same direction.

At any rate, taken by itself, the power of forgiveness of sins would
not be sufficient to characterize the new religious group as the possessor of an autonomous system. Only if it is placed next to two other
features—being sent out into the world and the possession of the
spirit and the "whole" truth—can the shape of this system be perceived.

The vision of the world: a) The adherents or components of the
Johannine community believe they possess the "truth" (*aletheia*) and
that they are therefore autonomous from the doctrinal point of view.
An essential part of what defines them as a group is the conviction
that they are possessed by the Holy Spirit (20:22). The Johannine
community is actually born at the moment when Jesus completes the
initiation of his own with the transmission of the vital breath of God
(20:19-23). The Johannine community lives under the constant influence of the supernatural inspiration of the Holy Spirit. It holds onto
the Jewish holy writings, but it believes it is in possession of a truer
interpretation, thanks to the new revelation granted by the Spirit
(16:13; cf., 2:17, 22).

b) The Johannine community shows its own individual identity in
the way in which it conceives its foundation and purpose. It believes

---

²² The fact that in the first century there were many Judaisms must not lead us to forget the central role of the religious system of the Temple.

²³ It has to be remembered that John the Baptist, in whose movement the beginnings of Jesus' own takes root, seemed already to attribute a function of forgiveness of sins to his own ritual of immersion (this can be seen both in Josephus, *Antiquities* 18:117, and in Mark 1:4 and Luke 3:3). That means that he questioned in some way the usefulness of the official rituals. On John the Baptist's baptism, cf., E. Lupieri, *Giovanni Battista nelle tradizioni sinottiche* (Brescia, 1998), 27.74, and his *Giovanni Battista fra storia e leggenda* (Brescia, 1998), pp. 31-36, 60-61, 119-131.

it was founded in an extra-human fashion by the *logos* of God himself (1:1, 12-14) and had received a divine command to preach the truth in the world (20:21b). According to John, the new community was formed because the *logos* of the Jewish God had descended to bring about a rebirth in all men (1:12-13). Jesus-*logos* had engaged in a battle with "the world" and, despite his apparent defeat, had emerged victorious, returning to life (chaps. 20-21) and expelling "the *archon* of this world" (12:31; 16:11). Before ascending again to his holy seat, he had infused the spirit into his disciples (20:22), enabling "birth from above" and thus guaranteeing a perpetual contact with the divine. According to John, the new community is born from the close interconnection of the descent, the victorious struggle and the reascent of the *logos*. As Esler[24] has pointed out, John "emphasizes the notion of salvation in the present more than other New Testament authors...he repeatedly introduces the idea that 'eternal life' is available to believers here and now: 'Truly, truly, I say to you, the person who hears my words and believes the one who sent me has eternal life, and does not come into judgment but has passed from death to life' (5:24)."

c) The redactor of John works out a spatial scheme dominated by the contrast of "above" and "below." The binary scheme (above-below, high-low, far-near, outside-inside) is one of the principal systems of cultural classification and serves to place people within the map of ideological and symbolic forms. This is so much the case that when the main binary references are shifted or altered, an operation of cultural re-ordering or the appearance of a new cosmology occurs.

In the culture of John, the "above" is the seat of God and evokes a cosmic order. God is situated above the heavens that lie over the earth;[25] and between the world up there and the world down here there is a clear contrast (3:31; 8:23). The Son of Man has descended from heaven (3:13) and his destiny is to be "lifted up" (3:14; 3:28); when he is lifted up to heaven, he will attract all men to himself (12:32-34).[26]

The opposition between the earth or the world on the one hand, and the seat of God on the other, and the impossibility of mediation between the two sides, is clearly expressed:

---

[24] Op. cit., p. 89.
[25] Destro and Pesce, *Come nasce una religione*, p. 126.
[26] On the relation between the vertical and horizontal action of God in John, cf., Brown, op. cit., cxxxix-cxli.

> You are from below. I am from above. You are from this world. I am not from this world (8:23).
>
> He who comes from above is above all others. He who is from the earth is from the earth and speaks from the earth. He who comes from heaven [is above all] (3:31).[27]

Johannine man is not from "below" but from "above." And this implies a new generation that takes the place of the former and that defines an imaginary space in a vertical sense. Essentially, the individual, in his/her bodily form itself, is not defined in a relation of identity with its own land (the Land of Israel), but with the "above," whence comes the regenerating divine power. The model John sets out therefore contains a dialectic between the relation above-below and that of the Temple and the land of Israel.[28]

3. *The System of the Community Rule*

Also for 1QS,[29] we shall examine the three main features of the religious system.[30]

The social group: A number of essential points can be listed for the definition of the nature of the social group that adheres to this religious system.

a) Adherence is voluntary: "This is the rule for the men of the Community who freely volunteer (*mtndbym*) to convert from all evil and to keep themselves steadfast in all he commanded in compliance with his will" (1QS 5:1).[31]

---

[27] "Is above all" is absent from some manuscripts, cf., G. Segalla, *Giovanni. Versione. Introduzione. Note* (Cinisello, 1990), p. 181.

[28] The former, however, does not totally substitute the latter. Cf., Destro and Pesce, *Come nasce una religione*, pp. 126-127.

[29] For the text of 1QS, see Martone, *La "Regola della Comunità". Edizione critica*; F. García Martínez and E.J.C. Tigchelaar, eds., *The Dead Sea Scrolls Study Edition. Volume One 1Q1-4Q273* (Leiden, 1997).

[30] For a systemic representation of the Qumran community or of the Community of 1QS, see M. Mach, "Conservative Revolution? The Intolerant Innovations of Qumran," in G.N. Stanton and G.G. Stroumsa, eds., *Tolerance and Intolerance in Early Judaism and Christianity* (Cambridge, 1998), pp. 61-79, Davies, op. cit., and J. Maier, *Die Qumran-Essener: Die Texte vom Toten Meer. Band I: Die Texte der Höhlen 1-3 und 5-11* (Munich, 1995).

[31] For the English translation of 1QS, we follow García Martínez and Tigchelaar, ibid., pp. 71-99.

b) The group is radically separated from the rest of Jewish society, called "a congregation of injustice:" "They should keep apart from the congregation of the men of injustice in order to constitute a Community in law and possessions" (1QS 5:1-2).

c) Entry into the community coincides with the stipulation of a new "covenant" with God: "And all those who enter in the Rule of the Community shall establish a covenant before God in order to carry out all that he commanded and in order not to stray from following him" (1:16-17).

d) Admission into the community requires the adept to bring all his own goods into the community: "All those who submit freely to his truth will convey all their knowledge, energies, and their riches to the Community of God in order to refine...all their riches in accordance with his just counsel" (1:11-13).

e) The community has a hierarchical structure, having at its head the priests, the "sons of Sadoq," who "keep the covenant" (5:9), followed by the Levites, and then by the people, divided up into degrees and orders:

> The priests shall enter in order foremost, one behind the other, according to their spirits. And the Levites shall enter after them. In third place all the people shall enter in order, one after another, in thousands, hundreds, fifties and tens, so that each Israelite may know his standing in God's Community in conformity with an eternal plan. And no one shall move down from his rank nor move up from the place of his lot (2:19-23).

f) The community is organized according to levels, determined by the degree of perfection (verified "year after year," 5:24), so that each person can always either improve his position or be demoted: "And they shall be recorded in order, one before the other, according to one's insight and one's deeds, in such a way that each one obeys another, the junior the senior" (5:23).

g) For breaking the rules of the covenant, a complex system of punishments is envisaged, going from demotion in the hierarchy and temporary isolation to expulsion (cf., 6:24-26; 7:1-27; 8:2-9:2).

h) A series of institutions for the government of the community is envisaged, as for example the *maskil* (9:12, 21), the "twelve men" and the "three priests" of which 8:1 speaks.

From all these features it emerges that the social group that calls itself "the Community of God" (*yahad 'el*) (2:22), thinks of itself as the true Israel. The rest of Jewish society is called "the congregation of the iniquitous." To enter the community a new covenant (*brit*) with God is necessary, implying the observance of the law as interpreted by the priests "sons of Sadoq." The relation between the true Israel and the rest of Jewish society is that of a radical separation, made effective by the fact that every member has to bring his possessions into the community (and therefore break off every kind of link with the rest of society) by the adoption of a different calendar that itself makes the break more acute and by the punishments of transgressions (the severest one being expulsion, and hence return into the overall Jewish society).[32] The fact that the group thinks of itself as the true Israel is shown also by the inner division into priests, Levites, and people, in which the highest directing function is given to the priests.

The religious practices: a) 1QS, like other documents discovered at Qumran, uses a calendar that regulates religious times in a different way from the one used by the rest of Palestinian Jewish society. This can be deduced from the insistence that those who adhere to the community will not only have to respect the laws but also to carry them out in the times established by the community: "They shall not stray from any one of all God's orders concerning their appointed times; they shall not advance their appointed times nor shall they retard any one of their feasts" (1:13-15).

b) The ritual of admission is fundamental (cf., 1:7-2:25; 6:13-23). For entry into the community (1QS 6:13-23),[33] it is envisaged that the people being initiated will themselves put forward their own candidacy. The first part of initiation foresees an examination by the *maskil*, instruction about "all the precepts of the community" and the passage from the "injustice" of their past life to the "truth" (6:15). These three features (examination, conversion, and instruction) are very closely connected to each other (1QS 6:13-16). After the collective scrutiny of the candidate follows admission to a probationary period of two years, each of which ends with an examination. In the first probationary year, the new adept does not pool his possessions with those of the community and cannot eat "the pure food of the many" (6:16-17). In the second year, he cannot "touch the drink of the many" (6:20) and hands his possessions over to the community, which, however, does not yet make use of them. Having passed the

---

[32] On the term "Israel," cf., also, 8:4 and 9:3.
[33] On Qumran initiation, cf., also Finn, op. cit., pp. 102-105.

examination after the second year, the adept is fully entitled to enter into the community way of life and into all its ritual occasions (1QS 6:16-23).

The admission ritual following on the examination and instruction by the *maskil* is described in 1:8-2:25. Precise parts are there attributed to the ritual agents: the priests and the Levites bless (1:19-20); the people being initiated confess their sins and those of their fathers; the priests bless and the Levites curse "men of the lot of Belial" (2:4-5). Finally, the priests and the Levites curse those who enter with evil intentions (2:11-17). In all three cases the people being initiated respond, "Amen, Amen."

The fact that the probationary period lasts two years brings out one of the most typical features of the ritual characteristics of the group. At the end of the first year the adept could eat the "pure food," but only at the end of the second year could he drink the "pure drink" of the community. Those who entered into the covenant, indeed, confessed their sins and committed themselves to following the law of God, but because of their previous life they remained contaminated for a very long time. A year of decontamination was necessary before they could eat "pure food" without contaminating it. And two years were necessary before they could have access to "pure drink," given that liquids are more vulnerable to contamination.[34]

The ritual of admission was envisaged once a year (1QS 2:18): "They shall act in this year after year, all the days of Belial's dominion" (1QS 2:19). This coincided with the whole community's renewal of the covenant with God. 1QS does not specify in which period of the year this renewal took place. The *Damascus Document* fixes it for *Shavuot*, the feast of the weeks (4Q266 18, V, 16-18).[35] It is probable that this was true also for 1QS.

The separateness of the group is cyclically re-emphasized through this confirmation of the covenant. The fact that the commitment to the covenant takes place not just once but must be repeated every year highlights its voluntary character and emphasizes the separation from the overall Jewish society.

---

[34] J. Licht, *The Rule Scroll: A Scroll from the Wilderness of Judea—1QS, 1QSa, 1QSb: Text, Introduction and Commentary* (Jerusalem, 1957), 148.294. See also Martone, op. cit., pp. 147-148.

[35] See Martone, op. cit., p. 140.

The vision of the world: a. According to 1QS the community possesses an overall vision about the entire destiny of humanity, which is fully presented in the long passage of 3:13-4:26,[36] as we can see in the opening sentence: "The Instructor should instruct and teach all the sons of light about the nature [literally: generations] of all the sons of man" (3:13).

This vision is essentially dualistic: on the one side lies the "spirit of truth," and on the other "the spirit of deceit" (3:18-19). The source of light generates the sons of truth, also called the sons of justice. The source of darkness generates the sons of deceit. Humanity is therefore divided into two sides over which preside two angels: on the one side "the angel of darkness," who makes men go astray; on the other "the prince of light," who helps the sons of light. God has divided people into two parts "until the appointed end and the new creation" (4:25).

This has led many interpreters to speak of an absolute determinism when referring to 1QS. Yet, it would seem that 1QS thinks the dualism is reproduced within each person: "Until now the spirits of truth and injustice feud in the heart of man" (4:23). In this way it would be possible for everyone to resist the spirit of injustice and the angel of darkness, thanks to the help of the prince of lights and God. As a matter of fact, the ritual of entry into the covenant presupposes the liberty to adhere to the community by abandoning the sons of darkness, as was also underlined by the confession of sins. The theories on the two spirits should hence be read bearing in mind the other 1QS theories and its ritual practices and not in isolation and independently of those. In addition, 1QS presupposes punishments of the members of the community: it is possible to distinguish between those that follow the rules rightly and those who break them.

---

[36] On the dualistic vision of 1QS 3:13-4:26 from a historical point of view, see Segalla, op. cit.; J.H. Charlesworth, "A Critical Comparison of the Dualism in 1QS 3:13-4:26 and the 'Dualism' Contained in the Gospel of John," in *NTS* 15, 1968-1969, pp. 389-418; R. Bauckham, "The Qumran Community and the Gospel of John" (1999), p. 14: "It was the publication of Qumran texts which effected a shift in Johannine scholarship towards recognizing the thoroughly Jewish character of Johannine theology. In retrospect this appears to have been a case of drawing the correct conclusion from the wrong evidence. There is no need to appeal to the Qumran texts in order to demonstrate the Jewishness of the Fourth Gospel's light/darkness imagery. This can be done more convincingly by comparison with other Jewish sources, which were already available before the discovery of the Dead Sea Scrolls."

b. The second feature typical of the conceptions of 1QS concerns the Law of Moses (*torat Mosheh*). Whoever enters into the covenant "shall swear with a binding oath to revert to the Law of Moses" (5:8).

By taking the Law of Moses as a fundamental point of reference, the community is referring to what is central to the vision of the world of every Jewish group. The general premise is that in Israel a deviation from the Law of Moses occurred. The insistence on the "return" implies that the community possesses the true interpretation of the Law. This claim is based on the conviction that the priests, "sons of Sadoq," who lead the community, possess a direct revelation from God that unveils the secrets contained in the Law of Moses. Those that are not part of the covenant "have neither sought nor examined his decrees in order to know the hidden matters in which they err by their own fault and because they treated revealed matters with disrespect" (5:11-12). The Community therefore possesses a direct revelation from God, which nevertheless does not substitute the Law of Moses but unveils its secrets so that it can be interpreted correctly.[37]

The functional relationship between the secrecy of the revelation and the social separateness of the group should not be missed. The divine truth of a separatist group can only be revealed secretly.

c. The 1QS' eschatological vision is the necessary counterpart to the dualistic perspective of the group. In the situation in which the world is dominated by Belial (2:18), the sons of light are forced to separate themselves radically from the overall Jewish society. But in the end, there will be divine punishment, the "retribution" for the "wicked" (8:7). Only at that moment may the religious ideal of the group be fulfilled, when "there will be no iniquity" (8:10) in Israel and throughout the land of Israel, for whose contamination, by that time, expiation will have been done (8:6, 10). 1QS seems to think that in that final moment there will no longer be a Temple because, "the community council shall be founded on truth to be an everlasting plantation, a holy house for Israel and the foundation of the holy of holies for Aaron" (8:5-6; see also 9:6).

The final stage, therefore, is not simply the turning upside down of

---

[37] On the relation between divine revelation and "human intellectual scrutiny on the process of shaping the halakhah," see Y. Shemesh and C. Werman, "Hidden Things and Their Revelation," in *Revue de Qumran* 18, 1998, pp. 409-427. See also Segalla, "Libri Sacri e rivelazione in Qumran," in *Libri Sacri e rivelazione* (Brescia, 1975), pp. 69-107.

the present situation but the construction of something new. It is not a restoration of the ancient Temple but its substitution by a different cult, "without the flesh of burnt offerings and without the fats of sacrifice—the offering of the lips in compliance with the decree will be like the pleasant aroma of justice, and the perfection of behavior will be acceptable like a freewill offering" (9:4-5).

d. A characteristic theory of 1QS 3:3-9 is that purification does take place through the spirit but also through submission to the Law of Moses and through water (3:6-9):

> It is by the spirit of the true counsel of God that are atoned the paths of man, all his iniquities, so that he can look at the light of life. And it is by the holy spirit of the community, in its truth, that he is cleansed of all his iniquities. And by the spirit of uprightness and of humility his sin is atoned. And by the compliance of his soul with all the laws of God his flesh is cleansed by being sprinkled with cleansing waters (*bmy ndh*) and being made holy with the waters (*bmy*) of repentance (*dwky*).

The conception that emerges in this text is that both the expiation of sins (*yekhupru khol awonotaw*) and the purification of the body (*yittaher besaro*) take place through an act of the Holy Spirit, together with observance of the precepts of God, not separate from a bodily purification through water (*lahazot bemei niddah ulehitqadesh bemei dokhi*). What is characteristic of 1QS is that on the one hand it is stated that purification does not take place until the rebellion against the precepts of God is brought to an end: "defiled, defiled shall he be all the days he spurns the decrees of God" (1QS 3: 5-6). On the other hand it is stated that the spirit has an expiatory (*lekapper*) and purification (*letaher*) function. As a matter of fact, 1QS also maintains that the adepts preserve the impurity of the body (for a year for solid foods and for two years for liquids) even after having confessed their sins and having joined the community. This means that a bodily contamination exists: it is not eliminated by the expiation worked through acts of justice, nor through the spirit.

It is methodologically mistaken to interpret every individual conception of 1QS independently of the others found in the same text. Even if originally the individual conceptions could have been independent and contradictory, the fact remains that whoever redacted 1QS in its present form did not think that there was a contradiction. He imagined a religious system in which a variety of conceptions contributed to a coherent whole. It is this coherence that we have to bring out. Impurity should certainly not be identified with moral evil but is only a bodily consequence of this.[38] Those who commit iniquity contaminate their bodies, and this bodily uncleanness persists for a long time also after conversion and after having moved away from iniquity. Purification by water therefore continues to be important in 1QS.

4. *A Systemic Comparison*

The systemic aim of the Johannine community is to produce a new birth in its adepts, provoked by a supernatural power; to practice the true cult of God, which takes place through the presence of the Holy Spirit in the body of the believer; and to maintain a supernatural union with Jesus/*logos*. In John, therefore, in place of the covenant, we find rebirth; in place of the cult, which substitutes the Temple, a meeting with God in one's own body through the spirit; and in place of purity, a total unity with Jesus/*logos*. The systemic aim of the 1QS community is to create the true Israel through radical separation from the surrounding Jewish world, installing a new covenant with God that fosters faithful observance of the law of Moses, rightly interpreted; and to prepare, for eschatological times, a pure Israel on the purified land of Israel.

These differences, however, turn out to be different modes of responding to related problems originating within Jewish society, though in different periods. Which identity should be pursued, given that the one pursued within Palestinian Jewish institutions is unsatisfactory? What is the true cult that should be practiced, given that the Jerusalem Temple is rejected and/or no longer exists? What behavior allows one to remain within the community?

The Two Social Groups

The socio-religious mechanisms to reach the systemic aim of the two groups are different. For the Johannine community they lie in an initiation process in which the adept has to take the same route as the master, making sure he or she continues to be supernaturally united to him. For the 1QS community they consist in an initiation process

---

[38] There is a different opinion in García Martínez, *The Dead Sea Scrolls Translated*, pp. 250-251.

that enables the adepts to separate themselves definitively from their society of origin and rigorously observe the precepts of the covenant in a state of absolute purity.

The criteria of legitimization of the two communities present both similarities and differences. In the first place, both communities claim to depend on *a direct revelation* from God, not available to others. In 1QS, however, the revelation God concedes concerns the secrets contained in the Torah and in the prophets of the Bible.[39] In John the "truth" (*aletheia*) is thought of not as a hidden knowledge already contained in the Bible but as a new revelation. The spirit also allows one to understand the Bible, but its revelation does not end there. John writes: "The Law was given by Moses, grace and truth came by Jesus Christ" (1:17).

Second, beside the claim for a direct revelation, the 1QS community claims it has another criterion of legitimacy, of a genealogical kind. The priesthood of 1QS is legitimate because it descends from Sadoq, the priest established by David. In John, genealogical legitimization is rejected: there are no criteria of legitimization within the Torah, Biblical history, or Jewish institutions. All those who "have faith in the name" of the Son are "generated by God" (*tekna tou theou*) and are born "not of blood, nor of the will of the flesh, nor of the will of man" (1:13). Essentially, in John, the Law of Moses and the genealogical principle do not have a legitimating function, because the Johannine community believes that its founder is Jesus/*logos* through whom the world was created (1:3). It is nevertheless important to remember that the cultural models that allow John to legitimate its founder, as if directly derived from God, are typically Jewish models, such as, for example, "the voice from heaven" in 12:28 or the holy spirit in 12:33 and 20:22.

These different criteria for legitimization are the expression of the different social make-up of the two communities. Speaking of 1QS community, Mach has argued that the Qumran texts appear to be expressions of a "declared conservatism" that in reality is a "conservative revolution." At Qumran, that is, the innovations produced by the community are presented as a recovery of ancient traditions betrayed or abandoned by the majority. According to Mach, this is shown by the self-definition as "sons of Sadoq" that serves the "group

---

[39] See Shemesh-Werman, op. cit.

as continuing a special kind of biblically legitimated priesthood" or by the fact that it has to defend an ancient calendar probably already abandoned at the time of 1 Enoch 72-82.[40]

In John, the situation is different: the group, though not physically separatist, no longer wishes to call itself Judean. The foundation derives from the fact that Jesus, the creator *logos* (1:14), has an authority superior to that of anyone in biblical or non-biblical history and even to the revelation of Moses itself. The Bible does not offer the model on which to base interpretation of present-day reality, but, on the contrary, it is present-day reality that serves to interpret the presumed true meaning of biblical history. The Bible is only a part of the truth and should be read in the light of the total truth possessed by the community and not vice versa. The Johannine community is not conservative but goes back to a refoundational radicalism that wishes to go beyond Jewish boundaries.

The modalities of admission to the community lend themselves to comparison. While in 1QS the adepts are received by a community well represented in its hierarchical structure (priests, Levites, and people differentiated according to degree) (cf., 1QS I:18-19: II:19-23), in John, only the leader of the group receives the adept (cf., 9:35-39; 11:26-27; 20:26-29).[41] The adepts do not have to declare their adherence to the Law but rather their faith in Jesus:

> Do you believe in the Son of God? ...I believe, Lord. And he prostrated himself before him (9:35.38).

> Whoever lives and believes in me shall never die. Do you believe this? She said to him, Yes Lord, I have believed that you are the Christ, the son of God who is coming in the world (11:26-27).[42]

The internal hierarchy of the 1QS community is the result of a distinctive process that at the social level is very effective. The adepts have separated themselves not just territorially but also through their goods. If their goods do not remain in the general society, separation from it will certainly be definitive. Separation and the hierarchical structure are guaranteed also by a liturgical calendar that is different from that in use in the overall Jewish society. This is not the case in

---

[40] M. Mach, op. cit., pp. 64-65
[41] See Destro-Pesce, *Come nasce una religione*, pp. 22-23.
[42] See Segalla, *Giovanni. Versione. Introduzione. Note*, pp. 323-324.

John, where adherence to Jesus implies leaving one's synagogue of origin, but not the world, nor entry into a community characterized by tightly-knit hierarchical levels.

The Johannine community, above all, is not socially homogeneous and is not defined by clear criteria of status. It does not tend towards economic equality and envisages differentiated institutional roles (as for example that of Peter and the beloved disciple; cf., chap. 21). The social difference between the two groups can easily summarized: the Johannine community is organized as a movement of disciples around a master and guide and is oriented towards the surrounding hostile world, to announce its message. The 1QS community is a separate society organized theocratically.

The Religious Practices of the Two Communities

The Cult. In 1QS, prayer and observance of the precepts in a state of purity transforms the community into a substitute for the Temple. 1QS does not imagine a reconstruction of the Temple even for the eschatological period. One can therefore speak of a non-sacrificial cult. In John, too, the cult is not sacrificial but an inner prostration before God; yet, it does not substitute the Temple but simply leaves it out of count. In fact, in John there is no further need for members' purity, nor for any priestly functions. The Temple does not exist even in a metaphorical sense.

The initiation. We have seen that among the religious practices a special role is played by the initiation process. In 1QS there is a) a period of examination, instruction, and conversion (with the immersion ritual and confession of sins), b) a probationary period of two years, and c) definitive admission to all the ritual activities of the community.

Three stages are also recognizable in John's initiation. The moment of the choice of disciples (1:35-51) is accompanied by the adept's declaration of adherence, after having received preliminary instruction.[43] The relation between the adept and the community in 1QS is of a voluntary nature, consisting in a project of explicit adher-

---

[43] The disciples have been taught about Jesus to some extent by John the Baptist (John 1:29-36), and Jesus seems to speak for a long while with the first two disciples who remain with him for quite a time. Also for Nathanael (1:45-51) there would seem to be some teaching, followed by his formal adherence.

ence by the adept. In John, too, the adept's voluntary orientation is necessary, but admission into the community is decided freely by the master, without any reference to the faithfulness or otherwise of the disciple towards the Law, as happens in 1QS. In John the second structural feature is there too, although not in the form of a probationary period. The disciples, during Jesus' activities in public (chaps. 2-12), are merely onlookers without being active or interactive subjects. In John, finally, the third feature consists in entry into the full exercise of the functions decided by Jesus.

There are other substantial points. a) The John initiation has to provide the means to face the fight that those being initiated have to undergo and that leads to victory over the world. The disciples have to receive a supernatural power that enables them to follow the master, and this is obtained through the spirit that keeps them in supernatural contact with him. The parable of the vines and the branches affirms two things simultaneously: "without me you can do nothing" (15:5) and "remain in me" (15:4). The spirit is what allows the disciples to remain in the Son even after his disappearance from the world. In 1QS, on the other hand, the initiation has to separate definitively "the sons of light" from the "men of the lot of Belial" (2:4-5). This is why a very long initiation is necessary, during which the complete decontamination of the adept's body takes place (2:16-22).[44] b) While purification occurs in 1QS through various features: "to do the truth," expiation through God, and purification through water, in John, purification occurs through the "word." The *logos* of God possesses the creational word that functions as purification (15:3) as well as sanctification (17:15-17). In 1QS, purity has a basic systemic function, whereas in John it has no systemic function at all. c) In John, the teaching of the group is transmitted to the adepts only at a central moment of their initiation and not at the beginning, as happens in 1QS: "He shall swear with a binding oath to revert to the Law of Moses, according to all that he commanded, with whole heart and whole soul, in compliance with all that has been revealed of it to the Sons of Zadok" (5:8-9).

---

[44] The procedure in 1QS is for entry into an already existing community, while for John it is a process that tends to the constitution of a new group. A distinction comes to light here between initiation rituals of admission to a community, and initiation rituals of institution (the case with John), with which a religious group is founded or refounded; cf., Destro and Pesce, *Come nasce una religione*, pp. 16-21.

The main object of acceptance is what is presented at the beginning of the initiation process: in 1QS it is the Law (obviously reformulated according to the 1QS vision), whereas in John it is the leader of the group. From this, the different function of the Law or of the precepts in the two groups becomes clear. In 1QS, there is a new covenant for the observance of the entire Law of Moses. In John, in the last analysis, there is just one precept, consisting of the repetition of the master's action: to love the way the master loved and to give one's life for one's friends (15:12-13).

Moreover, in 1QS the act of admission requires two fundamental features: a) a conversion, i.e., a confession of sins through which one condemns one's entire past and also the way of life typical of Jewish society; b) commitment to fulfil the ideal foreseen by Deut. 6:4, i.e., the adoration of the one God with all one's strength.[45] In John, as we have said already, entry into the community implies leaving the synagogue (9:22, 12:42) but does not consist of a radical alternative to the surrounding world. The Johannine principle is "you are not of the world," though you have to remain "in the world" (17:16-16).[46] One leaves the synagogue but enters into the world.

Unlike 1QS, the passage into the Johannine Community is not marked by a confession of sins or by conversion. Those who do not believe in the Son of God remain in sin, whereas those who believe are not subjected to the judgment that would condemn them because of their sin: "he that believes is not condemned; but he that does not believe has been already condemned because he did not believe in the name of the only begotten Son of God" (3:18). From the moment of the confession of faith onwards, the new Johannine adepts, united supernaturally to Jesus/*logos*, can take the route that will take them to "rebirth" and "eternal life:" "except a man be born of water and spirit, he cannot see the kingdom of God" (3:5).

Finally, in John as in 1QS, passage into the community is imagined as a passage from darkness to light:

> I came into the world, so that whoever believes in me should not remain in the darkness (12:46).

---

[45] The fact that the community is conceived as a priestly community, and therefore requires ritual purity for everyone in it, together with the need for radical separation from Judaic society, necessarily leads to mean the ideal of the adoration of God as a community of goods that is carried out in a separate society.

[46] In this context the "world" does not mean Judaism or the Judeans. The Judeans are only part of the "world" (cf., Esler, op. cit., p. 85).

Light is come into the world, but men loved darkness rather than light because their deeds were evil (3:19).

The difference lies in the fact that the passage from darkness to light in John is once again obtained by adherence to the leader of the group (Jesus/*Logos*). The contrast in both texts between darkness and light is insufficient to establish an affinity, because its function in the two systems is addressed to different purposes.

Two Visions of the World

The External World. In 1QS the separation between community and society produces the greatest possible estrangement. It creates an alternative world. This occurs through the specific and exclusive occupation of a territory and settlement that must have no contact with the world outside. In the case of John, the overall society exercises a powerful force of attraction. John responds to a vision of the world absent for the most part in 1QS. It originates in the inner conflict that the members of the Johannine community feel because of their difficulties over breaking with their original environment. This happens because the Johannine community is not organized theocratically, unlike that of 1QS. In John the dialectic between the force of attraction of the overall society and membership of a persecuted minority community is always present. In 1QS, by contrast, this attraction ends with entry into a community that is autonomous in religious, territorial, and economic ways.

In John there are moments of withdrawal into privacy, but they are only temporary and function to construct a community that has in any case to live and coexist with the overall society. For 1QS, the separation tends to be perpetual and will disappear only at the eschatological moment. Second, it is a community that tends to be totally self-sufficient and does not wish to integrate in any way with its surroundings. In 1QS, in fact, there is no trace of that missionary-in-the-world perspective that is fundamental for John: "As the Father has sent me, so I send you" (20:21).

The Johannine community accepts the organization of time of the overall society and does not think of transforming social organization on the basis of its own organization of time.[47]

---

[47] Destro and Pesce, *Come nasce una religione*, p. 121.

The fact that John's Jesus states "my father works until now and I also work" (5:17) means that the Gospel questions the cardinal feature of the synagogue's temporal system: the Sabbath. To discuss the necessity of resting on the Sabbath has in any case a specific social function. It means overcoming the division between religious groups determined by the interruption of work on the Sabbath day. The lessening of the Sabbath's importance allows social integration with those who normally carry out their everyday actions on the Sabbath. John does not have its own calendar, and is therefore disposed to accept any kind of calendar used by the society in which the community finds itself. In 1QS, on the contrary, the rhythm of time set out by the Jewish tradition is fully respected, even if interpreted according to calendar conceptions out of line with those in use in the overall Jewish society.[48]

The Temple and the Community. 1QS tries to construct a community that has all the characteristics of a temple, or rather of a substitute for a temple. In 1QS we are not dealing with a union between the believer and divinity but with the construction of a priestly society, radically pure, that can carry out the act of cult. As Davies has written, in 1QS the Temple, purification, and circumcision are not "abandoned, but...their efficacy was confined to the *yahad*. Every Jewish symbol is thus strictly disciplined into a single ideological and social construction: the yahad."[49]

1QS's points of reference are the people of Israel, the priesthood, and the Land. The *yahad* will constitute (8:5-10):

> [a] a holy house for Israel (*bet qodesh leyisrael*), [b] a foundation of the Holy of Holies for Aaron (*sod qodesh haqodashim le'aharon*); [c] true witnesses for the Judgment (*'ede 'emet lamishpat*); [d] and chosen by the will (of God) to atone for the land[50] (*lekhapper bad haares*) and to render the wicked their retribution.

The function of the community is to prepare the substitution for the

---

[48] Cf., Mach, op. cit., pp. 64-65 (with a bibliography). The fact remains that the rhythm of the Sabbath was fundamental for 1QS. Some have argued that John contains a calendar similar to the one in use in Qumran; cf., E. Ruckstuhl, *Chronology of the Last Days of Jesus: A Critical Study* (New York, 1965) and A. Jaubert, "The Calendar of Qumran and the Passion Narrative in John," in J.H. Charlesworth, ed., *John and the Dead Sea Scrolls* (London, 1972), pp. 62-75. On John 5:17, cf., Destro and Pesce, *Come nasce una relizione*, p. 122.

[49] Davies, op. cit., p. 191.

[50] *Ares* means "land," not "world."

Temple and the Saint of Saints in the eschatological time and to have a group of faithful who can judge the Judeans who have contaminated the land of Israel. In the judgment, they will be condemned, and the land of Israel will be purified once more. Thus the people of Israel will be able to live in its land under the guidance of its own legitimate priesthood. In John, the Temple is eliminated.

The Covenant and the Law. 1QS believes it enjoys a new covenant with God: it calls upon the Law of Moses, but it interprets it in an innovative way through claiming to possess its true meaning, thanks to a revelation received directly from God. In John, neither the Law of Moses nor the idea of a new covenant play a part.

5. *Conclusion*

If 1QS reformulates all the principal Jewish symbols, John reformulates only a few of them, eliminating others completely. The features eliminated are: Temple, circumcision, land of Israel, and expiation through sacrifices. These features are however preserved mainly in their metaphorical meaning. The Temple means the presence of God among men, and John believes that this presence is fulfilled through the holy spirit. The presence of the holy spirit does not imply the preparation of a new Temple in a purified future land of Israel. It simply means that God is present in the *kosmos* (not *ghe*). Also for circumcision, John preserves only the implicit cultural presupposition of pruning/purification (see the parable of the vine and the branches). Purification, however, takes place only through the acceptance of the "word" of Jesus: "you are pure through the word (*logos*) which I have spoken to you" (15:3).

This "word" is conceived following a Jewish concept as the original divine power (cf., 1:1). It has the same effect as circumcision, i.e., it purifies (cf., also, 13:3: "you are pure"). Essentially, acceptance of the preaching of Jesus[51] is conceived as a substitution for circumcision. For this reason it can be said that here John presents and justifies a break with one of the cardinal points of every Jewish religious system.

The concept of the land of Israel, on the other hand, does not even maintain a metaphorical function in John. The concept simply disap-

---

[51] See 15:7: "if you remain in me and my words remain in you."

pears and has no religious meaning. The determinants of space that acquire systemic significance in John are those of above and below: in John, belonging to the world from above completely takes the place of belonging to the land of Israel. In 1QS, on the contrary, in the eschatological moment the true Israel will once again inhabit the Land. Moreover, what is characteristic of John is that forgiveness of sins does not take place through a sacrificial system.

There is no trace in John of an idea such as that of the Qumran angelic liturgy found in 4QshirSabb, according to which the "above," where the celestial liturgy takes place, is the model for the "below," where the liturgy of the community takes place. In John, between above and below there is a relationship of conflict and opposition. There is no question of being able to imagine a modeling of the below on the basis of the ideal that can be found above.[52]

The conceptual and terminological affinities between John and the Qumran literature have often been stressed. The list of affinities includes for example expressions like "do the truth" (1QS 1:5; 5:3; 8:2; John 3:21); "light of life" (1QS 3:7; John 8:12); "works of God" (1QS 4:4; John 9:3); "spirit of truth" (1QS 4:21; John 14:17; 15:17; 16:13); "sons of light" (1QS 1:9; 2:16; 3:13 etc.; John 12:36);[53] or similarities such as "prince of this world" (John 12:31; 14:30; 16:11), etc. From the perspective of a systemic comparison, the use of similar or identical concepts or terms has little meaning where the systemic purpose and function are different. If the systemic purpose of John is rebirth, the use of concepts and terms such as purification and sanctification is wholly secondary, and serves only to express a profoundly different experience in traditional terms. Union with the master through the spirit is the fundamental instrument. Expressions such as "spirit," "truth," "do the truth," "injustice," "darkness," and "light" all acquire a profoundly different meaning. The other basic Jewish symbols—creational word (*logos*), spirit (*pneuma*), purification, sanctifica-

---

[52] Bauckham, op. cit., pp. 1-2, rightly observes that "the dualism of the Fourth Gospel is expressed in two different sets of images...the light/darkness opposition and the above/below and God/world opposition. It is very important to notice that these two sets of images never combine or overlap in the Fourth Gospel. Each is kept distinct from the other. Of these sets of images, the Qumran texts provide parallels only to the light/darkness opposition, which, of course, is found also in other Jewish texts." From this point of view the relevant systemic significance of the above/below opposition in John is clear.

[53] See M. Hengel, *La questione giovannea* (Brescia, 1998), pp. 270-271; Segalla, op. cit., pp. 41-44.

tion, and expiation—play a profoundly different role in John, despite the fact that they still preserve a metaphorical meaning.

1QS is a Jewish religious system, because it maintains it is the true Israel that is preparing the future people of Israel on the purified land of Israel and because it preserves and reformulates all the main Jewish symbols and rituals. John, on the contrary, reflects a religious system that is not Jewish because it is autonomous from the point of view of the social group (it defines the identity of the members independently of the land of Israel and the concept of Israel), from the point of view of religious practices (it has a cult that leaves out of account the Temple and has its own autonomous system of expiation), and from the point of view of the vision of the world (it believes it possesses a direct revelation of God that does not reveal the secrets of the Law of Moses, but is simply a new and complete revelation).

Bibliography

Ashton, J., *Understanding the Fourth Gospel* (Oxford, 1991).
Bauckham, R., "The Qumran Community and the Gospel of John" (1999, manuscript).
Bauckham, R., "Qumran and the Fourth Gospel: Is There a Connection?" in Porter, S.E., and C.A. Evans, eds., *The Scrolls and the Scriptures: Qumran Fifty Years After* (Sheffield, 1997), pp. 267-279.
Baumbach, G., *Qumrân und das Johannes-Evangelium. Eine vergleichende Untersuchung der dualistischen Aussagen der Ordensregel (1QS) von Qumrân und des Johannes-Evangeliums mit Berücksichtigung der spätjüdischen Apokalypsen* (Berlin, 1958).
Benoit, P., "Qumran et le Nouveau Testament," in *NTS* 7, 1960-1961, pp. 276-296.
Blockmuehl, M., "Redaction and Ideology in the Rule of the Community," in *Revue de Qumran* 18, 1998, pp. 541-560.
Böcher, O., *Der johanneische Dualismus im Zusammenhang des nachbiblischen Judentums* (Gütersloh, 1965).
Boismard, M.-E., and A. Lamouille, *Synopse des Quatre Evangiles en français. Tome III. L'Evangile de Jean* (Paris, 1987).
Braun, H., *Qumran und das Neue Testament, II Bände* (Tübingen, 1966).
Brown, R.E., *The Community of the Beloved Disciple* (New York and London, 1979).
Brown, R.E., *The Churches the Apostles Left Behind* (New York, 1984).
Brown, R.E., "The Dead Sea Scrolls and the New Testament," in *Expository Times* 78, 1966-1967, pp. 19-23.
Brown, R.E., *The Gospel according to John* (Garden City and New York, 1966-1970).
Brown, R.E., "The Qumran Scrolls and the Johannine Gospel and Epistles," in Brown, R.E., *New Testament Essays* (New York, 1965), pp. 102-131.
Charlesworth, J.H., "A Critical Comparison of the Dualism in 1QS 3:13-4:26 and the 'Dualism' Contained in the Gospel of John," in *NTS* 15, 1968-1969, pp. 389-418.
Charlesworth, J.H., "The Dead Sea Scrolls and the Gospel according to John," in Culpepper, R.A., and C.C. Black, eds., *Exploring the Gospel of John: In Honor of D. Moody Smith* (Louisville, 1996).

Charlesworth, J.H., ed., *John and the Dead Sea Scrolls* (New York, 1991).
Davies, P.R., "The Dead Sea Writings, The Judaisms of," in Neusner, J., A.J. Avery-Peck, and W.S. Green, eds., *The Encyclopaedia of Judaism* (Leiden, 2000), vol. 1, pp. 182-196.
Destro, A., and M. Pesce, *Antropologia delle origini cristiane* (Rome, 1997).
Destro, A., and M. Pesce, *Come nasce una religione. Antropologia ed esegesi del Vangelo di Giovanni* (Rome, 2000).
Destro, A., and M. Pesce, "La lavanda dei piedi di Gv 13,1-20, il *Romanzo di Esopo* e i *Saturnalia* di Macrobio," in *Biblica* 80/2, 1999, pp. 239-249.
Destro, A., and M. Pesce, "Lo spirito e il mondo vuoto. Prospettive esegetiche e antropologiche su Gv 4,21-24," in *Annali di Storia dell'esegesi* 12, 1995, pp. 9-32.
Dodd, C.H., *The Interpretation of the Fourth Gospel* (Cambridge, 1953).
Esler, P.F., "Introverted Sectarianism at Qumran and in the Johannine Community," in *The First Christians in Their Social Worlds* (London and New York, 1994), pp. 70-91.
Finn, T.M., *From Death to Rebirth. Ritual Conversion in Antiquity* (New York, 1997).
Fitzmyer, J.A., "The Qumran Scrolls and the New Testament after Forty Years," in *Revue de Qumran* 13, 1988, pp. 610-620.
García Martínez, F., and J. Trebolle Barrera, *Gli uomini di Qumran. Letteratura, struttura sociale e concezioni religiose* (Brescia, 1996).
García Martínez, F., *The Dead Sea Scrolls Translated. The Qumran Texts in English* (Leiden, 1996).
García Martínez, F., and E.J.C. Tigchelaar, eds., *The Dead Sea Scrolls Study Edition. Volume One 1QI-4Q273* (Leiden, 1997).
Geertz, C., *Interpretazione di culture* (Bologna, 1998) (= *The Interpretation of Cultures*, New York, Basic Books, 1973).
Hengel, M., *La questione giovannea* (Brescia, 1998).
Jaubert, A., "The Calendar of Qumran and the Passion Narrative in John," in Charlesworth, J.H, ed., *John and the Dead Sea Scrolls* (London, 1972), pp. 62-75.
Kuhn, K.G., "Die in Palästina gefundenen hebräischen Texte und das Neue Testament," in *ZTK* 47, 1950, pp. 192-211.
Licht, J., *The Rule Scroll: A Scroll from the Wilderness of Judea—1QS, 1QSa, 1QSb: Text, Introduction and Commentary* (Jerusalem, 1957) (Hebrew).
Lupieri, E., *L'apocalisse di Giovanni* (Milan, 1999).
Lupieri, E., *Giovanni Battista fra storia e leggenda* (Brescia, 1998).
Lupieri, E., *Giovanni Battista nelle tradizioni sinottiche* (Brescia, 1998).
Mach, M., "Conservative Revolution? The Intolerant Innovations of Qumran," in Stanton, G.N., and G.G. Stroumsa, eds., *Tolerance and Intolerance in Early Judaism and Christianity* (Cambridge, 1998), pp. 61-79.
Maier, J., "The Judaic System of the Dead Sea Scrolls," in Neusner, J., ed., *Judaism in Late Antiquity, Part Two. Historical Syntheses* (Leiden, 1996), pp. 84-108.
Maier, J., *Die Qumran-Essener: Die Texte vom Toten Meer. Band I: Die Texte der Höhlen 1-3 und 5-11* (Munich, 1995).
Malina, B.J., and R.L. Rohrbaugh, *Social-Science Commentary on the Gospel of John* (Minneapolis, 1998).
Martone, C., *La "Regola della Comunità." Edizione critica* (Turin, 1995).
Martone, C., *Testi di Qumran* a cura di Florentino García Martínez (Brescia, 1996).
Martyn, J.L., *History and Theology in the Fourth Gospel* (Nashville, 1979).
Metso, S., *The Textual Development of the Qumran Community Rule* (Leiden, 1997).
Neusner, J., *The Systemic Analysis of Judaism* (Atlanta, 1988).
Osiek, C., and D. Balch, *Families in the New Testament World. Households and House Churches* (Louisville, 1997).

Porter, S.E., ed., *Handbook to Exegesis of the New Testament* (Leiden, 1997).
Roloff, J., "Der johanneische 'LieblinJohnunger' und der Lehrer der Gerechtigkeit," in *NTS* 15, 1968-1969, pp. 129-151.
Ruckstuhl, E., *Chronology of the Last Days of Jesus: A Critical Study* (New York, 1965). (German: 1963).
Schnackenburg, R., "Die 'Anbetung in Geist und Wahrheit' (Joh 4,23) im Lichte von Qumrân-Texte," in *BZ* N.F. 3, 1959, pp. 88-94.
Schnackenburg, R., *Das Johannesevangelium* (Freiburg, 1965-1979), 3 vols.
Segalla, G., "Libri sacri e rivelazione in Qumran," in *Libri sacri e rivelazione* (Brescia, 1975), pp. 69-107.
Segalla, G., *Giovanni. Versione. Introduzione. Note* (Cinisello, 1990).
Segalla, G., "Qumran e la letteratura giovannea (Vangelo e Lettere). Il dualismo antitetico di luce-tenebra," in *Ricerche Storico-Bibliche* 9, 1997, pp. 117-153.
Shemesh, A., and C. Werman, "Hidden Things and Their Revelation," in *Revue de Qumran* 18, 1998, pp. 409-427.
Stegemann, E.W., and W. Stegemann, *Storia sociale del cristianesimo primitivo* (Bologna, 1998).

PART 5

CONCLUSION

17. READING THE SCROLLS SYSTEMICALLY

Bruce D. Chilton
Bard College

I. *The Order of the Findings*

Worldview, way of life, and view of the social order are the categories of description and analysis each of the essays in this volume has deployed in order to deal with the Judaism of Qumran. The contributors represent something of the ferment in matters historical, literary, and exegetical that still characterizes study of the Dead Sea Scrolls as a whole. Precisely because that variety has come through their work, the remarkable stability of their findings is all the more striking, when it concerns the systemic description of the religious structure articulated in the Scrolls.

The worldview portrays existence at the very edge of destruction and renewal. The way of life comports with the expectation of how God is effecting this transformation. The view of the social order is that only the faithful remnant will endure to inherit the promise of Israel.

These three structures of belief, action, and emotion are so tightly linked to one another, there is no perceptible interstice among them. The system positions both the community and the individual within a seamless whole of living. The integrally structural relationship of the categories set out in Jacob Neusner's initial, theoretical chapter is to that extent vindicated in the case of Qumran.

The linkage of those categories proves to be expressive of the life of Qumran's people as well as of their religious system. As these two volumes were assembled for publication, in fact, the editors found themselves re-ordering the categories. "Way of life" now enjoys relative precedence as well as what may seem at first sight to be disproportionate attention. A consequence of systemic analysis is that, by analyzing interfaces among belief, ethics, and social definition, the historically evidenced actions prompted by the system are put in clear relief. The assumption that the study of religion is an investigation of ideological constructs alone is therefore more than challenged:

a method is crafted that permits us to assess the power and influence of the system as a whole in its historical setting as well as within its own terms of reference.

The analytic essay on the archaeology of the site by James F. Strange and James Riley Strange disputes the thesis of a disruptive earthquake at Qumran and to that extent adjusts the received history of the group. Perhaps more surprisingly, their emphasis on the sparse conditions of living, hierarchical arrangements of accommodation, and commitment to the production of scrolls on an industrial scale represents a revival of the model of the sect Roland de Vaux suggested long ago, which has been subjected to keen (on occasion acerbic) criticism. Although this is no return to the alleged monasticism of Qumran, it does support the picture that the other articles endorse in regard to the way of life of the community.

Lawrence Schiffman's discussion of the significance of the discovery of phylacteries and *mezuzot* at Qumran, together with its exegetical emphasis on *nistar* ("hidden" knowledge), as distinct from both the emerging traditions of the Pharisees and the prevailing hierarchy in the Temple, only confirms that picture. When Eileen Schuller exposes how the prayers of Qumran combined individual and corporate devotion, eschatological and existential concerns, heavenly and earthly realities, that only underscores that way of life is inextricable from worldview and definition of the social order.

Johann Maier's deliberately controversial essay joins Schiffman's in providing a window into the affective life of the community. Schiffman's emphasis is on the elucidation of the Torah, and he rightly stresses the emotional engagement of binding oneself to God and Israel by means of this process. Maier, on the other hand, challenges the biblicism of much Qumran scholarship and demonstrates the vital importance of the practice of purity both in the geography and choreography of the Temple and in the liturgical dynamics of worshipping with angels. There is, in this case as in others, plenty of room for topical dispute over whether text or purity is at the center of gravity of the system as a whole. But in the midst of that debate, the emotional reward for the *yahad* of both correct interpretation and a purity commensurate with divine requirements should not be forgotten.

Martin G. Abegg's presentation of the calendar of Qumran stresses the theological, rather than observational, basis of the festal system; the interplay of darkness and light in both the regulation of the solar year and the experience within the community of those two forces underlines the emotional aspect of what might appear at first sight a purely intellectual element of the system. Peter W. Flint's elegant exposition of the constantly reshaping canonical process evidenced within the Scrolls attests this affective dimension active within what is still too often thought of as an antiquarian enterprise. Mayer I. Gruber's vigorous assertion of Qumran as an egalitarian "monument to a Judaism that might have been" is a stunning instance not only of objection to the putative patriarchy scholars may have brought to the Scrolls but of the way halakhic concerns highlight emotional resonances within the life of a community.

Edward Cook's article explicates how deeply integrative the work of the wise *maskil* was in opening the eyes and ears of the community to the secrets of God. The specificity of that claim, as compared to the more general but emphatic assertion in Dan. 12:2, joins worldview, individual and collective practice, and group identity into the single inheritance of privileged knowledge. Still, the emphasis on revelation throughout demonstrates that the leading category here is that of worldview, and this essay appropriately opens volume II. Likewise, Philip Davies presents a synthesis of the treatment of the Torah in the literature of Qumran that demonstrates the comprehensive sweep of that topic, but his emphasis rightly falls (especially in view of his analysis of the differentiated strategies of reading during the history of the group) on *how* the knowledge is assimilated, so that the group's way of life is the preeminent concern. In conjunction with this, Craig Evans shows that, for all that the technique of the *pesharim* is rooted in the divinatory confidence that the book of Daniel also attests, the form is a testimony to the sectarian self-consciousness of the Essenes. The complementarity of these three articles makes for a lucid introduction into how thought, practice, and social identity were interwoven at Qumran.

The structural relationship of the categories is so tight, one might wonder why historical developments of the sort Davies refers to ever took place. In the end, religious systems exist in worlds not entirely of their own making, and the Essenes' commitment to a precise calendar of the apocalypse proved vulnerable to historical experience. Todd S. Beall, who also provides as precise a historical sketch of the sect as its own eschatological orientation permits, shows that with admirable clarity. Adjustment to take account of disappointed expectations feeds into the stunning shift in worldview and way of life to which Davies calls attention, and to an emphasis on the increased authority of esoteric interpretation of the Torah. Worldview, way of life, and view of the social order move in a coordinated development in this case. All three are wrapped up in the *raz nihyeh* that Torleif Elgvin teases out, the mysterious plan for creation and history that only the elect can truly know.

Here it may be worth emphasizing that these interlocking, systemic studies prove to be coherent, even when the contributors do not fully agree on the history of the sect, on whether it is truly a sect (much less of Essenes), and on the relationship of the group to the "Pharisees" and "Sadducees" of the period. Those basic, now traditional questions will no doubt continue to be discussed, and the level of controversy in recent years is fully warranted in view of the differing exegetical possibilities that have been pursued and the fragmentary nature of much of the evidence. To that extent, the present, collaborative study is an example of how the analysis of religious systems need not entirely be held hostage to literary, historical, or archaeological inquiry. All those modes of investigation have their place in the elucidation of system, but none of them can replace or foreclose systemic scrutiny.

John J. Collins describes the group as both sectarian and reformist, with special reference to the probationary practice and the treatment of the covenant at Qumran. While not presented in any strict sequence, his essay moves us into articles that seek to evaluate the system as a whole, and he convincingly shows that the issue of "Israel" (particularly in contrast to the usage of the term within Christianity) is our appropriate point of departure. In this setting, Heikki Räisänen's particular comparison with Paul is important and amounts to a state of the art discussion of that apostle's theology.

II. *Systemic Analysis and Comparison*

Räisänen proposes a global, typological distinction between the Scrolls and Paul's theology. Where Qumran was a sect in its deviance from traditional beliefs, Paul's communities amounted to a cult in their embrace of novel beliefs and practices. It is a pleasure to see sociological categories deployed so easily and sensibly, and as a heuristic procedure such a refinement of Weberian types is to be welcomed. But I have a problem in deciding what is "traditional" and what is "novel," especially because (1) Räisänen demonstrates so many theological overlaps between Paul and Qumran, and (2) both systems manifest a fascinating blend of traditional and innovative elements. I am not at all sure we would be applying this distinction if Paul had been the end of the story of Christianity. Our conviction that Christianity was more novel than other forms of contemporary Judaism may owe more to our knowledge of where the system was heading than to our observation of its shape and character during the first century. And within Paul's own time, how would we describe the Christianities of a James or a Peter or a Barnabas? Would they be "sects" or "cults"? Since Paul himself had considerable difficulty with the influence of those teachers and others, it is in any case unclear that his "system" existed anywhere but in his head (at least, until the second century). This discussion takes us into the interface between describing a system and evaluating it comparatively, and into the relationship between religious system and the system of thought of a given theologian; here we press the limits of our certainty.

Adriana Destro and Mauro Pesce take us into better trodden ground within the comparative interface, because they limit their comparison to two texts that are commensurate: each of them is composite, and the articulation of a community (rather than a single author such as Paul). What they show us is that, by 100 C.E., Christianity indeed emerged within its own terms of reference as a religious system autonomous of Israel, because the category of "Israel" itself was no longer deployed to describe its way of life, view of the social order, or worldview. Then it was indeed a "cult," both in Räisänen's sociological sense and in the suspicious regard of the Greco-Roman world.

Even more to the point, Christianity had also become a cult within the terms of reference of some of its sources. A signal moment in the development of this self-consciousness is marked by the publication of the Epistle to the Hebrews (c. 95 C.E.). Hebrews' presentation of the worldview, way of life, and view of the social order of what was emerging as a distinct religious system invites comparison with the Mishnah and the Scrolls, because it turns on the presentation of the Day of Atonement, which is central to all three systems.

The superiority of what it styles a better covenant is spelled out in Hebrews through chapter 9, relying on the attachment to Jesus of God's promise in Ps. 110 (Heb. 7:28):

> For the law appoints men having weakness as high priests, but the word of the oath which is after the law appoints a son for ever perfected.

Perfection implies that daily offerings are beside the point. The son was perfected "once for all, when he offered himself up" (7:26-27). The author leaves nothing important to implication: Moses' prescriptions for the sanctuary were a pale imitation of the heavenly sanctuary that Jesus has actually entered (8:1-6). Accordingly, the covenant mediated by Jesus is "better," the "second" replacing the "first," the "new" replacing what is now "obsolete" (8:6-13).

Chapter 9 simply puts the cap on an argument that is already clear. In its elaboration of a self-consciously Christological interpretation, Hebrews develops a theory of the relationship between Jesus and the Scriptures of Israel.[1] The devotion to detail involved attests

---

[1] The Epistle has been compared to a homily and calls itself a "word of exhortation" in 13:22. "Word" here (*logos*, as in John's Gospel) bears the meaning of "discourse," and the choice of diction declares Hebrews' homiletic intent. It is a sustained argument on the basis of authoritative tradition that intends to convince its readers and hearers to embrace a fresh position and an invigorated sense of purpose in the world. Hebrews engages in a series of scriptural identifications of Jesus: both Scripture (in the form of the Septuagint) and God's son are the authoritative point of departure.

Scripture is held to show that the son, and the son's announcement of salvation, are superior to the angels and their message (1:1-2:18, see especially 2:1-4). Jesus is also held to be superior to Moses and Joshua, who did not truly bring those who left Egypt into the rest promised by God (3:1-4:13). Having set up a general assertion of the son's superiority on the basis of Scripture, the author proceeds to his main theme (4:14):

> Having, then, a great high priest who has passed into the heavens, Jesus the son of God, let us hold the confession fast.

That statement is the key to the central argument of Hebrews and therefore to an understanding of the Epistle.

The terms of reference in the statement are used freshly and—on first acquaintance with the Epistle—somewhat unexpectedly. Jesus, whom we have known as son, is now "great high priest." The term "high priest" is in fact used earlier, to speak of his having expiated sin (2:17), and in that role Jesus is also called the "apostle and high priest of our confession" (3:1). But now, in 4:14, Jesus is the "great high priest," whose position is heavenly. Now, too, the single confession of his heavenly location is the only means to obtain divine mercy.

Jesus' suffering is invoked again in 4:15 in order to make the link to what was said earlier of Jesus' expiation. But then 4:16 spells out the ethical point of the entire Epistle:

> Let us then draw near with assurance to the throne of grace, so that we might receive mercy and find grace for timely help.

With bold calculation, Jesus is presented as the unique means of access to God in the only sanctuary that matters, the divine throne in heaven.

The portrayal of Jesus as great high priest, exalted in heaven, proves to be the

the concern to develop that relationship fully. The chapter begins with the "first" covenant's regulations for sacrifice, involving the Temple in Jerusalem. Specific mention is made of the menorah, the table, and presented bread in the holy place, with the holy of holies empty but for the gold censer and ark. The reference to the censer's being in the holy of holies fixes the point in time of which the author speaks: it can only be the Day of Atonement, when the high priest made his single visit to that sanctum, censer in hand (Heb. 9:1-5).

That precise moment is only specified in order to be fixed, frozen forever. For Hebrews, what was a fleeting movement in the case of the high priest was an eternal truth in the case of Jesus. The movement of ordinary priests—in and out of the holy place, the "first tabernacle" (9:6) while the high priest could only enter "the second tabernacle," the holy of holies (9:7), once a year—was designed by the spirit of God as a parable: the way into the holy of holies could not be revealed while the first Temple, the first tabernacle and its service, continued (9:8-10). That way could only be opened, after the Temple was destroyed, by Christ, who became high priest and passed through "the greater and more perfect tabernacle" of his body (9:11) by the power of his own blood (9:12) so that he could find eternal redemption in the sanctuary.

---

center of the Epistle (Heb. 4-7). At first, the argument may seem abstruse, turning as it does on Melchizedek, a relatively obscure figure in Gen. 14. In Genesis, Abram is met by Melchizedek after his defeat of the king of Elam. Melchizedek is identified as king of Salem and as priest of God Most High (Gen. 14:18). He brings bread and wine and blesses Abram; in return, Abram gives Melchizedek one tenth of what he has in hand after the victory (Gen. 14:18-20).

The author of Hebrews hammers out a principle and a corollary from this narrative. First, "It is beyond all dispute that the lesser is blessed by the greater" (Heb. 7:7). From that straightforward assertion, the superiority of Melchizedek to Levitical priests is deduced. Levi, the founding father of the priesthood, was still in Abram's loins at the time Abram paid his tithe to Melchizedek. In that sense, the Levitical priests who were to receive tithes were themselves tithed by the greater priest (Heb. 7:8-10).

The importance of Melchizedek to the author of Hebrews, of course, is that he resembles Jesus, the son of God. His very name means "king of righteousness," and he is also "king of peace," Salem; he does not bear a genealogy, and his birth and death are not recorded (Heb. 7:2-4). In all these details, he adumbrates Jesus, true king of righteousness and peace, from a descent that is not priestly in a Levitical sense, of whom David prophesied in the Psalms, "You are a priest for ever, after the order of Melchizedek" (Heb. 7:11-25, citing Ps. 110:4 on several occasions, cf., 7:11, 15, 17, 21). Jesus is the guarantor by God's own promise of a better, everlasting covenant (7:22). His surety is linked to Melchizedek's as clearly as the bread and wine that both of them use as the seal of God's promise and blessing.

Signal motifs within the Gospels are developed in the passage. The identification of Jesus' death and the destruction of the Temple, which the Gospels achieve in symbolic terms by referring to the torn veil of the Temple (Matthew 27:51; Mark 15:38; Luke 23:45), is assumed to be complete. It is as if no significant time had passed between the crucifixion and the arson under Titus.

Moreover, Hebrews takes it for granted that Jesus' body was a kind of "tabernacle," an instrument of sacrifice (9:11), apparently because the Gospels speak of his offering his body and his blood in the words of Eucharistic institution. (And John, of course, actually has Jesus refer to "the temple of his body," 2:21.) The Epistle pursues the meaning of "body" and "blood" as Jesus' self-immolating means to his end as high priest. The Temple in Jerusalem has in Hebrews been replaced by a purely theological construct. The true high priest has entered once for all (9:12) within the innermost recess of sanctity, so that no further sacrificial action is necessary or appropriate.

In the conception of Hebrews, the Temple on earth was a copy and shadow of the heavenly sanctuary, of which Moses had seen "types." A type (*tupos* in Greek) is an impress, a derived version of a reality (the anti-type). Moses had seen the very throne of God, which was then approximated on earth. That approximation is called the "first covenant" (9:1), but the heavenly sanctuary, into which Christ has entered (9:24), offers us a "new covenant" (9:15) which is the truth that has been palely reflected all along.

The concluding three chapters of Hebrews recapitulate what has preceded in order to influence the behavior of those who read and hear the Epistle. Literal sacrifice is to be eschewed (10:1-18), and the approach to God in purity is now by means of Jesus (10:19-22). The confession is to be maintained, love and good works are to be encouraged, and communal gatherings are to continue as the day of the Lord approaches (10:23-25).

Above all, there is to be no turning back, no matter what the incentives (10:26-40). Faith in that sense is praised as the virtue of the patriarchs, prophets, and martyrs of old, although they were not perfected (11:1-40). Jesus alone offers perfection, as "the pioneer and perfecter of our faith" (12:1-3). Many incidental commandments follow: do not be afraid of shedding your blood (12:4), do not become immoral or irreligious in leaving old ways behind (12:16), give hospitality and care for prisoners and those who are mistreated (13:1-3), honor marriage and do not love money (13:4-5), respect leaders and beware false teaching (13:7, 9, 17), remember to share and to pray (13:16, 18). Interesting as those commands are individually (especially in drawing a social profile of the community addressed), the overriding theme is evident and carries the weight of the argument (12:14): "Pursue peace with all, and sanctification, apart from which no one will see God." Divine vision, the sanctification to stand before God, is in Hebrews the goal of human life, and the only means to such perfection is loyalty to Jesus as the great high priest.

The sense of finality, of a perfection from which one must not defect, is deliberately emphasized (12:22-4):

> But you have come to Mount Zion and the city of the living God, the heavenly Jerusalem, and to myriads of angels in festal gathering, and to the assembly of first-born enrolled in heaven, and to a judge—God of all, and to the spirits of the just who are made perfect, and to Jesus the mediator of a new covenant, and to sprinkled blood which speaks better than the blood of Abel.

Jesus, the only mediator of perfection, provides access to that heavenly place that is the city of the faithful, the heart's only sanctuary.

Hebrews so centrally locates Jesus as the locus of revelation that in due course it became inevitable to ask in a way that had not been current before about his natures—human and divine—and his consciousness. Hebrews reflects the development of a religious system that derives completely from Jesus. The ability of the author of Hebrews to relegate Israel to history (see 8:8, 10; 11:22) is related to the insistence, from the outset of the Epistle, that the son's authority is greater than that of Scripture. Once, God spoke in many and various ways through the prophets; now, at the end of days, he speaks to us by a son (Heb. 1:1, 2). The comparative judgment is reinforced when the author observes that, if the word delivered by angels (that is, the Torah) carried with it retribution for transgression, how much more should we attend to what we have heard concerning the son (Heb. 2:1-4). The implication of both statements is clear: Scripture is only authoritative to the extent that it attests the salvation mediated by the son (1:14; 2:3-4). The typology framed later in the Epistle between Jesus and the Temple derives directly from the conviction of the prior authority of the son of God in relation to Scripture.

Relativizing Israel and Israel's Scriptures, Hebrews traces its theology of Christ's replacement of every major institution, every principal term of reference, within the Judaism of its time. Before Hebrews, there were Christian Judaisms, in which Christ was in various ways conceived of as the key to the promises to Israel.[2] Hebrews' theology proceeds from those earlier theologies, and it remains a Christian Judaism, in the sense that its entire vocabulary of salvation is drawn from the same Scriptures that were axiomatic within the earlier circles. But the Christian Judaism of Hebrews is also and self-consciously a system of Christianity, indeed a cult (and at many levels), because all that is Judaic is held to have been provisional upon the coming of the son, after which point it is no longer meaningful. There is a single center within the theology of Hebrews. It is not Christ with Moses, Christ with Temple, Christ with David, Christ with Abraham, Christ with Scripture, Christ with Israel. In the end, the center is not really even Christ with Melchizedek (see n. 1), because Melchizedek disappears in the glory of his heavenly archetype. Christ is the beginning, middle, and end of theology in Hebrews, just as he is the same yesterday, today, and forever (Heb. 13:8). Everything else is provisional—and expendable—within the consuming fire that is God (12:29).

Both the sectarians of Qumran and the readers of Hebrews took part in a heavenly cult. But while in the Dead Sea Scrolls, at any level, that worship was Israel's eternal vocation, in Hebrews and the Gospel according to John, worship in the heavenly world had swallowed up the grounding conceptions of Israel itself. One reason for this shift, of course, was the physical burning of the Temple in 70 C.E.; the Zecharian program of Jesus, which understood Zion as the site of an eschatological and universal feast of Sukkot without the mediation of vendors (see Zech. 14 and Matt. 21:12-13; Mark 11:15-17; Luke 19:45-46; John 2:13-17),[3] was overtaken both by events and by the post-Pauline theology of authors such as the anonymous writer of Hebrews.[4]

The destruction of the Temple also occasioned the development of a sacrificial notion of eternity within Rabbinic Judaism, as may be

---

[2] See Jacob Neusner and Bruce Chilton, *Judaism in the New Testament. Practices and Beliefs* (London and New York, 1995).

[3] See my earlier work, *The Temple of Jesus. His Sacrificial Program within a Cultural History of Sacrifice* (University Park, 1992). This line of analysis has now been taken a step further; see Siegfried Bergler, "Jesus, Bar Kochba und das messianische Laubüttenfest," in *Journal for the Study of Judaism* 29.2, 1998, pp. 143-191.

[4] The Epistle passes itself off as part of the Pauline corpus by means of various allusions (see 13:18-24), but it has been recognized as pseudonymous since the time of Origen (see Eusebius, *History of the Church* 6.25).

appreciated by considering Mishnah Tractate Yoma, which treats of the same moment as Heb. 9:11, 12. In the Mishnah, the eternity involved is durative, rather than a single, arrested moment. Present participles persistently describe the preparation of the high priest. He is moved to a separate chamber seven days prior to the Day of Atonement, and a second is readied to take over in the event of his disqualification (1:1); he offers sacrifice during that week and receives instruction (1:2, 3); he fasts on the eve of the great day in order to stay alert (1:4) and is formally reminded to discharge the ritual correctly (1:5); the high priest spends the night before his special task in company, reading and being reminded or forced to remain awake (1:6, 7); the altar is cleaned early and victims prepared (1:8-2:7). The high priest goes out at the proper time, ritually immerses himself, vests and takes part in the slaughter of the Tamid offering (3:1-7). He presents his bull, laying on his hands and making confession (3:8), and proceeds to the north of the altar (3:9-11). Lots are cast for Azazel (4:1), and the scapegoat is released, with further confession over the bull (4:2); the bull can then be slaughtered, its blood contained (4:3), coals are removed for the censer, and other arrangements proper to the day are made (4:3-6). The high priest at last enters the sanctuary and the holy of holies, placing the censer on the bars of the ark (5:1), or on the low stone that replaced it (5:2), only to say a brief prayer and depart. He enters again to sprinkle blood (5:3), including the blood of a goat (5:4), and continues sprinkling from that point, especially the altar of incense and the altar itself (5:5, 6). The tractate continues to describe other provisions, but 5:7 gives the key to the whole:

> Every action on the Day of Atonement is here described in order. If he did one thing prematurely, before the action to precede, he did nothing.

To act out of order is to accomplish nothing whatever. The text goes on to specify the necessity of getting the order of sprinklings right, "because each of them is a separate atonement."

Tractate Yoma and Hebrews give us two priestly eternities relative to a Temple that no longer exists. In Yoma, the eternity is a set of preparations and gestures of sanctification, performed in a specific order. In Hebrews, the eternity is a moment fixed forever, literally unrepeatable, even in the imagination. The crucial moment of which Hebrews speaks can only be approached by means of the analogical language the Epistle actually employs. The durative eternity of Yoma invites further reflection on what might and should and must be done in order to perfect the order of sanctification. Thinking and discussion, the crafting of the perfect order, is the priestly sense that takes the place of actual gestures. In Hebrews, however, eternity has arrested progress. Once inside the veil, the high priest has nothing further to do.[5]

Taken together Hebrews and the Mishnaic tractate Yoma demonstrate that systems of religion respond to accidents of history, but that each does so within the nexus of practice and emotion and logic which conveys its particular character. In the case of the Essenes, no response to the events of 70 C.E. is audible (for reasons of simple chronology, *pace* revisionist attempts at a post-Christian dating of the Scrolls), and yet comparison with the eternities of the New Testament and the Mishnah is possible.

The Day of Atonement also features signally in the Dead Sea Scrolls, as Martin Abegg has here convincingly shown. The text of the Melchizedek fragments, which he cites along with the other textual bits and pieces that have been used to provide context, demonstrates the key importance of the day following the tenth jubilee (four hundred and ninety years; 11Q13 ii 7). Following the reconstruction and rendering of Joseph A. Fitzmyer[6] and James VanderKam,[7] the relevant passage reads:

> And this thing will [occur] in the first week of the Jubilee that follows the nine Jubilees. And the Day of Atonement is the e[nd of the] tenth Jubilee, when all the Sons of [Light] and the men of the lot of Mel[chi]zedek will be atoned for. [And] a statute concerns them [to prov]ide them with their rewards. For this is the moment of the Year of Grace for Melchizedek. [And h]e will, by his strength, judge the holy ones of God, executing judgment as it is written concerning him in the Songs of David, who said, Elohim has taken his place in the divine council; in the midst of the gods he holds judgment [Ps. 82:1]. And it was concerning him that he said, Return to the height above them; El

---

[5] Straining to make sense of what he describes in cultic terms, the author even speaks of Christ as an "anchor" that has entered the holy of holies (6:19). That image is deliberate: the author imagines all Christians entering the sanctuary by the way Jesus opened, sprinkled as the altars formerly were (10:19-22). The moment is neither to be repeated nor crafted further. It is perfection itself and it demands perfection, since sacrifice for sins no longer exists (10:26, 27). The exigent demands of an unchanging, eternal priest (cf., 13:8) make ethics the order of the day.

[6] "Further light on Melchizedek from Qumran Cave 11," in *Essays on the Semitic Background of the New Testament* (Missoula, 1974), pp. 245-267.

[7] *The Dead Sea Scrolls Today* (Grand Rapids and London, 1994), p. 53.

will judge the peoples (Ps. 7:7-8). And as for that which he s[aid, How long will you] judge unjustly and show partiality to the wicked? Selah (Ps. 82:2), its interpretation concerns Belial and the spirits of his lot [who] rebelled by turning away from the precepts of God to.... And Melchizedek will avenge the vengeance of the judgements of God...and he will drag [them from the hand of] Belial and from hands of all the sp[irits of] his [lot]. And all the gods [of Justice] will come to his aid [to] attend to the de[struction] of Belial.

Fitzmyer ably represents the cautious line taken by most scholars of the New Testament, who have been reserved about comparing the Melchizedek of Hebrews and that of 11Q13. The Qumran text does not develop out of a citation of Gen. 14:18-20 or of Ps. 110, as in Hebrews, and it certainly makes no case for an alternative priesthood derived from Melchizedek.[8]

A passage from the Songs of Sabbath Sacrifice (4Q 400-107) may at least attribute a priestly function to Melchizedek,[9] and it has recently been suggested that, even in 11Q13, Melchizedek's role is that "as priest he forgives sins."[10] But the contrast with the argument of Hebrews remains, and Barnabas Lindars has voiced the consensus that Melchizedek is in 11Q13 an eschatological figure of judgment.[11] Lindars also agrees with the identification of Melchizedek with Michael, but Fitzmyer urges caution here, too.[12] Marie E. Isaacs has more recently observed that Michael's role in the *War Scroll* (17:5-9) is more activist than juridical.[13] Obviously, the *War Scroll* can not be used to foreclose options of interpretation in 11Q13, but John J. Collins has pointed out that one could read the Melchizedek fragment as prelude to the outbreak of the eschatological war.[14]

From the point of view of interpreting the Epistle to the Hebrews,

---

[8] Fitzmyer is careful to observe, however, that this may be a result of the fragmentary nature of the evidence (p. 254).

[9] VanderKam, p. 171.

[10] Harmut Stegeman, *The Library of Qumran. On the Essenes, Qumran, John the Baptist, and Jesus* (Grand Rapids and Leiden, 1998), pp. 119-120.

[11] *The Theology of the Letter to the Hebrews* (Cambridge, 1991), pp. 74-75. Throughout, Lindars is a bit quick to use the term "messiah," however, when most interpreters have described Qumran's Melchizedek in angelic terms.

[12] Fitzmyer, p. 255.

[13] *Sacred Space. An Approach to the Theology of the Epistle to the Hebrews* (Sheffield, 1992), p. 163

[14] "The Expectation of the End in the Dead Sea Scrolls," in C.A. Evans and P.W. Flint, eds., *Eschatology, Messianism, and the Dead Sea Scrolls* (Grand Rapids, 1997), pp. 74-90, 86.

it is understandable that attention has been focused on identifying Melchizedek as closely as possible. (Indeed, the citation of Is. 61 at the opening of the fragment [not cited here] suggests a possible line of inquiry into the citation of the same passage by Jesus in Luke 4.) But from the point of view of reading the Scrolls systemically, what is far more important is Abegg's observation that the angelic Melchizedek signals judgment on the Day of Atonement. Here, as elsewhere, the calendar of the sectarians reveals their commitment to an eternity unlike the changeless perfection of Hebrews and the ceaseless readying of tractate Yoma. Melchizedek's eternity comes at a specifiable moment, in which heaven is rearranged so as to transform the reality on which the earth ultimately depends.

Our systemic analysis has traced the structural relations among worldview, way of life, and view of the social order in a manner that permits the Scrolls to articulate not only their theologies in regard to particular topics but the underlying theology they sought to understand, celebrated in their liturgies, and put into practice. The practitioners themselves have left behind the traces of their distinctive system, so that these categories of analysis may be defended in exegetical terms and do not require the a priori justification of many structuralist approaches.

At the same time, the present approach offers two other prospects of genuine progress in the study of religion. First, comparative analysis has proven possible, such that analogy (rather than alleged dependence) becomes the focus. The case of the Day of Atonement instances the persistent recourse within these volumes to comparison, such that the distinctiveness of systems becomes evident. Second, the dynamic relations among worldview, way of life, and view of the social order have provided a means of accounting for changes in all three, both within systems, and from system to system. Once we see that religions coordinate what people do, how they feel, and why they act and feel as they do, their tendency to change over time in response to alterations in any of those fields of action, feeling, and cognition becomes explicable. Historical and exegetical tools and insights are vital to systemic analysis, as it seeks to lay bare the forces that generated both the histories and the texts we seek to understand.

GENERAL INDEX

Note: Page references indicate volume and then page. *Italic* page references indicate graphic or tabular information.

Aaronic messiah, 2:140–141
Abraham, 2:184
Activities at Qumran, 1:63–67
Additions to Daniel, *2:54*
Additions to Esther, *2:54*
Adultery, 1:176n10
Agriculture, 1:64–65
Amos scrolls, 2:96
Angelic Liturgy, 2:40
Angels, 1:137–139
"Angry Lion," 2:129
Apocalypse of Weeks, 2:160
Apocalyptic writings, on Wisdom, 2:151–158
Apocrypha, 2:50–55
Apocryphal and Pseudepigraphal Scrolls, 2:101–103
Archeology
　of communal center, 1:96
　earthquake damage, 1:48–49, 2:234
　holy areas, 1:97–106
　living space of, 1:56–63
　pottery artifacts, 1:46, 1:53–56
　public/private space, 1:59–63, 1:67, *1:73*
　water system, 1:47–48, 1:65
Architecture, 1:47–48, 1:52
Atonement, 1:131–132

Baruch, *2:54*
Beckwith, Roger, 2:53
Belial, 1:139
Ben Judah, Rabbenu Gershom, 1:175n9
Ben Sira, 2:69–70, 2:101, 2:150–151
Bernstein, M.J., 2:51, 2:56
Bible, defined, 2:46–50
Bible, Masoretic, 2:50
Biblical interpretation. *see Pesher*
Biblical Scrolls, 2:87–100
Binah, 2:5–6
Bone deposits, 1:63–64
Book of *hhgw*, 2:31
Booths, Feast of, 1:164, 2:35
Bowls. *see* Pottery of Qumran

Boyce, Mary, 1:20
Bureaucracy, 1:67

Calendaric systems, 1:93–94, 1:135
　in Community Rule, 2:212
　competing solar, 1:146–147
　cycles of Qumran, 1:150–156, 1:165–171
　festival calendar, 1:157–164
　forty-nine year Jubilee, 1:156–157
　as indicator of sectarianism, 1:146–147
　intercalation, 1:149–150
　and Jubilees, Book of, 1:146, 1:147–148, 2:39
　lunar influences, 1:146, 1:148, 1:151–153
　lunar month, 1:151–153
　seven day week, 1:150–151
　six year priestly cycle, 1:156
　solar month, 1:153–154
　theological basis of, 1:149–150
　three year lunar cycle, 1:155–156
　364-day year, 1:154–155, 2:39–40
　294-year cycle of six Jubilees, 1:150–156
Calvin, 2:4
Canon, defined, 2:46–49
Canonical literature, 2:9
Canticles scrolls, 2:100
Celibacy, 1:50–51, 1:173–174
Cemetery, 1:49–51
Children, 1:50–51
Christ, 2:174–175, 2:176, 2:181, 2:184, 2:204–205, 2:239–242
Christianity, 1:3
Christian Judaism of Hebrews, 2:237–242
　persecution of, 2:175
　philosophical nature of, 2:3–4
　seen through John, 2:203–210, 2:237
　see also Christ; Johannine community; Paul of Tarsus
Chronicles, 2:71–72, 2:100

Circumcision, 2:181, 2:182–183, 2:184, 2:186–187, 2:225
"City of the Sanctuary," 1:103–105
Coin evidence, 1:47, 1:48
Communal prayer, 1:132–133
Community hymns, 2:165–167
Community Rule
  calendaric systems in, 2:212
  compared to Johannine system, 2:217–225
  dualism in, 2:214
  eschatology of, 2:137, 2:215–216
  Israel in, 1:30–34, 2:225–226
  pesharim in, 2:120–122
  religious system in, 1:131–132, 1:133–134, 2:210–217, 2:220–223, 2:227
  sectarianism in, 1:30–34, 1:36
  Shema reading in, 1:87
  social order in, 2:210–212, 2:217–220
  Torah in, 2:33–34
  view of God in, 2:126–127
  world vision in, 2:214–217, 2:223–225
Comparative religious studies, 1:15–17, 1:19
Congregation Rule, 1:75, 2:42–43, 2:136–137
Context, 1:18
Continuity, 2:198–200
Corinthian correspondence, of Paul, 2:176–177
Corpse impurity, 1:116
Cotton, Hannah, 1:174n7
Court of Israel, 1:102
Court of Men, 1:101
Covenant, 2:34–36, 2:225
  vs. holiness, 2:23–24
Cowley, R.W., 2:53
Creation, 2:148–149
Cults, 2:199–200, 2:220, 2:237

Daily Prayers, 1:135, 1:136, 1:137–138
Damascus Covenant, 1:29–30, 1:136, 2:32–33, 2:34–35, 2:36–37
Damascus Covenant groups, 1:112–115
Damascus Document
  eschatology of, 1:41, 2:133–134
  Israel in, 1:26–30
  Levitical origins, 2:80
  pesharim in, 2:120–121
  predestination in, 2:192–193
  sectarianism in, 1:26–30
  sin of humanity in, 2:5

Temple discussed, 1:131–132, 1:133, 1:136–137
  women in, 1:179, 1:183–187
Daniel scrolls, *2:54*, 2:62, 2:65–66, 2:100, 2:106–108
David, King, 1:182n33, 1:184
Davidic messiah, 2:137–140, 2:142
Day of Atonement, 1:164, 2:243–244
Day of Remembrance, 1:163–164
De Beauvoir, Simone, 1:176n10
De Vaux, Roland, 1:46–47
Dead, impurity of, 1:89–90
Dead Sea Scrolls. *see* Qumran scrolls (Dead Sea Scrolls)
Demons, 1:139
Deuteronomy, 2:23–24, 2:40
Deuteronomy scrolls, 2:61–62, 2:90–92
Discharge impurity, 1:116–117
Discipleship, 2:203–204
Discontinuity, 2:198–200
Divine wisdom, 2:147–158
Divorce, 1:182–183, 1:185n47
Dualism, 1:35–37, 2:21, 2:36, 2:39, 2:188–198, 2:214
Dûq, 1:149

Earthquake damage, 1:48–49, 2:234
Ecclesiastes, 2:70–71
Ecclesiasticus, *2:54*, 2:69–70
Ecology of religion, 1:15–17, 1:19–21
Ecstatic experience, 2:178
End of days, calculation of, 2:132–137
  see also Eschatology
Enoch scrolls, 1:93, *2:55*, 2:72, 2:74, 2:81, 2:101–102, 2:160
Epistle of Enoch, 2:160
Epistle of Jeremiah, *2:54*, 2:62, 2:64, 2:101
Eschatological war, 2:144–146, 2:178–179
Eschatology
  in Community Rule, 2:137, 2:215–216
  end of days, calculation of, 2:132–137
  eschatological war, 2:144–146, 2:178–179
  messianic expectations, 2:137–144
  Paul's views of, 2:174–175, 2:177–188
  pesharim, 2:117–120
  Teacher of Righteousness and, 2:130–135
  views of Qumran community, 2:128–130, 2:177–188, 2:215–216
  wisdom and, 2:151–162, 2:167–169

Esdras, *2:55*
Essenes, 1:26, 1:50, 1:81n29
Esther, *2:54*, 2:71
Ethiopian Narrower Canon, *2:53*
Exile, 1:25, 1:28–34, 1:37
Exodus scrolls, 2:60–61, 2:80, 2:88–89
Exorcism, 1:139
Ezekiel scrolls, 2:64–65, 2:74, 2:80, 2:95
Ezra, 1:25–26, 1:94
Ezra scrolls, 2:100
Ezra-Nehemiah, 2:72

Faith, 2:3
Feast of Booths, 1:164, 2:35
Feast of Unleavened Bread, 1:159
Feast of Weeks, 1:160–161, 2:35
Feminism, 1:175
Festival calendar at Qumran
    Day of Atonement, 1:164
    Day of Remembrance, 1:163–164
    Feast of Booths, 1:164
    Feast of Unleavened Bread, 1:159
    Feast of Weeks, 1:160–161
    first day of the first month, 1:158
    Firstfruit of the Oil, 1:162
    Firstfruit of the Wine, 1:162
    Passover, 1:158–159
    Second Passover, 1:160
    Waving of the Omer, 1:159–160
    Wood Offering, 1:162–163
Festival cycles, 1:93–94
Festival Prayers, 1:127
Fidelity, 1:176n10
    see also Adultery
First day of the first month, 1:158
    1 Enoch scrolls, *2:55*, 2:72, 2:74, 2:81, 2:101–102, 2:160
    1 Esdras, *2:55*
    1 Maccabees, *2:54*
Firstfruit of the Oil, 1:162
Firstfruit of the Wine, 1:162
Fitzmyer, Joseph A., 2:244–245
Flavius Josephus, 1:50, 1:96
Food preparation, 1:63
Formative Judaism, 1:6
    4 Maccabees, *2:55*

Galatians, 2:186
Gender issues, 1:173–194
Genesis Apocryphon, 2:26–27
Genesis scrolls, 2:60, 2:79, 2:80, 2:87–88
Gentile realm impurity, 1:118–119

Gentiles, 2:175, 2:182–184, 2:196
Ginzberg, Louis, 1:178n17
God
    attributes of, 2:18–21
    doctrine of, 2:14–22, 2:126–130
    Paul's and Qumran's, 2:177–188
    terms for, 2:14–15
Goodenough, Erwin R., 1:5
Grace, 2:179–188
Great Revolt, 1:85, 1:87
Greek Orthodox Canon, *2:53*
Greenfield, Jonas, 1:174n7

Habakkuk scrolls, 2:11, 2:96, 2:108, 2:114–115, 2:130–132
Haggai scrolls, 2:97
Halakhah of Qumran, 1:16, 2:28–29, 2:31–32
Halakhic Letter, 1:34, 1:79, 2:37–38, 2:122–123, 2:184
Hall with Annex, 1:58
Hasadim, 2:19–20
Hasmonean period, 1:78
Hellenistic period, 1:28, 1:47, 2:28
History, view of, 2:126–130
Hodayot, 1:127, 1:140–142, 2:163–165
Holiness, 2:23–24, 2:36–41
Holy areas, 1:97–106
Hosea scrolls, 2:95, 2:111–112
House of Absalom, 2:114, 2:115, 2:130
"House of prostration," 1:133
Human nature, 2:5, 2:190–198
"Hymns of the Community," 1:141
"Hymns of the Teacher," 1:140–141
Hypostatic Wisdom, 2:152

Idolatry, 1:118–119
Ilan, Tal, 1:174n7
Impurity of dead, 1:89–90
Index of Passages
    in Apocryphal and Pseudepigraphal Scrolls, 2:101–103
    in Biblical Scrolls, 2:87–100
Industrial activities, 1:66
Inhabitants, number of, 1:49, 1:60–62
Inner Court, 1:100–101
Interpretation. *see Pesher*
"Interpreter of Knowledge," 2:116
"Interpreter of the law," 2:142
Ioudaismos, 2:174
Isaiah scrolls, 2:64, 2:79, 2:93–95, 2:110–111

Isolationism, 1:51–52, 2:125, 2:173, 2:200, 2:223
Israel
  in Community Rule, 1:30–34, 2:225–226
  in Damascus Document, 1:26–30
  defined, 1:10, 1:12–13, 1:25
  in Deuteronomy, 1:25
  history of, 1:27–34
  identity of, 1:38
  new covenant with, 1:29–34
  purity and, 1:106–115
  Qumran community separation from, 1:26–42
  restoration of, 2:136–137

Janneus, Alexander, 2:112, 2:113
Jaubert, A., 1:147
Jeremiah, Epistle of, *2:54*, 2:62, 2:64, 2:101
Jeremiah scrolls, 2:64, 2:79, 2:95
Jerusalem, 1:103–105, 1:113, 2:39–40
Jesus, 2:174–175, 2:176, 2:181, 2:184, 2:204–205, 2:239–242
Jews, Paul and the, 2:177–190
Job, 2:67–68, 2:99
Joel scrolls, 2:96
Johannine community
  compared with Community Rule system, 2:217–225
  initiation into, 2:206–208, 2:220–223
  Israel in, 2:225–226
  religious system of, 2:204–208, 2:220–223
  social order of, 2:203–204, 2:217–220
  terminological affinities with 2:1QS, 2:226–227
  world vision of, 2:208–210, 2:223–225
John, Gospel of, 2:203–210, 2:217–225
Jonah scrolls, 2:96
Joshua scrolls, 2:63, 2:92
Jubilees
  on calendar, 1:146, 1:147–148, 1:156–157, 1:188
  Index of Passages, 2:102–103
  on purity, 1:92–94
  as Scripture at Qumran, *2:55*, 2:72–73, 2:74, 2:76n150, 2:79–80, 2:81
  Torah and, 2:26–27
Judaism, 1:5–6
Judaism, Christian, 2:237–242

Judaism(s)
  coherency of, 1:7, 1:16
  defining a single, 1:9–10
  diversity of, 2:202
  ecology of, 1:20–21
  formative, 1:6
  multiplicity of, 1:5, 1:9, 1:12, 1:16–17, 2:238–242
  philosophical nature of, 2:3–4
  sectarian *vs.* normative, 1:3
Judges scrolls, 2:63, 2:92
Judith, *2:54*

Kelim, 1:98
Kings scrolls, 2:63–64, 2:80, 2:93
Knibb, M., 1:28n10
Knowledge, religious, 2:3–7
  see also Wisdom

Lamentations scrolls, 2:71, 2:79, 2:100
Lasker, Daniel, 1:178n17
Last Judgement, 2:144–146, 2:181
Law, Jewish
  discrepancies in, 1:184n41
  history of, 1:75–79
  oral law, 1:80
  Qumran documents and, 1:75–79, 1:187–188, 2:30–31
  theology of, 1:80–82
  in Zadokite Fragments, 1:82–84
Laws, Sadducean, 1:77–78, 1:81
Lepers/leprosy, 1:104, 1:115–116
Levi, 1:107, 1:179n19
Leviticus, 2:23–24
Leviticus scrolls, 2:61, 2:79, 2:80, 2:89–90
Light and darkness, 1:35–37, 2:9, 2:21, 2:36, 2:127–128, 2:188–190
Liquids/oils impurity, 1:117–118
Liturgy, 2:14

Maccabees, *2:54*
Magness, Jodi, 1:46, 1:53–56
Main Building, 1:47, 1:56, 1:58
Malachi scrolls, 2:97
"Man of the Lie," 2:114, 2:115, 2:116, 2:130
Manual of Discipline, 2:9–10, 2:12, 2:16
Marriage, 1:50–51, 1:175–194
Maskilim, 2:7, 2:12–13, 2:33, 2:235
Masoretic Bible, 2:50
Mebin, 2:12–13

Melchiresha, 2:9–10
Melchizedek, 2:9–10, 2:118–119, 2:244–245
Merkabah (chariot) mysticism, 2:175
Messiah, Aaronic, 2:140–142, 2:144
Messiah, Davidic, 2:137–140, 2:142, 2:144
Messiahs, multiple, 2:140–142
Messianic age, 1:38–39, 1:40–41
Messianic expectations, 2:110–111, 2:117–118, 2:132–133, 2:137–144
Messianic prophet, 2:142–143
Messianic Rule, 1:38
Micah scrolls, 2:96, 2:112–113
Midrash, 1:82–84, 2:78
Milik, J.T., 1:146
Military camps, 1:106
Miqsat Ma'ase ha-Torah (MMT), 1:77, 1:84, 1:86, 1:88, 1:179n20
Mishnah, 1:82–84, 1:98, 1:189, 2:243
Monasticism, 1:174–175
Monogamy, 1:175–194
Moore, George F., 1:5
Murphy-O'Connor, J., 1:35–36

Nahum scrolls, 2:96, 2:113–114, 2:196–197
Natural History, 1:51
Nehemiah, 1:25–26, 1:94
Neusner, Jacob, 1:9, 1:173, 1:176–177, 1:179n18, 2:28
Normative Judaism, 1:3, 1:5
Northern Enclosure, 1:56
Numbers scrolls, 2:90

Obadiah scrolls, 2:96
One who Spouts the Lie, 2:114
Oral law, 1:80
Orthodox churches, *2:53*

Passover, 1:158–159
Pastoralism, 1:63–64
Paul and Palestinian Judaism, 1:5, 1:28n12
Paul of Tarsus
  acceptance into his communities, 2:198–200
  Christ vision of, 2:175–176
  Corinthian correspondence of, 2:176–177
  early religious life, 2:173–177
  eschatology of, 2:174–175, 2:177–188
  letters of, 2:176–177
  predestinarian beliefs of, 2:194–198
  theology of, 2:179–188, 2:236–237
Pauline communities, 2:188–190, 2:198–200
Peninah, 1:179n19
Perfection, 2:237–238, 2:240–241
Persian period, 1:27–28
Pesher, 2:77
  Community Rule, 2:120–122
  continuous *pesharim*, 2:109–117
  Damascus Document, 2:120–121
  defined, 2:106–109
  Habakkuk scrolls, 2:114–115, 2:130–132
  Halakhic Letter, 2:122–123
  Hosea, 2:111–112
  importance of interpretation, 2:105–106
  Isaiah, 2:110–111
  Micah, 2:112–113
  Nahum, 2:113–114
  thematic *pesharim*, 2:117–120
  types of *pesharim*, 2:109–120
  Zephaniah, 2:116
Pharisaic-Rabbinic tradition, 1:77–78
Pharisees, 1:81, 1:88, 2:173–174
Pharisee-Sadducean disputes, 1:75, 1:77
Philo, 1:10, 1:42
Physical defects, 1:104n38
Pliny, 1:51
Poetry. *see* Psalms
Polygamy, 1:175–194
Pottery of Qumran, 1:46, 1:53–56
Prayer of Manasseh, *2:55*
Prayer/prayer materials
  authorship of, 1:129–130
  communal, 1:132–133
  limitations of material, 1:126–129
  purpose of, 1:130–131
  schedules/cycles of, 1:86–87, 1:126–128, 1:132–137
  sectarian *vs.* nonsectarian, 1:130
  surveys of, 1:126, 1:128
Prayers for the Festivals, 1:127
Predestination, 2:190–198
Priestly messiah, 2:140–142, 2:144
Priests/priesthood, 1:34, 1:98–101, 1:156
Prophet, messianic, 2:142–143
Prophets, 2:11
Prophets scrolls, 2:62–66, 2:95–97
Prosper of Aquitance, 1:125

Protestant Old Testament, *2:46–47*
Proverbs scrolls, 2:68–69, 2:79, 2:100
Psalm 2:37, 2:116
Psalm 151, *2:55*
Psalms, 1:125, 1:127, 1:128, 1:130–131, 1:140–142, 2:62–63, 2:66–67, 2:76, 2:79, 2:81, 2:97–99
Psalms, Apocryphal, 2:101
Psalter, 1:130–131, 2:75
Pseudepigrapha, 2:50–51, 2:55–56
Public/private space, 1:59–63, 1:67, *1:73*
Purification, 1:119–120, 2:189, 2:216–217, 2:221, 2:225
Purity, of holy spaces, 1:98–107, 2:234
rules for, 1:107–120

Qimron, Elisha, 1:174n7
Qoheleth scrolls, 2:100
Qumran community
  acceptance into, 2:198–200, 2:212–213, 2:220–223
  activities, 1:63–67
  agriculture, 1:64–65
  architecture, 1:47–48, 1:52
  bureaucracy, 1:67
  calendaric system of, 1:145–171, 2:39–40, 2:234–235
  cemetery, 1:49–51
  communal center, 1:96
  compared with Paul, 2:173–200, 2:236–237
  divisible areas of, 1:56–59, *1:71, 1:72*
  doctrine of God at, 2:14–22, 2:126–130
  earthquake damage, 1:48–49, 2:234
  eschatology of, 2:128–146, 2:177–179, 2:190–198, 2:215–216
  existence of, 1:91
  halakhah of, 1:16, 2:28–29, 2:31–32
  holy areas, 1:97–106
  industrial activities, 1:66
  isolation, 1:51–52, 2:125, 2:173, 2:200, 2:223
  laws of, 1:75–79, 1:187–188, 2:30–31
  living space of, 1:56–63
  marriage in, 1:187
  messianic expectations, 2:110–111, 2:117–118, 2:132–133, 2:137–144
  number of inhabitants, 1:49, 1:60–62
  origin of, 1:47, 1:81n29, 2:125–126
  pottery artifacts, 1:46, 1:53–56
  predestinarianism of, 2:190–198
  priests/priesthood, 1:34, 1:99–101
  public/private space, 1:59–63, 1:67, *1:73*
  purity at, 1:91–124, 2:189, 2:216–217, 2:221, 2:225, 2:234
  revelation at, 2:7–11, 2:29–30
  separation from Israel, 1:26–34, 1:90, 2:24, 2:125, 2:173, 2:200, 2:223
  teacher-student relationship, 2:12–13
  Torah at, 2:30–34, 2:41–44
  view of history, 2:126–130
  water system, 1:47–48, 1:65
  women in, 1:173–194
  world vision of, 2:214–217
Qumran scrolls (Dead Sea Scrolls)
  Apocryphal and Pseudepigraphal Scrolls, Index of Passages in, 2:101–103
  authorship of, 2:125
  Bible-oriented approach to, 1:96–97, 2:234
  Biblical Scrolls, Index of Passages in, 2:87–100
  and calendar, 1:145–164
  canonical process of, 2:58–59
  dating of, 1:91
  historical readings of, 1:4
  and Jewish law, 1:75–90, 1:187–188, 2:30–31
  order of, 2:65
  pesher in, 2:109–123
  prayer/psalms in, 1:125–143, 2:234
  predestination in, 2:190–198
  Prophets, 2:62–66, 2:95–97
  Pseudepigrapha, 2:51, 2:101–103
  revelation in, 2:7–11
  sacred status of, 2:57–58, 2:73–81
  as sectarian literature, 1:91–92
  systemic analysis of, 1:3, 1:6–9, 2:233–246
  Torah, 2:59–62, 2:235
  wisdom writings in, 2:147–169
  Writings, 2:66–73
  see also individual manuscripts (e.g., Damascus Document)

Rabbinic Judaism, 1:85
Rabbis, and purity, 1:98–99
Radicalism, 2:173
Ragen, Naomi, 1:175–177
Raz nihyeh, 2:154, 2:157, 2:158, 2:162

Reason, 2:3
Reform of Israel, 1:41–42
Reich, Ronnie, 1:48
Religious systems, analyzing, 1:4, 1:8, 1:11–21, 2:201–203, 2:233–246
Remnant community, 2:158–162
Renewal of the Covenant, 1:136–137
Revelation, 2:7–11, 2:29–30, 2:152–153, 2:157
Revision, textual, 1:184n40
Riddle, Donald, 2:200
Ritual purity, 1:88–90, 1:107–124
Rohrhirsch, Ferdinand, 1:46
Roman Catholic Old Testament, *2:46–47*
Romans, 1:49
Rule of Blessings, 1:127, 1:142, 2:139
Ruth scrolls, 2:70, 2:100

Sabbath prayers, 1:136–138
Sacrifice, 1:85–86, 1:131–132, 2:187, 2:239
Sadducean laws, 1:77–78, 1:81
Sages, writings of, 2:154
Salvation, 2:179–188
Samaritans, 1:81n28, 1:95
Samuel b. Nahmani, 1:182n33
Samuel scrolls, 2:63, 2:92–93
Sanctuary, 1:102—103
Sanders, E.P., 1:5–6, 1:28n12, 1:38
Schechter, S., 1:181n30
Schremer, Adiel, 1:174n7
Schuller, E., 1:174
Scripture, Qumran scrolls' status as, 2:57–58, 2:73–81
Scrolls. *see* Qumran scrolls (Dead Sea Scrolls)
2 Esdras, *2:55*
2 Maccabees, *2:54*
Second Passover, 1:160
Second Temple Judaism, 1:85, 1:126, 1:139, 2:54, 2:179
Sect vs. cult, 2:199–200, 2:237
Sectarian Judaism, 1:3, 1:25–27, 1:83, 1:90, 1:147
Sectarian prayer, 1:130
Sectarian rule books. *see* Community Rule; Damascus Document
Sekel, 2:6–7
Self-Fulfilling Prophecy: Exile and Return in the History of Judaism, 1:13
Sexual impurity, 1:103–104, 1:115, 1:116–117

Sin, 2:4–5, 2:181–182
Slavonic Orthodox Canon, *2:53*
Social groups, 1:10
Social order
  in Community Rule, 2:210–212, 2:217–220
  of Johannine community, 2:203–204, 2:217–220
  as subject of analysis, 2:233, 2:235–236, 2:246
Social stratification, of Johannine community, 2:204
Sod 'emet, 2:5
Song of Songs, 2:70
Song of the Sage, 1:127, 1:139
Songs of the Sabbath Sacrifice, 1:138, 2:40, 2:245
Southeastern Area, 1:56, 1:59
Southern Enclosure, 1:56, 1:57–58
Stegemann, H., 1:36, 1:38–39, 1:60
Stock, Brian, 1:4
Sussman, 1:81n29
Systemic analysis
  comparative analysis, 2:246
  context in, 1:18
  defined, 1:11–13
  facts in, 1:17–19
  principles of, 1:15–17, 2:233–234
  of Qumran library, 1:3, 1:6–9, 2:233–246

Talmon, S., 1:146
Talmud, 2:114
Tannaitic literature, 1:80
Teacher hymns, 2:163–165
"Teacher of Righteousness," 2:11–12, 2:32–33, 2:42, 2:108, 2:114, 2:115, 2:116, 2:130–135
Teacher-student relationship, 2:12–13
Temple House, 1:100–101
Temple Scroll, 1:39–40, 1:76, 1:82
  literary character of, 1:83
  on sacrifice, 1:85–86
Testament of Kohath, 2:10–11
Testaments of the 12 Patriarchs, 2:103
Textual community, 1:4
Thanksgiving Scroll, 1:127, 1:140–142, 2:126
Theology
  of Jewish law, 1:80–82
  of purity/impurity, 1:120–124
3 Maccabees, *2:55*
Tobit scrolls, *2:54*, 2:68, 2:101

Torah
  allegorizing of, by Paul, 2:186–188
  in Community Rule, 2:33–34
  covenant vs. holiness, 2:23–24, 2:34–41
  development, in Second Temple Judaism, 2:28
  and Jubilees, 2:26–27
  Mosaic, 2:25–29, 2:215–216, 2:225
  role of, in Qumran community, 2:30–34, 2:41–44
  scrolls, at Qumran, 2:59–62, 2:235
Translations, 2:76–77
"Treatise of the Two Spirits," 2:9–10, 2:15–16, 2:127–128, 2:162–163, 2:191–192
Twelve (minor) Prophets, Book of the, 2:65, 2:95–97
Two-Spirit Treatise, 2:9–10, 2:15–16, 2:127–128, 2:162–163, 2:191–192

Understanding, 2:5–6
Universalism, 2:173, 2:200
Unleavened Bread, Feast of, 1:159
Utopian writings, 1:39–40

VanderKam, James, 2:244–245
Virginity, 1:191–193

Wacholder, B.Z., 2:26
War Rule, 1:36–37, 1:38, 1:75, 2:11–12, 2:42–43, 2:111, 2:189
Water system/basins, 1:47–48, 1:65, 1:96
Waving of the Omer, 1:159–160
Way of life, 2:233, 2:235–236, 2:246
Weeks, Feast of, 1:160–161, 2:35
Western Building, 1:56
"Wicked Priest," 2:114, 2:115, 2:116, 2:130
Wisdom
  community hymns, 2:165–167
  divine, 2:147–158

Lady Wisdom/Lady Folly, 2:147, 2:152, 2:153–154
  in Proverbs, 2:147–148
  sapiential traditions of, 2:147–151
  sapiential-apocalyptic traditions of, 2:151–158
  Teacher hymns, 2:163–165
Wisdom literature, 2:69–70
  in the *Yahad*, 2:163–169
Wisdom literature, 1:93
Wisdom of Jesus Ben Sira, 2:69–70, 2:101, 2:150–151
Wisdom of Solomon, *2:54*
Wise men, writings of, 2:154
Women
  feminist readings of Rabbinic texts, 1:173
  monogamy/polygamy issues, 1:175–194
Wood Offering, 1:162–163
Words of the Luminaries, 1:130, 1:135–136
World vision
  in Community Rule, 2:214–217, 2:223–225
  of Johannine community, 2:208–210, 2:223–225
  of Qumran community, 2:214–217
Worldview
  as subject of analysis, 2:233, 2:235–236, 2:246
Writings, 2:66–73, 2:74–81

Yadin, Y., 1:76
Yahad-Group, 1:108–112, 2:31, 2:32, 2:224
  wisdom writings and, 2:149, 2:150–151, 2:156, 2:159, 2:162–169
Yoma, 2:243–244

Zadokite Fragments, 1:82–84, 1:112
Zadokite groups, 1:112–115
Zephaniah scrolls, 2:96–97, 2:116
Zoroaster, 1:20

INDEX OF ANCIENT SOURCES

Note: Page references indicate volume and then page. The following Qumran documents are listed by name: *Hodayot*ᵃ, *Pesher Habakkuk*, *War Scroll*, *Rule of the Community*, and *Damascus Document*. Other scrolls are listed by item number of composition identification.

Bible		6:3-4	1:100
Genesis		12	2:79
1:1	2:148, 2:157	13-15	1:116
1:1-2:4a	1:184	15:1-15	1:116
1-3	1:187	15:31	2:79
1:14	1:155	16:6	1:187
1:16	1:149	17-26	2:24
1:23	1:124	18:5	2:14, 2:30
1:27	1:180, 2:79	18:13	1:189
2:2	1:150	18:18	1:175, 1:178, 1:182, 1:185, 1:186, 1:187, 1:189
7:9	1:180, 2:79		
14:18-20	2:245	23:6	1:188
15:6	2:123	23:11	1:159
18:16-33	2:150	23:15-16	1:160
20:12	1:188	23:24	1:163
40-41	2:154	23:42-43	1:164
49:8-12	2:117, 2:118	25:13	2:118
49:10	2:137, 2:138	*Numbers*	
Exodus		1-10:10	2:43
12:2	1:158	5:1-4	1:103
12:6	1:158	5:2	1:117
12:15	1:188	9:10-11	1:160
12:18	1:188	16:3	1:188
13:6	1:188	18:12	1:162
13:7	1:188	21:18	2:31, 2:41
19:15	1:117	22:13-22	1:192
21:19	2:77	24:15-17	2:143
22-35	2:80	24.16	2:15
23:7	1:110	24.17	2:121, 2:142
23:15	1:188	25:1-8	2:123
24:18	2:73	28:17	1:188
25:20	1:178	29:1-6	1:158
26:3	1:178	*Deuteronomy*	
26:5	1:178	4:6-8	2:151
26:6	1:178	4:37	2:14
26:17	1:178	5:28-29	2:143
28-29	2:77	6:4	2:222
28:42-43	1:100	6:4-9	1:87
34:6	2:19	7:13	1:162
34:18	1:188	10:15	2:14
Leviticus		15:2	2:14
2:34-35	2:24		

INDEX OF ANCIENT SOURCES

16:3	1:188	13:31	1:162
16:8	1:188	*Judith*	
17:17	1:180	9:5-6	2:16
18	2:142	*Tobit*	
18:15	2:142	3:8	1:139
20:1-4	2:111	*Esther*	
22:13-22	1:193	7-9	2:71
23:10-15	1:105	9:15	1:147
23:13-15	1:105	*Job*	
27-29	1:137	9:2	2:18
29:28	2:155	12:22	2:155
30:1-2	2:122	25:4	2:18
30:11-14	2:148	28:20-21	2:155
31:9	2:35	28:25	2:16
31:29	2:122	*Psalms*	
33:8-11	2:142	1	2:28, 2:147
Joshua		1:2	2:157
1:8	2:157	7:7-8	2:119, 2:120
8:30-35	1:137	33:6	2:148, 2:157
24:31	1:181	37	2:116
24:33, 29	1:181	69:29	2:20
Judges		82:1	2:119, 2:120, 2:244
2:7	1:181	82:2	2:119
2:13	1:181	106:31	2:122, 2:123
1 Samuel		107:40	2:14
1:6	1:179	110	2:244
6:10	1:182	119	2:147, 2:157
2 Samuel		*Psalms*	
7:11	2:78	1:1	2:78
7:12-14	2:117, 2:132, 2:142	2:1	2:78
23:1-7	2:67	3-4	2:67
1 Kings		5:10(?)	2:78
8	1:137	6:2-5	2:78
19:15	2:142	6:6	2:78
22:19-23	2:150	11:1-2	2:78
2 Kings		12:1	2:78
2:14-16	2:80	12:7	2:78
22-23	1:184	17:1	2:78
23:22-23	1:184	20-21	2:67
1 Chronicles		32	2:67
24:7-18	1:150, 1:156	41	2:67
Matthew		46	2:67
24:15	2:66	55	2:67
2 Chronicles		58	2:67
3:2	1:147	61	2:67
8:14	1:156	64-65	2:67
30	1:25	70	2:67
33:12	2:53	72-75	2:67
Nehemiah		80	2:67
9	1:137	87	2:67
9:29	2:14	90	2:67
10:34-35	1:162	108?	2:67

INDEX OF ANCIENT SOURCES   257

110	2:67	45:5	2:17
111	2:67	45:7	2:21
117	2:67	52:7	2:119
125:5	1:135	54:12	2:111
128:6	1:135	60:21	2:159
151A	2:67, 2:75, 2:76	61	2:118, 2:246
151B	2:67, 2:75, 2:76	61:1	2:118
154	2:67, 2:75	61:2	2:119, 2:120
155	2:67, 2:75	61:3	2:119, 2:159
213:2-3	2:78	63:7	2:20
213:5	2:78	*Jeremiah*	
Proverbs		10	2:148
1:1-6	2:79	10:12-13	2:148
1-2	2:69	10:23	2:16
1-9	2:151, 2:152	13:13	1:178
1:20-33	2:148	23:3	2:155
2:5	2:147	23:5	2:138
3:18	2:147	23:18	2:150
3:19	2:148, 2:157	23:25	1:178
8:22-31	2:157	25:31	2:18
8:23-31	2:148, 2:151	26	1:178
9:13-18	2:147	31:7	2:155
13-15	2:69	31:31	1:30
15:8	1:131, 2:79	40-44	2:79
16:9	2:16	52:12-13	2:79
Job		*Lamentations*	
5:1	2:149	1:1	2:79
6:10	2:149	1:1-7:5	2:53
8	2:68	*Ecclesiastes*	
9	2:68	8:1	2:106
12:22	2:149	*Ezekiel*	
13	2:68	1:9	1:178
14	2:68	3:13	1:178
28	2:149, 2:152	4:4-6	2:133
29:28	2:149	9:4	2:78
31-37	2:68	20:11ff	2:14
38-41	2:149	23	1:178
Isaiah		38-39	2:138
1	2:159, 2:160	40-48	1:39, 1:103
4	2:159	42:14	1:100
5	2:111	44:15	1:29, 2:74
6	2:150	44:17-19	1:100
9	2:159	47:1-12	2:164
10:34	2:111	124:23	1:178
10:34-11:5	2:110	*Ezra*	
11	2:159	9	1:137
11:1-5	2:137, 2:139	*Daniel*	
12	2:159, 2:160	2	2:106
14:24	2:16	2:4	2:106
28:16	2:79	2-5	2:154
31:8	2:12	2:5-7	2:106
40:3	2:79, 2:121	2:9	2:106

258 INDEX OF ANCIENT SOURCES

2:16	2:106	2:4	2:184, 2:185
2:18-19	2:107	2:4b	2:108, 2:115
2:22	2:155	*Nahum*	
2:24-26	2:106	2:12b	2:113
2:27-30	2:107	2:13	2:129
2:30	2:106	2:13b	2:113
2:36	2:106	3:6-14	2:114
2:45	2:106	*Zechariah*	
2:47	2:107	4:14	2:118, 2:144
4	2:106	6:11-13	2:144
4:6	2:107	13:1	2:160, 2:164
4:7	2:107	14	2:242
4:9	2:107	14:8	2:164
4:18-19	2:107	*Malachi*	
4:24	2:107	4:5	2:142
5	2:106	*Matthew*	
5:8	2:107	1:1-16	2:203
5:12	2:107	21:12-13	2:242
5:15-17	2:107	27:51	2:240
5:26	2:107	*Mark*	
7	2:106	11:15-17	2:242
7:13	2:140	12:26	2:49
7:16	2:107	13:14A	2:66
9	1:137	15:38	2:240
9:2	2:58	*Luke*	
9:24	2:127, 2:134	4	2:246
9:24-27	2:133	4:17	2:49
9:26	2:119	19:45-46	2:242
12:1-3	2:154	23:45	2:240
12:3	2:74	*John*	
12:10	2:62, 2:66	1:1	2:209, 2:225
Hosea		1:12	2:205
2:8	2:112	1:12-13	2:209
2:10	2:112	1:13	2:218
2:11-12	2:112	1:17	2:218
2:13	2:112	1:35-51	2:220
3:4	2:42	1:50	2:203
5:13-14	2:112	2:4-5	2:221
Amos		2-12	2:221
3:7	2:150	2:13-17	2:242
9:11	2:117	2:16-22	2:221
Micah		2:17	2:208
4:7	2:155	2:21	2:204, 2:240
5:6-7	2:155	2:22	2:208
Habbakuk		3:5	2:222
1:1-4a	2:115	3:13	2:209
1:4b	2:115	3:14	2:209
1:5	2:115	3:18	2:222
1:12b-13a	2:115	3:19	2:223
1:13	2:115	3:21	2:22
2:1-2	2:108	3:28	2:209
2:3a	2:108, 2:115	3:31	2:209, 2:210
2:3b	2:108	4:21-24	2:205

INDEX OF ANCIENT SOURCES

4:53	2:204	24:14	2:121
5:8-9	2:221	*Romans*	
5:17	2:224	1:2	2:58
5:24	2:205, 2:209	1:17	2:123
8:5-10	2:224	2:6-13	2:181
8:12	2:226	2:9ff	2:182
8:23	2:209, 2:210	2:14	2:182
9:3	2:226	2:25-29	2:186
9:22	2:222	3:9-12-24	2:181
9:35-36	2:203	3:10ff	2:182
9:35.38	2:219	3:19-20	2:182
9:35-39	2:205, 2:219	3:20, 28	2:123
11:25-27	2:203	3:24	2:180
11:26-27	2:205, 2:219	3:27-31	2:182
12-14	2:209	3:31	2:198
12:28	2:218	4:10-11	2:182
12:31	2:209, 2:226	8:28-30	2:193
12:32-34	2:209	9:1ff	2:193
12:33	2:218	9:2-4	2:194
12:36	2:226	9:6-13	2:194
12:42	2:203, 2:204, 2:222	9:14-18	2:194
12:46	2:222	9:22	2:195
13:3	2:225	9:24-29	2:195
13:33	2:206	9:30-10:21	2:195
13:34	2:206	9:30-33	2:195
14:17	2:226	11	2:197
14:30	2:226	11:1-2	2:195
15:3	2:221, 2:225	11:7	2:195
15:4	2:221	11:11-12	2:196
15:5	2:206, 2:221	11:17	2:196
15:12-13	2:222	11:17-24	2:196
15:13-15	2:204	11:17ff	2:199
15:17	2:226	11:20	2:196
16:11	2:209, 2:226	11:22	2:196
16:13	2:208, 2:226	11:23	2:196
17:15-17	2:221	11:25	2:196
17:16	2:222	11:29	2:196
17:17-19	2:207	12:14-21	2:190
18:10.15-27	2:206	*1 Corinthians*	
20:19-23	2:207, 2:208	3:16	2:187
20-21	2:209	9:19-22	2:187
20:21	2:207, 2:223	14:33-36	2:177
20:21b	2:209	*2 Corinthians*	
20-22	2:207	5:10	2:181
20:22	2:208, 2:209, 2:218	5:17	2:189
20:26-29	2:205, 2:219	*Galatians*	
20:31	2:205	1:15f	2:175
Acts of the Apostles		2:15-21	2:183
1:20	2:49	2:16	2:123, 2:189
9:2	2:121	2:16ff	2:199
19:9	2:121	3:2	2:123
22	2:121	3:6	2:123, 2:184
23	2:121	3:10	2:49

3:10-14	2:185	12:4	2:240
3:11	2:123	12:14	2:241
3:15-18	2:185	12:16	2:240
3:19-20	2:185	12:22-4	2:241
3:22-25	2:186	12:29	2:242
3:27-28	2:181	13:1-3	2:240
4	2:187	13:4-5	2:240
4:21-31	2:186	13:7	2:241
4:24-25	2:186	13:8	2:242
5	2:123	13:9	2:241
6:10	2:190	13:16	2:241
6:15	2:189	13:17	2:241
6:16	2:48, 2:186	13:18	2:241
20	2:123	13:22	2:238

Philippians
3:2-3	2:187	*Jude*	
		14-15	2:75

1 Thessalonians
Malachi
5:4-5	2:188	1:10	1:113, 1:131, 2:78

2 Timothy

Mishnah

Baba Qama
3:15	2:58	7:7	1:104
4:13	2:49		

Hebrews
Kelim
1:1	2:241	1:6-9	1:98
1:1-2:18	2:238		

Menahot
2:1-4	2:238, 2:241	10:3	1:161
2:17	2:238		

Middot
3:1	2:238	4:6	1:102
3:1-4:13	2:238		

Sheqalim
4:14	2:238	6.4	1:163
4:15	2:238		

Yadayim
4:16	2:238	4:6	2:58
7:26-27	2:238		

Yebamot
7:28	2:237	14:1	1:176
8:1-6	2:238		

Yoma
8:6-13	2:238	1:1	1:187
8:8	2:241	1:1-2:7	2:243
9:1	2:240	3:1-11	2:243
9:1-5	2:239	3.8	1:137
9:6	2:239	4:1-6	2:243
9:7	2:239	5:1-7	2:243
9:8-10	2:239		
9:11	2:239, 2:240		

Babylonian Talmud

Berakhot
9:12	2:239, 2:240	4b	1:87
9:15	2:240	27b	1:87
9:24	2:240		

Horayot
10	2:241	20b	1:163
10:1-18	2:240		

Pesahim
10:19-22	2:240	68b	1:161
10:23-25	2:240		

Shabbat
10:26-40	2:240	9b	1:87
11:1-40	2:240	31a	1:80
11:22	2:241		
12:1-3	2:240		

88a	1:161	11:23-24	1:141
Taanit		11:24	2:4
28b	1:163	11:29	2:145
		12	2:4
Qumran Scrolls		12:6	1:141
Hodayot (1QHa)		12:26	2:4
4:12	2:8	12:29	2:4
5:13	2:5	12:32	2:17
5:17	2:22	12:37	2:20
5:22-23	2:20	13	2:5
5:23	2:180	13:9	2:5
5:24-25	2:13	13:26	2:5, 2:6
5:31-33	1:141	13:27	2:4
6:8	2:6	14:9	2:19, 2:20
6:12	2:5	14:10	2:22
6:12-13	2:13	15:6	2:17
6:16	2:7	15:19-20	2:20
6:24	1:28, 2:18	15:28	2:18
6:25	2:4, 2:13, 2:19	15:30	2:19, 2:20
7	1:142	17:7	2:20
7:12	2:6	17:16-17	2:154
7:19-20	2:191	17:36	2:19
7:21	2:191	18:4	2:4
7:22-23	2:191	18:6	2:6, 2:22
8:22	1:141	18:9	2:20
8:24-25	2:19	18:10	2:17
8:28-29	1:141	18:12	2:22
9	2:165	18:20	2:7
9:7-8	2:191	19:3	2:4
9:10	2:22	19:4	2:5
9:16-20	2:126	19:6	1:141, 2:20
9:20	2:20	19:8	2:17, 2:18
9:21	2:4, 2:5, 2:8, 2:13	19:9	2:5, 2:19, 2:20
9:22	2:5	19:10-14	2:146
9:22:23	2:4	19:14-17	1:142
9:26-27	2:21	19:20-21	1:141
9:27	2:5	19:28	2:6
9:31	2:6	19:29	2:19
9:37	2:5	20:3	2:15
10:4	2:5	20:7-14	1:133
10:10	2:5	20:9-11	2:17
10:13	2:116	20:26	2:4
10:13, 18	2:13	20:33	2:5
10:17	2:6	21:12	2:4
10:22	1:141	22 iv 11	2:4
10:23	2:20	23:16	2:22
11:13	2:4	30	2:79
11:19-23	2:146	31	2:4
11:20	1:141	*Pesher Habakkuk (1QpHab)*	
11:20-21	2:189	1-2	2:114
11:20-37	1:142	1:11	2:130
11:21-22	2:177	1:13	2:114

INDEX OF ANCIENT SOURCES

2:1-2	2:114	1:2	1:37
2:1-3	2:115	1:9-10	2:130
2:2	2:11, 2:114	1:14	2:17
2:5	2:107	1:16	2:145
2:5-10	2:130	2:1-6	1:132
2:7-8	2:130	3:8	2:17
2:8-10	2:11	3:9	2:18
2:11-12	2:115	6:6	2:18
2:12-15	2:114	7	2:17
2:17-3:1	2:114	7:5-8	1:106
3:4-6	2:115	8-15	2:17
4:1-3	2:115	10:8-11	2:17
5:3-6	2:115	10:10-11	2:8
5:4	2:116	10-19	1:142
5:9-11	2:130	11	2:17
5:9-12	2:114, 2:115	11:1	2:17
5-13	2:115	11:1-3	2:17
6:1-2	2:115	11:2	2:15
6-12	2:115	11:4	2:17
6:14	2:108	11:6	2:8
7:1	2:11, 2:108	11:8	2:8, 2:11
7:1-8	2:168	11-12	2:17
7:1-14	2:135	12:1	2:17
7:4-5	2:130	12:2	2:17
7:5	2:11	12:3	2:17
7:10-12	2:136	12:8	2:17
8:1-2	2:184	13:7ff	2:190
8:1-3	2:115, 2:123	13:13	2:17
8:3	2:114	14	2:17
8:8-11	2:198	14:8	2:19
8:8-13	2:114	14:8-9o	1:37
8-12	2:115	15	2:17
8:16	2:114	16:15	2:8
9:2	2:114	17:5-9	2:245
9:4-7	2:115, 2:130	17:7-8	1:41
9:6-7	2:115	18:3	2:17
9:9-11	2:130	19:3	2:17
9:9-12	2:114	*Rule of the Community (1QS)*	
9-12	2:114	1-3	1:35
9-13	2:115	1:3	2:11, 2:74
10:3-5	2:18, 2:115	1:5	2:226
10:5	2:18	1:7	2:192
10:9-13	2:114	1:7-2:25	2:211
11:2-8	1:146	1:8-2:25	2:213
11:4-8	2:114, 2:130	1:9	2:226
12:2-10	2:114	1:9-10	2:188, 2:189
12:9	2:131	1:11-13	2:211
12:12-14	2:115	1:11-15	1:157
12-15	2:114	1:13-15	2:211
13:1-4	2:115	1:16-2:18	1:161
War Scroll (1QM)		1:16-2:26	2:35
1:1	2:128	1:16-17	2:211

INDEX OF ANCIENT SOURCES 263

1:16-18	1:139	4:23-26	2:127
1:18-2:18	1:136	4:25	2:214
1:19-20	2:213	4:29-22	1:121
1:22	2:20	5:1	2:192, 2:210
1:24-25	1:137	5:1-2	2:211
2:1	2:20	5:3	2:226
2:3	2:6	5:5	2:199
2:4-5	2:213	5:7-9	2:25
2:6	2:18	5:8	1:32, 2:215
2:8	2:18	5:9	2:211
2:9	2:19	5:11-12	2:155, 2:215
2:11-17	2:213	5:13-15	1:109
2:16	2:226	5:17	2:57
2:18	2:213, 2:215	5:20-22	2:33
2:19	2:213	5:21	2:6
2:19-23	2:211	5:21-23	2:7
2:21-23	1:136	5:22	1:32, 1:33
2:22	1:33, 2:211	5:23	2:6, 2:211
2:253:12a	1:121	5:24	2:211
3:1-4	1:121	5:24-26	2:189
3:3-9	2:216	6:3, 6	1:133
3-4	2:44	6:3-4	1:132
3:5-6	2:216	6:4	2:153
3:6-9	2:216	6:13	2:192
3:7	2:226	6:13-16	2:212
3:13	2:6, 2:9, 2:214, 2:226	6:13-23	2:211
3:13-4:26	1:121, 1:122, 2:9, 2:15, 2:36, 2:162, 2:191, 2:214	6:15	2:212
		6:16-17	2:212
		6:16-23	1:110, 2:213
3:13-15	2:128	6:20	2:212
3:15	2:20, 2:167	6:24	1:110
3:15-16	2:126, 2:191	6:24-26	2:211
3:15-17	2:15	6:27	2:15
3:17-4:1	2:127	7:1	1:110
3:18-19	2:9, 2:191, 2:192	7:1-27	2:211
3:20	2:192	7:7-8	1:132
3:24	2:14	7:15b	1:110
3:24-25	2:192	8:1	1:31
3:25	2:21, 2:192	8:1-4	1:109
4:1	2:19	8:2	2:226
4:4	2:20, 2:226	8:2-9:2	2:211
4:5	2:20	8:5-6	2:169, 2:187, 2:215
4:5-6	1:121	8:5-12	1:32, 2:40
4:6-8	2:145	8:6	2:215
4:8	1:142	8:7	2:79, 2:215
4:11-14	2:145	8:8-9	1:131
4:12	2:18	8:10	2:215
4:18-26	1:122	8:10b-12a	1:31
4:21	2:226	8:12-16	2:121
4:22	2:15	8:13-14	2:79
4:22-23	2:167	8:13-16	2:136
4:23	2:214	8:14	2:57

8:15-19	1:111	2:2	2:11
8:20-9:2	1:111	2:4	2:19
9:3	1:32	2:5-6	1:41
9:3-4	1:131	2:7-8	2:192
9:3-6	1:109	2:9-10	2:167
9:4-5	2:187, 2:216	2:14	2:7
9:6	2:215	3-4	1:29
9:7	1:33	3:10-13	2:34
9:9-11	2:136, 2:140, 2:142, 2:143	3:11	2:155
		3:11-12	2:188
9:12	2:211	3:12-16	2:30
9:12-21	2:12	3:17	2:5
9:15-16	2:7	3:20	1:41
9:17-18	2:192	3:20-4:2	2:74
9:18	2:7, 2:12	4:2	1:28
9:20	2:7	4:2-4	1:28
9:21	2:189, 2:211	4-5	2:30
9:21-10:5	2:12	4:9	2:34
9:26	1:132	4:10-11	1:30
10:1	1:133	4:15	1:28, 1:130, 1:139
10:6	2:16	4:19-5:1	2:79
10:6-11:22	2:12	4:19-5:5	1:185
10:7-9	2:16	4:20-5:2	1:189
10:9	2:22	4:20-5:6	1:179, 1:189
10:16	2:20	4:20-5:11	2:27A
10:16-17	2:18	4:21	1:182
10:17-18	2:71	5:2	2:58
10:20	1:28	5:6	1:131
11:2	2:180	5:7-11	1:189
11:3	2:8	5:9-10	1:193
11:3, 5	2:20	5:10	2:27
11:3-4	2:167	5:13	1:36
11:5-6	2:167	6	2:120
11:7	2:178	6:2-8	2:30, 2:32
11:7-8	2:168	6:2-11	2:41
11:10-11	2:180	6:5	1:28, 2:34
11:11	2:17, 2:20	6:7	2:142
11:11-15	2:179	6:11	2:42
11-12	2:155	6:11-13	1:131
11:12	2:20	6:11-21	1:113
11:14	2:20	6:12	2:37
11:14-15	2:5	6:12-7:6	2:36
11:19	2:8	6:13-14	2:40, 2:78
11:21	2:4	6:17	1:113
17:14	2:20	6:19	1:29
Damascus Document (CD)		7:4-7	1:32
1:1-6:10	1:94	7:9	2:18
1:4	2:33	7:18	2:142
1:4-9	1:27	7:18-21	2:121, 2:142
1:5-11	2:133	7:19	2:142
1:7-8	1:41	8:16	1:28
1:14-15	1:28	8:21	1:29

9:15	2:31	20:27	2:42
9-16	2:37	20:27-28	2:32
9:16-17	2:31	20:27-34	2:121
9:21	1:114	20:31-32	2:32
10:7-10	2:80	*Temple Scroll (11QT, 11QTa, 11Q19)*	
10:9-10	2:79	3-13:7	1:100
10:14	1:82	9-10	1:162
11:19-21	2:69, 2:79	11:9-14	1:158
11:21	1:131	11:10	1:158, 1:159
11:21-22	1:133	11:11	1:161
12	1:115	11:12	1:162
12:1	1:118	11:12-13	1:161
12:1-2	1:102, 1:103	14:9-10	1:158
12:1ff.	1:114	14:9-15:3	1:158
12:19ff.	1:114	17:6-9	1:159
12:21	2:163	17:10	2:57
12:23	2:42	17:10-16	1:159
12:23-13:1	2:140	18:10-13	1:161
12:43	2:40	19:11-14	1:162
13:9	2:189	19:11-25:10	1:161
13:12	1:36	21:12-22:16	1:162
13:22	2:163	23:03-3	1:163
14:4	1:30	25:3	1:164, 2:57
14:18-19	2:140	25:10-11	1:164
14:19	2:140	27:5	1:164
15:5	1:28	27:10-29:1	1:164
15:5-6	1:30	29:9-10	1:85
15:8-10	2:24	31-32	1:100
15:9-10	2:199	34-35	1:100
15:12-14	2:25	35:1-9	1:100
15:15-17	1:112	40	1:100
16:1-5	2:25	40:5-45:2	1:102
16:2	2:74	42:12-17	1:164
16:2-3	2:26	42:14	1:100
16:2-4	2:75, 2:127	43:1-12a	1:102
16:3	2:160	43:3	1:162
16:4-5	1:139	43:3-10	1:162
19:10-11	2:140	43:6	1:161
19:11	2:8	44:17-19	1:100
19:11-12	2:78	45:7-12	1:104
19:31-32	2:19	45:7b-46	1:102
19:33-4	2:34	45:7b-48	1:102
19:33-34	1:29	45:10	1:103
20	1:41	45:10-12	1:117
20:1	2:140	45:10-12a	1:103
20:11-12	2:121	45:12b-14	1:104
20:13-14	2:42	45:15-17	1:117
20:13-19	2:134	45-46	1:104
20:17	1:28	46:3-4	1:102
20:19	2:58	46:5-8	1:102
20:20	2:20	46:9-12	1:102
20:23	1:131	46:13-16a	1:105

46:16b-47:2	1:104	1QPsb	2:67
46-47	1:104	1QPsc	2:67
47	1:106	1QSa	1:38, 1:39, 1:40, 1:42, 1:190, 1:191, 1:192, 1:193, 2:42
47:3-7a	1:103		
47:7b-18	1:105		
48:14-17	1:106	1QSa 1:1	2:133
49:5-51:6	1:116	1QSa 1:1-6	2:196
49:6-8	1:117	1QSa 1:3	2:187
51:19-54:7	1:118	1QSa 2:11-22	2:140
52:13b-19a	1:105	1QSa 2:17-22	2:133, 2:177
52:16b-19a	1:105	1QSam	2:63
52:19b-21	1:105	1QSb+d	1:33
52-53	1:105	1QSc	1:35
57:11-15	2:139	1QSd	1:32, 1:33
57:17	1:187	1QSe	1:33
57:17-18	1:185	1QTa	2:79
57:17-19	1:189	2Q18	2:150
57:18	1:187	2QDeut^a	2:61
58:18-19	2:139	2QDeut^b	2:61
63:10ff.	1:119	2QDeut^c	2:61
394b-11	1:101	2QExod^a	2:60
Other Scrolls		2QExod^b	2:60
1Q14	2:109, 2:112, 2:113	2QExod^c	2:60
1Q16	1:130	2QGen	2:60
1Q26	2:154	2QJer	2:64
1Q27	2:22, 2:161, 2:162	2QJob	2:67, 2:68
1Q28b	1:127, 1:142	2QJuba	2:73
1Q34	1:127, 2:17	2QJubb	2:73
1Q34bis	1:127, 1:164	2QNuma	2:61
1Q35	1:127	2QNumb	2:61
1Q37-40	1:127	2QNumc	2:61
1Q171	1:130	2QNumd?	2:61
1QDan^a	2:65	2QpaleoLev	2:61
1QDan^b	2:65	2QPs	2:67
1QDeut^a	2:61	2QRuth^a	2:70
1QDeut^b	2:61	2QRuth^b	2:70
1QExod	2:60	2QSir	2:69
1QEzek	2:64	3QEzek	2:64
1QGen	2:60	3QJub	2:73
1QGenAp	2:15	3QLam	2:71
1QHE 12:31	2:15	3QPs	2:67
1QH FG. 4:12	2:6	4Q38'97	1:107
1QIsa^a	2:63, 2:64	4Q159	1:92, 1:192, 2:30
1QIsa^b	2:64	4Q161	2:109, 2:110, 2:138
1QJub^a	2:73	4Q162	2:109, 2:111
1QJub^b	2:73	4Q163	2:78, 2:109, 2:110, 2:111
1QJudg	2:63		
1QMA 10:10	2:6	4Q164	2:109, 2:111
1QpaleoLev	2:61	4Q165	2:109, 2:111
1QpH 7:1	2:8	4Q166	2:109, 2:112
1QpPs	2:77	4Q167	2:109, 2:112
1QPsa	2:67	4Q169	2:113, 2:114

INDEX OF ANCIENT SOURCES

4Q170	2:116	4Q319	1:149, 1:155, 1:156, 1:157, 1:159, 1:164
4Q171	2:116	4Q320	1:151, 1:153, 1:156, 1:158, 1:159, 1:160, 1:161, 1:163, 1:164
4Q173	2:116		
4Q174	1:101, 2:58, 2:62, 2:66, 2:74, 2:117, 2:132, 2:133, 2:142, 2:168	4Q320 1 i 1-5	1:148, 1:149, 1:154
4Q175	2:63, 2:143	4Q320-4Q321a	1:161
4Q177	2:78, 2:117, 2:132	4Q320-321a	1:148, 1:151
4Q179	2:79	4Q321	1:151, 1:159, 1:160, 1:161, 1:164
4Q184	2:79		
4Q185	2:79, 2:152	4Q324	1:161, 1:164
4Q208-211	1:151	4Q325	1:160, 1:161, 1:162
4Q215a	2:161	4Q326	1:159, 1:160
4Q228	2:74	4Q328	1:153
4Q246	2:139	4Q329	1:151, 1:153
4Q247	2:77	4Q329a	1:159
4Q249	1:92	4Q365	1:162, 1:163, 1:164
4Q251	1:92, 2:77, 2:80	4Q365a	1:83, 1:159
4Q252	1:154, 2:8, 2:117, 2:137	4Q372	2:18
		4Q377	2:8
4Q254	2:117, 2:118	4Q380	1:130
4Q255	2:58	4Q380-381	1:128
4Q255-4Q264	1:91	4Q381	1:130
4Q264a	1:92	4Q382	2:80
4Q265	1:92, 2:80	4Q385	2:15, 2:146
4Q266	1:109, 1:116, 1:129, 1:136, 1:139, 1:161, 2:11e2:8, 2:14, 2:35, 2:213	4Q385-88	2:80
		4Q385b	2:79
		4Q392	2:21
		4Q394	1:101, 1:104, 1:107, 1:118, 1:119, 1:124, 1:154, 1:161, 1:162, 1:163
4Q266-4Q273	1:92, 1:112		
4Q267	1:36, 1:109		
4Q268	2:8	4Q396	1:104, 1:107, 1:116, 1:118, 1:124
4Q269	1:109, 1:115		
4Q270	1:109, 1:115, 2:35	4Q397	2:59
4Q271	1:115, 1:133	4Q398	2:180
4Q274	1:109, 1:117, 1:118, 1:119, 1:120	4Q400	1:138, 2:18
		4Q400-107	2:245
4Q274-4Q283	1:92	4Q400-407	1:128, 1:138, 2:12, 2:40
4Q276	1:120		
4Q277	1:116, 1:120	4Q403	2:18
4Q280	2:9	4Q404	2:18
4Q284	1:92, 1:119, 1:121	4Q405	2:18
4Q284a	1:92, 1:118	4Q409	1:161, 1:163, 1:164, 2:15
4Q285	1:142, 2:8, 2:110, 2:111, 2:131, 2:139		
		4Q414	1:92, 1:119, 1:121, 1:129, 2:6
4Q286	2:5, 2:6		
4Q286-290	1:128, 1:129	4Q415	2:16, 2:154
4Q287	1:132, 2:15	4Q416	2:6, 2:18, 2:154, 2:156
4Q299	2:161	4Q417	2:5, 2:6, 2:13, 2:19, 2:58, 2:154, 2:157
4Q300	2:5, 2:161		
4Q301	2:161		
4Q317	1:152	4Q418	2:6, 2:12, 2:13, 2:16,

	2:154, 2:156, 2:157, 2:158	4QDeut^d	2:62
		4QDeut^e	2:62
4Q418a	2:154	4QDeut^f	2:62
4Q420	2:152, 2:153	4QDeut^g	2:62
4Q421	2:12, 2:152, 2:153	4QDeut^h	2:62
4Q422	2:77	4QDeut^i	2:62
4Q423	2:154, 2:158	4QDeut^j	2:62
4Q427	2:7, 2:12, 2:18	4QDeut^{k1}	2:62
4Q427-432	1:128	4QDeut^{k2}	2:62
4Q433	1:128	4QDeut^{k3}	2:62
4Q433a	1:128	4QDeut^l	2:62
4Q434	2:16, 2:19	4QDeut^m	2:62
4Q434-38	1:128	4QDeut^n	2:62
4Q440	1:128	4QDeut^o	2:62
4Q444	2:13	4QDeut^p	2:62
4Q472a	1:92	4QDeut^q	2:62
4Q474	2:58	4QEna ar	2:72
4Q481a	2:80	4QEnastr^a ar	2:72
4Q491	1:37, 1:92, 2:58	4QEnastr^b ar	2:72
4Q493	2:14	4QEnastr^c ar	2:72
4Q496	1:104	4QEnastr^d ar	2:72
4Q503	1:132, 1:135, 1:136, 1:137, 1:152	4QEn^b ar	2:72
		4QEn^c ar	2:72
4Q504	1:130, 1:132, 1:135, 2:58	4QEn^d ar	2:72
		4QEn^e ar	2:72
4Q509	1:127	4QEn^f ar	2:72
4Q510	1:139	4QEn^g ar	2:72
4Q510-511	1:139, 2:12	4QEnoch	2:160
4Q511	1:127, 1:140	4QExod^b	2:60
4Q512	1:92, 1:116, 1:119, 1:129	4QExod^c	2:60
		4QExod^d	2:60
		4QExod^e	2:60
4Q513-514	1:92	4QExod^g	2:60
4Q521	2:143, 2:146	4QExod^h	2:60
4Q524	1:92	4QExod^j	2:60
4Q525	2:13, 2:15, 2:79, 2:152	4QExod^k	2:60
4Q536	2:10	4QExod-Lev^f	2:60, 2:61
4Q541	2:140	4QEzek^a	2:65
4Q542	2:10	4QEzek^b	2:65
4Q560	1:139	4QFlor	2:57, 2:78
4QCanta	2:70	4QGen^b	2:60
4QCantb	2:70	4QGen^c	2:60
4QCantc	2:70	4QGen^d	2:60
4QCatena	2:57	4QGen^e	2:60
4QChron	2:71	4QGen-Exod^a	2:60, 2:61
4QDan^a	2:65, 2:66	4QGen^f	2:60
4QDan^b	2:65	4QGen^g	2:60
4QDan^c	2:65, 2:66	4QGen^{h1}	2:60
4QDan^d	2:65	4QGen^{h2}	2:60
4QDan^e	2:65, 2:66	4QGen^h-title	2:60
4QDeut^a	2:62	4QGen^j	2:60
4QDeut^b	2:62	4QGen^k	2:60
4QDeut^c	2:62		

INDEX OF ANCIENT SOURCES

4QGen^n	2:60		1:103, 1:104, 1:114, 2:37, 2:38, 2:40, 2:58, 2:59, 2:74, 2:122–2:123
4QH180	2:126		
4QHa	1:142, 2:155, 2:166, 2:167		
4QHb	2:163, 2:164	4QMmt	2:174
4QHe	1:142	4QNum^b	2:61
4QIsa^a	2:64	4QpaleoDeut^r	2:62
4QIsa^b	2:64	4QpaleoDeut^s	2:62
4QIsa^c	2:64	4QpaleoExod^m	2:60
4QIsa^d	2:64	4QpaleoGen-Exod^l	2:60, 2:61
4QIsa^e	2:64	4QpaleoGen^m	2:60
4QIsa^f	2:64	4QpaleoJob^c	2:67, 2:68
4QIsa^g	2:64	4QpapTobit^a ar	2:68
4QIsa^h	2:64	4QpHab	2:77, 2:112
4QIsa^i	2:64	4QpHos^a	2:77
4QIsa^j	2:64	4QpHos^b	2:77
4QIsa^k	2:64	4QpIsa^a	2:77
4QIsa^l	2:64	4QpIsa^b	2:77
4QIsa^m	2:64	4QpIsa^c	2:77
4QIsa^n	2:64	4QpIsa^d	2:77
4QIsa^o	2:64	4QpIsa^e	2:77
4QIsa^q	2:64	4QpMic	2:77
4QJer^a	2:64	4QpNah	2:77, 2:109, 2:129
4QJer^b	2:64	4QpNah 3:3-5	2:197
4QJer^c	2:64	4QpPs^a	2:77
4QJer^d	2:64	4QpPs^b	2:77
4QJer^e	2:64	4QProv^a	2:69
4QJob^a	2:67	4QProv^b	2:69
4QJob^b	2:67	4QPs^a	2:66, 2:67
4QJosh^a	2:63	4QPs^b	2:67
4QJosh^b	2:63	4QPs^c	2:66, 2:67
4QJub^a	2:73	4QPs^d	2:67
4QJub^c	2:73f	4QPs^e	2:67
4QJub^d	2:73	4QPs^f	2:67
4QJub^e	2:73	4QPs^g	2:67
4QJub^f	2:73	4QPs^h	2:67
4QJub^g	2:73	4QPs^j	2:67
4QJudg^a	2:63	4QPs^k	2:67
4QJudg^b	2:63	4QPs^l	2:67
4QKgs	2:63	4QPs^m	2:67
4QLam	2:7171, 7171	4QPs^n	2:67
4QLev^b	2:61	4QPs^o	2:67
4QLev^c	2:61	4QPs^p	2:67
4QLev^d	2:61	4QPs^q	2:67
4QLev^e	2:61	4QPs^r	2:67
4QLev^g	2:61	4QPs^s	2:67
4QLev-Num^a	2:61	4QPs^t	2:67
4QLXXDeut	2:62, 2:77	4QPs^u	2:67
4QLXXLev^a	2:61, 2:77	4QPs^v	2:67
4QLXXNum	2:61, 2:77	4QPs^w	2:67
4QMMT	1:27, 1:34, 1:38, 1:75, 1:79, 1:81, 1:92, 1:95,	4QPs^x	2:67
		4QpZeph	2:77

4QpZeph^a	2:77	11Q17	1:138, 2:12
4QRuth^a	2:70	11Q20	1:92, 1:163
4QRuth^b	2:70	11Q21	1:92, 1:104
4QS	1:97	11QapocPs	2:67
4QSam^a	2:63	11QapPs	1:139
4QSam^b	2:63	11QDeut	2:62
4QSam^c	2:63	11QEzek	2:64
4QS^d	1:30, 1:31, 1:32	11QJub	2:73
4QS^e	1:30, 1:31	11QLev^b	2:61
4QtgJob	2:68, 2:77	11QMelch	2:39, 2:58, 2:118–2:119, 2:127, 2:145, 2:154
4QTobit^a ar	2:68		
4QTobit^b ar	2:68		
4QTobit^c ar	2:68	11QpaleoLev^a	2:61
4QTobit^d ar	2:68	11QPs^a	1:127, 1:130, 1:134, 1:139, 2:62, 2:67, 2:69–2:70, 2:75, 2:148, 2:150, 2:152, 2:153, 2:157
4QTobit^e	2:68		
4QTohorot A-G	2:39		
4QXII^a	2:65		
4QXII^b	2:65		
4QXIIc	2:65	11QPs^b	2:67
4QXII^d	2:65	11QPs^c	2:67
4QXII^e	2:65	11QPs^d	2:67
4QXII^f	2:65	11QPs^e	2:67
4QXII^g	2:65	11QPs^f	1:130
5/6HevNum	2:61	11QtgJob	2:68, 2:77
5/6HevPs	2:67	MasDeut	2:62
5Q13	1:92	MasEzek	2:65
5q391	2:80	MasGen	2:60
5QAmos	2:65	MasLev^a	2:61
5QDeut	2:62	MasLev^b	2:61
5QIsa	2:64	MasPs^a	2:67
5QKgs	2:63	MasPs^b	2:67
5QLam^a	2:71	MasSir	2:69
5QLam^b	2:71	MurExod	2:60
5QPs	2:67	MurGen	2:60
6QCant	2:70	MurGen 1	2:60
6QDan	2:65	MurIsa	2:64
6QGen	2:60	MurNum	2:61
6QpaleoLev	2:61	MurXII	2:65
7Q4.1	2:72	pap4QEn gr	2:72
7Q4.2	2:72	pap4QGen	2:60
7Q8	2:72	pap4QJub^b(?)	2:73
7Q11	2:72	pap4QJub^h	2:73
7Q12	2:72	pap4QLXXLev^b	2:61, 2:77
7Q13	2:72	pap6QDeut?	2:62
8HevXII gr	2:65	pap6QKgs	2:63
8QGen	2:60	pap6QPs	2:67
8QPs	2:67	pap7QEn gr	2:77
11Q5	1:155	pap7QLXXExod	2:60, 2:77
11Q13	1:164, 2:9, 2:244, 2:245	QHalakhaa 17 1	1:82
		SdeirGen	2:60
11Q14	1:142, 2:43	XHev/SeNum^a	2:61

Apocrypha
1 Maccabees
12:9   2:58
Ben Sira
1   2:69
1:1-20   2:151
6   2:69
23:20   2:16
24:1-22   2:151
24:1-29   2:151
24:30-34   2:151
39:1-5   2:28
39-44   2:69
51:13-19   2:147
51:13-30   2:67, 2:69, 2:75
Tobit
1-7   2:68
12-14   2:68

Pseudepigrapha
1 Enoch
1:2   2:75
5:6   2:154
10:1-11:2   2:75
12:4   2:154
15:1   2:154
72-82   1:151, 2:219
81:1-2   2:75
90:19   1:109
92:1   2:154
93:1   2:75
93:10   2:154, 2:160
93+91   2:39
98:11   2:72
100:12   2:72
103:3-4   2:72
103:7-8   2:72
105:17   2:72
Jubilees
1:5-18   2:75
3:8-14   2:75, 2:79
3:27   1:134
3:31   2:75
6:14   1:134
6:23   1:153
6:36-38a   1:148, 1:151
10:1   1:139
22:16ff.   1:118
23:11   2:79, 2:80
23:26-31   2:160

32:13   1:102
33:7   1:124
49:19   1:134
Levi, Testament of
Col. C 9-20   1:162

1 Clement   2:48
53:1   2:58

Hippolytus of Rome
Refutation of All Heresies
9.27   2:146

Irenaeus
Against Heresies
1.9.4-5   2:48
3.2.1   2:48
3.11.1   2:48

Josephus
Antiquities of the Jews
3:261-263   1:77
5:224   1:102
10 §§249, 266-267   2:66
12:138-144   1:95
12:138-153   1:105
13.13.5-14.1 §372-378 2:113
13.14.2 §380-383   2:113
13:171-173   1:77
18:11-17   1:77
Contra Apionem
1:282   1:104
Wars of the Jews
2.8.5 §154-55   2:146
2:119-166   1:77
2:123   1:118
2:149   1:105
5:227   1:77

Philo
De decalogo
§45   1:120
De specialibus legibus
I §261   1:120
III §64   1:120

Pliny
Historia Naturalis
V.17.73   1:51

HANDBUCH DER ORIENTALISTIK

Abt. I: DER NAHE UND MITTLERE OSTEN

ISSN 0169-9423

Band 1. Ägyptologie
1. *Ägyptische Schrift und Sprache.* Mit Beiträgen von H. Brunner, H. Kees, S. Morenz, E. Otto, S. Schott. Mit Zusätzen von H. Brunner. Nachdruck der Erstausgabe (1959). 1973. ISBN 90 04 03777 2
2. *Literatur.* Mit Beiträgen von H. Altenmüller, H. Brunner, G. Fecht, H. Grapow, H. Kees, S. Morenz, E. Otto, S. Schott, J. Spiegel, W. Westendorf. 2. verbesserte und erweiterte Auflage. 1970. ISBN 90 04 00849 7
3. Helck, W. *Geschichte des alten Ägypten.* Nachdruck mit Berichtigungen und Ergänzungen. 1981. ISBN 90 04 06497 4

Band 2. Keilschriftforschung und alte Geschichte Vorderasiens
1-2/2. *Altkleinasiatische Sprachen [und Elamitisch].* Mit Beiträgen von J. Friedrich, E. Reiner, A. Kammenhuber, G. Neumann, A. Heubeck. 1969. ISBN 90 04 00852 7
3. Schmökel, H. *Geschichte des alten Vorderasien.* Reprint. 1979. ISBN 90 04 00853 5
4/2. *Orientalische Geschichte von Kyros bis Mohammed.* Mit Beiträgen von A. Dietrich, G. Widengren, F. M. Heichelheim. 1966. ISBN 90 04 00854 3

Band 3. Semitistik
Semitistik. Mit Beiträgen von A. Baumstark, C. Brockelmann, E. L. Dietrich, J. Fück, M. Höfner, E. Littmann, A. Rücker, B. Spuler. Nachdruck der Erstausgabe (1953-1954). 1964. ISBN 90 04 00855 1

Band 4. Iranistik
1. *Linguistik.* Mit Beiträgen von K. Hoffmann, W. B. Henning, H. W. Bailey, G. Morgenstierne, W. Lentz. Nachdruck der Erstausgabe (1958). 1967. ISBN 90 04 03017 4
2/1. *Literatur.* Mit Beiträgen von I. Gershevitch, M. Boyce, O. Hansen, B. Spuler, M. J. Dresden. 1968. ISBN 90 04 00857 8
2/2. *History of Persian Literature from the Beginning of the Islamic Period to the Present Day.* With Contributions by G. Morrison, J. Baldick and Sh. Kadkanī. 1981. ISBN 90 04 06481 8
3. Krause, W. *Tocharisch.* Nachdruck der Erstausgabe (1955) mit Zusätzen und Berichtigungen. 1971. ISBN 90 04 03194 4

Band 5. Altaistik
1. *Turkologie.* Mit Beiträgen von A. von Gabain, O. Pritsak, J. Benzing, K. H. Menges, A. Temir, Z. V. Togan, F. Taeschner, O. Spies, A. Caferoglu, A. Battal-Tamays. Reprint with additions of the 1st (1963) ed. 1982. ISBN 90 04 06555 5
2. *Mongolistik.* Mit Beiträgen von N. Poppe, U. Posch, G. Doerfer, P. Aalto, D. Schröder, O. Pritsak, W. Heissig. 1964. ISBN 90 04 00859 4
3. *Tungusologie.* Mit Beiträgen von W. Fuchs, I. A. Lopatin, K. H. Menges, D. Sinor. 1968. ISBN 90 04 00860 8

Band 6. Geschichte der islamischen Länder
5/1. *Regierung und Verwaltung des Vorderen Orients in islamischer Zeit.* Mit Beiträgen von H. R. Idris und K. Röhrborn. 1979. ISBN 90 04 05915 6
5/2. *Regierung und Verwaltung des Vorderen Orients in islamischer Zeit.* 2. Mit Beiträgen von D. Sourdel und J. Bosch Vilá. 1988. ISBN 90 04 08550 5
6/1. *Wirtschaftsgeschichte des Vorderen Orients in islamischer Zeit.* Mit Beiträgen von B. Lewis, M. Rodinson, G. Baer, H. Müller, A. S. Ehrenkreutz, E. Ashtor, B. Spuler, A. K. S. Lambton, R. C. Cooper, B. Rosenberger, R. Arié, L. Bolens, T. Fahd. 1977. ISBN 90 04 04802 2

Band 7
Armenisch und *Kaukasische Sprachen.* Mit Beiträgen von G. Deeters, G. R. Solta, V. Inglisian. 1963. ISBN 90 04 00862 4

Band 8. Religion
1/1. *Religionsgeschichte des alten Orients.* Mit Beiträgen von E. Otto, O. Eissfeldt, H. Otten, J. Hempel. 1964. ISBN 90 04 00863 2
1/2/2/1. Boyce, M. *A History of Zoroastrianism. The Early Period.* Rev. ed. 1989. ISBN 90 04 08847 4

1/2/2/2. Boyce, M. *A History of Zoroastrianism. Under the Achaemenians*. 1982.
ISBN 90 04 06506 7
1/2/2/3. Boyce, M. and Grenet, F. *A History of Zoroastrianism. Zoroastrianism under Macedonian and Roman Rule*. With a Contribution by R. Beck. 1991. ISBN 90 04 09271 4
2. *Religionsgeschichte des Orients in der Zeit der Weltreligionen*. Mit Beiträgen von A. Adam, A. J. Arberry, E. L. Dietrich, J. W. Fück, A. von Gabain, J. Leipoldt, B. Spuler, R. Strothman, G. Widengren. 1961. ISBN 90 04 00864 0

Ergänzungsband 1
1. Hinz, W. *Islamische Maße und Gewichte umgerechnet ins metrische System*. Nachdruck der Erstausgabe (1955) mit Zusätzen und Berichtigungen. 1970. ISBN 90 04 00865 9

Ergänzungsband 2
1. Grohmann, A. *Arabische Chronologie* und *Arabische Papyruskunde*. Mit Beiträgen von J. Mayr und W. C. Till. 1966. ISBN 90 04 00866 7
2. Khoury, R. G. *Chrestomathie de papyrologie arabe*. Documents relatifs à la vie privée, sociale et administrative dans les premiers siècles islamiques. 1992. ISBN 90 04 09551 9

Ergänzungsband 3
Orientalisches Recht. Mit Beiträgen von E. Seidl, V. Korošc, E. Pritsch, O. Spies, E. Tyan, J. Baz, Ch. Chehata, Ch. Samaran, J. Roussier, J. Lapanne-Joinville, S. Ş. Ansay. 1964.
ISBN 90 04 00867 5

Ergänzungsband 5
1/1. Borger, R. *Einleitung in die assyrischen Königsinschriften*. 1. Das zweite Jahrtausend vor Chr. Mit Verbesserungen und Zusätzen. Nachdruck der Erstausgabe (1961). 1964.
ISBN 90 04 00869 1
1/2. Schramm, W. *Einleitung in die assyrischen Königsinschriften*. 2. 934-722 v. Chr. 1973.
ISBN 90 04 03783 7

Ergänzungsband 6
1. Ullmann, M. *Die Medizin im Islam*. 1970. ISBN 90 04 00870 5
2. Ullmann, M. *Die Natur- und Geheimwissenschaften im Islam*. 1972. ISBN 90 04 03423 4

Ergänzungsband 7
Gomaa, I. *A Historical Chart of the Muslim World*. 1972. ISBN 90 04 03333 5

Ergänzungsband 8
Kornrumpf, H.-J. *Osmanische Bibliographie mit besonderer Berücksichtigung der Türkei in Europa*. Unter Mitarbeit von J. Kornrumpf. 1973. ISBN 90 04 03549 4

Ergänzungsband 9
Firro, K. M. *A History of the Druzes*. 1992. ISBN 90 04 09437 7

Band 10
Strijp, R. *Cultural Anthropology of the Middle East. A Bibliography*. Vol. 1: 1965-1987. 1992.
ISBN 90 04 09604 3

Band 11
Endress, G. & Gutas, D. (eds.). *A Greek and Arabic Lexicon. (GALex)*. Materials for a Dictionary of the Mediæval Translations from Greek into Arabic.
Fascicle 1. Introduction—Sources—ʾ – ʾ-kh-r. Compiled by G. Endress & D. Gutas, with the assistance of K. Alshut, R. Arnzen, Chr. Hein, St. Pohl, M. Schmeink. 1992.
ISBN 90 04 09494 6
Fascicle 2. ʾ-kh-r – ʾ-ṣ-l. Compiled by G. Endress & D. Gutas, with the assistance of K. Alshut, R. Arnzen, Chr. Hein, St. Pohl, M. Schmeink. 1993. ISBN 90 04 09893 3
Fascicle 3. ʾ-ṣ-l – ʾ-l-y. Compiled by G. Endress, D. Gutas & R. Arnzen, with the assistance of Chr. Hein, St. Pohl. 1995. ISBN 90 04 10216 7
Fascicle 4. Ilā – inna. Compiled by R. Arnzen, G. Endress & D. Gutas, with the assistance of Chr. Hein & J. Thielmann. 1997. ISBN 90 04 10489 5.

Band 12
Jayyusi, S. K. (ed.). *The Legacy of Muslim Spain*. Chief consultant to the editor, M. Marín. 2nd ed. 1994. ISBN 90 04 09599 3

Band 13
Hunwick, J. O. and O'Fahey, R. S. (eds.). *Arabic Literature of Africa*. Editorial Consultant: Albrecht Hofheinz.
Volume I. *The Writings of Eastern Sudanic Africa to c. 1900*. Compiled by R. S. O'Fahey, with the assistance of M. I. Abu Salim, A. Hofheinz, Y. M. Ibrahim, B. Radtke and K. S. Vikør. 1994. ISBN 90 04 09450 4
Volume II. *The Writings of Central Sudanic Africa*. Compiled by John O. Hunwick, with the assistance of Razaq Abubakre, Hamidu Bobboyi, Roman Loimeier, Stefan Reichmuth and Muhammad Sani Umar. 1995. ISBN 90 04 10494 1

Band 14
Decker, W. und Herb, M. *Bildatlas zum Sport im alten Ägypten. Corpus der bildlichen Quellen zu Leibesübungen, Spiel, Jagd, Tanz und verwandten Themen.* Bd.1: Text. Bd. 2: Ab-bildungen. 1994. ISBN 90 04 09974 3 *(Set)*
Band 15
Haas, V. *Geschichte der hethitischen Religion.* 1994. ISBN 90 04 09799 6
Band 16
Neusner, J. (ed.). *Judaism in Late Antiquity.* Part One: The Literary and Archaeological Sources. 1994. ISBN 90 04 10129 2
Band 17
Neusner, J. (ed.). *Judaism in Late Antiquity.* Part Two: Historical Syntheses. 1994.
ISBN 90 04 09799 6
Band 18
Orel, V. E. and Stolbova, O. V. (eds.). *Hamito-Semitic Etymological Dictionary.* Materials for a Reconstruction. 1994. ISBN 90 04 10051 2
Band 19
al-Zwaini, L. and Peters, R. *A Bibliography of Islamic Law, 1980-1993.* 1994.
ISBN 90 04 10009 1
Band 20
Krings, V. (éd.). *La civilisation phénicienne et punique.* Manuel de recherche. 1995.
ISBN 90 04 10068 7
Band 21
Hoftijzer, J. and Jongeling, K. *Dictionary of the North-West Semitic Inscriptions.* With appendices by R.C. Steiner, A. Mosak Moshavi and B. Porten. 1995. 2 Parts.
ISBN Set (2 Parts) 90 04 09821 6   Part One: ʾ - L. ISBN 90 04 09817 8   Part Two: M - T. ISBN 90 04 9820 8.
Band 22
Lagarde, M. *Index du Grand Commentaire de Faḫr al-Dīn al-Rāzī.* 1996.
ISBN 90 04 10362 7
Band 23
Kinberg, N. *A Lexicon of al-Farrāʾ's Terminology in his Qurʾān Commentary.* With Full Definitions, English Summaries and Extensive Citations. 1996. ISBN 90 04 10421 6
Band 24
Fähnrich, H. und Sardshweladse, S. *Etymologisches Wörterbuch der Kartwel-Sprachen.* 1995.
ISBN 90 04 10444 5
Band 25
Rainey, A.F. *Canaanite in the Amarna Tablets.* A Linguistic Analysis of the Mixed Dialect used by Scribes from Canaan. 1996. ISBN *Set (4 Volumes)* 90 04 10503 4
Volume I. Orthography, Phonology. Morphosyntactic Analysis of the Pronouns, Nouns, Numerals. ISBN 90 04 10521 2   Volume II. Morphosyntactic Analysis of the Verbal System. ISBN 90 04 10522 0   Volume III. Morphosyntactic Analysis of the Particles and Adverbs. ISBN 90 04 10523 9   Volume IV. References and Index of Texts Cited. ISBN 90 04 10524 7
Band 26
Halm, H. *The Empire of the Mahdi.* The Rise of the Fatimids. Translated from the German by M. Bonner. 1996. ISBN 90 04 10056 3
Band 27
Strijp, R. *Cultural Anthropology of the Middle East.* A Bibliography. Vol. 2: 1988-1992. 1997.
ISBN 90 04 010745 2
Band 28
Sivan, D. *A Grammar of the Ugaritic Language.* 1997. ISBN 90 04 10614 6
Band 29
Corriente, F. *A Dictionary of Andalusi Arabic.* 1997. ISBN 90 04 09846 1
Band 30
Sharon, M. *Corpus Inscriptionum Arabicarum Palaestinae (CIAP).* Vol. 1: A. 1997.
ISBN 90 04 010745 2   Vol.1: B. 1999. ISBN 90 04 110836
Band 31
Török, L. *The Kingdom of Kush.* Handbook of the Napatan-Meroitic Civilization. 1997.
ISBN 90 04 010448 8
Band 32
Muraoka, T. and Porten, B. *A Grammar of Egyptian Aramaic.* 1998. ISBN 90 04 10499 2

Band 33
Gessel, B.H.L. van. *Onomasticon of the Hittite Pantheon.* 1998.
ISBN *Set (2 parts)* 90 04 10809 2
Band 34
Klengel, H. *Geschichte des hethitischen Reiches* 1998. ISBN 90 04 10201 9
Band 35
Hachlili, R. *Ancient Jewish Art and Archaeology in the Diaspora* 1998. ISBN 90 04 10878 5
Band 36
Westendorf, W. *Handbuch der altägyptischen Medizin.* 1999.
ISBN *Set (2 Bände)* 90 04 10319 8
Band 37
Civil, M. *Mesopotamian Lexicography.* 1999. ISBN 90 04 11007 0
Band 38
Siegelová, J. and Souček, V. *Systematische Bibliographie der Hethitologie.* 1999.
ISBN *Set (3 Bände)* 90 04 11205 7
Band 39
Watson, W.G.E. and Wyatt, N. *Handbook of Ugaritic Studies.* 1999.
ISBN 90 04 10988 9
Band 40
Neusner, J. *Judaism in Late Antiquity, III,1.* 1999. ISBN 90 04 11186 7
Band 41
Neusner, J. *Judaism in Late Antiquity, III,2.* 1999. ISBN 90 04 11282 0
Band 42
Drijvers, H.J.W. and Healey, J.F. *The Old Syriac Inscriptions of Edessa and Osrhoene.* 1999.
ISBN 90 04 11284 7
Band 43
Daiber, H. *Bibliography of Philosophical Thought in Islam.* 2 Volumes.
ISBN *Set (2 Volumes)* 90 04 11347 9
Volume I. Alphabetical List of Publications 1999. ISBN 90 04 09648 5
Volume II. Index of Names, Terms and Topics. 1999. ISBN 90 04 11348 7
Band 44
Hunger, H. and Pingree, D. *Astral Sciences in Mesopotamia.* 1999. ISBN 90 04 10127 6
Band 45
Neusner, J. *The Mishnah.* Religious Perspectives 1999. ISBN 90 04 11492 0
Band 46
Neusner, J. *The Mishnah.* Social Perspectives 1999. ISBN 90 04 11491 2
Band 47
Khan, G. *A Grammar of Neo-Aramaic.* 1999. ISBN 90 04 11510 2
Band 48
Takács, G. *Etymological Dictionary of Egyptian.* Vol. 1. 1999. ISBN 90 04 11538 2
Band 49
Avery-Peck, A.J. and Neusner, J. *Judaism in Late Antiquity IV.* 2000. ISBN 90 04 11262 6
Band 50
Tal, A. *A Dictionary of Samaritan Aramaic.* (2 Volumes) 2000. ISBN 90 04 11858 6 (dl. 1)
ISBN 90 04 11859 4 (dl. 2) ISBN 90 04 11645 1 (set)
Band 51
Holes, C. *Dialect, Culture, and Society in Eastern Arabia.* Vol. 1 : Glossary 2001.
ISBN 90 04 10763 0
Band 52
Jong, R.E. de. *A Grammar of the Bedouin Dialects of the Northern Sinai Littoral.* Bridging the Linguistic Gap between the Eastern and Western Arab World. 2000. ISBN 90 04 11868 3
Band 53
Avery-Peck, A.J. and Neusner, J. *Judaism in Late Antiquity III,3.* Where we stand: Issues and Debates in Ancient Judaism. 2000. ISBN 90 04 11892 6
Band 54
Krahmalkov, Ch. R. *A Phoenician-Punic Grammar.* 2001. ISBN 90 04 11771 7
Band 55
Avery-Peck, A.J. and Neusner, J. *Judaism in Late Antiquity III,4.* Where we stand: Issues and Debates in Ancient Judaism.. *The Special Problem of the Synagogue.* 2001.
ISBN 90 04 12000 9.

WITHDRAWN